D1174530

ASA Essays in Social Anthropology

GENERAL EDITOR: EDWIN ARDENER

VOLUME 1

Transaction and Meaning:
Directions in the Anthropology
of Exchange and Symbolic Behavior

TRANSACTION
AND
MEANING _____

Directions in the Anthropology
of Exchange and Symbolic Behavior

edited by Bruce Kapferer

A Publication of the
Institute for the Study of Human Issues
Philadelphia

Library
I.U.P.
Indiana, Pa.

301.21 T687r
C.1

Copyright © 1976 by ISHI,
Institute for the Study of Human Issues, Inc.
All Rights Reserved
No part of this book may be reproduced in any form or by any electronic or mechanical
means including information storage and retrieval systems without permission in writing
from the publisher, except by a reviewer who may quote brief passages in a review.

Manufactured in the United States of America

Library of Congress Cataloging in Publication Data:

Main entry under title:

Transaction and meaning.

(ASA essays in social anthropology; v. 1)
Includes bibliographies and indexes.
1. Ethnology—Addresses, essays, lectures. 2. Social interaction—Addresses,
essays, lectures. 3. Communication—Addresses, essays, lectures. I. Kapferer, Bruce.
II. Institute for the Study of Human Issues. III. Series: Association of Social Anthropolo-
gists of the Commonwealth. ASA essays in social anthropology; v. 1.
GN320.T72   302.2'1   76–12644
ISBN 0–915980–04–5

For information, write:

Director of Publications
ISHI
3401 Science Center
Philadelphia, Pennsylvania 19104
U.S.A.

General Editor's Note

The essays in this and several other volumes largely derive from the 1973 Decennial Conference of the Association of Social Anthropologists of the Commonwealth. The conference was entitled "New Directions in Social Anthropology" and was held at St. John's College, Oxford, 4–11 July 1973. The present volume, edited by Bruce Kapferer, is based on the session of 9 July, which examined the increasingly discussed transactional perspective in social anthropology.

Under today's conditions the economics of publishing specialized academic volumes is becoming increasingly complex, and even more daunting is the task of publishing a considerable number of them simultaneously, or as nearly so as possible. In the case of the studies arising from the Decennial Conference it was especially important that they should appear within two or three years of the conference itself. There were originally eleven sessions of papers. Even with a greatly pruned list of related volumes, our aim has been achieved only by the successive efforts of two publishers. Three volumes of essays have been published by Malaby Press, London, under the general title of ASA Studies.* It has subsequently become possible, through the present welcome arrangement with the Institute for the Study of Human Issues (ISHI), to publish two or three further volumes, of which this is one, at reasonable price for the buyer and with minimal publishing delays— both overriding factors in academic publishing today. The ISHI volumes will appear in a series whose overall title is ASA Essays in Social Anthropology. The Chairman and Committee of the Association of Social Anthropologists consider that any unavoidable bibliographical complexity that results from the inclusion of the Decennial volumes in two series will be far outweighed in the minds of readers by the advantages in economy and speedy publication.

The ASA would like to thank the President and Fellows of St. John's College, Oxford, and the Warden of Rhodes House, Oxford, for providing the home for the conference, and the staff of both for their willing assistance. The major convening task was shared with me by Shirley Ardener, and I would like to acknowledge also the help of Nigel Barley, Martin Cantor, Christine Cooper, Robert Heath, Joy Hendry, John Mathias, David Price, Matt Schaffer, and Drid Williams, then mostly graduate students of the Oxford University Institute of Social Anthropology.

As General Editor I warmly acknowledge the role of Dr. Jean La Fontaine, the

*The ASA Studies volumes (all published by Malaby Press in 1975) are: *Biosocial Anthropology*, edited by Robin Fox; *Marxist Analyses and Social Anthropology*, edited by Maurice Bloch; and *The Interpretation of Symbolism*, edited by Roy Willis. These volumes contain a fuller account of the topics covered by the Decennial Conference and of its organization.

present Chairman of the ASA, and the directors and staff of the Institute for the Study of Human Issues in making the arrangements under which this series appears.

EDWIN ARDENER

Editor's Acknowledgments

I would like to thank many at the conference, aside from the contributors to this volume, who participated in the discussion. In particular I wish to state our collective debt to Alice Dewey, John Davis, and Keith Hart, who played a significant part as discussants of the papers. Others also were important in the organization and general debate of the issues raised, and these were Edwin Ardener, Derek Allcorn, and Jeremy Boissevain. Finally, I wish to record my thanks to Gwen Rice, who typed the manuscript in its final form, and to Beverley Jones and Raylene Mulvihill, who assisted with the many aspects of editorial work.

BRUCE KAPFERER

Contents

Introduction:
Transactional Models Reconsidered

BRUCE KAPFERER

The major focus of the contributions to this volume is on the process of interaction, transaction, and exchange, between individuals and groups participating in defined social and cultural contexts. Approaches to the study of transactional and exchange behavior are extremely diverse. In their broadest usage the terms "transaction" and "exchange" refer to the patterned transference of "items," both material (shells, animals, food, labor) and immaterial (status, power), between individuals and groups. Most anthropology deals with such processes. The social and cultural principles, the norms, values, and ideologies which direct transactions and exchanges, are a fundamental concern of anthropological analysis.

Their elucidation has been a major area of theoretical debate from the beginnings of modern anthropology and sociology, in the studies of Spencer, Frazer, Marx, Durkheim, and Mauss, up to the present day. Ekeh (1974), who has examined the major formal statements concerning the processes of transaction and exchange, distinguishes "individualistic" theories of social exchange from "collectivistic" theories. The former, Ekeh states, derive from the British social anthropological tradition, although there are similar currents among American anthropologists and sociologists. The major recent exponent of an "individualistic" theory of social exchange is Homans, a scholar steeped in the British sócial anthropological tradition but not averse, as perhaps many British anthropologists are, to drawing extensively on such related disciplines as economics and psychology. "Collectivistic" social exchange theory emerges more from the European sociological tradition and is best typified by the early work of Lévi-Strauss, which in itself is a development of the approaches of Durkheim and Mauss.

There are difficulties with such a broad characterization. For example, Ekeh argues that the "individualistic" perspective of British social anthropology owes much to the adaptation of Durkheim's ideas by Radcliffe-Brown. I suspect that on both sides of the Atlantic many anthropologists, influenced by the work of Radcliffe-Brown, would object to such a judgment. Indeed, there is much concern by both American and British anthropologists, and not simply those who are breaking with established positions in the discipline, about the "individualistic" turn of much social exchange theory and what they view as the neglect of the structure of the cultural and social systems in which exchanges and transactions take place.

1

Nevertheless, the distinction between "individualistic" and "collectivistic" is useful, for whatever the antecedents or the reasons, formal theories of social exchange as they have emerged in America and Britain have tended to be of an "individualistic" variety. The anthropologist who has given the greatest impetus to the development of such theory in recent years is Fredrik Barth, whose seminal empirical and theoretical studies date from the mid fifties.

There is a large body of critical comment in the discipline on the general approach of which Barth's is but one example (see Abrahamson 1970; Ekeh 1968, 1974; Heath 1968; Mulkay 1971), and some of the prevailing criticisms as well as new ones are included in the essays in this volume. Barth's method does not encompass all the various approaches to the study of transactional and exchange behavior, or even those with similar conceptual frameworks of decision making and strategy (see Whitten and Whitten 1972). However, Barth's orientation provides a useful starting point, since many of the difficulties his approach encounters apply also to others. In addition, many of the chapters in this volume take Barth as their main point of departure, although they also explore alternative perspectives on the study of transactional activity.

Barth's *Models of Social Organization* (1966b), which built upon work among the Swat Pathans (1956, 1959a, 1959b) and in Norway (1963), can be conceived as marking a "paradigm" shift in British social anthropology. In it Barth attacked the dominant orthodoxies of normative consensus and structural-functionalism, which regarded society as a system of morals, logically prior to behavior, and did not "depict any intervening social process between the moral injunction and the pattern" (p. 2). Furthermore, he criticized the general assumption that culture was a structurally integrated whole. He argued that anthropologists, rather than assuming this, should concentrate on the process whereby the various institutional elements within a society become integrated, and the conditions and processes which do or do not produce generally shared meanings and understandings. Barth held that normative and structural-functional approaches could not satisfactorily deal with a major problem area in anthropology—the matter of social change—and that this fact was closely linked with the inability of these approaches to deal with social behavior as process. The alternative approach he proposed could, he claimed, overcome these deficiencies and lead to the development of a "science of social life" with hypotheses capable of being tested. He suggested that this approach would also circumvent some of the difficulties then inherent in much comparative anthropology, whose "procedure of comparison has consisted of a morphological matching of forms so as to locate differences, and a concentration of attention on the correlation of the morphological differences," a process that "does not lead to any procedure which differs from that utilized in cross-cultural area files." The prevailing method, he objected, "leaves the field open for *ad hoc* hypotheses to explain concomitance" (1966b: 22).

The major reasons for his disaffection with the reigning anthropological orthodoxies were also being expressed by others. Leach (1954) attacked the emphasis of structural-functional anthropology on models of static equilibrium and later (1961) criticized certain aspects of comparative anthropology and the legitimacy of terms such as "marriage," "patrilineal," and "matrilineal" as organizing concepts for cross-cultural comparison. Geertz (1957), Bailey (1960), and Van Velsen (1964) among others criticized modes of anthropological analysis which assumed a close integration of standardized modes of thought with observed patterns of social activity. These scholars stressed the need for a more dynamic anthropological analysis and an approach which accounted for variation as well as conformity of observed behavior.

Barth's orientation also has much in common with other approaches already well established in anthropology and elsewhere. It cannot be divorced from the earlier work in anthropology and sociology of Simmel, Mauss, Malinowski, and Firth and should, in many ways, be seen as one development from the studies of these scholars. Like Barth, they were concerned with processes of exchange, the values underlying them, competition, and the principles governing choice and the allocation of resources. The issues raised by their studies are equally pertinent to the approach outlined by Barth. Questions concerning Malinowski's focus on individual "needs" and motives are relevant to a discussion of Barth, as are issues emerging from Firth's work, specifically his emphasis on individual choice behavior and his application of certain aspects of Western economic theories. Debates which revolved around the formalist/substantivist controversy in economic anthropology—focusing on such concepts as "rationality," "maximization," and "profit"—also relate to Barth's work and the transactional orientation in general.

ASSUMPTIONS AND PROBLEMS IN ANALYSIS

The keynote of Barth's approach is that anthropological analysis must be processual, that it must explain how various social forms—such as types of segmentary lineage structure, units of economic production, and kinds of political alliance—are generated. This could be achieved, Barth said, by focusing explicitly on transactional behavior, defined as "sequences of interaction systematically governed by reciprocity." The transactions would be viewed as subject to the rules of strategy put forward in decision and game-theory models, according to which the value gained is greater than or equivalent to the value lost. In the elucidation of the basic assumptions of his model, Barth makes frequent reference to actors pursuing "self-interest" and the maximization of profit. Such a perspective, held to be useful in cross-cultural analysis, immediately raises a number of questions, especially since its exponents have consistently emphasized the fact of cultural difference—the fact that cultural and structural principles specific to certain contexts are likely to govern behavior differently. Can human behavior in its various forms, we then may ask, be reduced to guiding principles such as Barth's? This is an important question, especially because anthropological opinion is increasingly critical of attempts to import Western principles (which are themselves under attack) into the analysis and description of other cultures. The question is critical, too, in the light of one of Barth's own declared aims: to develop a model whose tenets fit closely with observed patterns of behavior. Given the variety of cultural contexts which anthropologists study, there may well be a divergency between the assumptions of his model and the particular activities and processes described by anthropologists. While there might be a relatively high degree of fit in some contexts, such as that of New Guinea "big-men," we cannot assume that Barth's principles are applicable to all situations.

Barth, to some extent, recognizes these problems and seeks to overcome them. For example, he emphasizes the methodological nature of anthropological enquiry. In the course of field work, as the anthropologist learns a language and participates in the everyday life of a society, he roots his categories and concepts in terms understood by native actors and concentrates on their difficulties and problems with relative independence of his analytical model. Since this model generates only approximations to the social forms he has recorded, some aspects of the model, the explanatory variables fed into it, and the hypotheses generated can be falsified. Barth constantly asserts that the problems to which anthropological explanations are addressed must be substantively located in the context of study (1966a; 1967). This approach, which is followed by his own empirical studies, does circumvent certain criticisms. It preserves the integrity of the different cultures studied by anthropologists.

Even so, the obvious difficulties remain. How independent of the analytical model are the anthropologist's field observations? The model seems very likely to intrude consciously or unconsciously into the process of data selection and the recording of behavior. Insofar as it does intrude, the "testability" of propositions generated by the model is limited; the analyst produces nothing but a tautology. As Cancian stresses in a discussion of the maximization principle, "If [the analyst] cannot see the act as maximization, he immediately assumes that his statements of norms, motives, etc., and conditions are not yet correct and seeks to 'balance the equation' so that it will work. He does not reject the idea that people will maximize, for it is the basis of his scientific strategy" (1968: 231).

A. F. Heath's chapter in this volume discusses aspects of this problem with reference to what is termed the "sure-thing" principle. This principle is a special case of the utility maximization principle. As Heath says, "It holds for simple situations where one alternative is better than the other in some respects and identical in all others. It therefore suggests that the 'mistakes' which occur in utility maximization arise when the actor has to 'trade-off' advantages from course of action A against different advantages from course of action B." The problem here is that the sure-thing principle, although frequently used, is severely limited as an explanation for behavior. It explains only why actors behave differently under different conditions; it does not explain the patterning of behavior under the same conditions. Heath suggests a possible solution to this problem. In a reexamination of Barth's Norwegian fishermen example, he applies a decision-making model which includes risk and uncertainty as basic elements (many anthropologists, while acknowledging risk as an important factor, have continued to employ a model based on riskless choice). He postulates that choice will be affected by actors' past experiences and pursuit of information in situations where they must balance a complex set of outcomes, many of which are uncertain. Heath recognizes that a number of difficulties are likely to remain, especially in gaining independent evidence with which to test the validity of the model.

A degree of control over the adequacy and validity of a transactional model can be gained by exploring alternative explanatory principles, through reanalysis of behavior recorded by others. But reanalysis is difficult, especially if the working assumptions of the first anthropologist have intruded markedly into the collection and selection of data. This can render impossible the successful application of an alternative perspective. Although Heath engages in a reanalysis of Barth he is limited by the data which Barth presents.

Our ability to overcome this difficulty is critical, for reanalysis can point up necessary modifications in the model and significant limitations in its use. Recently Asad (1972) has reanalyzed Barth's early work among the Swat Pathans (1959a, 1959b) using a Marxist class model. Asad is able to show how many of Barth's assumptions entered into his description of Swat society, directing his attention away from other possibilities. He criticizes Barth's assumption that the Swat political system can be understood as the sum of all individual choices, as a system in which individuals can voluntarily choose and in which, when faced with a choice between individual and group interests, they choose the former. According to Barth's perspective, the Pakhtun landlord exerts domination over landless Pathans by bartering economic gain for political authority. Alternatively, Asad argues, the political authority of Pakhtun landlords can be seen simply as a result of their membership in a politically dominant class which has control over scarce land resources. Contrary to Barth's notions, "The fact that the landless greatly outnumber the landowners is not a source of weakness but of strength ... the landlords do not need to worry about how to make themselves indispensable to the landless: it is the latter who must worry about making themselves acceptable to the landlords" (p. 87). This relationship between landed and landless cannot be seen as a contract defined in a pure market system "in which individual buyer meets individual seller as just equal in the unceasing pursuit of profit" (p. 87).

Barth's analysis indicates that the overall political system exhibits an alternating pattern of opposed political blocs. This argument, Asad states, obscures the fact that the smaller landowners are progressively eliminated and that the option to shift alliance is open only to the more powerful, ambitious landlords. Over time, as these smaller landlords are eliminated and land comes to be controlled by fewer families, it is likely that a more stable class domination will be established; this, in turn, will facilitate the emergence of a princely agrarian state, to be further stabilized by the British imperial presence. Asad points to the importance of the need for additional data on such matters as agricultural debt and the ideology and consciousness of different social groups. One critical omission in Barth's analysis is his failure to take into account broader historical processes bearing on Swat political structure, and this relates to Asad's central argument. The results of historical research, Asad suggests, would yield a greater understanding of the pattern of political process in Swat. Through insufficient attention to this, Barth has committed some of the same errors as the functionalist studies he himself criticizes. He treats Swat society as a "logically closed system . . . located at a point in linear time" (p. 90), not as a developing reality. His assumption of individuals freely pursuing self-interest does not permit processual analysis accounting for the progressive accumulation of land and power; rather, like many functionalist analyses, Barth's reveals a mechanism for the maintenance of political equilibrium.

A key point thus emerges. Because a political system at any point in time is the product of different combinations of factors operating at different periods, it is inappropriate, as Asad argues, to specify a single mechanism for a political structure as a developing form. This kind of criticism need not be reserved for Barth; it presumably can be applied to other work in anthropology, such as Sahlins' on the emergence of predatory segmentary lineage systems and the evolution from stateless segmentary societies to states.

The influence of assumptions on ethnographic description is by no means unique to Barth's kind of theoretical orientation. It is a problem which anthropological analyses, whatever their theoretical underpinnings, must confront. Perhaps only reanalysis, like that of Asad, is going to provide the necessary corrections, indicating where assumptions have intruded into ethnographic description and where significant data have been excluded from analysis. Of course, if it can be shown that the omission of important data is a problem inherent in the general structure of transactional analysis, not just in one application of it, then transactionists are swimming in troubled waters. Some of the problems isolated by Asad, such as Barth's inattention to the ideologies of various social groups and to historical factors, are not necessarily inherent in the model. Many of the essays in this volume take as their explicit concern the role of ideology in the organization of transactional behavior (Cohen and Comaroff, Parkin, and Gilsenan, for example). Historical events and the relationship these have to various choices and the formation of interpersonal and group relationships should be capable of analysis. This is one of the features of Handelman's analysis of client-welfare agency relationships in Jerusalem, and of Strathern's description of ceremonial exchange in the New Guinea Highlands.

Barth's orientation toward the use of a choice/decision-making model shows a spirit in common with Firth. He resists, it would seem, the application of Western market principles as norms of behavior in other cultural contexts. "We are not committed to any prejudged 'view of society'—the adequacy of the transactional model for any and every particular relationship is continually on trial" (1966b: 5). But Barth's notions of maximization and profit are relatively weak: for instance, his idea that actors enter into transactions where they receive value greater than or equivalent to what they give out. Transactional activity, according to this principle, is facilitated by actors' having differential access to information and varying value preferences.

There are, of course, methodological problems here. The empirical determination of individual or group motives and value preferences might not be easy. Individuals in many contexts are not likely to have clear objectives or to have them organized and ranked according to a means-end schema. This is especially so in contexts where a multitude of factors have bearing on the actors' decisions. Also, the separation of actors' value scales from the social relationships produced by transactional activity is problematic. It is a well-known phenomenon that actors will reinterpret their own motives, readjust their perspectives, on the basis of their current commitments and relationships. Their declared motives and value scales, rather than generating their relationships, can be retroactively produced by those relationships.

It seems that a transactional orientation like Barth's is at once too broad and too restrictive. The broadness of the model, the potential all-encompassing quality of some of the guiding concepts and assumptions, as well as their looseness of definition, could contribute to the danger of tautology and reduce the model's explanatory efficacy. But it is also too restrictive in the sense that it forces too much behavior which can be viewed as transaction (the communication of information, the sharing of ideas, and even the passage of goods, services, and the like) into a unidimensional model. By so doing one might rob the explanation of social phenomena of much of its manifold richness and thereby subvert one of the model's own objectives, which is to depict observed behavior in a manner as close as possible to "reality." Furthermore, such a model might not simply direct the analyst away from alternative explanatory principles; it might lead to a neglect of aspects of social behavior—for instance, behavior's symbolic mode—which might be critical to successful explanation.

There have been a number of attempts to modify and refine some of the guiding concepts in Barth's model and other related transaction and exchange models, such as those proposed by Homans (1961) and Blau (1964). Skvoretz and Conviser, following Meeker (1971), devise a set of exchange rules which specify various outcomes according to whether individuals organize their actions in terms of rules pertaining to "individualism," "competition," "group gain," "equity," or "reciprocity" (1974: 60). In doing this they are extending Barth's distinction between relationships built on transactions in which individuals pursue self-interest, and relationships in which individuals pursue benefits for the group (see also Paine's essay in this volume). They also suggest a clearer definition of the concept of "interest" and a replacement of the notion that individuals pursue maximal benefit with the assumption that individuals orient their activity to obtaining *satisfactory* benefit (see also Salisbury's chapter in this volume). All this constitutes a valuable revision of Barth's initial model but it still confines the analysis of transactional activity to a restrictive idea of "rationality"; activity continues to be seen in terms of receiving benefit or gain. The adoption of a notion of "satisfactory benefit" to replace "maximal benefit" is only a slight adjustment of the maximization-of-value principle.

TRANSACTIONS, CODES, AND MEANING

The essays in this volume (with the exception of those by Heath and Salisbury), by strongly directing attention toward the control and management of meaning, and the cognitive framework and symbolic processes which direct and organize transactional activity, suggest important refinements for transactional models. But more than this, they indicate significant limitations in the application of a model founded on the notion that "benefits" or "rewards" equalize or exceed "costs." Negotiation and bargaining processes, stressed by the Barthian maximizing model, are expressly excluded from much transactional activity constrained by the nature of some symbolic systems.

The application of a model of rational decision making is often distinctly inappropriate given the nature of the symbols and metaphors which can guide and instigate activity viewed as transaction. Turner (1974), for example, has brilliantly demonstrated the force of symbol and metaphor in social and political action and has shown the limitation of many formal models of cognitive and social processes including those based on the rules of strategy and a principle of maximization. A Barthian type of model, by treating the units transferred in transactional activity solely on the basis of accounting procedures, of profit and loss, not only can obscure the meaning of such activity for the actors but also can systematically fail to capture the significance of the behavior in the overall context of the empirical study.

It is a major problem of formal exchange or transactional theory that the meaning of the act is to be interpreted within the paradigm of a restricted notion of rationality attached to a maximizing principle. There are numerous other ways in which individuals can be regarded as proceeding rationally (Schutz 1967; Garfinkel 1967), and these alternative conceptions of rational activity do not require us to view individuals as pursuing "benefit." Interpretation of behavior in terms of the rational principle adopted by many transactional theorists gives little attention to how actors recognize and establish rates of exchange. In Blau's exchange theory there is little specification, apart from the application of principles largely independent of empirical setting, of "how actor and researcher learn, recognize, and use standards as universalistic or particularistic, [or of] the kind of interpretative procedures the actor must process to carry out social exchanges that enable him to recognize what standards are appropriate for particular social settings" (Cicourel 1970: 19).

Paine's essay in this volume emphasizes the need to examine more completely the role of mediation and of communicative codes in which transactional and exchange activity is couched. Expanding Barth's distinction between transaction (T) and incorporation (I), Paine examines the process of transmission and receipt of messages concerning value and relates it to aspects of power, social control, and brokerage. Drawing extensively on the work of Bernstein and Bateson, he notes that a restricted code of communication is likely to be associated with exchange in the *I* mode and an elaborated code with exchange in the *T* mode. Bargaining and negotiation are a feature of the latter but not of the former. Table 2 in Paine's essay sets out clearly the implications of his argument. Many of the assumptions and guiding principles of conventional transactional theory are shown not always to hold. Thus, whether transactional activity leads, for example, to the development of shared values, or is integrative, as both Barth and Blau argue, is dependent on whether it is set in a restricted or elaborated code. If transaction occurs on the basis of a restricted code, value disjunctions are likely to be maintained. The extent to which individuals can be seen as themselves responsible for exchange is again dependent on the nature of the communicative code: responsibility is generally higher in *I* modes where the code is restrictive than in *T* modes where the role of third parties is significant. In presenting these arguments, Paine examines the role of the broker, specifically in the field of political dealings.

This is more substantively examined in Cohen and Comaroff's essay, as is the general significance of the communicative code as part of transactional activity. Particular stress is placed on the constructive process of meaning and the way in which this defines relationships and the activity pursued in reference to them. Cohen and Comaroff are concerned with the image of self and others communicated by actors; this is an important consideration, they suggest, in examining political process. Barth, Blau, and more recently Kapferer (1972) have drawn attention to this. However, Cohen and Comaroff extend the implications for the analysis of transactions.

Their chapter deals with the management of meaning by political brokers in Newfoundland and the political significance of the constructive process surrounding marriage and chiefly succession among the Barolong boo Ratshidi of South Africa. A feature of the first part of the chapter is the exploration of how political brokers operate within the meaning code or constructs of clients, maintaining the disjunction (as Paine suggests in his essay) between a locally derived and restricted set of meanings and those encountered in the loci of centralized government institutions. They show how the legitimacy and ability of an individual as a political broker are dependent not just on successful presentation of a personal image but on his success in translating a more elaborated set of understandings into the restricted meaning framework of his clients. The implication is that the ability to control the actions of others is not so much emergent from the structure of the transactional relationship itself, the patterned imbalance in the transfer of goods and services, as argued in the studies of Barth and Blau; rather it is a property of the successful management of meaning and presentation of self by a political actor.

The second part of the chapter extends this argument, focusing on the process of communication, construction, and fixing of meaning as a ''fundamental property of political interaction.'' Cohen and Comaroff show that the labels which designate particular forms of marriage are assigned as the result of activity within a political arena. The process of definition and its acceptance govern how a particular marriage is to be read—as an FBD or MBD marriage, for example, as an indicator of political alliance or competition. The demonstration that marriage labels are mutable and that the existence of marriage ties does not necessarily suggest political alliance, as is often assumed in ethnographic analysis, constitutes a general contribution to anthropology. But, of more specific relevance to this volume, the authors' approach emphasizes the danger of generalizing from the substantive values apparently exchanged to the overall significance of the relationship without examining closely the cognitive framework underlying the transaction and the symbolic quality of the transaction itself. Concentration on the "currency" of the transaction, on surface appearances, might not reveal the rules or principles governing transactional activity; the cognitive aspects, the meaning sets, the verbal idiom surrounding the transactional activity must also be considered.

These ideas are further elaborated in the chapters of Sansom and Parkin. Sansom examines the intriguing context of Pedi marriage. Here cash derived from participation in a market economy is used in the payment of bridewealth, but is nominally treated and verbally referred to as "cattle, sheep, and goats." While factors relevant to involvement in a market economy surround the choice and acceptance of suitors and affect the deliberations on a "price" for a bride, the marriage ceremonial is "always described as if unspoiled by monetary intrusion." The idiom employed by Pedi is both transformative and expressive of the fact that the rules which govern transactional activity in the marketplace are not applicable in the sphere of marriage, even though the transactional units used could imply this. The idiom is transformative in the sense that the procedure whereby money is treated as animals permits the breakdown of a complex exchange occasioned by marriage into its multifarious components. Each cash amount treated as an "animal" has its various characteristics commented upon and tied to particular transfers of rights over persons. Furthermore, the idiom facilitates the creation and definition of new forms of behavior and status.

Sansom's chapter draws attention to the failure of symbolic interactionist analyses, like those of Barth and Blau (also Davis 1973: 161), to define various transactional types. He distinguishes between "market" and what he terms "signal" transactions, and there is much in the distinction which bears comparison with Paine's discussion of two codes in which transactional activity can be effected. Market transactions are affected by standardized processes that determine value in a market; they are pursued within an elaborated code. Signal transactions operate within a restricted code. They define exchange items in relation to highly specific ends and impose a limitation on bargaining and negotiation.

Sansom argues that in the Pedi situation there is an opposition between market value and signal value, and that the idiom of the latter serves to suppress and limit behavior with reference to the former in various spheres of social activity. Parkin pursues a similar theme when he contrasts the "altruistic" custom-based ideology of Giriama elders with the "negotiable" ideology of the younger men who have become engaged in entrepreneurial activity. Government policy geared toward economic development and progress supports a negotiable maximizing ideology but is faced with the difficulty of overcoming "altruistic" views of customary Giriama behavior. The starting point of Parkin's analysis is that words, the verbal symbols which Giriama employ in everyday discourse, identify forms of social conduct according to the respective ideologies. Words are a means whereby action is fitted into wider systems of classification, of meaning and roles. A point which Parkin elaborates is that activity expressive of one system of classification does not exclude activity premised in accordance with another. Indeed words, and the manipulation of their meaning, provide a means whereby young Giriama entrepreneurs can circumvent the restrictions of the traditional system adhered to by the elders and even legitimate their status and activities in terms of it. The key to this process rests in the ambiguous property of verbal symbols themselves. Parkin demonstrates this, for example, through an analysis of the meaning and usage of the traditional respectful term for elders, *mutumia*.

Many of the chapters in this volume touch on the interpretative procedures employed by actors in their transactional activity. The authors accentuate the importance of adopting symbolic interactionist or phenomenological approaches. Gilsenan's essay is a particularly sensitive treatment of transactional activity in a symbolic interactionist mode. He takes as his theme deception or "lying," a common element in most social activity, and analyzes its manifestations in a Lebanese village. He examines the conditions for the emergence, maintenance, and subversion of images of self in interpersonal interaction, focusing on the subtleties and intricacies of word play, of action and performance. Gilsenan's concern is with modes of public and tacit communication, whereby publicly projected identities are compared with the private knowledge of persons either to authenticate the public image or to reveal the truth underneath. This is shown in his account of the visit of a foreign *sheikh* to the village he studied. In the *zikr* ritual the projected "holiness" of the visiting *sheikh* failed to receive public authentication, because he did not recognize the deception of a "disciple" from the village. The *sheikh* was discredited both by the knowledge other villagers had of the supposed disciple's irreligious behavior and by the latter's revealing that he had broken important ritual conventions. The visiting *sheikh* acted in accordance with an elaborated code of "holy" behavior in the context of a restricted code which determined the understanding and response of his audience. It was through this restricted code, and the locally derived cues and knowledge, that a "value" was placed on the visitor's behavior and the "holiness" of the local *sheikh* authenticated by comparison. Gilsenan's analysis underlines points made by the other essays: it is important to examine the process of communication and meaning in transactional activity; what is apparently transacted or communicated is not necessarily what is received or understood; what is being transacted cannot be separated from the transactor; the actor, as Mauss argued, also transacts aspects of his own identity; transactions are symbolic and their symbolic properties themselves control and direct action.

Many transaction or exchange theorists certainly advocate a symbolic interactionist or phenomenological approach (Barth 1966b; Blau 1964; McCall and Simmons 1966; Singelmann 1973). But there is some debate about how this is to be achieved and about the merit of it for the respective orientations involved (see Abbott et al. 1973; Singelmann 1973). It can be argued, for example, that there is an inherent opposition between symbolic interactionist approaches and formal transactional approaches. A transactional approach sees values, meanings, and so forth as part of an environment, all of whose elements are brought into association through the search for benefits and rewards. Interaction is promoted according to this principle. This is not so with symbolic interactionism, which sees cognitive systems, values, and meanings as being created and as creating behavior independently of such principles as benefit and reward. This does not deny some degree of overlap between the two approaches. Both view interaction and the nature of the relationships so formed as sustaining and modifying the ideas, values, and meanings which have entered into the process of social activity.

The extent to which transactional analysis can legitimately incorporate aspects of symbolic interactionist and phenomenological approaches depends on its reliance on decision-making/maximization principles. My own view, shared by Parkin, is that the analysts of transactional activity, rather than assuming that men maximize, should examine the conditions which permit the pursuit of such activity. Furthermore, attention should be paid, as in Marriott's essay in this volume, to the particular cultural understandings which underlie maximization or any other tactic or strategy, and to how these understandings relate to the frequency patterns of transactions. A totally Western-oriented or "scientific" view of maximizing behavior could fail to take account of important factors. Marriott, for example, shows for South Asia that "Transactions, notably nonreceivings and receivings as well as initiations of action, both demonstrate and bring about natural or substantial rankings through what are thought to be the actors' biomoral losses and gains." That is, transactional behavior, and the rules which occasion it, relate not only to the structure of social relationships but also to the individual bodily make-up. The individual, through transaction, affects his own internal order.

The question now arises as to whether the abandonment of universal, nonculturally specific assumptions reduces the ability of transactional theory to account for the emergence and change of social forms and decreases its effectiveness as a tool in comparative analysis. My own opinion is that, while such an approach must have limitations, it can still help to explain the generation of social forms and perhaps even the variations within them. Marriott's essay is a clear move in this direction. By taking a set of culturally specific assumptions he is able to define certain strategies and tactics for particular castes and account for variations among them. That his approach is restricted to specific cultural assumptions limits its range of applicability and exposure to comparative test. He does suggest, however, that his approach is relevant across a wide and diverse region.

One further problem requires brief elaboration. I stated that Barth developed his model in opposition to theorists who saw a moral system as prior to behavior and consequently depicted social behavior in static terms. The return to a consideration of cultural and cognitive rules in this volume does not imply a return to the static moral view which Barth opposed. Indeed, many of the essays in this volume clearly show that meaning sets, understanding, and the like are not immutable but fluid; that ambiguities (Cohen and Comaroff, Parkin, Gilsenan) in symbolic activities and in the rules underlying behavior emerge in the process of interaction. Cultural rules have a dynamic quality, capable of producing transformations in meaning and changing or redirecting behavior along new paths. This is not to say that the problems connected with this question do not require more investigation. For example, little attention (except for Handelman's chapter here) has been focused on the way social relationships emergent from transactional activity "feed back," either sustaining the constructions placed on relationships or setting up processes of redefinition.

PROCESS AND CHANGE: REDUCTIONISM VERSUS EMERGENT PROPERTIES

I now turn more explicitly to problems connected with the analysis of process and change from the transactional orientation. The issue here is the individualistic, actor-oriented perspective of transactional theory: whether, for example, it is legitimate to explain social forms and changes in them as the result of factors governing the actions of individuals. A major criticism of transaction or exchange theory is that it is ego-centered, and tends to see individuals as voluntarily involved in, relatively unrestrained by, their social systems, relationships, and settings.

Salisbury's chapter in this volume approaches this issue directly. He considers that under certain circumstances it might be more legitimate to examine the factors governing the decisions of individuals independently of their relationships with those toward whom they are orienting their strategies. In a sense, he criticizes Barth from the opposite direction to that from which Barth draws most of his critics. Like many of the other authors in this volume, he questions a view which focuses on the negotiative, bargaining aspects of transactional activity. But rather than concentrate on the mode or media of transactions or on their symbolic quality, he wishes to examine the factors relating to an individual's decisions. These factors would be connected with the specific life-situation of the individual, and would be isolated from the transactional activity or relationships which are to be explained. Salisbury also stresses, as Heath does, the need to apply economic analysis more rigorously.

Salisbury notes that there are situations where it is legitimate to focus on the decision making of individuals *qua* individuals and where the form and content of their transactions are of reduced significance in explaining their activity. The specific example he takes is the relationship between agents of the Hudson's Bay Company and Indian trappers. He shows, for example, that the different strategies of Indian trappers in the organization of their subsistence economy can be deduced in isolation from their relationship with HBC stores and agents. The nature of the context in which the Indians participate permits this kind of explanation; if they were more dependent on HBC stores, we might have to give greater attention to their transactional relationships with the stores.

Salisbury's aim is a corrective one. He does not exclude as legitimate other modes of transactional analysis. Although he is critical of Barth, he in fact is arguing in much the same spirit. He advocates a firmer adherence to decision-theory principles of economics and stresses the importance of reviewing alternatives "systematically, rather than considering them on an ad hoc basis when the initial analysis proves insufficient." His concern is to demonstrate the possibility of accounting for certain behavior between actors without applying concepts such as "reciprocity" which imply some overall normative framework governing the transactions. By looking for "the internal logic of the decisions made by two separate actors," he "leaves open the question of whether both parties are deciding on the same basis."

The essay by Salisbury indicates that there are important areas of social activity in which an individual and his specific situation can be taken in isolation from others with whom he transacts. But there are many contexts where this could be less readily argued. It is important, therefore, to examine the "individualistic" character of much exchange theory in greater detail. This analytical bias is not necessarily overcome by a focus on the cognitive frameworks underlying and guiding the participation of actors or by a concentration on the codes of conduct and images of self which actors project in the course of their interaction. Such aspects can be treated in a highly individualistic way, with the failure or success of individuals being gauged in terms of how adequately they have read a situation or performed in it. But clearly the properties of the situation, of the form and patterning of relationships themselves and the organization of power within them, might reduce an individual's control over his own actions and the behavior of others. The why of behavior, why individuals opt for one course of action rather than another, cannot be simply reduced to a failure in their accounting procedures, the complexity of factors bearing on their individual decisions, their lack of information, and so on. These aspects related to individual decision making might themselves be produced by the form and content of the relationships which interrelate individuals and by the nature of the symbols through which they communicate.

Barth and Blau, in setting out the basic mechanisms, certainly reduce the importance of extraindividual factors, structures, and institutions to a bare minimum. They are impelled to this because of the nature of their objective, which is to deduce social forms and the structures of relationships from principles held to direct individual behavior. It is here that they are most exposed to the criticism of methodological individualism. Barth, of course, devotes considerable attention to factors located in the environment which constrain individual choice. But he treats the various constraints he isolates, as Asad (1972: 84) notes in relation to the Swat Pathan material, in a highly individuated manner. Thus ecological factors, kinship and rank positions and occupational roles—slots into which individuals fit— influence the choice of strategy; they are brought into relation through individual action. Although I agree with this view to some extent, it is also true that these factors might be structurally connected in themselves and their interrelations might direct individual action. It is this point which I stress: the various elements occurring in an environment stand in such a relation to each other that they might organize behavior and establish frequency patterns independently of the choices and decisions of actors. In a study of clothing factory workers in Zambia (1972), I showed that there were many unintended consequences of individual choice behavior which could be accounted for only by the way various elements stood in a structural relationship to each other.

All this is not completely fair to Barth. He is aware of the dangers of a reductionist approach and he makes an explicit attempt to correct some of them in the second essay in *Models*. Thus he makes use of the concept of feedback, a concept that links his approach to modern systems theory (see, for example, Buckley 1967). He states that it "absolves us from the difficulties inherent in the provisional, linear form of the model used in the first chapter, where social forms were generated from values" (1966b: 15). It absolves him in the sense that he can argue that while "every instance of transaction takes place in a matrix of values and statuses, the latter being a basic social arrangement, a distribution of values" (*ibid.*), these can be seen as themselves the product of individual choices which then feed back to canalize further choices. Blau also attempts to overcome the reductionist implications of an exchange model and places an emphasis on the emergent properties of social relationships, organizations, and institutions. Social relationships generated through individual activity, in his view, exert a force over individual behavior independently of the choices, perceptions, and interests of particular individuals.

A concern with the emergent properties of action has deep roots in anthropology and sociology; it is by no means the special preserve of modern exchange theory or a contribution of exchange analysis to the development of sociological theory in general. "Emergence" is a major organizing concept developed by McHugh, following G. H. Mead, in *Defining the Situation*; it refers "to the definition, and transformations in definition, of an event over time" (1968: 31). Nadel (1951) explicitly uses the concept "emergence" in an attempt to link individuals to the institutionalized forms in which they participate. He states that emergence is

> possible only under two conditions: first, the mental and organic events materializing in the action of an individual must be capable of being *experienced by* others; and secondly, this experiencing by others must *once more evoke action*. Expressed differently, the mental event-become-action must add to the environment of objects in

which all experiences and actions take place. We assume, therefore, that once the initial action materializes, it is there to be perceived, remembered, perhaps felt, and responded to; it thus, in some measure, delimits the random experiences of others, and hence their random behaviour, providing "objects" for the former and models, goals, or constraints for the latter. If the objects and models endure, and if they are uniformly responded to, the resulting novel combination of events in many minds and organisms is the social fact "emerged" [1951: 217].

The concept of emergence is critical to exchange theory and the analysis of transactional activity in general for two important reasons. It is a means whereby the actions of individuals can be linked to the wider institutional arrangements in which they participate and whereby "culture" as a set of shared agreements affecting and guiding action can be studied. Furthermore, as is indicated in the use of the term, it is a concept vital to the analysis of process and change. It is this last aspect to which I will direct most of the remainder of this Introduction. Before I do this, however, it is important to note some of the difficulties for a theory premised on individual decision making once the significance of emergence is recognized.

Attention to the emergent properties of action allows us to link the activities of individuals to the social systems in which they participate. However, it also shows the limitations of an approach which is biased toward the examination of the choices and decisions of individuals. Once it is recognized that relationships and systems of relationships can exert an independent effect upon the behavior of individuals, the futility of reducing all study of social behavior to individual components becomes clear. Webster (1973) makes this point expressly in relation to the concept of emergent properties: "Thus a study of molecular properties of water would not ordinarily prepare the student for the fact that a glass of water is *transparent*. . . . Molecular properties say nothing about molar properties" (p. 269). He argues that while the concept of emergent property is not incompatible with methodological individualism, it is absurd to state that propositions about social phenomena are generally reducible to individual component parts.

The position which I put forward is this. Attention in transactional analysis should be more explicitly focused on the structure, form, and content of social relationships produced through transactional activity, whatever the guiding assumptions; on the complex networks in which relationships are set; on the processes of flow and feedback between the organizations and institutions in which individuals are active. Although Barth's model is based on the processes of individual decision making, many of his ethnographic cases describe complex patterns of flow and feedback between, for example, units of domestic production, the nature of the product, forms of festivity, and the organization of customary obligations (1966c, 1967). The itemization of a system of flow and feedback imparts to the contexts he studies their dynamic quality and their transformational properties.

The essays by Handelman and Strathern in this volume, both concerned with aspects of change, illustrate and extend parts of my argument. Handelman examines the social relationship between a welfare agency and a client and treats it as an emergent property of the history of the social contacts of the partners to the relationship. The particular extended case he takes, which he documents in considerable ethnographic detail, is analyzed in seven phases covering a period of twenty years. He addresses himself to the problem that, despite the separate but common interests of the welfare agency and clients in terminating their relationship speedily, it nonetheless endures over a long time span. Handelman explains this by focusing on factors emergent from the relationship itself: in the course of transactions the conceptions, the ideas, in terms of which the relationship was initiated, and also the resources, opportunities, and goals of the participants, are progressively altered. For example, he explains the procedures employed by agency and client in negotiating a fair exchange for the termination of their affiliation. He shows how the client initially presented himself as the single representative of a solidary household unit. As the agency entered into the relationship on this basis, it became aware of diverse interests, many of which were opposed to each other, within the household. The demands on the agency were thereby increased, and this in turn raised the value of the fair exchange. Furthermore, the agency sought the assistance of other organizations in a bid to sever the affiliation. But their involvement restricted the ability of the agency and client to agree upon the value of fair exchange for termination. The structure and development of the client's career-line in relation to the agency are not just emergent from transactional activity; they feed back and prevent the agency from terminating the relationship.

Although Handelman pursues his analysis in terms of concepts familiar in formal transactional theory—concepts of benefits, costs, investment, and fair exchange—he avoids what I consider to be the often static modes of analysis of those who interpret transactional activity in decision-theory terms. He does not view the decisions of individuals as related to a fixed set of resources, goals, and opportunities located at one point in time. Rather, he sees these factors as continually changing, and the change in itself as a product of the emergent forms of relationships. A mode of analysis which seeks to explain the frequency pattern of behavior through consideration of a fixed set of resources, opportunities, and the like might be able to account for the presence of a particular social form; change in this social form could in turn be explained by any alteration in the resources and opportunities. But such an analysis couched in decision-theory terms is not necessarily any more processual than, for example, conventional modes of structural-functional analysis. No account is given of how new resources and opportunities enter the situation or alter the patterns of behavior observed. Handelman, on the other hand, has shown how the emergent form of a relationship developing in response to a series of transactions can systematically introduce and alter resources, opportunities, and objectives.

The next step is to examine how resources and goals change as a result of factors *external* to the relationship being examined. Strathern discusses just such a situation, showing as well how factors emergent from sets of relationships modify certain potentially disruptive aspects of the outside elements.

Strathern's essay concentrates on changes which have occurred in the Mount Hagen area of Papua New Guinea since the arrival of Europeans in the early 1930s. He focuses on the factors maintaining the continuity of the *moka* system of ceremonial exchange, and, in particular, on the change of the transactional medium from shells to cash. Certain themes in the chapter can be usefully compared with the essays of Sansom and Parkin: for example, the use of cash derived from participation in a money economy in "traditional" spheres of social activity and the opposition between those Strathern calls "traditionalists" and those he names "progressives," the older and younger generation of Hageners.

Strathern states that the explicit cultural role of the *moka* is that the "*moka* maker" must give more than he has received by way of "solicitory" gifts. The operation of this principle creates a debt or imbalance in relationships and also sets up a process of delayed exchange, since it takes time to gather and produce the goods needed for *moka*. A problem which Strathern selects for analysis is the extent to which the entry of new valuables into the ceremonial exchange system, specifically money which links the system to wider and alternative fields of action, will threaten its continuity. This problem involves the emergent phenomenon of delayed exchange, which necessitates the eventual participation of younger, "progressive" men whose interests in the accumulation and distribution of wealth through the medium of money might lead them to direct their activities outside an institution of ceremonial exchange altogether. Strathern is able to show that the rules of *moka*—the mode of calculation governing transaction—enabled money to replace shells and sustained a system of delayed exchange. He explains how over time the units of *moka* transactions changed—for example, a shift from the use of pearl shells to cowrie shell rope—and how a system of establishing equivalences emerged.

It was in terms of this emergent system that cash as a major unit of transaction was introduced. Cash units were treated in much the same way as the new types of shells that had earlier been introduced as currency units. Furthermore, Strathern describes how the rules of *moka* lead to the emergence of large-scale and complex sets of exchange relationships. These aspects, which can be viewed as emergent properties of the *moka* system of ceremonial exchange, are important in under-standing how the system is able to continue. Young progressive men engaged in a market economy can plough the money they earn into *moka* and can legitimate their prestige and political influence in terms of their participation in *moka*. Additionally, the development of extended networks of exchange relationships reduces the extent to which an individual *moka* maker must depend on his land to produce the valuables required for participation in *moka*. As Strathern states, "Men can obtain the pigs they need by careful management of their auxiliary exchange networks." Strathern contrasts the situation he describes with that of the neighboring Chimbu, where cash has not been able to enter a traditional system of ceremonial exchange as a major unit of transaction, and where there is greater dependency on the productive value of land for participation in the exchange system. Here the opposition between "progressives" and "traditionalists" is more intense and the continuity of the ceremonial exchange system exposed to greater threat.

The chapters by Handelman and Strathern demonstrate the importance of considering the role of emergent properties in the study of transactional behavior. They show how a transactional approach can be adapted to the analysis of events over historical time, that it can treat events as linked in a sequential process. In particular, Handelman's analysis with its focus on the consequences of decisions indicates how these decisions themselves can alter the character of goals and resources. Neither essay can be viewed as an analysis of equilibrium, in the sense in which Asad criticizes Barth's description of the Swat Pathans, or as the type of structural-functional analysis which Barth opposes. Moreover, change or continuity is not seen as simply a crude function of external forces, or as merely the net result of shifts in the strategies and decisions of individuals. Change or continuity is seen as a product of both: strategies and decisions evolve as a response to one another and to external forces. And the analyses of Handelman and Strathern point out that the transformational potential of social relationships, their ability to change, continue, or disappear, can be a property of the form and content of the relationships themselves.

A concern with the emergent properties of action argues against reducing social behavior to the actions of individuals or reducing anthropological analysis to the dynamics of individual decision making. If such reductions continue to constitute the main thrust of transactional analysis, then it seems likely that transactionalists will be largely limited to the study of subinstitutional behavior and will maintain a restricted view of "the social reality as a negotiated settlement, a network of ego-centred manipulating individuals" (Davis 1973: 159).

I have discussed the essays in this volume largely in relation to the transactional model outlined by Barth. Many of the essays point to the methodological and theoretical limitations contained in that model's basic assumptions. They also indicate a range of ethnographic problems and material to which the model in its stated form cannot easily be addressed. As a general theory purporting to take account of a wide variety of ethnographic evidence and problems, formal exchange theory has encountered difficulties, and will continue to encounter them if it remains in an unmodified form. This does not mean that in certain contexts and given specific problems the approach or some development of it could not prove fruitful and insightful. Problems connected with the organization of entrepreneurial and trading activity, or the analysis of power brokers, might be particularly well suited to a formal exchange or transactional theory approach. But, as many of the detailed analyses in this volume show, the would-be user of such a mode of analysis should be attuned to the limitations it might impose. Not only might it be relatively insensitive to other factors guiding and influencing behavior, but also it might direct attention away from ethnographically relevant problems. Transactional theory, of course, is not alone in this. Any theory once it takes hold in a discipline demands a concentration on its conceptual supports. The critical problem for anthropology or sociology is that ethnographic contexts become reduced merely to the means for the elaboration and resolution of theoretical debate. While theoretical debate is essential, it should not continue in such a way as to overlook the key problems of specific ethnographic contexts (see Glaser and Strauss 1967).

It is possible to modify and develop the transactional model so that it is both more closely rooted in the realities of a certain context and capable of wider application. Clearly this can be achieved by examining transactional activity in terms of specific guiding cultural rules rather than constraining it within an abstract principle of gains exceeding or equalling costs; by examining the code within which transactional activity is cast; and by attending to the procedures whereby actors assign symbolic meaning to their transactions. The model can be developed by drawing on the ideas of phenomenology, symbolic interactionism, linguistics, and communication theory. However, in some ways these various perspectives constitute competing paradigms, and the inclusion of elements drawn from them in the one model might reduce their explanatory efficacy. The contribution of Barth has been to draw attention to the importance of a focus on transaction and to suggest one way in which this focus could yield explanations concerning the generation of social forms. The authors represented in this volume share this interest but at the same time point to new directions in the analysis of transactional behavior.

ACKNOWLEDGMENTS

I wish to thank Tom Ernst, Roy Fitzhenry, Adrian Peace, and Basil Sansom for the long discussions I have had with them in the course of writing this Introduction. While their ideas and views have been influential and have sharpened my approach to the problem of transactional analysis, they are in no way responsible for any errors which the reader might detect. I would also like to express my gratitude for the helpful suggestions offered by the directors and staff of the Institute for the Study of Human Issues.

REFERENCES

Abbott, C. W., C. R. Brown, and P. V. Crosbie. 1973. Exchange as symbolic interaction: for what? *American Sociological Review,* 38: 504–506.
Abrahamson, Bengt. 1970. Homans on exchange: hedonism revisited. *American Journal of Sociology,* 76: 273–285.
Asad, Talal. 1972. Market model, class structure and consent: a reconsideration of Swat political organisation. *Man,* n.s., 7 (1): 74–94.
Bailey, F. 1960. *Tribe, Caste and Nation.* Manchester: Manchester University Press.
Barth, F. 1956. Ecologic relationships of ethnic groups in Swat, North Pakistan. *American Anthropologist,* 58: 1079–1089.

_____. 1959a. *Political Leadership Among the Swat Pathans*. London: Athlone Press.

_____. 1959b. Segmentary opposition and the theory of games: a study of Pathan organization. *Journal of the Royal Anthropological Institute,* 89: 5–21.

_____. 1963. *The Role of the Entrepreneur in Social Change in Northern Norway*. Bergen.

_____. 1966a. Anthropological models and social reality. The Second Royal Society Nuffield Lecture. In *Proceedings of the Royal Society*. London.

_____. 1966b. *Models of Social Organization*. Royal Anthropological Institute Occasional Paper No. 23. London.

_____. 1966c. On the study of social change. *American Anthropologist,* 69: 661–669.

_____. 1967. Economic spheres in Darfur. In R. Firth, ed., *Themes in Economic Anthropology*. ASA Monograph No. 6. London: Tavistock.

Blau, Peter M. 1964. *Exchange and Power in Social Life*. New York: John Wiley.

Buckley, Walter. 1967. *Sociology and Modern Systems Theory*. Englewood Cliffs, N.J.: Prentice-Hall.

Cancian, F. 1968. Maximization as norm, strategy, and theory: a comment on programmatic statements in economic anthropology. In E. E. LeClair and H. K. Schneider, eds., *Economic Anthropology*. New York: Holt, Rinehart and Winston.

Cicourel, A. 1970. Basic and narrative rules in the negotiation of status and role. In H. P. Dretzel, ed., *Recent Sociology*. Vol. 2. London: Macmillan.

Davis, J. 1973. Forms and norms: the economy of social relations. *Man,* n.s., 8 (2): 159–176.

Ekeh, Peter P. 1968. Issues in social exchange theory. *Berkeley Journal of Sociology,* 13: 42–58.

_____. 1974. *Social Exchange Theory: The Two Traditions*. London: Heinemann.

Garfinkel, H. 1967. *Studies in Ethnomethodology*. Englewood Cliffs, N.J.: Prentice-Hall.

Geertz, C. 1957. Ritual and social change: a Javanese example. *American Anthropologist,* 59: 32–54.

Glaser, Barney G., and Anselm Strauss. 1967. *The Discovery of Grounded Theory*. Chicago: Aldine.

Goffman, E. 1970. *Strategic Interaction*. Oxford: Basil Blackwell.

Heath, A. 1968. Economic theory and sociology: a critique of P. M. Blau's *Exchange and Power in Social Life*. *Sociology,* 2: 273–292.

Homans, G. C. 1961. *Social Behavior: Its Elementary Forms*. New York: Harcourt, Brace and World.

Kapferer, B. 1972. *Strategy and Transaction in an African Factory: African Workers and Indian Management in a Zambian Town*. Manchester: Manchester University Press.

Leach, E. R. 1954. *Political Systems of Highland Burma*. London: G. Bell and Sons.

_____. 1961. *Rethinking Anthropology*. London School of Economics Monographs on Social Anthropology No. 22. London.

Lindesmith, Alfred R., Anselm L. Strauss, and Norman K. Denzin. 1975. A statement of position: symbolic interactionism as perspective and method. In Alfred R. Lindesmith et al., eds., *Readings in Social Psychology*. New York: Holt, Rinehart and Winston.

McCall, G. J., and J. L. Simmons. 1966. *Identities and Interactions*. New York: Free Press.

McHugh, Peter. 1968. *Defining the Situation: The Organization of Meaning in Social Interaction*. Indianapolis: Bobbs-Merrill.

Meeker, B. F. 1971. Decisions and exchange. *American Sociological Review,* 36: 485–495.

Mulkay, M. J. 1971. *Functionalism, Exchange, and Theoretical Strategy*. New York: Schocken.

Nadel, S. F. 1951. *The Foundations of Social Anthropology*. London: Cohen and West.

Schutz, A. 1967. *Collected Papers, Vol. I: The Problems of Social Reality*. The Hague: Martinus Nijhoff.

Singelmann, P. 1973. On the deification of paradigms: reply to Abbott, Brown and Crosbie. *American Sociological Review*, 38: 504–507.

Skvoretz, W. H., Jr., and R. H. Conviser. 1974. Interests and alliances: a reformulation of Barth's *Models of Social Organization*. *Man*, n.s., 9 (1): 53–67.

Turner, Victor. 1974. *Dramas, Fields and Metaphors: Symbolic Action in Human Society*. Ithaca, N.Y., and London: Cornell University Press.

Van Velsen, J. 1964. *The Politics of Kinship*. Manchester: Manchester University Press.

Webster, M., Jr. 1973. Psychological reductionism, methodological individualism, and large-scale problems. *American Sociological Review*, 38: 259–273.

Whitten, N. E., Jr., and D. S. Whitten. 1972. Social strategies and social relationship. *Annual Review of Anthropology*, 1: 247–270.

Part One

TRANSACTIONS AND THE
ANALYSIS OF DECISIONS

Library
I.U.P.
Indiana, Pa.

301.21 T687r
c.1

Decision Making and Transactional Theory

A. F. HEATH

MODELS OF DECISION MAKING

No longer can it be said that "economics is all about how people make choices. Sociology is all about why they don't have any choices to make."[1] Decision-making models, often borrowed from economics itself, have become increasingly popular in sociology and anthropology. According to this new approach, the existence of norms and rules (the sociologist's traditional concerns) does not mean that men have no choices to make; instead, norms and rules become simply one set among many of "the constraints and incentives that canalize choices."

This new approach has become particularly influential in the study of transactions. Blau in sociology and Barth in anthropology have both developed what are in effect decision-making models. Both emphasize the importance of choice. Thus Blau writes: "The only assumption made is that human beings choose between alternative potential associates or courses of action by evaluating the experiences or expected experiences with each in terms of a preference ranking and then selecting the best alternative" (1964: 18). Barth writes: "The most simple and general model available to us is one of an aggregate of people exercising *choice* while influenced by certain constraints and incentives" (1966: 1; Barth's emphasis).

This approach is by no means restricted to what has been called exchange theory or transactional theory. It seems to me that Jarvie's "logic of the situation" amounts to very much the same thing. He writes: "A man, for the purposes of the social sciences, can be viewed as in pursuit of certain goals or aims, within a framework of natural, social, psychological and ethical circumstances. These circumstances constitute both means of achieving his aims and constraints on that achievement. A man's conscious or unconscious appraisal of how he can achieve his aims might be called sorting out the logic of the situation he is in" (1972: 4). It might, indeed, but it could equally be called decision making. The same kind of approach is becoming increasingly popular in sociology too. Thus Matza: "Since man occupies a position in a complex and loosely organized social system, since he is the object of unclear and often conflicting forces, and since he is himself an integral part of his social system, he possesses some leeway of choice" (1964: 11).

Strangely, however, users of this new approach have paid relatively little

25

attention to the process of choice itself. It is not enough to know what men's goals are and what constraints they perceive. We must have some theory of decision making before we can explain their behavior. Without such a theory we have a crucial lacuna at the heart of the explanation. We could even adapt Barth himself and suggest that "one form, in the sense of a set of regular patterns of behaviour, is translated into another, virtually congruent form, made up of constraints and incentives, which are made logically prior to behaviour. The model does not depict any intervening social process between the constraints and incentives and the pattern. There is indeed no science of social life in this procedure, no explanation of how actual forms, much less frequency distributions in behaviour, come about, beyond the axiomatic: what people do is influenced by constraints and incentives" (see Barth 1966: 2).

This would, however, be a distinctly uncharitable comment. Most of the writers whom I have mentioned do make some attempt to fill the lacuna. My main criticism of them is that they make no attempt to assess the soundness of their theories of decision making. They make brief and unexplicated assumptions, and then move quickly on to the (no doubt) more interesting business of identifying the constraints and incentives.

In almost all cases the assumption is made that men choose rationally. Either the actor chooses the most effective means to his goals, given his understanding of the situation (Jarvie), or he chooses a course of action which ensures that the value gained is greater than or equal to the value lost (Barth), or he selects the alternative which ranks highest in his preference ranking (Blau). Blau's version is identical to the economist's principle of utility maximization. This assumes that the actor can rank in order of preference all the states into which he can get and then select the course of action which leads to his most preferred state. It is essentially a theory of *riskless* choice, since it assumes that the actor knows exactly what the outcome of any course of action will be.[2] It is by far the simplest and most popular model, but I am very doubtful about its general applicability in sociology or anthropology.

To cope with the presumably rather more common situations of risk and uncertainty, economists have developed two other main principles, the *expected* utility maximization and the minimax loss principles. The former is a straightforward extension to deal with risky choices—that is, with choices where some numerical probability can be assigned to the likelihood that a particular outcome will follow a particular course of action. First, the expected utility of a course of action is found by multiplying the utility of each possible outcome by its probability of occurrence and summing these products across all possible outcomes. That is,

$$\text{EU} = p_1 u_1 + p_2 u_2 + \cdots + p_n u_n,$$

where p stands for the probability of an outcome, u stands for the utility of an outcome, and $p_1 + p_2 + \cdots + p_n = 1$. The expected utility maximization principle then simply states that the actor will choose the course of action which has the highest expected utility. I take it that Jarvie's principle is something close to this.

The most effective means to a goal is presumably the one which has the highest probability of achieving the goal; by selecting the most effective means one is thus maximizing expected utility.[3]

The minimax loss principle, on the other hand, is most commonly used to deal with *uncertain* choices—that is, with situations where numerical probabilities cannot be assigned. The principle states that the actor will consider the worst outcome which could follow from each course of action and will then select the course which will have the least ill effects if the worst outcome occurs. It is most commonly used in the theory of games and, although sometimes used for explanatory purposes (as in Davenport's study of Jamaican fishing),[4] it is most often regarded as a normative principle rather than as a descriptive one.

These three principles, the utility maximization, expected utility maximization, and minimax loss principles, are the most rigorously defined and most commonly used models of rational choice. If we intend to use a decision-making approach to the study of transactions, they are the most obvious candidates to fill the gap between the "constraints and incentives" and the observed patterns of behavior. It seems to me that the potentialities, and limitations, of these models are not often enough recognized in the anthropological and sociological literature, and it is on these models, therefore, that I wish to concentrate in this chapter. This means that I will be concerned primarily with the psychological assumptions which lie, or perhaps *should* lie, behind transactional theory and not with the transactions themselves.

Before I examine the models in detail, I would like to make some preliminary points. In particular I would like to stress that, if we wish to borrow these models of rational choice from economics, we do not also have to make the other assumptions that are sometimes made by economists. First, none of the models entails the assumption that men maximize money profit or that men behave self-interestedly: none specifies what it is that gives utility. Of course, there is still the problem of how one actually identifies and measures preferences or utilities. The conventional approach to this in economics (or by Homans in sociology) has been to infer them from men's actual choices, but if we do this the utility maximization principle at least becomes almost tautological. However, I see no need to adopt such a behaviorist approach. It is commonplace in sociology and anthropology, if not in economics, to deal with "subjective" or "meaningful" categories such as men's values, intentions, or perceptions, and I cannot see that utility or preference is any different in kind. It is "unobservable" and thus not directly accessible to the social scientist; to get at it we have to rely on the traditional methods of getting at "subjective" categories, namely interviews, accounts, and questionnaires. The problems with these are considerable and well known but not in my view of such weight that we must resort to behaviorism.

Second, we do not need to assume that the actors have perfect knowledge. Certainly economists frequently make this assumption when they use the utility maximization and expected utility maximization principles, but I do not think there is any need to follow them in this. There is no reason, in principle, why we should not develop realistic theories according to which the actor behaves rationally in the light of the information available to him. Thus in the case of the utility maximization principle I see no difficulty in assuming that men choose the most preferred alternative which they *believe* open to them. (Of course, with this model we must still require that men feel certain about what the outcomes of their actions will be, whether or not this certainty is justified, since otherwise we would need to use theories of risky or uncertain choices.) Similarly, I see no special difficulty in taking into account men's own estimates of the probabilities that particular outcomes will follow particular actions. True, there is no guarantee that these "subjective probabilities" will sum to unity, but I see no harm in removing this requirement.

There is a third assumption, made not so much by economists as by writers like Homans and Jarvie, which I think could be dispensed with too. This is the assumption that the models of rational choice can be applied to both conscious and unconscious decisions. My own view is that it is rather unlikely that the same principles would apply to both kinds of decision, and I would be inclined to use, say, learning theory for habitual and unreflective choices and to retain the rational-choice principles for those decisions which involve more conscious calculation. I might add that I doubt if this would prove a very serious restriction. Certainly all the examples at which I shall be looking in this chapter would appear to involve conscious thought processes. However, whether the same principles apply to both conscious and unconscious processes is an empirical matter, not one to be settled a priori.

As regards the first two of these assumptions, if not the third, I take it that I would be in fairly close agreement with the writers such as Barth whom I mentioned at the beginning of this chapter. They are presumably concerned with the way in which the actor chooses, given his own definition of the situation and his own set of goals or preferences. Where I differ from them is simply in my concern with the economist's more rigorously defined notions of what constitute rational decision rules, and in my concern with the question of whether men actually follow these decision rules.

THE MODELS EXAMINED

Consider, then, the principle of utility maximization. For it to have any explanatory usefulness it clearly requires that men have stable preferences. It then simply amounts to the decision rule: "Act consistently with your preferences." Strangely, there is no research (that I know of) directly relevant to this. Rather, the research effort has largely concentrated on transitivity. (An individual chooses transitively if he chooses A in preference to B, B in preference to C, and therefore also A in preference to C.) The evidence so far on transitivity is rather equivocal. The conventional view seems to be that people choose transitively when faced with simple payoffs but begin to make appreciable numbers of intransitive choices when faced with multidimensional payoffs, such as phonograph records or girl friends (see Simon and Stedry 1969).

Strictly, however, it is not clear whether the intransitivity so far discovered is evidence that people fail to follow the utility maximization principle. If someone actually has intransitive preferences, then the decision rule "Act consistently with your preferences" is of no help: it does not give a determinate answer. It is only if someone actually has transitive preferences but then chooses intransitively that we can say that he is not following the rule. Again, there is no direct evidence on this, but I am inclined to think that actual intransitive preferences are very rare. Most examples of intransitive choices seem to be due to people "making mistakes" (or perhaps choosing randomly between equally preferred alternatives). In one of the few studies which actually confronted people with their intransitive choices, only two of the thirty-eight subjects wished to stand by their original choices. The others all claimed they had made mistakes (MacCrimmon 1968).

Nevertheless, if people do make appreciable numbers of mistakes, then the explanatory power of the utility maximization principle would seem much reduced and we should need to look elsewhere for our theories of choice. A number of factors incline me against this view, however, and I suggest that the attention paid to intransitivity in the economic and psychological literature is grossly disproportionate to its importance for the explanation of those choices with which sociologists and anthropologists are concerned. First, many of the studies involve bets for trivial sums in a laboratory or hypothetical choices between, say, a girl friend described simply as "pretty, very charming, well-to-do," one described as "beautiful, fairly charming, poor," and so on. I hardly find it surprising that people make careless choices in situations like these, and I do not find them a good guide to the decision rules that people employ in more realistic or serious situations. Indeed, in a study of my own which gave subjects choices somewhat more realistic than usual (but still unfortunately hypothetical), virtually no examples of intransitivity occurred.[5]

Second, even if people do make mistakes, in the situations with which sociologists are concerned the "sure-thing" principle is frequently the only one required. "The sure-thing principle asserts that if course of action A is at least as good as course of action B in all possible future states of the world, and is definitely better in one or more, then B should never be preferred to A: it is about the only universally accepted and universally empirically confirmed principle in decision theory" (Edwards 1961: 477). The sure-thing principle is of course simply a special case of the utility maximization principle. It holds for simple situations where one alternative is better than the other in some respects and identical in all others. It therefore suggests that the "mistakes" which occur in utility maximization arise when the actor has to "trade-off" advantages from course of action A against different advantages from course of action B.

Let us consider, then, some examples of these principles at work. My favorite one comes from Latané and Darley (1970). They start with the puzzle provided by such incidents as the Kitty Genovese murder. Kitty Genovese was set upon by a maniac as she returned home from work at 3:00 A.M. Thirty-eight of her neighbors came to their windows when she cried out in terror, but none came to her assistance even though the murderer took half an hour to finish the job. No one even called the police. Why?

Latané and Darley suggest that the explanation may lie in the very fact which so surprises us: the number of onlookers present. They suggest, *inter alia*, that the presence of other people can alter the rewards and costs facing each individual. "Perhaps most importantly, the presence of other people can reduce the cost of not acting. If only one bystander is present at an emergency, he carries all the responsibility for dealing with it; he will feel all of the guilt for not acting; he will bear all of any blame others may level for nonintervention. If others are present, the onus of responsibility is diffused, and the individual may be more likely to resolve his conflict between intervening and not intervening in favor of the latter alternative" (p. 21).

This example, I think, nicely illustrates the character of a rational-choice approach at work. The main explanatory interest comes from the description of the "constraints and incentives" present. Latané and Darley suggest that, the more people are present, the less blame is attached to any one individual. They do not give any independent evidence for this, but it appears to be a plausible and readily testable hypothesis. They then, equally plausibly, assume that individuals find blame a cost and hence that the costs of not acting are greater when an individual is on his own than when he is in the company of others. Having dealt with the constraints and incentives, Latané and Darley show little interest in the decision rule; but they could use something akin to the sure-thing principle, since they are essentially comparing two situations which are identical apart from the fact that one involves an extra cost. This example differs from the sure-thing situation, of course, since the individual is not choosing between helping when someone else is present and helping when he is alone. We are instead comparing choices between helping and not helping under two different conditions. I would guess that the sure-thing principle could be extended to cover this and that we could reasonably conclude, as do Latané and Darley, that the individual is less likely to help under the one condition than the other.

This means that we can explain *differences* in the rates of behavior, but we cannot say that we have now explained why no one actually went to help Kitty Genovese. To take a rather simplistic example, the probability that John Smith will go to the help of Kitty Genovese may well be lower if there are thirty-seven other people present than if there are only four others, but this does not allow us to conclude that *none* of the thirty-eight will go to her help. If the probability that John Smith will go to her help is 0.1 when there are thirty-seven others and 0.4 when there are four others, and if the probabilities are the same for the other individuals as well, then elementary probability theory tells us that we can expect *more* people to go to Kitty Genovese's help in the former case than in the latter. After the fact, we will be inclined to think that the probability must have been much lower than 0.1 in the former case, but we have in no sense explained this. To do so we need to know at least what the other rewards and costs are and, most important, what the individual's trade-offs are between the different rewards and costs. It is not enough to know that he prefers less blame to more, less effort to more, and so on. We also need to know, for example, how much effort he is prepared to exchange for a given amount of blame. Of course, we can always postulate some set of rewards and costs and some set of trade-offs to give us the right answer, but then we have to obtain independent evidence that these were the actual sets involved. Even if we can do this (and I am rather doubtful that people's preferences are sufficiently stable to enable us to do so), there still remains the problem that it may be in cases such as these—with multidimensional payoffs involving trade-offs—that the individual makes mistakes.

Of course, gaps are bound to occur in any explanation and it is silly to criticize an argument solely on the grounds that not every assumption has been rigorously spelled out and tested. However, I do not think that the gaps which I have mentioned in Latané and Darley's arguments are wholly venial. Rather, if we are to explain why no one came to Kitty Genovese's assistance, it is precisely our task to fill these gaps. Unless this is done, one's initial intuitive view that, when there are more people present, there is a better chance of receiving assistance will not be shaken.[6]

Many examples of rational-choice arguments with a similar general structure could easily be found. For example, Kapferer in his study *Strategy and Transaction in an African Factory* (1972) explains why married men are less likely than single men to seek jobs in other towns by suggesting that married men incur greater costs in moving to another town (by virtue of having to transport and find housing for a whole family). Kapferer gives no independent evidence for the existence of this constraint, but his claim seems quite reasonable. All he then needs is an extension of the sure-thing principle to conclude the explanation.

However, Kapferer also seems to want to explain why married men do not move *at all* to different towns (or at least why they do so very rarely). He therefore suggests that the costs of moving would exceed the possible gains from new employment, but he does not tell us what these possible gains are nor does he give any evidence of the trade-offs involved. Again, we would be inclined to accept the idea that the costs must have outweighed the benefits, but this of course does not provide us with an explanation.

A much more serious worry than the absence of information about men's preferences is the fact that a theory of riskless choice is being used in a situation which is quite clearly one of risk or uncertainty. This is not perhaps quite so important when we are simply comparing the married and the single men (since our extension of the sure-thing principle can presumably be applied to risky situations too), but it is crucial when we wish to explain why the married men do not move. Kapferer, and for that matter Latané and Darley, are by no means alone in this omission. Indeed, apart from the occasional uses of game theory, there are very few rational-choice explanations in anthropology or sociology which explicitly employ a model based on uncertainty or risk.

The crucial problem for someone interested in offering such explanations is whether people actually do follow the expected utility and the minimax loss principles which I outlined earlier. The conventional wisdom among psychologists and economists seems to be that these are normative rather than descriptive principles and hence that they are not useful for explanatory purposes. For example, Simon (1959: 260) has concluded that "even in an extremely simple situation subjects do not behave in the way predicted by a straightforward application of utility theory." He based this view on a survey of binary-choice experiments. In these the subject is required in each of a series of trials to choose one or the other of two symbols—for example, plus or minus. When he has chosen, he is told whether his choice was right or wrong, and he may also receive a reward for the correct choice. Now suppose that the experimenter arranges for plus to be the correct choice on one-third of the trials and minus to be correct on the other two-thirds. The subject is faced, on each trial, with a choice between one course of action which has a probability of one-third of bringing a reward (and hence utility) and another course of action which has a probability of two-thirds of bringing the same reward. A subject who is maximizing expected utility should therefore *always* choose the latter course (namely, selecting minus). "Unfortunately for the classical theory of utility," Simon reports, "few subjects behave in this way. The most commonly observed behavior is what is called event matching. The subject chooses the two alternatives (not necessarily at random) with relative frequencies roughly proportional to the relative frequencies with which they are rewarded" (p. 260).

Before abandoning the expected utility principle, however, we should notice a number of points. First, the rewards used in those experiments are usually quite trivial and it is quite possible that the subjects are willing to forego them in order to add some variety to the experiment. Thus the utilities being maximized *may* be rather different from those postulated by the experimenters. (Of course, as I have suggested earlier, we can always postulate some set of utilities to make the behavior seem "rational," but we also need independent evidence to show that these are in fact the relevant utilities. This is rather difficult to obtain.) Second, it is quite likely that the subjects fall prey to the gambler's fallacy. They may well suppose that, because two minuses have come up consecutively, a plus is more likely to come up on the third trial. This is certainly irrational in the sense that the subjects have misunderstood probability theory and made incorrect inferences, but it does not follow that the subjects failed to use an expected utility principle. Quite the contrary. If the subject believes that a plus is more likely than a minus on the third trial, the principle indicates that he should choose plus. The results of the binary-choice experiments may thus falsify only the assumption made in classical utility theory that men have perfect knowledge (an assumption which we have already rejected). The rest of the theory may still stand untouched.

However, while subjects in the binary-choice experiments *may* be following the expected utility principle, it is hard to demonstrate that conclusively. We usually have too many unknowns, and we can juggle them to give us any answer we want. Consider, for example, the following case. Suppose that you are given a choice between on the one hand a certainty of one thousand pounds, and on the other hand a fifty-fifty chance of getting either four thousand pounds or nothing. Most people to whom I have so far suggested this example (none of them very rich) have chosen the certain one thousand pounds. On the face of it, this looks as though they are following the minimax loss rather than the expected utility principle. Clearly, the *money* expectation from the gamble is much larger than one thousand pounds and so we might expect the expected utility to be larger too. Unfortunately, we cannot be sure that it is. Given the declining marginal utility of money, it is quite possible that the difference in utility between nothing and one thousand pounds is greater than that between one and four thousand pounds, in which case the expected utility principle would indicate that the certainty should be chosen. To discover which rule people are following, then, we need to measure the utility of money on an interval scale, but unfortunately the only convincing attempts to do so assume the truth of the expected utility principle.

This might seem to suggest that the lacuna at the heart of rational-choice theories of decision making is likely to remain. However, I suspect that some headway can be made. In the first place it seems perfectly possible to obtain interval scales of utility by directly questioning subjects. In one preliminary piece of research I have asked some sociology postgraduate students to state their liking for a number of teaching and research jobs of the kind for which they would shortly be looking in earnest. I asked them not only to rank the jobs but also to say which one, ''as regards your personal liking for it,'' came halfway in between the most liked and the least liked. This was repeated for various lists of jobs.

I then gave the subjects choices analogous to that between the certain one thousand pounds and the gamble for four thousand pounds or nothing. I asked them to suppose that they had been offered two jobs (on one of which they had to make an immediate decision) and had applied for a third which, they were to assume, they had a fifty-fifty chance of obtaining. For this third job I chose one for which they had a relatively strong preference; the job on which no decision was required was one for which they had a relatively weak preference; and the one on which they had to make an immediate decision was either just above or just below the midpoint (in utility terms) between the other two. Subjects following the expected utility rule should choose the gamble when the job on which they had to make the immediate decision came below their midpoint, and they should reject the gamble when it came above. Minimaxing subjects, on the other hand, should always reject the gamble. By and large the results showed that it was the expected utility principle which subjects were following.[7]

Presenting subjects with hypothetical choices rather than with real ones has obvious drawbacks, but otherwise the situation was a fairly realistic and familiar one. We are often faced with the choice between continuing with our present course of action (with its known and certain outcomes) and on the other hand adopting a riskier course which could turn out either better or worse. This is presumably the kind of situation that faced Kapferer's workers. Each could either continue in his present job with its known outcomes or move to another town with the possibility of getting a better job and the certainty of incurring extra expense.

A number of further points are worth making about the subjects' responses to the experiments. First, none of the subjects balked at the notion of a fifty-fifty chance of obtaining a job. This fits in with common sense, although strictly the matter is likely to involve not risk, to which probability applies, but uncertainty. I suspect that for most people, who do not understand probability theory anyway, the distinction between risk and uncertainty is really immaterial. My guess is that, while the distinction may be important normatively, it has little explanatory value. True, there will be people who, for reasons of personality, follow the minimax (or maximax) principle rather than the expected utility principle, but there is no evidence to support the view that in situations of uncertainty different principles are employed than in situations of risk. And indeed there is some evidence against this view (see MacCrimmon 1968).

Second, it appeared that the subjects not only made choices which could be predicted from an expected utility principle but also followed something akin to the principle in their reasoning. A typical explanation for a particular choice was: "I would accept Brunel [the job for which the immediate decision was required] because my preference for Oxford over Brunel was not so great as to make the risk of waiting for the Oxford job worthwhile." From further questioning it appeared that in deciding whether a risk was worthwhile the subjects were in fact comparing the two intervals. If they judged the difference between the least liked and the intermediate job to be not as great as that between the intermediate and the most liked, then the risk was worth taking.

Notice, however, what the subjects were not doing. They were not multiplying the utility they would get from the Oxford job by 0.5. Of course they had no need to in this particular situation in order to get the "right" answer, since it was a fifty-fifty gamble. However, had it been a sixty-forty gamble, simple estimation of the intervals would not give the same answer as the expected utility principle. Now I cannot believe that even in situations where computation of the expected utilities is "required" people do carry it out. Possibly they weight the intervals instead, according to the relevant probabilities. Alternatively, people may use the minimax principle (although this would mean discarding what could be important information). However, my own suggestion is that, unless there is a fairly simple way of reaching a decision, people will try to obtain further information. If the intervals are similar but the probabilities very different, a decision can easily be made. Equally, if the probabilities are very similar but the intervals very different, there is no difficulty. However, when a judgment based on probabilities contradicts one based on intervals, rather than attempting computations people will tend to adopt the other choice that is almost always open to them—to collect further information.[8]

BARTH'S HERRING SKIPPERS: AN EXAMPLE

If this argument is correct, then it should help to illuminate some actual decisions. I propose therefore to consider one of the classic choices in transactional theory, namely that facing Barth's herring skippers. The choice is where to search for herring and, says Barth, "the skipper's dilemma is continual: the vessel has to go or be somewhere always, so the decision can never be ignored or postponed. Success or failure depends on it" (1966: 10). Further, the choice is a splendid example of one made under conditions of uncertainty. While the skippers have a wide range of information available—from radio reports and forecasts, from use of the vessel's own asdic, and from watching the movements of other vessels nearby—the information taken together is still "very incomplete and fragmentary as the basis for a rational decision" (*ibid.*).

The decisions which do emerge, moreover, seem to result in "grotesquely unadaptive patterns of movement and congregation." "The several hundred vessels of the fleet constantly tend to congregate in small areas of the immense, and potentially bountiful, expanse of sea; most attention is concentrated on discovering the movements of other vessels, and most time is spent chasing other vessels to such unplanned and fruitless rendezvous" (*ibid.*). Furthermore, these patterns occur despite the fact, presumably known to all skippers, that a vessel's chance of finding herring is greater if it strikes out on its own than if it follows other vessels.

Barth's own explanation for these strange patterns focuses on the transactions between skipper and crew and on the importance of *relative* catch. He argues:

> If a skipper, without special information to justify the move, decides to go elsewhere than where other vessels go, he demands more trust in his transaction with the crew. They are asked to respect his judgement, as opposed to that of the other skippers; they are thus asked to make greater prestations of submission than they would otherwise have had to. The skipper also risks more by not joining the cluster: if a few vessels among many make a catch, the crew and the netboss can claim that it might have been them, had the skipper only given them the chance. If the vessel on the other hand follows the rest, they are no worse off than most, and the onus of failure does not fall on the skipper.
>
> Secondly, the absence of a catch matters less, so long as other vessels *also* fail—the measure of a skipper's competence and success is not absolute, but relative to the catch of other vessels. The factor affecting the skipper's ability to recruit a good crew next season is his position in the catch statistics, not the gross amount.
>
> These patterns are self-confirming: good skippers with good and stable crews will have greater freedom of choice because greater prestations of trust can be demanded; the same boats and skippers will consistently top the lists of resultant catch, and they will be regarded as elite boats, who most often find the herring and whom it is an advantage to follow. Being first, they *will* tend to get best results, and so on [*ibid.*].

This explanation can certainly account for the fact that good skippers more readily go off on their own: that they can demand greater prestations of trust presumably means that they incur fewer costs in going on their own than do the skippers with poorer records. However, neither this nor the rest of Barth's argument can explain the actual pattern of movement, the observed clustering of vessels. The situation is identical to that with Latané and Darley's bystanders or Kapferer's workers. By postulating an extra reward or cost (and using the extension of the sure-thing principle) we can explain why some men are more likely to act than others or more likely to act under some conditions than others. But we cannot explain why the rate of behavior is what it is: we can explain only differences in rates.

Let us reconsider Barth's explanation. The majority of skippers incur extra costs by going on their own and they also run the risk of doing worse than average. However, they have a better chance of a relatively *good* catch if they go on their own, and presumably this is a valued objective too. There are therefore both advantages and disadvantages to going on one's own, and it is not self-evident that the latter outweigh the former. Of course, it may be that the skippers follow the minimax principle; this would certainly account for the decisions of the majority, but we have no good grounds for supposing that they do. In the absence of evidence to the contrary, I think that we should assume that people follow the expected utility principle.

If we are to make any progress, then, we must begin with some assumptions about the utilities skippers derive from varying sizes of catch. Furthermore, it is crucial to make assumptions that can be checked independently; as I have said repeatedly, it is no help to say that the advantages must have outweighed the disadvantages. There is of course one assumption which can readily be made and for which there is independent evidence, namely that of diminishing marginal utility. On its own this assumption is not particularly powerful, but it becomes much more useful to us if we ally it with the assumption that the individual incurs diminishing marginal *dis*utility as he obtains increasingly *less* than he is accustomed to. This gives us a combined utility-disutility curve as in Figure 1. I have no direct evidence that the curve does have this general shape, but the shape is readily testable. In addition, there is some evidence from the psychological literature on level of aspiration that the individual's past record of success will be crucial in determining the positioning of the curve.

Let us consider now the choices facing, say, skippers with average, below average, and above average records. I assume that a skipper with an above average record will have a utility curve such as AA' in Figure 2. (That it is further to the right than the other curve indicates that the successful skipper gets less utility than do the others from any given catch.[9]) He is faced with the choice between keeping in contact with other ships or going on his own. If he stays with the others he is highly likely to get an average catch (OQ) and hence little utility (OG). There will not be complete certainty, of course: he is faced, like everyone else, with a probability distribution, but this will presumably have a relatively small variance. If he goes on his own, on the other hand, he can expect on average a rather better catch, but the distribution will have a larger variance. He might thus obtain a very

FIGURE 1

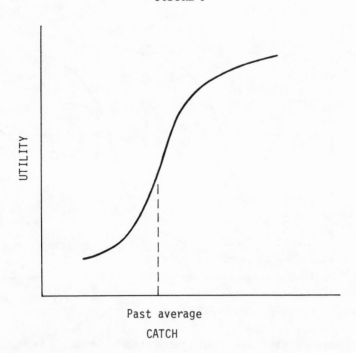

large catch (*OR*) giving a great deal of utility (*OL*) or a very small catch (*OP*) giving much less utility (*OF*). We can assume that a particularly good outcome is no more likely than a particularly bad one. Then, since *GL* is a great deal larger than *FG*, the expected utility principle clearly indicates that the skipper should go on his own.

Consider next a skipper with a below average record. I assume that his utility curve (*BB'* in Figure 2) is further to the left than those of his peers, indicating that he gets more utility from any given catch. If he keeps in contact with the other vessels he can be fairly sure of an average catch (*OQ*), giving him a great deal of utility (*OM*). If he goes on his own he might get a very large catch (*OR*) giving even more utility (*ON*) or a very poor catch (*OP*) giving very little utility (*OH*). However, since *MN* is much smaller than *HM*, the expected utility principle indicates that he should go with the fleet.

To put the situation in this way is clearly to oversimplify grossly, but I hope that the general structure, and hence the general conclusion, is sound. That is, the better a skipper's past record, the more likely he is to go on his own; and the poorer the record, the more likely he is to go with the fleet. However, the closer to the average the skipper's record is, the less clear-cut is the answer given by the expected utility principle. According to my earlier reasoning, this should mean that the skippers will attempt to acquire further information. There is one clear way

FIGURE 2

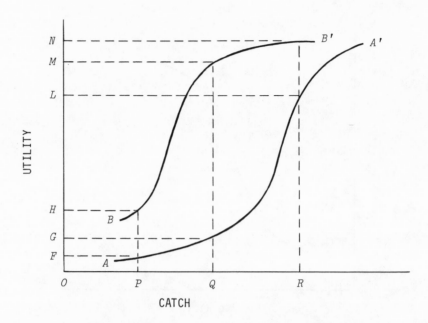

to do this, namely to stay in contact with the other ships. On Barth's own account, the movements of other ships are an important source of information and to go on one's own is therefore to cut oneself off from that source.[10]

I cannot be confident that the explanation I have offered is the correct one, since it has involved a considerable number of assumptions, although none of them I hope are either wholly implausible or wholly unsupported. It is quite possible that new evidence will necessitate a quite different explanation. However, I think my explanation does indicate the kind of assumption which must be made if we are to explain not only differences in rate but also the actual patterns of behavior. In the first place we must assume some more sophisticated decision rule than simple utility maximization if we are to deal with situations of risk and uncertainty. The minimax loss principle would be the most convenient for the sociologist (since it requires information only about the ranking of worst outcomes). But unfortunately I suspect that we shall need something based on the expected utility principle. If we do, then we shall need to be able to construct not merely ordinal scales but also interval scales of utility. In principle there is no reason why this should not be done, but in practice it proves very difficult to obtain independent evidence for them. This is likely to be a crucial difficulty with the rational-choice approach. Anything can be "explained" if we postulate particular preference rankings (either ordinal or interval) without requiring independent evidence, but the resulting explanations will never (and should never) convince. If we can demonstrate the existence of some general principles governing utilities (such as the principle of diminishing marginal utility or the more complicated one which I have offered), then we may make some progress. But these will not always be useful if we are dealing with an array of different rewards. In the Kitty Genovese case, for example, we need to balance quite different rewards and costs and probabilities— the rewards gained from helping people and the costs incurred if one gets hurt, if one is blamed for not acting, and so on. Of course it may be that in situations such as this it is difficult not only for the sociologist but also for the actor himself, who therefore decides to collect further information by simply watching from his window. But we cannot rely on this notion. We may have to recognize that there are some patterns of behavior which we are simply not going to explain on rational-choice lines.

NOTES

1. J. S. Duesenberry, quoted in G. Hawthorn, *The Sociology of Fertility* (London: Collier Macmillan, 1970), p. 59.

2. Blau is of course very well aware of the importance of risk and uncertainty in social life, but he does not formally take account of them in his general statement of psychological assumptions, quoted at the beginning of this chapter.

3. Jarvie, however, unlike the economist, is not at all clear as to the principle on which the actor makes his choice when he has a variety of goals. Indeed, he says "there is *no* suggestion that there exists some perfect scrutiny of the situation which yields a uniquely effective move" (1972: 4). This is not very helpful, although it may of course be true.

4. See Davenport 1960: 3–11. Whether Davenport actually succeeds in providing an explanation is another matter. I am inclined to think that he does not.

5. Details of this research are given later in the chapter.

6. It is only fair to point out that Latané and Darley do mention another argument which could provide an alternative explanation for the failure of anyone to help Kitty Genovese. They argue that American males try to appear calm in times of stress. Further, "if each member of a group is, at the same time, trying to appear calm and also looking around at the other members to gauge their reactions, all members may be led (or misled) by each other to define the situation as less critical than they would if alone. Until someone acts, each person sees only other nonresponding bystanders and is likely to be influenced not to act himself. A state of 'pluralistic ignorance' may develop" (p. 15.). This argument may well be correct, but it is quite separate from the argument about the effect of group size on the costs of not acting. It essentially claims that, in a crowd, people may define a situation as a non-emergency and hence one in which *acting* gives no payoff.

7. There were eight subjects and they were each given six choices to make. A number of these were discarded when a follow-up showed that the relevant parts of some subjects' preference orderings were unstable. This left a total of 39 choices. The expected utility model predicted correctly on 27 occasions; the minimax on 20.

Further experience has suggested to me that the technique of asking subjects to identify midpoints is not a particularly satisfactory one. I suspect that better results will be obtained by asking subjects to rate the difference (in terms of utility) between items or even to assign a number proportional to the utility of each item.

8. We can put the same point a little differently. The expected utility of collecting further information will increase with the likelihood that further information will affect one's

decision. It will tend to be at a maximum when the choice between two alternatives is more or less balanced.

9. In this, and in a few following points, I am assuming that we can make interpersonal comparisons of utility. This assumption is often made by ordinary people but is abhorrent to economists. No important stages of my argument depend on it, however, and it is intended mainly to make the argument more intelligible to noneconomists. If the assumption were removed I would need to present the curves AA' and BB' on two separate graphs, not one.

10. To put the argument in this way is to adopt a sequential model in which the costs and benefits of information are considered only if a prior appraisal of the situation yields no clear answer.

REFERENCES

Barth, F. 1966. *Models of Social Organization*. Royal Anthropological Institute Occasional Paper No. 23. London.

Blau, P. M. 1964. *Exchange and Power in Social Life*. New York: Wiley.

Davenport, W. 1960. *Jamaican Fishing: A Game Theory Analysis*. Yale University Publications in Anthropology, 59. New Haven.

Edwards, W. 1961. Behavioral decision theory. *Annual Review of Psychology,* 13.

Jarvie, I. C. 1972. *Concepts and Society*. London: Routledge and Kegan Paul.

Kapferer, B. 1972. *Strategy and Transaction in an African Factory*. Manchester: Manchester University Press.

Latané, B., and J. M. Darley. 1970. Social determinants of bystander intervention in emergencies. In J. Macaulay and L. Berkowitz, eds., *Altruism and Helping Behavior*. New York: Academic Press.

MacCrimmon, K. R. 1968. Descriptive and normative implications of the decision-theory postulates. In K. Borch and J. Mossin, eds., *Risk and Uncertainty*. London: Macmillan.

Matza, D. 1964. *Delinquency and Drift*. New York: Wiley.

Simon, H. A. 1959. Theories of decision-making in economics and behavioral science. *American Economic Review,* 49.

Simon, H. A., and A. C. Stedry. 1969. Psychology and economics. In G. Lindzey and E. Aronson, eds., *Handbook of Social Psychology,* 2nd ed. Reading, Mass.: Addison-Wesley.

Transactions or Transactors?
An Economic Anthropologist's View

RICHARD F. SALISBURY

Can one understand the behavior of two individuals better by looking at each one separately, or by considering them as two poles of a dyad? Is what they do a single "transaction" or is it two "actions," each of which has an effect on the other actor? Phrased thus crudely the question appears an unreal one: for some purposes the interaction of two individuals *is* a single event, which both participants and any observer will describe in the same terms; but for many other purposes it is significant that both parties to a transaction have different goals in mind and would each describe what is happening in different terms. The film "Rashomon" made this latter point so tellingly in the postwar cinema that it has become commonplace: how appearances deceive, how the observer's view differs from the participants', and how each participant's view may differ from the other's.

The simple resolution of the problem is to say that *both* types of analysis are indeed valid and necessary, but any particular analyst may choose to concentrate on one particular aspect. Most social anthropologists since the publication of Barth's *Models of Social Organization* have adopted the view that the transaction, or the dyad, is the unit for study, and have left the study of individual decision making to other disciplines. Insofar as Barth himself in some places reifies the "transaction," the "model," and "reciprocity," this stricture applies to him also. There is of course ample precedent for studying dyads rather than individuals. Durkheim, while accepting the validity of explanations of behavior in terms of factors working on individuals, deliberately searched for "social" explanations at a different "level." He argued that social phenomena such as transactions were scientific facts observable unequivocally by outsiders and that these phenomena should be the basis for social science. The debt of transactionalists to Durkheim, through Mauss, in their choice of subject matter and in their positivistic approach needs no further mention. It is clear that viewing transactions from outside, seeing a process of interaction or bargaining, and relating the observed outcomes to what occurred during the interaction has produced major insights.

By contrast, analysis of individual decisions has been underemphasized in anthropology.[1] It is true that Barth sees the focusing on transactions as a way of moving from the dynamic of the individual event to the "generation" of the model of the total system, thereby including individual decision making in the system of explanation. But in fact inferences about individual decisions are most often

41

derived from the observation of transactions or from a priori assumptions about human nature. The fact that two transacting parties reach an agreement is often taken to imply that both parties come with the same understandings, values, and expectations—particularly expectations about reciprocity. Though this *may* be true, I find myself, Rashomon-like, questioning whether it is a valid assumption.

I find myself arguing that if one is to contribute to the understanding of transactions, it may be important to gain a fuller understanding of *transactors*. Like Homans (1964), though less chauvinistically, I want to "bring the people back in." I want to consider the individual as the locus of decision making, and to investigate how in individual transactions his choices are influenced by the other activities he is involved in.

I wish to take an explicitly economic stance. I would argue, as I have done since 1957, following Robbins (1935), Firth (1939), and Belshaw (1954), that any behavior can be looked at as the outcome of an allocative choice, a decision of how to apply scarce means to alternative ends. I wish to look at individual strategies of choice, at their opportunity costs—what other possible choices are eliminated when one positive choice is made—and at the indications of preference maps given by behavior *outside* the specific transaction. In this way I hope to see how far one can interpret what happens in transactions in the light of the factors affecting *individual* decisions. While the nature of the choices made is clearly influenced by constraints—limited means available, the choices that other people have already made, or the events in the transaction themselves—and a series of generalizations is possible about the effects of constraints, the individual decision is the point at which these constraints enter into behavior. Transactional analysis will be greatly strengthened if it applies economic reasoning about decision making more closely to the formulation of its propositions.

NORMATIVE AGREEMENT AND TRANSACTIONS

Before discussing the more general situation in which normative agreement between transactors is *not* assumed, a word might first be said about transactions within single "moral communities." In this area traditional utility economics can sharpen the analysis of transactionalists.

Economists have long insisted, like Durkheimian positivists, that one must sharply distinguish the commodities that change hands during a transaction—the "values given in exchange"—from the "subjective values" placed by the individual on those commodities. The "value" of an object *is* what it is exchanged for. Yet what is obtained by a transaction is not clear in most cases: for example, a businessman making a generous donation to a charity may gain a quiet conscience, merit in the next world, or more prosaically the prospect of an eventual seat on the board of the charity. An economist may use various techniques to assess the cash value of having a seat on the board, and may try to determine whether the donation is a worthwhile investment. He may bring progressively more intangible factors into his calculations and demonstrate that each can be shown to have a measurable "value in exchange." It is clear that the number of such intangibles exchanged in a transaction is potentially infinite. One may glibly say that everything has a value, but it is another thing entirely to quantify values. Even if one ignores problems of quantification a paradox remains. If one observes over time that donors of sums over $10,000 in a particular city do receive seats on the charity boards, it may be possible to generalize for that society or culture that $10,000 and a seat are equal in exchange value. Why then do exchanges take place? If one says that the impecunious charity places a higher subjective value on the money, and that the wealthy businessman places a higher subjective value on the seat, one is merely postponing empirical analysis. How can one determine subjective values? And does the existence of different subjective values imply that the society is not a single moral community, that it has multiple cultures?

Classical utility economics sidesteps both questions. The transactors may (but need not necessarily) have a similar culture, similar value *standards,* but these take the form of preference *maps.* Even when the preference map is stable, the choices made by an individual at any one time depend on his situation at that time. If you are a millionaire you are in a different situation from a pauper, and you will behave differently in giving to a charity, though you may both agree on the merit of the charity. Marshall's concept of declining marginal utility and Hicks's formulation of indifference curves express this idea mathematically and indicate how both transactors may be viewed as increasing their total satisfactions by exchanging. Microeconomic analysis of transactions within a single moral community leads directly into a consideration of how the various "situations" of individuals affect their transactional behavior vis-à-vis individuals in other situations. The variables defining "situations" include levels of wealth, age, and education, access to information or other resources, geographical location, and so on. The variables are ones commonly analyzed by social anthropologists, but there is a difference. While social anthropologists most often use these variables as though they define groups or aggregates possessing an interest in common, economists treat them more as external continua affecting decisions made by independent individuals.

To illustrate the matter using Hicks's terminology, it could be argued that a New Guinea Highlander might be indifferent to which one of the following sets he owned: (no pig and 50 pearl shells), (1 pig and 20 shells), (2 pigs and 10 shells), (3 pigs and 5 shells), or (4 pigs and 2 shells). Even if all Highlanders shared the same preference map for evaluating pigs and shells, the man with no pigs would be desperate to obtain the nucleus for a herd. By contrast, the man with enough pigs to provide for his anticipated needs for ceremonial distribution would prefer to increase his supply of other valuables rather than increase the strain on his gardens and on his wife by having a larger herd. At the same time, any individual given a choice between (1 pig and 20 shells) and (1 pig and 21 shells) would naturally opt for the second. In such a situation exchanges will occur. As long as a man with four pigs and two shells can get more than three shells for a pig, he will see a gain in exchanging one pig (but not two), since three pigs and six shells is better than three pigs and five shells; as long as a man with 50 shells and no pig can obtain a pig for less than 30 shells, he too will gain by exchanging.

Classical economists also spell out how aggregate effects alter the "situation" for individual transactors. In the pig/shell example it can readily be seen that the unevenness in the distribution of wealth in the population affects the number of transactions taking place and the exchange rate at which they occur. Moreover, if the total number of pigs changes, so too will the pattern of transactions. But it should be noted that the classical formulations of market reaction to aggregate supply and demand imply assumptions about the distribution of goods within a population and about even access to knowledge. For pig/shell exchanges to stabilize at a market rate of four shells for a pig implies several things, according to classical theory: (1) there are many more people with four pigs and two shells than with one pig and twenty shells; (2) all people with few pigs will rapidly obtain more by transactions; and (3) people needing shells will be able to get in touch with people needing pigs and will have heard about other transactions.

These may be reasonable assumptions for predicting aggregate patterns. But to analyze the individual transaction an economist uses such generalizations about "the market" only as first approximations. He considers how deviations from the assumptions of an open market—monopoly in the ownership of one good, or an individual's lack of knowledge about other transactions—make specific transactors prepared to exchange at rates other than the "market rate." Barth's analysis of Darfur (1967), Firth's study of Tikopia (1939), and my own study of Siane (1962a) have all followed in this tradition, analyzing how social definitions of what constitute appropriate nexuses of exchange act as constraints on particular transactors, providing them with standards that they can use to calculate their personal costs and benefits.

Most social anthropologists looking at transactions have focused differently. They have tended to look at those features *within the transaction itself* that determine its particular form. Since bargaining is the most commonly observed element in transactions, and since bargaining usually involves discussion by transactors of the terms of trade, the anthropological analysis is most commonly an analysis of bargaining. It is assumed that while the aggregate market conditions may be one determinant of the likely terms of trade for a specific transaction, it is the bargaining process that fixes the price actually paid. It is a short step to seeing the bargaining process as the paradigm for all social transactions. The limitations of a bargaining approach are not significant when one is dealing with a single moral community. Although the logic of bargaining implies that a politically powerful transactor should be able to dictate terms to a less powerful one, common membership in a single moral community can be seen as providing the sanctions that prevent the terms from becoming too disadvantageous for the less powerful. These sanctions can even enjoin particular exchange terms. Reciprocity, the imbeddedness of particular transactions in long-term relationships, and standard prices are some ways of expressing this idea. In practical terms these social concepts are the equivalent of the concepts used by economists. The two approaches do not differ significantly in their results.

But immediately the question arises: What are the constraints on bargaining that prevent exploitative behavior from being carried to its logical conclusion when transactors are *not* members of a single moral community? Such situations are commonly studied by anthropologists from the Arctic to the Amazon, from Norway to New Guinea. Here one cannot posit agreements on standard prices, relationships are not imbedded, and reciprocity is not an enforceable norm. I shall argue that the economist's approach of looking for factors impinging on the individual transactor may be more productive in such situations.

TRANSACTIONS UNDER CONDITIONS OF NORMATIVE DISAGREEMENT

My own questioning of the importance of the bargaining process in determining the terms of trade when transactors do not agree on standards of evaluation is colored by an experience I had in 1952. As an interested but almost penniless student, passing through Port Said by ship en route for Australia, I had spent most of the three hours ashore sightseeing and sampling Egyptian cuisine, and only at the last minute did I discover that I needed materials to darn my clothing. Nearby was a large self-service department store, resembling Woolworth's, where I could quickly buy needles and thread without speaking Arabic. But on the counter near the needles was a pile of fezzes, and on impulse I bought one as a souvenir, paying the price marked. On return to the ship the passengers conversed eagerly about their experiences of bargaining for souvenirs with itinerant vendors, and it turned out that almost everyone had bought a fez—all of identical manufacture. I shamefacedly kept quiet, having done no bargaining. The discussion of prices paid developed only slowly, but it finally emerged that not a single bargainer had paid as low a price as he could have paid in buying over the counter in Woolworth's. Needless to say, I preserved my silence after that, to avoid alienating my fellow passengers.

Generalizing widely from a single case is dangerous, but the case will illustrate the multiple levels at which such complex situations can be analyzed.

In the first place, one can make an orthodox social anthropological analysis, focusing on the evident role relationships involved—among the tourists, the itinerant vendors, the resident shopkeepers, the local residents, and the nontourist maritime population. These relationships appear to lend themselves to a simple analysis of role complementarity and interdependence, and to an interpretation of what happens in each individual transaction in bargaining terms. Vendors always get the better of tourists, but local stores deal with local residents on a basis of equality. The analysis would go beyond the single dyad: each dyadic relationship would be one example in a system of category relationships. Treating the tourist trade as a system also permits a structural analysis, according to which the relative

numbers of role players influence the nature of the system, as does the interconnec-
tedness or rapidity of information flow among fellow passengers or fellow vendors. For some purposes the existence of normative disagreement can be ignored
without too much difficulty.

Perhaps the major transactional analysis to give explicit recognition to normative disagreement is the one based on what has been called (following Berreman
and Goffman) "impression management" (see Paine 1971). This is, in economic
terms, an attempt to limit the flow of information from one party to the other—to
persuade the other person, for example, that the vendor is really penniless, or that
the tourist is really a sophisticated traveler. Each party then hopes that transactions
will take place in terms of his own standards and not those of the other party.

If we shift to economic analyses, several frameworks are possible. Simplest but
somewhat trite is the microeconomic analysis of the dyad, which we have already
sketched. Each pair of individuals would be considered in isolation, one with a pile
of fezzes and the other with a pocket full of money; they would arrive at an
exchange rate because of their indifference curves for money and fezzes.

A more complex and less trite analysis would consider the aggregate of transacting pairs, or the fact that each member of each pair can choose to transact with
someone else if the terms of trade are unsatisfactory. This market analysis would
require us to consider such variables as rates of information flow or numbers of
buyers and sellers. Even more complex is an analysis which does not take even
these variables as "fixed" for each specific transaction, but considers how they
themselves change with different parameters—with differing flows of tourists at
different seasons or changing costs of fez production at the factory. All these
analyses, being primarily dependent on quantification of the commodities exchanged, can be carried out with little consideration of whether the transactors
share a common frame of reference.

The type of economic analysis which I wish to expand on in this chapter is not
one that builds on basic units of dyads and transactions, but one which takes each
actor independently. It asks, for example: Why did a particular person choose to
buy a fez at a particular price, or why did a vendor sell at a particular price?
Empirically, in my decision to buy, the fact that the vendors demanded five
piastres for a fez was only one factor. My status and preferences as a student
anthropologist explained why I had spent time sightseeing and visiting cafes; my
wealth (or lack of it) partially explained why I had bought no souvenirs; my wish
not to appear a tourist explained my refusal to haggle with vendors on the dock, my
readiness to enter a store frequented by local people, and also my readiness to make
a transaction in which ignorance of Arabic would be no handicap. The price of one
piastre marked on the fezzes in the store was within what even my limited finances
allowed. I bought a souvenir. The costs in time, status, linguistic difficulties, were
all as important as the monetary costs and all entered into my decision not to buy
from a vendor and my revised decision to buy in a self-service store.

In economic terms this sort of analysis has been most commonly applied to the
decisions that producers make, regarding what they will produce and what compo-

nents they will use in the production. Generalized as "the theory of the firm," it can involve an examination of production functions, using probability estimates under conditions of uncertainty and other involved mathematical operations. For the anthropologist the mathematical precision may be spurious, but the approach is important. It leads one to look at the internal logic of the decisions made by two separate actors, and it leaves open the question of whether both parties are deciding on the same basis. Anthropologists pride themselves on rendering generally understandable the decisions that people make, and on testing whether the analysis is accurate by producing or predicting behavior. Decision analysis would appear ideal for anthropology.

Numerous workers (e.g., Ortiz and Howard 1971; Heath in this volume) have discussed the application of decision analysis in anthropology to situations where there is only one actor. I have already indicated (Salisbury 1968) how a variety of decision procedures may occur even within a single culture, that of Rossel Island, and how different individuals, while making decisions using different strategies, may still complement each other and so transact. Prattis (1973) has recently confirmed this analysis and amplified it at some points. The idea that is proposed here is that the existence of nonagreement, on both cultural rules and strategies used in decision making, should be taken as likely in any transaction, and that the calculations and decisions of *both* individual transactors should be examined independently when action depends on two decisions.[2]

This is not to say that such an analysis excludes all the other analyses mentioned. Unless the category characteristics of tourists, vendors, shopkeepers, students, and so on are isolated, and the individual's behavior related to his category characteristics, the analysis of his decisions cannot be generalized. Unless the quantitative features of markets, their timing, and the flow of goods through them are studied in their own terms, our knowledge of the constraints operating on the individual decision remains unsatisfactory. Unless we study the processes of bargaining and interaction within dyads, we can predict only the limits of what transactions might be acceptable to particular transactors, and not what will empirically occur. The analyses are complementary, but all are needed, and to ignore the existence of differences in cultural rules and strategies used in decision making is to weaken the strength of any analysis.

A CASE ILLUSTRATION:
THE HUDSON'S BAY COMPANY AGENT AS A TRANSACTOR

To illustrate the different conclusions arrived at using an individual decision analysis and a more conventional anthropological analysis, let us consider recent studies of the role of Hudson's Bay Company (HBC) agents in Indian communities in the eastern Arctic. A "traditional" view of these communities (Leacock 1954; Dunning 1959; Steward and Murphy 1956) was that the advent of the HBC in 1670 rapidly made them highly dependent on the fur trade. The organizing focus of each community was its relations with the HBC agent, who was the main patron and/or broker in any settlement until the advent of the Anglican missions and the Canadian government late in the nineteenth century. Between 1870, when administration of Rupert's Land was transferred from the HBC to the Canadian government, and 1947, change was very slow in the eastern Arctic. Since then, however, the number of southern Canadian agencies— schools, medical services, meteorological and radar stations, aircraft companies, and most recently oil companies—has grown rapidly. At the same time, the communities have become increasingly involved in a monetary economy, utilizing outboard motors and snowmobiles instead of paddles and sled dogs.

There have been excellent analyses of the role of the HBC agent, starting from Dunning (1959) and his characterization of the agents as "marginal men," and including most recently the work of Paine (1971) and his associates Briggs, Henriksen, and Freeman. But with the work of Paine and others the focus has changed from a role study to analyzing how the transactions involving HBC agents and other patrons can be seen as part of a "game."[3] The "game" is one in which "reciprocity"—in the limited sense of the term as used by Barth (1966) and Sahlins (1965)—is the key word. That is to say, both patron and client adopt strategies in order to increase the "values" which they obtain from the other transactor. Paine concludes, for example, that a crucial difference between a patron and client, within this analysis, is that the patron chooses what values he will provide, while a client must provide what the patron chooses (p. 15).

I must confess to being disturbed at this usage of the term "reciprocity," and the present case brings out the reason for this disturbance. Certainly there is "give-and-take" or "vice-versa movement" (Sahlins 1965: 141), and the "social fact of sides is inescapable" (p. 142). But for me an implication of "reciprocity" is that there is some "balance." There is certainly not an easy give-and-take of "generalised reciprocity." Yet to follow Barth (1966: 4) and call the relationship a "balanced" one, because one side uses accounting procedures to total up the goods and services exchanged, for me appears to beg the question. There is indeed willingness on both sides "to give for that which is received" (Sahlins 1965: 178)—to advance credit or to repay advances. But in realistic terms there is not balance but incommensurability in the commodities that change hands between a trader and an Indian customer. Even if one ignores the intangible services involved, the goods are different. It would be ethnocentric to assume that the somewhat arbitrary "prices" posted in the stores constitute an "agreed" rate for exchange or conversion of the goods.

Sahlins' argument, that "balanced reciprocity" inherently means "unbalanced reciprocity" (p. 178), for balance would destroy the relationship, may be true, but is to me a subtle way of trying to preserve a concept that has no real referent. It would be more useful to call such situations "successive transactions" (Barth 1966: 4) than examples of "reciprocity."

At least Sahlins' solution is more realistic than the alternative approach of arguing that where reciprocal flows of goods do not balance, compensating flows must be assumed to be occurring in intangibles—support, prestige, loyalty, reputation, or salvation (Paine 1971: 19). In this approach balance does not require proof; it is assumed to exist. Thus balance cannot be used as an independent explanatory force. That is not to say that nonmaterial "prestations" (or their availability as resources) should be ignored, but assigning them values in exchange to balance equations means that these values cannot be used predictively (however, *"costs"* can be assigned separately for each transactor, as I shall argue).

It is perhaps unfair to link an ethnographic citation from Paine with discussion of "balance," for Paine argues explicitly *against* the idea that "reciprocity" in Arctic communities (or even more generally) necessarily involves balance (1971: 17). He is content to use "reciprocity" to mean "successive transactions," even where these transactions are "directed" instead of alternating in direction (*ibid.*). Unfortunately this usage loses the sense of "accounting" that is central to Mauss and to Barth.

Paine's analysis goes beyond the traditional one, and its major contribution is novel. Based on a case study by Henriksen (1971), it looks at the "bargaining" procedures by which individual patrons in the Arctic set themselves up "in business." Briggs (1971) analyzes how individual patrons "manage their identities" so as to preserve their own and other persons' views of their status within the communities. These are brilliant studies, using the dramaturgical idiom of Goffman, and they branch out in new directions. I shall not follow those directions.

I wish to present an economic analysis, focusing particularly on the individual decisions of the two main categories of transactor—the trader and the individual Indian, head of a household. What I shall try to show is how one can assess the "cost" to each transactor of his interaction with the other, perhaps not in absolute terms but in terms of his own individual values, and in relation to other activities he must forego or opt not to undertake. It will appear that the value scales differ markedly, both from one another and from the idealized picture presented earlier. Yet it is in terms of those value scales that each transactor makes his decisions about when and how to interact. Negotiation or bargaining occurs only after initial decisions have been made on an individual basis, and it takes place within the framework set by these decisions.

Let us consider the Indian transactor first. Compared to earlier studies, recent close investigations of Indian economies (Elberg et al. 1972; Feit 1969, 1974; La Rusic 1969; Watt 1971) give a very different impression of the degree of dependency of Indian settlements on the Hudson's Bay post. For most bands, even now when family allowances, old-age insurance, wage employment by band councils, medical posts, or schools subsidized by federal funds provide major injections of cash into the local economy, 70 percent of all food consumed (by number of meals, and a higher proportion by value) is from hunting, trapping, or fishing. The proportion must have been higher before 1947. The amount of foodstuffs *purchased* clearly varies according to the occupation and degree of sedentarization of the individual Indian family, with full-time wage employees buying the most.

Purchases of necessities for hunting—shotgun shells, steel traps, fishing nets and line, rifles, ice chisels, gasoline and oil, and so on—are very seasonal, and by definition very closely linked with the carrying out of subsistence activities.

Even so, it is curious to note that the largest purchasers of the shotgun shells are often those in wage employment, for whom hunting is a weekend activity. In other words, full-time hunters tend to use hunting strategies and technologies that economize on store-bought items. Purchases of major items of equipment—snowmobiles, canoes, and outboard motors—are irregular, and they depend on a variety of factors, not the least of which is the readiness of the store manager to advance credit to the individual wishing to buy. However, all investigators are impressed by the near-universality of all these items; households differ only in number, degree of care given, and the serviceability of the equipment. Clothing, household equipment, and leisure products now form a major part of Hudson's Bay Company sales, but the degree to which particular households purchase them naturally varies most markedly with the family cash income and degree of sedentarization.

Looking at this description in terms of the degree of dependence—and more specifically, the qualitative foci for dependence—of Indians upon the HBC, one can generalize in the following way. The wage-earning family with permanent residence in the settlement near the post purchases much more from the HBC, but such a family tends to have a relatively high cash income earned independently of the HBC. Such families may be particularly concerned about the prices charged by the HBC, and may be on the lookout for ways of making their cash income stretch to meet their needs, but for them the two major areas of dependence are that (1) they need a store of some kind and (2) they may require credit to purchase major items of household equipment.

For the family committed to full-time hunting, day-to-day dependence on the HBC is minimal. The option of *not* utilizing store-bought foods is always open, although tea, flour, and lard have for centuries been accepted as standbys that any family always has available and buys periodically from the HBC. More critical for such families is that there be a store stocking hunting supplies; there must be an outlet for the sale of furs. Traditionally this has been the HBC. But provided that the sale of furs produces enough for equipment for the new hunting or fishing season, the hunter has little to worry him. He is "dependent" only when adverse exchange rates or hunting failures result in a lack of stock for next year's hunting; or when he needs a large capital item—a gun or a snowmobile—that would have to be bought on credit.

There is a range of family types intermediate between the two I have mentioned, with varying combinations of the types of dependency. There is also a range of other factors which interrelate with the degree of sedentariness or the involvement in hunting of any particular family. A family with children below school age is more likely to be absent from the settlement all winter than is one with children of elementary-school age. Postsecondary education for a family head is likely to mean wage employment in an administrative position; on the other hand, a distantly located family hunting territory and few siblings may predispose a young man for hunting.

What emerges from even this cursory review of Indian subsistence is that an Indian family head has many means available to him to avoid dependence on the HBC, if he feels that the terms of transactions with the HBC are unsatisfactory. He does not depend on having to bargain with the HBC agent. The benefits/costs to him of trading with the HBC are measurable in terms of the costs/benefits of his other activities.

Different strategies for relating these costs and benefits can be isolated. In hunting, for example, beaver trapping provides the major cash returns, but trapping beaver involves a much greater input of work per pound of meat than do other types of hunting (moose or caribou or bear) or fishing. Beaver are most predictable: the hunter knows that with hard work some beaver can be caught at any active beaver dam, while moose and caribou can be readily killed only when snow and weather conditions are right. A hunter thus normally practices a mixed hunting strategy, concentrating on big game for meat when the appropriate conditions are present, systematically catching beaver when the conditions for big game are not present, and catching small game or fish at odd times. Within this general strategy, modifications are made in response to the need for cash. If the need is low, there is more emphasis on hunting large game for meat. If the cash need is moderate, systematic beaver hunting is undertaken as soon as the winter camp has been set up in late October and a moose killed to provide a food reserve; beaver hunting then continues until enough have been caught to repay the costs of equipping for the winter, after which the hunting is almost entirely aimed at obtaining meat. If the cash need is high, a hunter may deliberately decide to "trap out" his territory, concentrating on beaver all winter and ending the season with as much as $5,000 worth of furs. For areas that a single hunting group can cover this is not an ecologically destructive course of action; beaver families, colonizing an area that has been "trapped out," multiply faster than do those in populated areas, and in three years a trapped-out area is likely to have reattained equilibrium beaver densities. In fact periodic "trapping out," by encouraging rapid breeding, produces a larger take-off of beaver over the long run than does steady hunting (Feit 1974).

With "trapping out" it is possible to pay off a major capital purchase or credit by one year of intensive hunting. This option provides the hunter with a way of avoiding the most serious dependency situation—that of indebtedness for capital items. Any major purchase can be considered equivalent to a single winter's hard work.

But "trapping out" does not provide a solution for the other major problem— arbitrary buying/selling prices at the store (that is, exchange rates of furs and goods). Here there appears (and has appeared for a long time, especially when only the storekeeper was literate and could keep account of credit advances) a major discrepancy. Prices appear to be fixed solely by the HBC agent, and minimal modification of them in the course of bargaining is reported. Fur prices have fluctuated wildly with world market prices, while store prices have shown steady inflation. Yet one is struck, over the long term, by the apparent stability of the total volume of furs from the area (with the exception of the near-extinction of the beaver in the 1930s) and by the way in which the cash receipts for furs have almost exactly equalled the outfitting requirements of the trappers. The "cost" of time and effort spent in beaver trapping and preparation of the skins, as compared to the "cost" of other bush activities, is presumably judged to be "fair" by hunters. In effect, a hunter can exchange the by-products of a subsistence life in the bush for the tools (and now also the air transportation) that make subsistence much easier to obtain. If hunters are dissatisfied with the HBC, they could largely withdraw from dependence on it, as they have done at numerous times and places. On the other hand, a few individuals do adopt the "trapping out" strategy, with its concomitant hard work and increased dependence.

Our individual decision analysis of the HBC agent will necessarily be more cursory, partly because sufficiently detailed data have not been published. The lifelong career pattern of HBC agents is a major decision factor. Of predominantly Scottish background, they tend to have lived much of their adult lives in the Canadian north, spending several years at each of a number of different posts. They know their colleagues at all the other posts, who clearly serve as a major reference group and source of information; yet, at the same time, all the agents are fierce individualists, each one running his own store entirely independently. No agent is likely to achieve personal wealth from operating a northern store, but in few occupations elsewhere in Canada is the smooth running of daily life so much a matter of personal decision and personal attention to detail. Success from the company's point of view may be evidenced by steady increases in volume of furs shipped, in turnover, and in profit margin. But for the HBC agent himself, though these may be desirable to please the company, the major challenge is merely to keep the operation going, despite communication difficulties, delays of the supply barge, impossible demands by paper-bound clerks in Winnipeg, and the climatic and living difficulties of the north.

Living in the north is a distinctive way of life. True, most HBC stores and their adjoining houses are set well apart from the Indian community on its Reserve land, so that the everyday personal life of agents and their wives is not mainly with Indians. But other administrators (of churches, police departments, air charter companies, Indian affairs, and so on) visit not infrequently, and there is a flow of transients—one or two in most weeks. It can be a busy, involved, and active life even if it includes few of the Indian community. This is the life that Dunning (1959) characterized as "marginal"—neither southern Canadian nor Indian.

At work the agent meets many members of the local Indian community every day. Knowing who is leaving or who has just returned from the bush, where each hunting group is trapping, who is having a baby, and who is about to get married is vitally important to an agent who has to grant credit, make out orders for supplies months in advance, and arrange for flying in furs from a "trapping out" camp in time to catch the January sale. Gossip is vital for keeping his business running.

Even if local Indian store clerks do most of the actual buying and selling, the store manager in his office must interest himself, through the gossip, in the major community activities. He should know everyone's credit rating and abilities. The "marginal man," in short, has a distinctive economic position; he can have access to varied knowledge and resources without being personally involved in community social life.

In reality there is an immense variation in the degree of involvement in the community, ranging from the agent who has married a wife from the community to the newcomer who tries to keep business apart from social life and to run the store as if he were in southern Canada. It is this variation, I would maintain, that is the major influence in determining what exchange rates are acceptable to an HBC agent and how liberal he is in advancing credit.

Given a liking for the north, a career within the HBC and "company loyalty," an independent posting, a pleasant family life, and reasonable practical ability, the agent has little to gain by pressing for the maximum number of furs at the lowest prices, or by inflating the prices of merchandise for sale and trying to push the major appliances. By being liberal, he can involve himself comfortably in community affairs, can reduce the unpleasantness which a more forceful policy might produce, can reduce many of the difficulties of management, and can possibly even increase the volume of business, although he may not increase profits to the same extent. Set against this tendency (of which the head office is aware) is the fact that the manager knows he is not basically dependent on the community; he will move on and retire elsewhere, and his salary is paid by the HBC. He must not be *too* liberal.

In short, for the "typical" manager, provided he runs an effective and profitable store, the level to which he raises prices, takes credit risks, or bargains harshly for furs is a matter of personal discretion. Whether any particular manager is harsh or easygoing is determined by his degrees of commitment to the community and to the company, and by his comparison of the satisfactions provided by northern life with those of mobility within a southern Canadian business. In short, the total life situation of the manager is the best predictor of the strategy he will take vis-à-vis any community member, and of how his role will be structured.

It is at this point that we can return to the traditional bargaining analysis. The Indian–manager transactions take place within a range of parameters—or constraints—determined externally. The demands of the HBC head office on the manager are influenced by factors outside the scope of local personnel to alter—the costs of operating a fleet of supply barges northward from Moose Factory, for example. So too the minimal demands of population subsistence or cultural survival or the level of federal family allowances must be taken as given for Indian families. But these limits allow a very wide range of possible "terms of trade" that could apply in Indian–manager relations.

If bargaining were the principal process affecting where, within that range, the actual terms of trade were fixed, then one would expect the terms to follow closely the balance in resources and power between the two transactors. Since this balance is overwhelmingly in favor of the HBC, it would be expected that the terms of trade would be overwhelmingly tipped against the Indians. Yet the northern Cree Indians do not consider themselves exploited; their typical diet of three pounds of fresh meat per adult per day is one that many other Canadians would envy. They see their way of life as something to be preserved, and view modern development, in the form of a hydroelectric project, as destructive of a highly rewarding existence. The bargaining interpretation can therefore be questioned.

Before turning to decision analysis we must discuss an alternative interpretation. Maybe it is wrong to say that the HBC has more "resources" or "power" than the Indians. If "resources" are considered in the widest sense, they may include, for the Indians, such alternatives as collaborative importing by air freight, community boycotts of the HBC, gradual escalation of the credit balances owed to the company, and long-term political bargaining to increase employment in the stores. In this light the Indians may not be so powerless. But considering these alternatives as resources is in fact doing decision analysis under another name. The advantage of recognizing that one is analyzing decisions is that one's first step is then to review alternatives systematically, rather than considering them on an ad hoc basis when the initial analysis proves insufficient.

Of course, individual decision analysis does not preclude other analyses. Bargaining occurs, and the bargaining is influenced both by a transactor's view of his own costs and benefits and by his perception of the other party's evaluation of alternatives. In short, where a straightforward decision analysis leaves a degree of indeterminacy in the terms of trade between two parties, one can reduce the indeterminacy if one knows how much information each party has about the other's decision making. One would predict that terms of trade would tend to favor the better-informed party.

The effect of better information is clear in the Canadian north. Even five years ago it was striking how much more was known by HBC managers about local decision making than was known by local people about how decisions were made by HBC managers. The increase over the last five years in local knowledge of southern Canadian society, through a multitude of sources—including now TV by satellite—is dramatic. It is reducing the indeterminacy in the exchanges with HBC managers, and making them resemble much more closely a situation of cultural uniformity and bargaining in an open market. But until the information flow is perfect there is a place for individual decision analysis.

Although predicting the future would be a good empirical test of the usefulness of decision analysis, it is easier to see whether it enables us to understand the past—1947, 1922, or even 1822. The contrast in northern Canada between the period since 1947 and the time before that date is striking. Cash has largely replaced credit, and welfare and other federal payments are now made through band officials rather than through HBC accounts. Administrative services have expanded greatly, and the HBC now appears as only one among many white institutions, rather than as the leading horse in a troika of HBC, church, and RCMP. But the effect of this change on the role of the agent has not been a direct one. Economically, the HBC plays much the same role as it did earlier. The resources and knowledge available to the agent have changed little over the period—if anything, they have grown; and although Indian resources have also grown, the relation between the two has remained fairly stable. There has been little change in the volume of the fur trade since 1947. What has happened is that a wide range of new alternatives has emerged. The presence of new alternatives has influenced the decisions of both transactors. The HBC agent has been able to withdraw from areas of behavior that "cost" too much in ill will—administration of welfare, for example—and has concentrated more on the storekeeper role; the Indian who wishes to continue subsistence hunting has been able to do so, and because of a decrease in his dependence on the HBC has been able to increase his returns from family life, education, and social activities. The category of Indian most affected by the alternative activities, the wage employee, has changed most in relations with the HBC.

To understand the 1920s within this framework, two external factors need to be known. First is the fact that at this period the French firm of Révillon Frères (Usher 1971) was attempting to break the HBC monopoly in the fur trade by opening competitive stores in the eastern Arctic. Secondly, the HBC head office was concerned over the large sums tied up in inventory and credit accounts at its stores. Presumably the two facts were linked, for credit accounts became risky if a hunter could sell his furs to another firm. The result was that agents were forced by the head office to restrict credit. They themselves made only slight changes in the direction of less liberal behavior. But the effect on the Indian opportunity-cost structure, at those critical points already analyzed, was great. The rough balance between subsistence "by-products" (fur) and equipment needs, which could be adjusted next year if it was a little off this year, could not be maintained. Even before fur prices fell in the depression, hunters were opting in large numbers for short-term "trapping-out" tactics to meet urgent requirements for everyday credit—not only when major purchases were in prospect.[4] As beaver became "trapped out" the pressure became even greater, and a result was the virtual extermination of the beaver in the mid thirties. With the depression occurring simultaneously, a major return to subsistence hunting occurred. Révillon Frères went out of business, and eventually the HBC reverted to its earlier credit policies.

For earlier years the historical data are less clear, but Lips (1947) cites the diaries of HBC agents of the 1820s. Leacock (1954) has subsequently cited Lips in order to argue that family hunting territories were a major innovation following the advent of the HBC. What these diaries show, in fact, is the same picture as the recent data. If conditions were right for large game, nothing could stop Indians from hunting it where they would. Even the presence of an HBC agent with a hunting group, helping them with his more accurate weapons, made the Cree feel no "gratitude" and no greater desire to meet his demands that they go fur hunting. As now, beaver trapping must have had its place as a standby activity when large-game hunting was impossible and meat scarce. Winter residence had to be planned as it is now so that standby resources were available when large-game hunting was inappropriate; this could only be achieved by conservational use of beaver resources and a consistent return to known areas. Then as now, catching small game was the least productive use of hunting time. In short, it seems likely that the advent of the HBC had little effect on the pattern of hunting decisions, and that the modern pattern of spaced territories, their size based on the availability of big game but their regularity of use based on consistent planning within groups of kinsmen about the trapping of beaver,[5] has existed as long as subsistence hunting.

CONCLUSION

Many of the data cited will be recognized as amenable to a bargaining analysis of transactions, a market analysis of the fur trade, or an ecological analysis of metropolis-hinterland relationships. However, looking at the two transactors separately, in order to see their transactional behavior as a result of each one's arriving at an individual decision in his own terms, has brought order to a wide range of data. Otherwise these data would appear random, introduced into the analysis on an ad hoc basis.

The analysis has not assumed that each transactor is trying to achieve the maximum possible returns through antagonistic bargaining. In fact, it has indicated that a flexible exchange rate was likely (this is empirically documented), and that prices would have little effect in either raising or curtailing production (again this is empirically documented). By assuming that each transactor in each decision is trying to increase his level of satisfaction over what he can expect from other options, it is possible to interpret many data without assuming that HBC agents and Indians were members of a single moral community, committed to balanced reciprocity.

Barth's introduction of transactional analysis is entirely to be welcomed. It has led anthropologists to recognize that an analysis of the situational logic of individual behavior can fruitfully be combined with an analysis of normative features in social roles. Such analyses have long been implicit in economic analysis. The defect in the present state of transactional analysis is that it still often uses a terminology more appropriate to organismic functional social analysis. Indeed, in the case of the concept of "reciprocity," the implied reversion to normative thinking becomes a positive danger. The study of situational logics is not enough; we need to study also the individually specific decision logics of each transactor.

EPILOGUE

When this essay was read at the ASA meetings in July 1973, the following epilogue was included:

"In a world involved in an 'energy crisis,' discussion of tourists in Port Said or fur traders in the Canadian north may appear remote, yet the sort of analysis here proposed is highly relevant in the context of the energy crisis. When oil leases were negotiated originally between major companies and the Arab states, the terms arrived at were not based on agreement on relative values or on hard bargaining. For oil companies, any price that enabled them to sell at a profit at prices then current in the U.S. and Europe would have been acceptable. For the exporting countries at that time, any revenue from oil seemed like affluence compared to their previous state. The low price agreed on was fixed more by the opportunity costs of the individual transactors than by any open market price or bargaining process.

"Bargaining and negotiation have, since then, raised the price paid closer to the limits importers could pay, and further from the minimum exporters would accept. But it is also true that the exporters' opportunity costs have risen as they have developed industrial economies. What is now becoming apparent is that decisions about U.S. oil imports, from Canada as from the Arab states, are not merely a matter of world market prices and bargaining; they are critically related to opportunity-cost structures within the United States. To what extent are people prepared to buy smaller cars and drive more slowly? Should energy be used to create jobs at the cost of private discomfort? To what extent are the costs of pollution tolerable? Would low-grade coal provide a securer and lower-cost fuel?

"Negotiating between the parties must continue, but the decisions made internally by each transacting country are going to be critical."

Though the situation has changed by 1976, the logic is still relevant.

NOTES

1. I here except a major group of younger and predominantly American scholars working in formal or mathematical analysis in economic anthropology. At the risk of omitting names I would include Sutti Ortiz, Alan Howard, Roger Keesing, Hugh Gladwin, Christine Gladwin, Naomi Quinn, Stuart Plattner, Ian Prattis, Henry Rutz, Carol Smith, Geoff Stiles, Sidney Greenfield, and Ira Buchler, as a minimum.

2. Though I am deliberately *not* raising the issue here, I am consciously supporting the position most cogently argued by Wallace (1961): that every individual's culture is different, and that "norms" are shared in only the most general sense. For my own views on idiosyncratic individual cultures, see Salisbury 1962b.

3. Elsewhere I have discussed briefly the "impression-management" aspect of the analysis, particularly with respect to Briggs, and I will not present it here. It does raise the question of whether one should regard the communication of information as a transaction. Information has the interesting property that "giving" it to someone else does not mean that one loses as much as the receiver gains. In many cases giving *exclusive* information may mean some loss to the person who communicates, but he may often be rewarded disproportionately by the receiver, who gains greatly from his new knowledge. This is a further example of two transactors valuing the commodity transferred in different ways, but the basis for the different valuations is not the different opportunity-cost structures of the transactors.

4. I am particularly indebted to Professor Harvey Feit (personal communication) for this interpretation and for the historical information about the HBC credit policies. I am placing it in a different context than he would.

5. Again Feit (1974) provides the major documentation and discussion of this issue in an ecological context. Personal discussion with him has clarified my thinking about decision-making and hunting strategies.

REFERENCES

Barth, F. 1966. *Models of Social Organization*. Royal Anthropological Institute Occasional Paper No. 23. London.
_____. 1967. Economic spheres in Darfur. In R. Firth, ed., *Themes in Economic Anthropology*. ASA Monograph No. 6. London: Tavistock.
Belshaw, C. S. 1954. *Changing Melanesia*. Oxford: Oxford University Press.
Briggs, J. 1971. Strategies of perception: management of ethnic identity. In R. Paine, ed., *Patrons and Brokers in the East Arctic*. St. John's: Institute of Social and Economic Research, Memorial University.
Dunning, R. W. 1959. Ethnic relations and the marginal man in Canada. *Human Organization*, 18: 117–122.
Elberg, N., J. Hyman, K. Hyman, and R. F. Salisbury. 1972. *Not by Bread Alone: Subsistence Activities Among the James Bay Cree*. Montreal: Indians of Quebec Association.
Feit, H. A. 1969. Mistassini hunters of the boreal forest: ecosystem dynamics and multiple subsistence patterns. M.A. thesis, McGill University.
_____. 1972. L'ethno-écologie des Cris Waswanipi. *Recherches amérindiennes au Québec*, 1: 84–93.
_____. 1974. Waswanipi realities and adaptations: human ecology as cognitive structure and as ecosystem. Ph.D. dissertation, McGill University.
Firth, R. 1939. *Primitive Polynesian Economy*. London: Routledge.
Henriksen, G. 1971. The transactional basis of influence. In R. Paine, ed., *Patrons and Brokers in the East Arctic*. St. John's: Institute of Social and Economic Research, Memorial University.
Homans, G. C. 1964. Bringing men back in. *American Sociological Review*, 29: 809–818.
La Rusic, I. 1969. From hunter to proletarian. In N. A. Chance, ed., *Developmental Change Among the Cree Indians of Quebec*. Ottawa: Department of Forestry and Rural Development.
Leacock, E. 1954. *The Montagnais Hunting Territory and the Fur Trade*. American Anthropological Association Memoirs, No. 78. Menasha, Wis.
Lips, J. E. 1947. *Naskapi Law*. Transactions of the American Philosophical Society, Vol. 37. Philadelphia.
Ortiz, S., and A. Howard. 1971. Decision making and the study of social process. *Acta Sociologica*, 14: 213–226.
Paine, R. 1971. A theory of patronage and brokerage. In R. Paine, ed., *Patrons and Brokers in the East Arctic*. St. John's: Institute of Social and Economic Research, Memorial University.
Prattis, I. J. 1973. Strategising man. *Man*, N.S., 8: 46–58.
Robbins, L. 1935. *An Essay on the Nature and Significance of Economic Science*. London: Macmillan.
Sahlins, M. D. 1965. On the sociology of primitive exchange. In *The Relevance of Models for Social Anthropology*. London: Tavistock.

Salisbury, R. F. 1962a. *From Stone to Steel*. Cambridge, Eng.: Cambridge University Press.

———. 1962b. *Structures of Custodial Care*. University of California Publications in Culture and Society, No. 8. Los Angeles.

———. 1968. Formal analysis in anthropological economics: the Rossel Island case. In E. Buchler and H. Nutini, eds., *Game Theory in the Behavioral Sciences*. Pittsburgh: University of Pittsburgh Press.

Steward, J. H., and R. F. Murphy. 1956. Tappers and trappers: parallel processes in acculturation. *Economic Development and Cultural Change,* 4: 335–355.

Usher, P. J. 1971. *Fur Trade Posts of the Northwest Territories*. Northern Science Research Group Paper 71–4. Ottawa: Department of Indian Affairs and Northern Development.

Wallace, A. F. C. 1961. *Culture and Personality*. New York: Random House.

Watt, J., ed. 1971. *The Round Lake Ojibwa 1968–1970*. Toronto: Department of Lands and Forests.

Part Two

TRANSACTIONS, COGNITIVE SYSTEMS, AND THE COMMUNICATION OF MEANING

Two Modes of Exchange and Mediation

ROBERT PAINE

INTRODUCTION

This formal analysis derives principally from Barth's (1966) seminal work on exchange; it attempts to deal constructively with some of the points raised in an earlier essay (Paine 1974) on the Barthian schema. We begin with a brief overview of the issues that are to come under discussion.

Two Modes of Exchange

I will refer to the two modes of exchange that appear in the title as *T* and *I*, derived as they are from Barth's (1966) transaction and incorporation, respectively. In Barth's essay, the *I* mode of exchange is introduced as the analytic opposite of *T* (p. 4) but languishes as a wallflower through most of the ensuing discussion, which is given over to the *T* mode. My intention is to attempt to restore the balance. For it is the *I* mode that reminds one how exchange can be independent of the notion of competition or even of contract; how exchange can be conducted between partners who offer not different but similar, even identical, commodities; and how exchange need not posit a debt relationship (or be based on altruism).

Nowadays, the *T* mode is frequently spoken of as though it is the only mode of exchange,[1] and the uneven treatment in Barth (1966) pushed the notion of transaction up to a new pinnacle of notoriety. This state of affairs is seemingly grounded in the belief of a number of writers that exchange is *exclusively* based on principles of game theory.[2]

Treatment of the theme of love is a case in point. As Hampden-Turner (1971: 13–14) notes, "While Romeo can say to Juliet 'The more I give you the more I have,'" Blau (1964: 78) analyzes the behavior of lovers in transactional terms. Lyman and Scott (1970) carry this tendency even further and, regrettably, are able to cite Simmel (1959: 249–252) in support. They posit that "the fundamental structure of human action is conflict" (p. 5). From a general reading of their book it seems that they could have given that place to exchange just as well as to conflict; but they put it the way they did because, for them, exchange is subsumed by conflict. They continue (*loc. cit.*): "this is true even if individuals are pursuing the same ends, since each is out to maximize his own interests. Thus, even two lovers in an erotic embrace, as Simmel once noted, may be regarded in conflict since each may be seeking to outdo the other in demonstrating affection or providing the other

63

with feeling.'' It may often be so, but why forward this as *the* explanation? Hampden-Turner's comment of disapproval on the apparent need for this kind of interpretation is plausible: to admit ''love flowing from one person to another destroys the logical distinction between A and not-A'' (*loc. cit.*).

Now, it is precisely this distinction on which the T mode[3] depends but which is negated—or subdued or rendered irrelevant—in the I mode of exchange. In other words, the existence of the distinction ''between A and not-A'' is itself a variable, and one should attend to the circumstances in which it holds and those in which it is superseded by another principle.

The essence of the I mode of exchange and the contrast with T are found in this passage in Barth:

> Between shareholders in an estate there must emerge a relationship of jointness, or incorporation, since for certain purposes their interests are identical and inseparable. Their activities *vis-à-vis* each other with respect to the rights they share can never have a transactional form; their strategy must be directed towards maximizing the sum of their assets [pp. 23–24].

However, his delineation of the I mode is made with less sure a hand than is the case with the T mode. For example, he holds that parties to an incorporation do not come together, or continue to stay together, without measuring their respective self-interests (pp. 24, 26–27). Once again, competition and bargaining and contract appear to belong to all social situations. But if the heralded opposition between the two modes is blurred here, in another passage the opposition, once more reinstated, appears no longer to be between alternative modes of exchange at all: incorporation is alluded to as an alternative to exchange (p. 29), as though exchange is restricted to bargaining.

Communication and Mediation

This essay will also be concerned with the place of communication in exchange. The view throughout is that (1) exchanges, no less than other events, must be explained socially—that is, rendered ''intelligible'' for those engaging in them, and (2) exchanges are themselves events that explain—that is, people ''use'' their exchanges to render their life experiences more intelligible. Both these things happen through a process of *mediation,* in which the factual and evaluational are inextricably entwined (cf. Hymes 1964: 19; Dreitzel 1970: xix; Boulding 1971: 174). The simple but fundamental distinction should therefore be made between information as data that are yet to be rendered socially intelligible, and communication as a socially inteliigible message. Communication is mediated information. Bateson (1951: 209) puts a finer point on it: mediation is ''communication about communication'' or metacommunication.

All exchange includes metacommunicative or mediating activity on the part of all parties, in both "sender" and "receiver" roles. The relevance of this idea for analysis is in the emphasis it places upon exchange as an instrument of evaluation. Consider the mundane example of two schoolboys swapping postage stamps of different catalogue value. If the catalogue were the only determinant of value, then the boy proffering the stamp of higher catalogue value would lose; but because it is a "swap" we can assume he is as pleased as the other with the exchange. Each collector considers not only the catalogue value of a stamp but also its value to his own collection (the stamp may be the one needed to complete a set); the catalogue listing of a stamp provides an exchange rate *in lieu of,* or prior to, separate mediation by both parties to the swap. Accordingly, that aspect of value with which I am concerned here is the contextually perceived. True, the same commodities may be exchanged in a number of contexts, but what interests me is the process whereby their values are mediated by each party in each instance. For it is only then that one is able to take account of the salient feature of human exchange, namely, that a prestation "received" is not necessarily the same as the prestation that was sent. With this established, one can appreciate how a value may be enhanced or attained through exchange, *without itself being exchanged.* Often it is messages about values that are exchanged, and these are usually messages about the supposed values of the other party.

This whole matter of mediation is too often neglected, and one consequence is the assumption that prestations received are, in fact, the same as those sent. Consider, for example, Barth's basic paradigm of a transaction (p. 13):

$$A \, {}^x \underset{\leftarrow}{\rightarrow} \, {}_yB.$$

Each party appears to be imposing something upon the other without mediation: the sender role is, in each case, afforded spurious dominance over the receiver role, and prestations—called values, as it happens—move from one person to another unaltered in content and meaning. It all happens rather as though the persons are psychic, social, and cultural facsimiles of each other.

Mediation belongs to both the modes of exchange; how it is handled in each is another dimension of the *T/I* difference that I want to explore in the body of this essay.

Power

Of related interest is the place of power in exchange. Viewing exchange as a communicative event, we must concern ourselves with the balance of power between the sender of a message, as one mediator, and the receiver, as the other. If, as Bateson (1951: 210) argues, messages are "tailored to fit" by the sender, according to his ideas about the receiver, and they include instructions on how the receiver should interpret their content, what kind of defenses are available against such metacommunicative "attack"? It is in respect to this question, among other things, that I introduce into the argument some of the work of Bernstein (see references) on codes and social control. This grafting of Bernstein onto Barth (1966) also provides the T/I distinction with some of the necessary sociological underpinnings.

Reference to metacommunicative "attack" also raises the issue of the definition one attaches to the general term "exchange." For Blau (1964: 6), it is "actions that are contingent upon rewarding reactions." But, surely, exchanges may also be unrewarding for one, both, or all the parties; they may then be accounted for as mistakes that become a matter for regret, but they are exchanges nonetheless. Are there not also exchanges into which persons are more or less forced and which are regretted even at the time they are made? The view of exchange adopted in this essay shows how the devices of communication—mediation and codification—are potential devices of power, whereby it is possible for the options of a party to an exchange to be practically predetermined (even in some cases without the party's realizing the fact).

The Blau definition, then, is altogether too naive in its neglect of power; as he himself notes (p. 22), "exchange processes give rise to differentiation of power." It is as if Blau, in this definition, were delineating *good* exchanges.[4] For the present, our view of exchange is that (a) each party transmits a message, and (b) each party mediates the message transmitted to him. Here, too, there are T/I differences that I want to discuss. They are associated with the choice of code which, in turn, is associated with the kind of knowledge particular individuals and groups are able to have and wish to have about themselves and about each other.

Brokerage

Finally, there is the place that brokerage has in exchange. It is inadequate to analyze exchange as an event limited to two parties (though that is the usual approach), for exchange which is ostensibly based on mediation by the principal protagonists may in fact depend on mediation by a third party.

A methodological point: the inclusion of a third person does not necessarily break the dyadic form of interaction. As Simmel (1950: 136) put it, a triad usually results in "three parties of two persons each." In a paradigm of exchange in which there is a broker and two clients, there may actually be only two dyads activated: those of the broker with each of his clients. The "original" dyad (between A and B, now the clients of a broker) is likely to be displaced; this is probably in the interests of the broker (cf. Paine 1974: 24–28), and the clients themselves may reject the original dyad for the reasons that led them to seek a broker in the first place. At any rate there is a plurality of dyads and the situation is likely to be more complex than the "two against one" alignment discussed by Caplow (1968) as a likely outcome of a triadic situation. Indeed, the situation generated by the broker consists of *two* such alignments: the *raison d'être* of brokerage, one might say, is to defy Caplow's "law." Capitalizing upon this situation, the broker, it may be expected, resembles Simmel's *tertius gaudens,* "the third who enjoys," as he makes the exchanges yield "a means for his own purposes" (p. 154). He is a "fixer" of exchanges.

What I want to focus upon is the significance of certain affinities that will emerge in this essay—affinities between particular modes of exchange, modes of mediation, modes of social control, and modes of codification—for the opportunity of brokerage and for its management.

An Example

I will conclude these preliminary notes with a scenario from Lévi-Strauss (1969), in which both of the alternative modes of exchange are present in their rudiments and the decisive development of the one or the other hangs in the balance.

> In the small restaurant [in the south of France] where wine is included in the price of the meal, each customer finds in front of his plate a modest bottle of wine. . . . The little bottle may contain exactly one glassful, yet the contents will be poured out, not into the owner's glass, but into his neighbour's. And his neighbour will immediately make a corresponding gesture of reciprocity [p. 58].

The question is put:

> What has happened? The two bottles are identical in volume, and their contents similar in quality. Each person in this revealing scene has, in the final analysis, received no more than if he had consumed his own wine. From an economic viewpoint, no one has gained and no one has lost. But the point is that there is much more in the exchange itself than in the things exchanged [p. 59].

Perhaps this is a situation from which the *I* mode of exchange emerges?

> The partner who was entitled to maintain his reserve is persuaded to give it up. Wine offered calls for wine returned, cordiality requires cordiality. . . . There is no way of refusing the neighbour's offer of his glass of wine without being insulting [p. 59].

Even so, there is the likelihood of one of the partners controlling the exchange more than the other:

> The person beginning the cycle seizes the initiative, and the greater social ease which he has displayed puts him at an advantage [pp. 59–60].

But there is also the real possibility of a *T* mode of exchange developing between the diners:

> . . . the table-companion may respond to the drink offered with a less generous glass, or . . . he will take the liberty to bid higher, obliging the one who made the first offer

(and we must not forget that the bottle is small) either to lose his last trump as his last drop, or to sacrifice another bottle for the sake of his prestige [p. 59].

MEDIATION

All exchange includes two mediating roles for each message passed: the roles of sender and receiver. Thus, in ideal terms for the moment, the decoding phase of metacommunication is as strong as the encoding. Both parties (assuming an exchange between two persons) steer the interaction and do so in both receiver and sender roles; hence the information passed between them is without a spurious autonomy and is broken down mutually into communications. Moreover, neither party is forced into accepting the other's evaluation of a prestation.

This process is most clearly evidenced in the paradigm of the T mode of exchange (Figure 1). In the example of a stamp swap, x and y are the stamps, the

FIGURE 1

The T *Mode of Exchange*

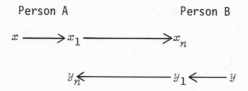

exchange commodities. The equations $x_1{\rightarrow}x_n$ and $y_1{\rightarrow}y_n$ are the messages about value; x_1 is A's suggestion about the value of x, while x_n is B's estimation of its value to himself.

The T mode is characterized by the expectations of choice and a "value optimum" for *each* party (Barth, p. 4). But the realization of these expectations may be difficult. It is predicated on bargaining over rates of exchange $(x{:}y)$ and even over which commodities are to be exchanged (for example, whether x or z will be traded for y). And inequalities of bargaining position are likely to occur, robbing an actual T exchange of its ideal quality of being complementary for both parties. The exchange may be complementary from the viewpoint of only one of the parties—if, for instance, A imposes x on B, who would have preferred z in exchange for y. Such an exchange is exploitative, and I will have more to say about this in the next section.

Effective bargaining may be expected to depend on information about a number of factors, and the possession of information with the skill to render it relevant should itself be considered a resource in all T exchanges. Person A, for example, is likely to wish to measure:

1. The loss to him of a portion of x against the gain to him of a portion of y.
2. The loss to him of some of x against the loss to B of some of y.
3. The use he can make of y (in the form of y_n) against the use B can make of x (in the form of x_n).

Next, we can consider the I mode. Here "value optimum" is sought for the *sum* of the partners (Barth, p. 4), whose solidarity may be based on a contract or simply on common prior commitment to a certain value. Mutuality in this mode of exchange is forged out of a bond at once more enduring and more onerous than that of bargained complementarity; it reaches out toward co-identity: "for certain purposes their interests are identical and inseparable" (Barth, p. 23). Nonetheless, the basic process of mediation pertains; as I said earlier, one depends on mediation to render experience intelligible. The difference from the T mode is that the receiver's mediation always confirms the sender's mediation. Figure 2 puts this statement in a graphic form: $x_1 \longleftrightarrow x_1$.

FIGURE 2

The I Mode of Exchange

Person A   Person B

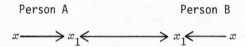

We were told (Lévi-Strauss) that "Wine offered calls for wine returned, cordiality requires cordiality," and so it is with the Masonic handshake or the lovers' embrace. In all exchanges of this "I-Thou" kind it is as though the receiver intones an "Amen!" as his mediation of the message. Between those who enjoy a compact in regard to an intrinsic value there is, then, reflexive mediation, and the course taken by such an exchange is likely to be not only predictable but also self-validating in character. Exchange in the I mode, incidentally, demonstrates how mediation—the process of evaluation—occurs even where there are not evaluative differences between persons; it affirms what had only been a presumption.

But there is a distinction to be made among exchanges of the I mode itself. In the examples mentioned so far, persons share a single resource (viz., wine, love, group membership) and status differences between them are either absent or irrelevant. A principle of replication governs. However, the I mode also can involve persons bringing different resources and separate statuses to their compact. Patron-client relationships are an example (Figure 3).

The patron brings resource x, "influence"; the client accepts his patron's

FIGURE 3

A Variation of the I *Mode:*
Patron-Client Exchange

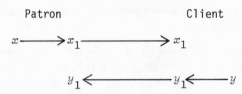

mediation of this resource as "protection" (x_1). Thus $x{\to}x_1{\to}x_1$ is one message about the value around which the compact is established. Resource y, which the client brings, is his "custom," and the patron accepts its mediation as "loyalty and esteem" (y_1). Thus $y{\to}y_1{\to}y_1$ is the other message about the value underlying the compact. The value is, of course, the bond or compact of patronage itself. A good illustration of the bonding of a patron and his client is found in Campbell (1964):

> In effect, patronage converts impersonal and ephemeral connexions into permanent and personal relationships; for in Greek society it is, generally, only in established personal relationships, of which the archetypal forms are found in the family, that any considerable element of moral obligation exists. . . . when such a relationship endures for any length of time it takes on a strong moral quality. . . . *The social reputations of the two men are now linked.* . . . More generally, patronage links persons of different social status, introducing into their social relations a common area of shared values which would otherwise not exist [pp. 259, 261; emphasis added].

A methodological point not to be lost is that the presence of two resources and two statuses does not mean that an exchange is necessarily in the T mode.[5] However, co-identity is less pervasive in those I mode exchanges based on two resources. Where there is only one resource, role separation in the I exchange is likely to be negligible and also deliberately undercommunicated; both of these conditions are unlikely when each party contributes a separate resource. Thus it is only in the consummation (or the failure) of their compact, and not in their respective contributions to it, that the patron and client share an identity.

TRANSFORMATIONS AND EXPLOITATION

So far the modes of exchange have been considered as formally separated and internally consistent structures, each forwarding the due processes of mediation. It is now necessary to break these molds so as to take account of changes and of formal inconsistencies within a mode; to consider exploitation within exchange; to notice how, in the course of its own development, a social or economic relationship may change its mode of exchange. Such change may be toward an extreme position within the same mode or it may be from one mode to the other; in the latter case, the change may be restricted to the encapsulation of just a few elements of the other mode.

It is particularly in T mode exchanges that governance by external factors can be a source of serious inequality. Barth (p. 5), for example, concedes that "transactional behaviour takes place with reference to a pre-established matrix of statuses." While this type of constraint is likely to affect parties unequally, it cannot be supposed that the advantage always goes to the person of higher status.[6] For this reason the term "status" is best left alone here and reference made simply to the constraints of the normative structure; in this way, too, it is easier to capture the sense of Schelling's (1956: 282) crucial point: "the power to constrain an adversary may depend on the power to bind oneself." This power is not predetermined by relative status in any clear way; it is likely to owe something to accidents of ascription, and still more to bargaining skill, which is Schelling's concern. He notes, paradoxically, that "in bargaining, weakness is often strength, freedom may be freedom to capitulate" (*ibid.*). In other circumstances, however, to find oneself bound means simply that one cannot escape from a commitment. Here it is important to note how constraints put upon a person in a T exchange may refer to his involvement in an I exchange: in other words, an appeal is made to him in the name of a "higher loyalty" that he recognizes (cf. constraints placed upon backbenchers by party whips).

Another source of inequality can be the means by which such higher loyalties are themselves established—a matter of particular relevance to the I mode. Metaphysical points of interpretation lurk here but we will evade them. However, one cannot escape from some consideration of the various associations between "incorporation" and bondage. On the one hand, there are religious messages of incorporation such as St. Paul's to the early Christian communities: "all being predestinated according to His purpose. . . . Thou has put all things in subjection under His feet" (Ephesians, 1:11; Hebrews, 2:8). On the other hand, there is incorporation achieved by brainwashing (cf. Sargant 1959: passim). That the one kind is not always easily separable from the other is evident from much of the history of evangelical movements, religious and political (Sargant 1959: 79ff.; Hinton 1966: passim). The only distinction proposed here is between incorporation that heightens self-awareness and raises self-esteem, and incorporation that violates these qualities perhaps to the point of destroying them. It is only the latter kind that is regarded as exploitative and as a debased form of exchange. A notable ethnographic example is South American debt peonage (Wolf and Hansen 1972: 145–147):

> One way of getting people to work for you was to extend credit to them . . . force them into debt, and then allow them to work off that debt by laboring on the estate. Over time, this arrangement could be made hereditary. . . . Through such means hacienda owners also forced their laborers to recognize no other lords than themselves. The

hacienda owner adopted the role of the dominant father, prepared to guide the steps of his worker-children.[7]

In general terms, it seems that the excessive and arbitrary control by one party over another which is the sign of exploitation in an exchange is achieved through (1) control of the selection of commodities to be exchanged, and the exchange rates; and (2) control of the other party's capacity for mediation so that he may be subjected at will to "learning to learn" (Bateson) programs, i.e. the Pavlovian model of communication (Bateson 1951: 215; Sargant 1959: passim). These two means are frequently found in combination. This was probably the case with South American peonage (cf. Wolf 1959); an important part of the explanation of that exploitative relationship is the personalization of a T mode of exchange (Wolf and Hansen, p. 156: "In Latin America . . . relationships based on economic transactions . . . are strongly personalized"). Upon this basis, the additional bonding of an I mode of exchange was fabricated. However, exploitative relationships in exchange can also develop through the reverse process of accretion of the T mode to an original I mode of exchange.

But changes in exchange patterns do not flow only in the direction of exploitation: differences within the patron-client relationship are interesting in this respect. On the one hand, the bargaining power of many native clients in the Canadian Arctic (1960s) has been minimal (Paine 1971: passim): clients are "directed" by their patrons (p. 17) who create the need for patronage (p. 14). In this frontier situation, the patron-client relationship often came close to being conducted along the lines of the Pavlovian model of communication. On the other hand, the bargaining power of clients in Sicily is "such [that] a social accounting is the basis upon which a system of patronage rests" (Boissevain 1966: 22): the I mode is tempered by elements of T exchange. (This is still properly referred to as a patron-client relationship, however, on account of the importance of the esteem paid to the patron by his clients; see Boissevain, p. 27, and Foster 1963: 1290.) Because the patron-client relationship is based upon the exchange of different resources (Figure 3), it is open to market influences—notwithstanding its anchoring to the I mode—and it is some of these that are now contributing to a change in patronage in the Arctic area toward the Sicilian pattern: that is, clients enjoy increased options concerning choice of patrons and a growing sophistication of knowledge about the outside world.

CODING AND SOCIAL CONTROL

In this section the formal analysis will be continued. The original statement by Barth of the T/I distinction concerned *value optimum*, but it is only by exploring beyond this point and adding other diacritica that the explanatory utility of the distinction may be enhanced. We have already explored alternative modes of mediation; I now want to look at alternative modes of coding and social control.

The phenomenological relationship between coding and social control is, of course, a close one. For it is not just messages that are passed in communication, but encoded messages. Indeed, a code has been described as that which "controls both the creation and organization of specific meanings and the conditions for their transmission and reception" (Bernstein 1972b: 474). Codification (encoding) is the attempt to ensure that a message will be understood in the precise way its sender intends; or as Bateson (1951: 158) puts it, coding is "instructions on how to interpret a given message." But as there are alternative kinds of messages or instructions, so there are alternative codes to impart *different kinds of control* over messages. On the one hand, control may be directed toward uniformity and consensus: we can call this the closed message; on the other hand, control may be an arrangement to ensure that alternative interpretations of a message are not lost or hidden or subjugated: the open message.

In sum, the choice of code is an important instrument in the mediation of meaning.[8] Once again, Bateson (1951: 209) sums up the matter: "propositions about codification are also implicit or explicit propositions about relationships and vice versa." In other words, because social relationships vary, so will codes.[9] Thus it may be expected that the *T* and *I* modes of exchange, as ideal propositions about relationships, will each have its typical code, and this will be an instrument of the mode of social control prevailing in the relationship.

Just how propositions about codes are, indeed, propositions about modes of social control, and vice versa, is the precise and recurrent theme of much of Bernstein's writings (e.g., 1964, 1965, 1972a, 1972b). Let me summarize.

The intention of the closed-message system of control is to "increase the similarity of the regulated with others of his social group" (1972b: 486), and this system is associated with *position-oriented* groups. Here the status aspect of any social relation is salient, and status the cardinal means by which group consensus is maintained (1964: 58, 59; 1965: 154). Loss of personal autonomy is compensated through a heightened sense of social identity (1972a: 175). In the open-message system, however, social control is "very much at the level of individual intention, motive, and disposition" (1972b: 487); hence this system is associated with groups that Bernstein calls *person-oriented*. Here role discretion is wide (1972b: 483), though there may be a relative loss in the sense of social identity (1972a: 175).

So far this schema is a recognizable paraphrase of various writers in the Grand Theory tradition (Durkheim, Marx, Parsons, Tönnies, Weber); however, Bernstein uses the schema as scaffolding by which he reaches "differences in the norms or social rules underlying the informants' communicative behavior, differences which affect their perceptions of social relationships" (Gumperz 1971: 223). Hence codes.

Because social relations in a position-oriented group are most likely to be "of an inclusive kind . . . refracted through a common cultural identity" (Bernstein 1965: 155; cf. 1972a: 171), what becomes important is "*how* things are said, *when* they are said, rather than what is said" (1965: 156). And I think that among the diacritica of the code associated with this situation, the most significant is that "the intent of the listener is likely to be taken for granted"; in other words, "the unique meaning of the individual is likely to be implicit" (1965: 156).[10] The change to person-oriented groups, on the other hand, is a change to relations in which the listener's intent cannot be taken for granted, in which what matters is precisely what is said. The "listener is dependent upon the verbal elaboration of meaning" (1964: 63; 1965: 156). There is a necessary substitution of codes.

If we speak of position- and person-oriented *situations* instead of groups, the strait jacket of ideal, dichotomous propositions is loosened considerably, and we surely have a model of considerable relevance. The code of the closed-message system of position-oriented situations is given the name *restricted (R) code* by Bernstein; the other he calls the *elaborated (E) code*. My proposal is that the R code is the archetypal code of the I mode of exchange, just as the E code is that of the T mode of exchange. (See Table 1.) Let us explore this further.

The I mode of exchange itself constitutes a closed-message system. As the interests of the parties are identical and inseparable, so their exchange is based on empathy or co-identity, not bargaining, and the mediation of messages between the parties is mutually supportive or reflexive: choice is not a value of the exchange. And the code (R) of the closed-message system "is concerned with control rather than information" (Robinson 1971: 82); it operates in relationships in which cognitive boundaries are well defined, in which there are "condensed" symbols and strong constraints in support of the legitimating values (Bernstein 1972a: 164). A consequence of these characteristics is that "inside" such an exchange relationship predictability and comprehension of messages are both high, but both are low, or absent, for those who may be listening to the messages from outside the relationship.

The T mode of exchange is, of course, based on bargaining. Each party has his separate interests to take care of, and each makes his own evaluation of messages that are received: choice *is* a value of the exchange. Thus the T mode constitutes an open-message system, and the code (E) has been described as allowing each person to behave as "an emancipated self-organizing system" (Robinson, p. 86). The boundary distinctions of the closed-message system are collapsed, with the result that predictability concerning the kinds of messages that are likely to be passed is low. On the other hand, the comprehension of messages, notwithstanding their variety, need not suffer, since there is verbal elaboration of meaning beyond that normally occurring in the I mode of exchange.

The fact that the two modes of exchange are, at the same time, different kinds of communication becomes still clearer when we note that the likelihood of self-validating evaluations is greater in the I mode, less in the T mode. Bateson (1951) has written of I mode communication as "value-seeking" activity whereby a person or group achieves "coincidence or congruence between something in his head . . . and something external . . . *by altering the external objects and events*" (p. 179; emphasis added). Such communication is tautological, and on account of its particular dependency on symbols for the maintenance of commitment (cf. the "condensed" symbol structure that Bernstein attributes to the position-oriented groups), persons who take part in it "sometimes perceive less freedom for action than they really have" (Katz 1969: 135; cf. the fact that choice is not a value in the *I* mode of exchange). The observation that the coding process reduces the world to "a few meaningful and simplified categories" (Katz and Kahn 1969: 96) is particularly true in this context (cf. the closed-message system of social control directed toward consensus).

Exchanges in the *T* mode are by no means purged of the self-validating evaluation; but because each party makes his own evaluations in the light of his

TABLE 1 *Properties of the Two Modes of Exchange*

	I Mode of Exchange (Incorporation)	*T* Mode of Exchange (Transactions)
General structure	Value sought jointly for sum of partners	Each seeks his own value
	Choice not a value	Choice is a value
	Exchange based on co-identity—sharing	Exchange based on bargained complementarity
Mediation	Receiver confirms sender's mediation	Receiver makes own evaluation of sender's message
	No ascendancy in roles, or receiver accepts ascendancy of sender	An ascendancy likely to be gained and can be won by either role
Social control	Position-oriented	Person-oriented
	Little role discretion	High role discretion
	Strong social identity	Weak social identity
Cognitive boundaries	Well-defined	Indeterminate
	Condensed symbols around group-legitimated values	Individuated symbols
Code	*R*: closed-message system	*E*: open-message system
	Intent of listener taken for granted	Verbal elaboration of meaning
	Self-validating communication ("value-seeking")	Corrective learning ("information-seeking")
	Code hallowed	Code open to exchange
Value and code	Congruent	Differentiated
	Both axiomatic	Both propositional

These diacritica are discussed in the text; they derive from Barth, Bateson, Bernstein, and the present writer. Additional tabulation of the *T/I* difference is found in Table 1 of Paine (1974), where the distinctions made by Barth are related to those of Durkheim, Parsons and Shils, Gluckman, and Blau.

separate interests, there will not be the collusion in this matter that is characteristic of the *I* mode. If we accept Bateson's axiom that "man lives by those propositions whose validity is a function of his belief in them" (1951: 212), the important question is how that "belief" is reached and maintained. The effort of each party in a *T* exchange to maximize his own interests and, accordingly, the consideration he gives to relative utility, make corrective learning, or negative feedback (to which the *I* mode is antipathetic), a strong likelihood. In Bateson's terms again, value-seeking activity is now supplemented by "information-seeking," whereby a person attempts to achieve congruence between something in his head and something external *by altering what is in his head* (p. 179; cf. the use of the open-message system of social control to ensure that alternative interpretations of a message are not lost).

There is the question of the relation between value and code; indeed, what meaning may "value" have that is not already attributed to code? Bateson draws the two closely together, as though the one is the epiphenomenon of the other (p. 176); but he seems to be concerned at this point only with the self-validating system of communication, and the relationship between value and code will assuredly be a different one where there is corrective learning. This is reason enough for keeping value and code separated conceptually, and I suggest[11] that values are standards to which incoming behavior is compared, and that codes serve to limit the standards available for comparison. In the *I* mode of exchange, comparison of values is severely limited, but this is always less true in the *T* mode. Similarly, the code of an *I* mode of exchange is unlikely to be held in question but, instead, becomes hallowed through usage (cf. the axiomatic character of the *R* code); in the *T* mode, on the other hand, codes themselves are liable to be items of transaction (cf. the propositional character of the *E* code).

Earlier, reference was made to the possibility of metacommunicative "attack" in the process of mediation. But we now see that it is really only in the *T* mode of exchange that there is a struggle between sender and receiver roles, for in the *I* mode the tailored-to-fit messages that are sent are mutually held to be "correct." There is, then, this rule-of-thumb difference between the two modes of exchange: in the *I* exchange there is an expectancy of no ascendancy at all or an ascendancy, accepted by the receiver, of the sender's role; in the *T* exchange, by contrast, either role may gain ascendancy against the wishes of the other and the expectancy is that one of them will.

PRIVATIZATION AND BROKERAGE OF MEANING

So far we have considered codification as supportive of communication, but account must also be taken of the ways in which it is, at the same time, expressive of systemic *disjunctions* in social life. These disjunctions can place individuals or groups "out of communication" with each other. After all, a code provides instructions on how to interpret a message only to those who master it, and those who do not may be effectively excluded from communication and exchange. Although we have considered a general schema of codification based on verbal communication only, even that provides a proliferation of separate codes within each basic type (R and E),[12] and in one of these kinds (R), decoding is always predicated on the possession of intimate knowledge of social context. Bernstein's own field-research problem is an example of systemic disjunction.

His research is concerned with the fact that, against expectations, universal education in England has done little to break down class disparities; on the contrary, these have been ushered into a new arena, the school, where middle-class children, it is reported, do conspicuously better than lower-class children. The disjunction resides, ethnographically, in the fact that the schools themselves are middle-class institutions.[13] Cybernetically, the disjunction resides in problems of code repertoire and code switching. In general, "systems can react only to those information signals to which they are attuned" (Katz and Kahn 1969: 96); in this particular case, it is lower-class children and middle-class teachers who are insufficiently attuned to each other's codes.

The issue of linguistic competence (particularly in E codes), and of the function of social class as a variable, need not concern us here.[14] Rather, I want to raise the general proposition that such situations of disjunction are, in fact, dramatic expressions of a dialectical opposition that is always likely to be present in the politics of exchange. On the one hand, there are the well-known Maussian obligations of reciprocity. On the other hand, there are forces of self-enclosure or withdrawal producing, in the evocative paraphrase of Hannah Arendt (cited by Mueller 1970), *privatization of meaning*. Where privatization of meaning prevails, value-seeking activity is taken a crucial step beyond self-validating coding of messages; there is a refusal to pass messages beyond the borders of one's group—or, in the case of "privatized" individuals, to pass messages at all.

For example, privatization of meaning in archetypal position-oriented groups is generated by ordinances that create a boundary around the group; the boundary is of symbolic importance to the group's members, and communication and exchange may be terminated there. The boundary marker is an R code: its usage upholds an internally legitimated value system. The "withdrawal" of a group can occur as a consequence of its renouncing all codes other than its "own," whose R code qualities will become exaggerated. Thus, in the English classroom, teachers. and some of the children are on the "outside" of each others' cognitive boundaries; each has difficulty in catching the others' cues (different R codes). Eventually, one or both parties may begin to reject the cues of the other.

Efforts to escape privatization are common, but so is the likelihood of their being resisted and thwarted—resisted because others perceive such efforts as directed either toward the dismantling of their closed group or toward intrusion *into* it; thwarted because of defenders' tactical advantages in this matter. Would-be intruders on the R codes of others find these codes not easily assailable by learning (cf. Schutz 1944: 505); they are also defended with a passion because they articulate the domains of "personal space" (Hall) and "backstage" (Goffman), of "subjective plausibility" (Mueller) and "identity reinforcement" (Bernstein). Against those who attempt to acquire familiarity in some of the different institutionalized E codes of public life, an efficacious countermove is to render the public use of E codes politically insensitive. This emasculation of the role of an E code may be achieved essentially by withdrawing information from it; thus the assault brings no more than a Pyrrhic victory and power retains its elusive privacy by retreating behind doors that are still closed. This may not provoke protest if in the place of verbal elaboration of meaning (E code) symbols are judiciously introduced into the public discourse to maximize the emotive rather than the logical impact of messages (cf. Bernstein 1959: 317). Thus what began as an attempt by one party to open an exchange in the T mode with those in power may end as ritual communication (R code) and an exchange in the I mode, perhaps along the lines of the patron-client exchange of Figure 3.

The absence of protest in this turn of events would itself be a clue that self-validating messages are being passed; and the paradox that the more one knows, the less one learns, is likely to prevail. This is also the probable outcome when people are left feeling "out of communication" through failure to receive or understand a message that *was* sent:[15] individuals attempt to rectify the situation by using their *own* experience to fill gaps in their knowledge (cf. Shibutani 1966: passim).[16] Here information (or rather its pretense) is "planted" on a person, not by the other party to the exchange but by himself. Value-seeking activity is used *as if* it were information-seeking. Indeed, what we see here is "exchange" being conducted even in the absence of a partner, or of an input from a partner: his input is imagined. This should not surprise us too much in view of what has already been said of exchange as a mediated process whereby each partner's input is, in the ordinary course of events, evaluated by the other.

But the forces of privatization have a dialectical relation with those of reciprocity: no act of self-enclosure or withdrawal from the larger world is ever likely to be complete, and relations persist across boundaries fashioned by value preferences. Hence the role of brokerage in exchange. Whereas privatization is associated with the breakdown of communication and exchange, or at least their restriction to the I mode, brokerage is an important means for the restitution of T exchanges, even between groups that have strong and mutually exclusive I mode commitments.

Systems theorists care to belabor the point that any closed system eventually "runs down and perishes" (Katz and Kahn 1969: 95);[17] but what is surely of greater importance to us is the human, or cultural, characteristic of living in "as if" closed systems[18] such as we have been discussing. This characteristic provides the ultimate explanation of brokerage. By means of brokerage, individuals and groups can avoid paying the ultimate penalty—perishing—of living in a closed system; at the same time brokerage helps to maintain the facade of a closed system. That is, brokerage is supportive of I modes: by having a broker *transact* on his behalf, the client himself avoids having to go "outside" his own domains (or appearing to do so). A broker is able to perform this function because exchange, in the T mode, is not a sharing relationship (something that it is unlikely a broker could achieve for a client); it is sufficient that each party is able to decode (or have decoded) the message of the other.[19]

The point I am urging is that the use clients have for a broker is based upon his relatively open-system location in contrast to their relatively closed-system locations. This is also the source of the broker's control over his clients. Accordingly, a broker may be expected to strive (a) to retain his open-system capabilities, and (b) to keep his clients happy in their own "as if" closed systems. This state of affairs implies more than that parties with different R codes cannot communicate directly with each other through them. There are also difficulties with E codes. The fact that verbal meaning is elaborated and hence may be learned (in the sense that is not true of R codes) does not mean that it will be learned. Indeed, it is perhaps particularly among the E code-conditioned middle class (here I am following Bernstein) that there is awareness of a "Tower of Babel" effect of different E codes; the greater facility in E codes of this class of people does not make up for the concomitant factor of the greater enmeshment of their lives in a complex world of crisscrossing E codes. As Bateson (1972: 418) has reminded us: "the logician's dream that men should communicate only by unambiguous digital signals has not come true and is unlikely to." The point, then, is the generality of limits of actual (as opposed to potential) resources for encoding and decoding; the limits may vary in kind with social status, but are probably surprisingly constant in their extent. The possibility of privatization in interaction is present even in a world of E codes.

Much of the expertise of the broker's role lies in the manipulation of the codes to which he has access and others do not. In Bernstein's terms, he may be expected to retain the dependence of his clients by not attempting to improve their E code abilities and by not teaching them each other's R codes. In Barth-derived terms, he does not try to remove the obstacles in the way of direct T exchanges between his clients (cf. Paine 1974: 24–28). At the same time, a broker must be perceived by each client as working on behalf of his particular interests. This means, in Bateson's terms, that a broker becomes involved both in his clients' own value-seeking activity and in information-seeking on their behalf. He may have to direct and control the privatization of meaning by a client in order to minimize its social and economic costs, but only in exceptional cases would he set out to destroy it. Where introducing information from outside means modifying a client's values, the broker has to avoid subjectively placing that client in a conflict of values.

Such considerations call attention to the other principal locus of broker expertise: broker-client intersubjectivity[20] and its politics.[21] On behalf of his clients, a broker engages in exchanges in the T mode, but R codes have as important a place as E codes in the process. To look first at brokerage on behalf of clients who remain in the shelter of their "as if" closed worlds: only R codes can satisfy two of the prerequisites. First, their use *retains* interclient distance—distance that symbolizes important values held by each—and relieves fears, which clients may otherwise have, that brokerage would erode this distance.[22] Secondly, by conducting his dialogues in the respective R codes of the clients, a broker *reduces* the distance between himself and each client. However, this has to be qualified by yet a third prerequisite which demonstrates the use a broker, in these circumstances, may make of E codes: the *alternation* of social distance with a client. The reason is that the broker has to be concerned not only with how clients perceive the world, but also with how the world perceives them. This means that he must not allow himself to be caught in the web of his clients' symbols, even when he undertakes to interpret these symbols to third parties.

In the case of brokerage to resolve an impasse arising out of the use of one or more E codes by a client, the task falling to the broker is to show the client how his logical, rather than emotive, perception of the world is not necessarily consistent with the realization of all his interests. This inversion of the problem leads to an inversion also in what may be regarded as the usual procedure of brokerage: instead of the broker's moderating a client's value-seeking activity in the light of information external to it, the broker urges subjectivity on his client.

In all cases a broker has to achieve a high level of intersubjectivity with his client, yet success in the role is ultimately dependent on a *limit*'s being called—for the broker "has to place in question nearly everything that seems to be unquestionable" to his client.[23]

What we have said of breakdowns in exchanges and the manner in which a broker restitutes exchange suggests another explanation besides the one Blau had in mind of *how* exchange gives rise to differences in power. Not only are there inequalities within individual exchanges, there are also inequalities of opportunity to make exchanges, and in both cases the power that manifests itself in these inequalities is closely connected with control over communication as a political resource. The options that a person has *in* an exchange or his options to institute an exchange may be predetermined by another's control of the mediation process; this control is not easily challenged once it is established. This is true even with E codes: they are not necessarily available to all who may learn them—or when learned they may be found to be no longer particularly useful.

Perhaps the key summarizing concept is what we termed "disjunctions" in the structure of communication. Grounded in differences of socialization and social perception and expressed in differences of code, these disjunctions are likely to be manipulated as nodules of power by certain parties. For whoever controls the edges around a disjunction should be in a good position to direct exchanges across it, as has been amply demonstrated in the context of economic anthropology. What is being controlled in this case are the codes in which exchanges may be conducted: power is *encoded*. In his search for power, the aspiring politician, for example, looks for a situation—or creates one—in which there are disjunctions that inhibit action for others but not for himself: it is he, not they, who can make the connections or transformations. The broker role is an exemplar of this whole notion, and our discussion has suggested certain formulae of power based on brokers' manipulation of codes and social distance. Politicians may assume broker roles themselves; they may also—with greater sophistication—"own" brokers.[24]

CONCLUSION: ASSUMPTIONS ABOUT EXCHANGE

The governing premise of this essay has been that when engaging in exchanges persons are concerned to render them intelligible. In exploring this premise, two analytic connections have been paramount: (1) between exchange and communication—how a person renders his own exchanges intelligible; and (2) between these and power—how another person imposes "intelligibility" upon one's exchanges. In pursuing this course I have called upon the work of others; in particular, the distinction found in Barth (1966) between transaction and incorporation was developed, and it was related to the distinctions between kinds of

TABLE 2 *Assumptions About Exchange*

Assumptions by Various Authors	Refinements or Counterassumptions
Exchanges may be explained by game theory.	Not those of the *I* mode (cf. Table 1).
Exchanges are voluntary.	Not necessarily (and the circumstances of the involuntary differ in the two modes).
Along with commodities, values are exchanged.	It is messages about values that are exchanged along with commodities.
Prestations received by a party are the same as those sent to him.	Possible in the *I* mode (cf. Figure 2); otherwise the meanings of prestations change in the process of delivery.
Exchange is integrative; it breaks down divisions and brings people into sharing relationships.	Exchange can integrate (e.g., within the *I* mode), or it can be a process whereby people find the means to live apart or are kept apart; only in the *I* mode can there be a sharing relationship.
We save ourselves from repeating our mistakes through corrective learning (or negative feedback) in exchanges.	Most unlikely in the *I* mode, somewhat more likely in the *T* mode. (The conditions under which corrective learning occurs are rather special and not well understood, whereas the contrary process in exchange, self-validating communication, is widespread and better understood.)
The parties who are exchanging are themselves responsible for the exchange.	Generally true within the *I* mode, but third-party mediation is common in the *T* mode and exchanges can occur at the will of the third party rather than of the exchange partners themselves.

communication made by Bateson (1951) and Bernstein (see references). The argument placed in question various assumptions apparent in other writings about exchange. Table 2, in conclusion, collects these assumptions and matches them with the refinements, or counterassumptions, made in this essay.

ACKNOWLEDGMENT

This essay replaces the paper circulated at the 1973 ASA conference under the title "Transactions as Communicative Events." My thanks to Peter Harries-Jones for his stimulating comments in the formative phase of this essay.

NOTES

1. It is one whose "structure . . . permits analysis by means of a strategic model, as a game of strategy" (Barth, p. 4).

2. Davis (1972, 1973) voices the same complaint. He notices "the way that as the attributed scope of exchange has become all-embracing, the principles on which decisions and exchanges are said to be made have been narrowed until we are left with only one: that is, that men maximize rewards less costs." He suggests that "much confusion seems to result from pan-transactionalist assumptions. . . . Are we really to assume," he asks, "that these [exchanges] are all governed by the same sort of rules—are the same sort of transaction?" (1973: 160; 1972: 408).

3. In the *T* mode ". . . each actor's social adjustment to the other party in the transaction is depicted in terms of alter's possible moves, and how they in turn affect ego's value gains" (Barth 1966, p. 4).

4. For a parallel criticism of Barth's treatment, see Paine 1974: 6–10.

5. This interpretation of the patronage relationship is a development of an earlier one (Paine 1971), in which resources were not distinguished or the *I* mode separated from the *T*.

6. On the other hand, this is not to deny Harries-Jones' idea (personal communication) that any liberal progression in the change from status to contract posited by Maine is largely illusory, since contract itself is a common instrument of status.

7. For treatments of this kind of relationship in another cultural setting, the "truck" system of trade in Atlantic fishing communities, see Paine (1965: 170–174) on Norwegian merchants and Wadel (1969: passim) on Newfoundland merchants.

8. This is demonstrated, through attention to the strong situational aspect of choice of code, in the Norwegian study of Blom and Gumperz (1972), where code switching (between a dialect and a standard form of Norwegian) is related to association with the "local team"; and in an earlier piece, Gumperz (1964) suggests an analysis of code switching in connection with changes between "two types of interaction: transactional and personal."

9. Cf. Bernstein (1965: 157): "the ability to switch codes controls the ability to switch roles." There is the possibility for a misunderstanding in connection with this statement: the point is not to posit a primacy, whether developmental or logical, of code over role. Rather, it is to stress their interrelationship and to demonstrate how codification is a necessary aspect of role. This is made clear elsewhere in his writings: "role is defined as a complex coding

activity," and "if you cannot manage the role, you can't produce the appropriate speech" (1972a: 158, 166; cf. 1964: 64, and 1972b: 473–474).

10. It should *not* be understood that the use of this code—the *R* code, as I will explain in a moment—removes all possibility for the expression of individual differences; this is a common misconception of Bernstein's analysis. Rather, these differences are more likely to be expressed through extraverbal channels (gesture, pause, stress, etc.) characteristically associated with this code (cf. Bernstein 1965: 155). But even this characteristic of the code is sometimes cited in criticism of the schema: it is alleged that the code implies a lack of fundamental capacity for logical analysis and conceptual thought among its users (cf. Jensen 1968: 118; Labov 1972a: 183). This is a travesty of the thesis; cf. Bernstein 1972c: 16f.

11. With prompting from Peter Harries-Jones.

12. Within each type there is, first, a subdivision into "object"-oriented and "person"-oriented, and a further division into "means" and "ends" variants. See Gumperz and Hymes 1972: 468f.

13. Bernstein (1972a: 176) says that "the value system of the middle-class penetrates the texture of the very learning context itself."

14. Besides Bernstein's writings, see Cazden 1972; Labov 1972a and 1972b; and Mueller 1973: Chapter 2.

15. The message may be insufficiently encoded to protect it from "noise," in which case it becomes garbled. Or the encoding may be such the message is rejected by the receiver as being outside his cognitive experience; in this case the failure of the sender is that he is unable to alter what is "in the head" of the receiver.

16. Shibutani's book is an analysis of rumor along these lines.

17. Closed systems perish because they lack "a continuous inflow of energy from the external environment and a continuous export of the products of the system" (Katz and Kahn, p. 96).

18. Indeed, is not "a culture," in one essential aspect of its definition, an "as if" closed system?

19. Cf. Wallace 1964 and the discussion in Paine 1974: 19–23.

20. "The experience of my 'understanding' the other, and his 'understanding' me" (Schutz 1970: 319).

21. "[One is] also concerned with the processes which lead and allow certain individuals to control the perceptions of and the behaviour of others, and with the processes which generate changes in their perceptions and related social activity" (Kapferer 1972: 205).

22. Where a broker is forcing his good offices upon clients who, conceivably, could mediate their own exchanges, it helps to *create* the interclient distance that is a prerequisite of brokerage (cf. Paine 1974: 24–28).

23. The quotation is from Schutz's (1944) essay on the stranger (p. 502); cf. Simmel's (1950) essay on the same subject, where he speaks of objectivity as composed of "distance and nearness, indifference and involvement," so that the stranger "as a group member . . . is near and far at the same time" (pp. 404, 407). I think there are insights to be gained from considering the broker sociologically as a kind of stranger.

24. That is, a particularly strong client may force a broker to abandon the ideal stance of equal concern for all clients: the broker becomes the creature of that particular client (the politician). In this way the politician himself can more easily remain uncommitted, where this is an advantage, regarding exchanges (prospective or ongoing) arranged between

different sectors of *his* political clientele. "Watergate" is an interesting example of such stratagems.

REFERENCES

Barth, F. 1966. *Models of Social Organization*. Royal Anthropological Institute Occasional Paper No. 23. London.

Bateson, Gregory. 1951. Chapters 7 and 8 in J. Reusch and G. Bateson, *Communication: The Social Matrix of Psychiatry*. New York: W. W. Norton.

———. 1972. *Steps to an Ecology of Mind*. San Francisco: Chandler.

Bernstein, Basil. 1959. A public language: some sociological implications of a linguistic form. *British Journal of Sociology*, 10: 311–325.

———. 1964. Elaborated and restricted codes: their social origins and some consequences. In J. J. Gumperz and D. Hymes, eds., *The Ethnography of Communication*. Special publication of the *American Anthropologist*. Washington, D.C.

———. 1965. A socio-linguistic approach to social learning. In Julius Gold, ed., *Penguin Survey of the Social Sciences 1965*. Harmondsworth, Middlesex: Penguin.

———. 1972a. A brief account of the theory of codes. Typescript.

———. 1972b. Social class, language and socialization. In P. P. Giglioli, ed., *Language and Social Context*. Harmondsworth, Middlesex: Penguin.

———. 1972c. A sociolinguistic approach to socialization, with some reference to educability. In J. J. Gumperz and D. Hymes, eds., *Directions in Sociolinguistics*. New York: Holt, Rinehart and Winston.

Blau, P. M. 1964. *Exchange and Power in Social Life*. New York: John Wiley.

Blom, J. P., and J. J. Gumperz. 1972. Some social determinants of verbal behavior. In J. J. Gumperz and D. Hymes, eds., *Directions in Sociolinguistics*. New York: Holt, Rinehart and Winston.

Boissevain, Jeremy. 1966. Patronage in Sicily. *Man*, N.S., 1: 18–33.

Boulding, Kenneth E. 1971. *The Image*. Ann Arbor: University of Michigan Press.

Campbell, J. K. 1964. *Honour, Family and Patronage*. Oxford: Clarendon Press.

Caplow, Theodore. 1968. *Two Against One: Coalitions in Triads*. Englewood Cliffs, N.J.: Prentice-Hall.

Cazden, C. B. 1972. The situation: a neglected source of social class differences in language use. In J. B. Pride and J. Holmes, eds., *Sociolinguistics*. Harmondsworth, Middlesex: Penguin.

Davis, J. 1972. Gifts and the U.K. economy. *Man*, N.S., 7: 408–429.

———. 1973. Forms and norms: the economy of social relations. *Man*, N.S., 8: 159–176.

Dreitzel, Hans Pieter. 1970. Introduction: patterns of communicative behavior. In H. P. Dreitzel, ed., *Recent Sociology No. 2*. New York: Macmillan.

Foster, G. M. 1963. The dyadic contract in Tzintzuntzan: patron-client relationship. *American Anthropologist*, 65: 1280–1294.

Gumperz, J. J. 1964. Linguistic and social interaction in two communities. In J. J. Gumperz and D. Hymes, eds., *The Ethnography of Communication*. Special publication of the *American Anthropologist*.

———. 1971. *Language in Social Groups: Essays by John J. Gumperz Selected and Introduced by A. S. Dil*. Stanford: Stanford University Press.

Gumperz, J. J., and D. Hymes, eds. 1972. *Directions in Sociolinguistics*. New York: Holt, Rinehart and Winston.

Hampden-Turner, Charles. 1971. *Radical Man*. New York: Doubleday.

Hinton, William. 1966. *Fanshen*. New York: Vintage Books.

Hymes, Dell. 1964. Introduction: towards ethnographies of communication. In J. J. Gumperz and D. Hymes, eds., *The Ethnography of Communication*. Special publication of the *American Anthropologist*. Washington, D.C.

Jensen, A. 1968. Social class and verbal learning. In M. Deutsch, I. Katz, and A. R. Jensen, eds., *Social Class, Race and Psychological Development*. New York: Holt, Rinehart and Winston.

Kapferer, Bruce. 1972. *Strategy and Transaction in an African Factory: African Workers and Indian Management in a Zambian Town*. Manchester: Manchester University Press.

Katz, D. 1969. Group process and social integration: a system analysis of two movements of social protest. In H. P. Dreitzel, ed., *Recent Sociology No. 1*. New York: Macmillan.

Katz, D., and R. L. Kahn. 1969. Common characteristics of open systems. In F. E. Emery, ed., *Systems Thinking*. Harmondsworth, Middlesex: Penguin.

Labov, W. 1972a. The logic of nonstandard English. In P. P. Giglioli, ed., *Language and Social Context*. Harmondsworth, Middlesex: Penguin.

———. 1972b. The study of language in its social context. In P. P. Giglioli, ed., *Language and Social Context*. Harmondsworth, Middlesex: Penguin.

Lévi-Strauss, Claude. 1969. *The Elementary Structures of Kinship*. London: Eyre and Spottiswoode.

Lyman, S. M., and M. B. Scott. 1970. *A Sociology of the Absurd*. New York: Appleton-Century-Crofts.

Mueller, Claus. 1970. Notes on the repression of communicative behavior. In H. P. Dreitzel, ed., *Recent Sociology No. 2*. New York: Macmillan.

———. 1973. *The Politics of Communication*. New York: Oxford University Press.

Paine, Robert. 1965. *Coast Lapp Society II: A Study of Economic Development and Social Values*. Oslo: Universitetsforlaget.

———. 1971. A theory of patronage and brokerage. In Robert Paine, ed., *Patrons and Brokers in the East Arctic*. St. John's: Institute of Social and Economic Research, Memorial University.

———. 1974. *Second Thoughts About Barth's "Models."* Royal Anthropological Institute Occasional Paper No. 32. London.

Reusch, J., and G. Bateson. 1951. *Communication: The Social Matrix of Psychiatry*. New York: W. W. Norton.

Robinson, W. P. 1971. Restricted codes in socio-linguistics and the sociology of education. In W. H. Whiteley, ed., *Language Use and Social Change*. Oxford: Oxford University Press.

Sargant, W. 1959. *Battle for the Mind*. London: Pan Books.

Schelling, T. C. 1956. An essay on bargaining. *American Economic Review*, 46: 281–306.

Schutz, Alfred. 1944. The stranger: an essay in social psychology. *American Journal of Sociology*, 49: 499–507.

———. 1970. *On Phenomenology and Social Relations*, ed. with an introduction by H. R. Wagner. Chicago: University of Chicago Press.

Shibutani, Tamotsu. 1966. *Improvised News: A Sociological Study of Rumor*. New York: Bobbs-Merrill.

Simmel, Georg. 1950. *The Sociology of Georg Simmel*, trans., ed., and with an introduction by Kurt H. Wolff. New York: Free Press.

———. 1959. *Georg Simmel, 1858–1918*, ed. Kurt H. Wolff. Columbus: Ohio State University Press.

Wadel, Cato. 1969. *Marginal Adaptations and Modernization in Newfoundland*. St. John's: Institute of Social and Economic Research, Memorial University.
Wallace, A. F. C. 1964. *Culture and Personality*. New York: Random House.
Wolf, E. R. 1959. *Sons of the Shaking Earth*. Chicago: University of Chicago Press.
Wolf, E. R., and E. C. Hansen. 1972. *The Human Condition in Latin America*. New York: Oxford University Press.

The Management of Meaning:
On the Phenomenology
of Political Transactions

A. P. COHEN AND J. L. COMAROFF

Since the publication of *African Political Systems* in 1940, there has been an observable trend in political anthropology toward the adoption of processual models of political behavior,[1] in which "politics" is rendered increasingly diffuse by being definitionally dissociated from institutional frameworks and, latterly, from specific structural referents and loci.[2] We consider that the ultimate logic of this trend may be expressed in the notion of politics as behavior associated with the unequal distribution of valued social resources. In this chapter, we propose to examine two examples of such distributive inequality. In the first, the valued resource is indispensability; in the second, it lies in the actors' capacity to identify and manipulate sources of political support and, alternatively, of competition. Both instances are concerned with a fundamental aspect of political process: the management of meanings to produce particular constructions of political behavior.

The ethnographic examples we have chosen suggest to us that such management of meanings underpins political action. This leads us to argue for a more obviously cognitive emphasis in political analysis, and one which takes into account phenomenological dimensions of political behavior. We do not make this argument simply as partisans of phenomenology but rather because ethnographic attention to the actor's perception of his and others' strategies is warranted by the recognition of the emic realities of political process.

Like the other contributors to this volume, we were originally invited to consider transactional analysis as a "new direction in anthropology," the theme of the Decennial Conference of the ASA. We chose not to undertake a systematic review of the literature on transactional analysis or exchange theory, as such reviews already abound.[3] Rather, we take these analytical paradigms as a point of departure for the exploration of a "new direction": the cognitive dimension of political process. We do not suggest that previous transactional or exchange theorists have ignored this dimension; rather, the foundations which they have already laid seem to us to warrant further development.

Our presentations of the two ethnographies will follow similar patterns. First, we will briefly evaluate the ways in which brokerage or marriage forms have been treated in the literature of transaction, and suggest how and why increased attention to the phenomenology may provide a clearer conceptualization. We will then set out the ethnography, giving emphasis to the indigenous view of transaction as a property of brokerage or marriage. Finally, we will argue that the *power* which informs the political relations expressed in, and created by, brokerage and marriage is crucially related to the actors' success in contriving particular interpretations of these relations. We will conclude that the management of meaning must be regarded as a fundamental property of political interaction, to be explicated through adequate consideration of the phenomenological realities of situations, insofar as these are ascertainable.

BROKERAGE IN NEWFOUNDLAND

Our first ethnographic case concerns brokerage in a Newfoundland community, Focaltown. Following the idea of politics which we elaborated above, we conceptualize the broker as a *political* actor by virtue of his observable attempt to create relations of inequality structured by the unequal distribution of the valued resource of indispensability: he seeks to make the other parties to brokerage relations—patron and client—dependent upon his services.

The Concept of Broker

Much of the difficulty with the concept of broker derives, perhaps, from the associated discussions of patron-client roles and particularly from the need to distinguish the broker role both from the patron and from other intervening roles (see Boissevain 1966: 25; Foster 1963; Mayer 1967; Paine 1971: 19ff.; Silverman 1965). We suggest that the broker role has been infrequently recognized in the literature as embodying the essential attribute of power: the capacity to construct and purvey meanings concerning a variety of relationships and interactions. We hope that the crucial nature of this attribute will become apparent as our argument proceeds.

It is common to distinguish the roles of "go-between," "middleman," "mediator," "intermediary," and so on, and all of these have been variously attributed to the broker. However, the relationship between a patron and a client obviously varies with the kinds of intervention articulated into it. Paine suggests that the broker be distinguished from those in other intermediary roles by his peculiar activity of mediating or "processing" information, with the intention of changing its emphasis and/or content (1971: 21; 1973: 27ff.). But, allowing the broker this mediatory role, how do we explain his *presence* in the relation at all? Again the theories proliferate, and the broker's presence is variously explained in terms of the distance between patron and client, the stage of societal "development" and the consequences of structural change, the exigencies of career, and so forth. All of these generalizations may well be true, and there seems little point in bringing them into question. However, there is a further explanation to be added, drawn from the logic of the concept of the mediator. The function of the broker has usually been seen, in social science, to be the bringing together of a patron and clients in response to *their* mutual needs. We suggest, however, that the broker may actually provoke those needs himself. He may create a demand for values among potential clients, and persuade a "patron" that he, indeed, has resources of patronage to dispense and that it is desirable to have clients obligated to him. In so doing, the broker creates a demand for his services by both patron and clients. While this consideration does not contradict the asymmetry frequently postulated for the patron-client relation, it does tend to qualify the assumption of Paine (1971) and others that the values circulating in the relation are of the patron's choosing: they may well have been dictated by the broker. Thus we suggest that the broker role is not called into being simply by the desire of two parties to transact valued items: rather, it creates or may create the demand for those values in the "transacting" parties.[4]

The broker emerges from this model as an actor who, potentially, has considerable power, and as one who is clearly distinct from the patron; he gives access to the resources of patronage, but does not dispense them himself. He gains or seeks to gain values of his own choosing from performing his broker's role, not the least being his indispensability (cf. Paine 1974; Bailey 1969: 167ff.). We would suggest that it is his attempt to create and maintain the need for his services in patron-client relations which distinguishes the broker, as an *empirical* type, from other kinds of middleman. It is this indispensability that constitutes the unequally distributed valued resource which structures the *political* relation between the broker and those he "serves."

This dimension of indispensability is not given to the broker role by the transactional paradigm within which the broker has most often been examined. Rather, power is seen, within the logic of the paradigm, to be an "emergent property" of the transaction (Blau 1964) which is, itself, only minimally constrained by the structural correlates of power (Barth 1966: 5). Our model of the broker, on the other hand, emphasizes the strategic manipulation of *apparently* transactional relationships, and the empirical propagation of frameworks for the contrived interpretation of these relationships. The broker, then, is one who manages the meanings which people attribute to kinds of social phenomena,[5] and the character of his role is therefore to be captured by attention to the phenomenology of the situation within which he operates. How does he perceive and present himself? How is he perceived by others?

The empirical salience of the broker role in Focaltown, Newfoundland, may be ascertained by a brief examination of the patronal mode of articulation which has typically characterized interaction between rural communities (*outports*) in Newfoundland and the Newfoundland government. We shall then look at instances of contemporary leadership behavior in Focaltown as examples of attempts to create *political* relationships, structured around the value of indispensability, through the interpretive mediation or cognitive management of *apparently* transactional interaction.

Traditions of Brokerage

Traditionally, leadership in the Newfoundland community was attached to exclusive roles.[6] The merchant, whose dominion was built on his monopolistic position as both a source of credit and an outlet for the fishermen's catch, exercised a fundamental control over communal affairs. The only roles that impinged on his power were those of the priest—if it was a Catholic community, which Focaltown is not[7]—and the magistrate, who was resident only in the largest of the outports. The merchant, as leader, provided the only link between the outport and the capital, St. John's. It was a link through which the outport sought entry into the typical patronal relations emanating from the capital. Center-periphery relations in Newfoundland, both within and between communities, were typically articulated through patronage. In this regard, the community leader, as "link man," was identifiable as a broker between the outport and the central patron, and possibly also as a patron *within* the community itself.

The dispensation of services is still a typical and prominent feature of leadership behavior in Newfoundland. After Newfoundland entered the Canadian Confederation in 1949, the government, led and dominated by Joseph Smallwood until 1972, continued traditional practice and ruthlessly used its control of the "public chest" as a potent political resource (see Gwyn 1968: 125; Perlin 1971). At the local level, confederation afforded massive opportunities to would-be brokers, for the government was now increasingly able to provide such valued services as roads, electricity, mains water, sewerage, schools, community wharves, and so forth. At this level, then, a man's acuity as a leader came to be evaluated by his success in procuring amenities for the community.

Brokerage as Politics

Political leadership in Newfoundland has been typically populistic and, perhaps as a consequence, highly personalized. The leader made himself available to clients; he was identified in personal terms rather than by partisan labels or institutional affiliations.[8] Indeed, customary styles of leadership have been so nonbureaucratic that a condition of the leader's success has been his ability to transcend, in the public mind, the nonpersonal paraphernalia of his status-role.[9] Thus the distance separating the client outports from the patronal government was *conceptual* rather than merely geographical. The outporter could not approach the government because he could make no sense of it; it was a bureaucratic monolith which struck no chord of familiarity in his cognitive experience, *except insofar as it was mediated by an actor with whom he could establish a sense of personal affinity*. At the community level, these mediatory services were provided by brokers.

Such a man is Mr. L. He says of his clients, "They don't really know what the government is and they look at government as some big organization that is far from their reach." The broker translates the unknown and inaccessible into the familiar and the possible. He manages the meanings in terms of which his clients construe their interactions with the outside world. Without the services of the broker, the client outports would often stagnate completely. This amazing state of dependency is not a new phenomenon. It was noted by a royal commission appointed by the British government to enquire into Newfoundland's political and economic condition in 1933,[10] and it was maintained during the long years of Smallwood's government through the patronal allocation of services and welfare. Many local leaders built their careers upon it as brokers, and in so doing reinforced it, for in creating a need for their own services they rendered grass-roots or communal organization unnecessary.

Mr. L. exemplifies the broker strategy in all of these dimensions. He is a Focaltown motel owner who is associated through kinship, commerce, co-residence, and friendship with the traditional mercantile-oligarchic leadership of the community. Because of his *manifest* political ambitions, he occupies a lower evaluative status than his associates in the eyes of Focaltowners. However, his brokerage is directed not toward Focaltowners themselves but toward the residents of the small settlements in Focaltown's hinterland. Typically, these communities subsist on welfare.[11] They have no tradition of communal organization, nor even the basic social skills and inclinations to organize themselves.[12] The broker, then, must so contrive the collective definition of the situation of the settlement that the acquisition of services from outside appears both desirable *and* possible, and can be effected without the perceived difficulties of collective organization or entry into the unknown. For example, Mr. L. told the ethnographer of going to one of these small settlements and finding that a fisherman had not resumed fishing in the new season because the flashing light on the end of the pier had not been re-lit. So simple a procedural matter had brought his subsistence activity to a complete halt. He had no idea of how to rectify the situation. As Mr. L. reported,

> He told me that he was waiting for this light to be lit that goes in the harbor, you see. I said, "That's simple." He said, "What do you mean?" I said it was just a matter of me knowing the right person. He just didn't believe that this could be done. This is something big. I just picked up the phone and called this guy in St. John's and told him about this particular light, and I said, "We want this lit." I said, "We would like to have it lit as soon as you can get word to somebody to light it." It's as simple as that. This is one thing that I proved to these people. They laughed when I said, "Well, I can have that done." I said to them, "If I thought there was going to be any trouble, I would . . . call the minister of transport and that thing will be lit before the end of this month."

In similar fashion, Mr. L. claims to have single-handedly persuaded the government to grant municipal status to one community, make water systems available to two others, provide vital constructional modifications during the paving of Focaltown's access road to the Trans-Canada Highway, and finance a $300,000 extension to Focaltown's hospital.

The element of his strategy which must be noted here is his personalizing of the interaction. *He* knows how to engage advantageously with the government.

Moreover, he does so (or presents himself as doing so) by "knowing someone" in the government: *he* knows the *person* with whom to engage.

> I have been very closely connected with the premier and his cabinet for the past several years and I am privileged, in a sense, to be able to go into St. John's and in the Confederation [government] Building, and without any appointment or anything I can pretty well see any of these fellows at any time.

This personalization is the means by which Mr. L. accounts for his success. But, more significantly, it provides the terms with which he can make his interaction with the government intelligible to his clients and thereby make them aware of *their* need for *his* services. They cannot comprehend an individual—a neighbor— taking on the government and emerging with some profit. But a friend's approach to a friend is a different matter. Such partiality has always been a feature of patronage in Newfoundland (cf. Noel 1971) and is wholly familiar within the outporters' cultural experience. Mr. L. tells his listeners:

> I am not saying that this is the way it should be, but I am saying that this is the way it has been and always will be. Any member of the government is either a friend of yours or he is not. If he's not, you don't expect to get the same results—if you do, you're crazy. As I have said, I can go to the Confederation Building today and I venture to say that by six o'clock this evening I could see every department head that is in there. . . .

Similarly, his closest political associate, the mayor of Focaltown, says,

> It's not what you know—it's who you know. You need the proper contacts, you can't do it alone. . . . You've got to have connections to the right contacts. . . . You've got to have the cooperation of the right people in the right places. . . .

And Mr. L. adds, "if you are trying to do anything for the community, if you don't have any close contact with the people concerned—ministers and so on—you can't do anything."

The broker thus performs his services and renders himself indispensable to his clients in two ways. First, he provides access to the substantive resources of patronage. Secondly, he manages the meaning of his interaction with the patron in order to render it intelligible within the clients' cognitive and cultural idioms; he does this in such a way as to imply the exclusivity of his skills and knowledge and therefore his clients' need for his services.

Brokerage as Exchange

While outporters have traditionally left themselves at the mercy of a governmental system which articulates through patronage, and have yielded their autonomy to the contrived indispensability of local brokers, they retain a realistic view of the advantages of office. In a way, they expect the politician to feather his own nest, and they find instances of such behavior unremarkable. But they are less tolerant of their *local* leaders, and tend to be somewhat cynical in their evaluations of them. Given the history of Newfoundland's political and mercantile organization, it is hardly surprising that ulterior motives should be imputed to voluntary service. To Focaltowners, it appears to be almost incomprehensible that a man should engage in community activity without the incentive of material gain. The leaders are aware of these suspicions. One of Mr. L.'s rivals in the Focaltown leadership expressed the difficulty in this way: "They see me, Mr. E., a Focaltown businessman, and they think, 'Well, that guy wants to get his hands in our pockets. We're not going to help him.' "

To some extent, this is a rationalization of Mr. E.'s long and manifest failure to secure any public support, a failure that derives largely from the assertive nature of his leadership. This is colloquially expressed in the use of the term *businessman,* which suggests aggressive, entrepreneurial modernity, in contrast with the term *merchant,* applied locally to the legitimated leaders who operate in a customary political style. Mr. E.'s credentials as a leader are not helped by the fact that he is an outsider—he was not born in the community. One of his associates, similarly placed, articulates both dimensions of the difficulty, which he encountered when he was trying, with Mr. E., to establish local branches of the Herring Bay Economic Development Association: "You know, I could see them thinking, 'Well, he must be in it for something—what's he getting out of it? He's an outsider and he's a businessman.' They weren't going to help us—no, sir! They didn't see we was trying to help them."

Thus the local leader, if he is to be successful as a broker, must somehow contrive to present himself as lacking any self-interest in whatever transaction he effectuates between client and patron. He must employ a rhetoric of legitimation which condemns any reward for himself. Mr. L. explains:

> a hundred people have said to me, "Well, what are you getting out of this and what kind of salary are you being paid?" or some sort of thing like this. I say to them, "If you knew what this is costing me personally out of my own pocket, you would be frightened still. This costs me literally hundreds of dollars a year." Well . . . possibly there are a lot of other people that benefit more from my efforts than I do myself.

The broker must also try to present himself, not as a willing leader—for that would be an idiomatic expression of assertiveness[13]—but as a man who reluctantly dons the mantle of leadership in recognition of his public duty. Mr. L. presented his manifesto for election to the town council by saying, "For quite some time I have been approached by several of our citizens to seek a position on the council in the forthcoming election, and after some thought I decided that I should offer my services." It was, in fact, his third attempt to win a seat on the council. His friend and associate, the mayor, adopted a similar style: "After much consideration I decided to seek re-election for another term . . . at least ten people felt my experience over the past eight years should be helpful . . . and, therefore, urged and

encouraged me to again run as a candidate.'' Mr. L. explains his brokerage
activities simply in terms of providing a service:

> I tell you that people who feel that I am getting something personally out of the actual
> work that I am trying to do just don't see it at all. I don't have to go out through the
> doors of my house for the rest of my days if I don't want to. I could just stay in
> Focaltown. I don't *have* to get aboard a boat and go out to the Long Island, and at
> eleven or twelve o'clock at night get aboard of a skidoo and go two or three miles in
> subzero weather, and this sort of thing, to make a living. I would just do it because I
> like to; I do it because I am the type who likes to help other people, and to get this
> message across is not simple.

The image that he presents of himself is so unlikely, in terms of their political
experience, that his clients find themselves having to acknowledge that it might
just possibly be true. But stressing the altruism of his motives is not enough. The
broker must also present himself in terms with which his clients can identify. He
must stress his social affinity to them. Such affinity is a condition of their trust and
is necessary to his portrayal of unfamiliar social processes as comprehensible
within their terms.[14] The broker's strategy is to reduce the apparent social distance
which separates him from his clients, and to stress those components of his identity
with which they can most easily associate themselves.

Mr. L. is helped considerably in the strategic presentation of self by the
juxtaposition within Focaltown's leadership of his group—indigenous activists,
associated with the traditional mercantile oligarchy and with Smallwoodism—
with a clique of businessmen and professionals (Mr. E.'s group), all of whom are
outsiders, who reject the personalism of customary Newfoundland political style,
and who are opposed to Smallwood. Mr. L. appears politically legitimate simply
by contrast to them. But he also contrives legitimacy. He expresses his long
association with the community and area by prefacing all his speeches with, ''I
don't need to introduce myself to you: you all know me, some of you since I was
born.'' His family was among the first to inhabit Focaltown, in the 1890s, and he
has extensive kin relationships in the community and the locality. He tells his
audience, ''There are more L.'s down here than there are fish in Herring Bay.''
And, despite the fact that he is a businessman and belongs to Focaltown, he
presents himself locally as a ''common man,'' suffering from the same disadvantages as his clients. He uses his faulty grammar and strong local accent to suggest
that he is no better educated than they are: ''Dere were no big schools in our time.
Hif dere 'ad been modern schools in our time, bye, I reckons we would've made
it.'' Campaigning for the presidency of the Herring Bay District Liberal Association, against a young, articulate, and highly trained high-school teacher, he said,
''The Liberalism in my heart makes up for what I haven't got in the head.'' Finally,
he stresses, on every possible occasion, the intimacy of his association with
Smallwood, for this is to identify himself with terms of political experience which
are familiar to his clients.

As a manager of meaning, then, the broker's strategy lies along two dimensions. First, he contrives meanings for the interaction between client and patron, creating a role for himself, and he makes that role intelligible within the terms of his clients' cultural experience. It is on such meanings that his indispensability is founded. Secondly, he contrives a meaning for the nature of his own behavior as broker; this is tantamount to legitimation, and it reconciles the clients to their dependence on behavior of which they are intuitively suspicious.

What this ethnography is intended to suggest is that an important part of the capacity to play the broker role resides in the ability to manage meanings. Therefore the management of meaning is an essential aspect of power.

MARRIAGE IN A TSWANA CHIEFDOM

Time and again, I was struck by the repetition of the view that people behave among themselves in a certain way and there-fore they are related in a certain way: not that people are related in a certain way and therefore they behave in a certain way. This is true of relationships of wider scale, or political kinship.

I. CUNNISON (1959: 75)

We continue our exploration of the cognitive dimension of power by considering aspects of royal marriage in a Tswana chiefdom.[15] Among the Barolong boo Ratshidi,[16] marriage is constantly emphasized as a political transaction par excellence, since it is a formal and public means of creating and manipulating support and alliance. In this section, we hope to demonstrate that Tshidi royal marriage provides the actors with a conceptual framework within which meanings may be managed in order to negotiate and articulate the realities of power relations.

Approaches to Marriage Among the Tswana

The significant feature of Tswana marriage with which we are concerned here is that all forms of cousin marriage are preferred. The previous literature on the subject—most notably, that of Schapera—tends to treat the various forms of marriage as objectifiable realities: that is, a man has an FBD or MBD and marries her; therefore, an FBD or MBD marriage has occurred. With such an immutable fact recorded, it becomes possible to count up incidences of FBD or MBD marriages in order to produce analyses of the structural implications and/or political significance of such marriage forms. There is, however, a problem in this well-established procedure: the relationship categories involved in Tshidi cousin marriage are anything but immutable. They are a matter of actor definition. As we shall show, FBD marriage is FBD marriage when the actors involved manage to invest it with such meaning. Rival factions may and do compete over such meanings. To treat Tswana marriage forms as immutable phenomena is to confuse models with reality. We shall argue that the marriage forms, insofar as they convey meanings, are *outcomes* of competition for power—that they represent an indigenous mode of constructing and expressing the state of relations between the parties involved. As such, they are to be understood not as objective facts in their own right, but as part of the phenomenological dimension of a process of political transaction between and within factions.[17]

Marriage Among the Tshidi: Indigenous Perspectives

In order to substantiate these statements, it is necessary first to introduce *indigenous* views concerning (1) agnation, affinity, and matrilaterality, and (2) the politics of marriage.

1. *Agnation, affinity, and matrilaterality.* The Tshidi chiefdom (*setshaba; morafe*) is composed of a series of increasingly inclusive local politico-residential units (households, local lineage segments, wards, and sections). In Tshidi theory, all such units are based on agnation. A local lineage segment is ideally composed of two or more households whose heads are agnatically related, with the genealogically senior as the elder (*mogolwane*). Similarly, wards contain two or more segments whose elders are also agnatically related, again with the senior being the ward headman (*tlhogo*). The actual composition of Tswana chiefdoms has been thoroughly reported, and we do not intend to describe it here (cf. Schapera 1938, 1940; Comaroff 1973). However, Tshidi have clearly defined ideas concerning the nature of kinship relations which are of relevance to our discussion. The polygamous household provides a folk paradigm for the conceptualization of higher-order political units. The household is, in relation to the outside, a solidary unit with a single legal identity. Its head is responsible for ensuring that each house has sufficient economic resources to serve its needs. The sons of such households should, ideally, cooperate; but the Tshidi point out that this does not often occur. For reasons which will be explained later, genealogical rank and, therefore, rights to succession and inheritance are distinctly mutable; they give rise to competition between the groups of full siblings which comprise the respective constituent houses.

Tshidi have, at one level at least, a conflict model of agnation. They assume that as (half-) brothers become adults they will come into conflict over rank and property and, after the death of the household head, will "fight and separate." As one informant put it, "it is just a matter of time." Each of the brothers will establish an independent household unit. But the agnatic relationships between these units will be recognized; they will be ranked and, in theory, will live contiguously as members of a local lineage segment.[18] Conflict does not end there, however. For Tshidi assume that the houses (now households) will continue to compete over rank, that disputes over genealogical seniority, and hence the position of elder, are perpetual. (As an aside, we may remark that Tshidi theory on the origin and dynamics of structural units is based on this notion of inevitable conflict. For, in the process of fission, units at every structural level come into being.) Conflict between agnatically related elders surrounds the ward headmanship as well. This status is held by a genealogically defined segment; and if agnatic rank can be redefined or manipulated, it follows that segment elders may try to assert their seniority. In this sense, all political conflict is couched in terms of agnation. Indeed, Tshidi see the chiefship as being held by the head of the senior household of the senior local lineage segment of the senior ward of the senior section of the chiefdom! Accession to the chiefship is, therefore, no different in kind (at least as far as the Tshidi are concerned) from accession to any other agnatically defined status.

In all this, the Tshidi assume that certain relationships are especially characterized by conflict. It is already implicit in the description that half-brothers tend to come into conflict. Although "half-brother" is not distinguished linguistically from "full brother" as a term of address or reference, there is a vernacular term, *setsalo,* for "children of one house," "group of full siblings." The other point of conflict which is stressed is that between FB and BS. This the Tshidi see primarily as a continuation of the conflict of half-brothers into the next generation.[19] It is, as one informant stated, "just a man protecting his son against his BS," to ensure that his son may attain or retain the highest possible genealogical rank. He may also try to weaken the descendants of his brother's house through the promotion of conflict between the full siblings in that house. A high proportion of agnatic disputes are blamed on FB interference—even when, to the ethnographer, it is patently clear that this has not occurred.[20] The essential point, however, is that Tshidi assume that close agnates will fight over rank and access to property and position. In apparent contradiction to this, agnatic groupings are expected by the Tshidi to act as support groups. When a man competes for office, it is believed that his close agnates who are also co-residents in his ward will be among his primary supporters. Tshidi do not attempt to resolve this paradox. Agnates fight and cooperate; it is a fact of life. It is also, of course, a well-recognized feature of segmentary lineage systems.

In contrast, Tshidi stress the supportive nature of affinal and matrilateral ties. The two points of alliance within the household derive from the mother-child and brother-sister relationships. Despite the fact that mother-son disputes do occur occasionally, Tshidi ignore this in the elaboration of their model. Apart from property[21] and protection, the mother bestows upon her children a series of relationships with her kinsmen and, in particular, with her brothers. The special relationship between a man and his mother's brother is characterized by reciprocal exchange and, as Tshidi emphasize, support against competitive agnates. A man and his mother's brother have no cause to compete and, in addition, the latter may become the father-in-law of the former. Informants often stress the supportive significance of mothers' brothers, and Tshidi frequently ascribe the success of a candidate for office to the political power of his matrilateral kin. These kin are not shared by the sons of a (polygamous) house*hold;* they relate to the sons of one house alone. This, again, emphasizes the significance of the *house* as a political unit, since each has its own matrilateral support. The brothers of a woman usually look after her interests and those of her children, and the rank of the house may depend on their efforts.

There is one important dualism in the Tshidi theory of affinity. On the one hand, they tend to stress that affines and matrilateral kin fall outside of the agnatic and hence the co-residential group. In emphasizing these relationships as a supportive counterbalance to the conflicts characteristic of agnatic ties, they articulate the difference as one between insiders and outsiders. They do not mean simply that matrilateral and affinal kinsmen fall outside a metaphorical sphere of conflict. Because they correlate agnation and co-residence, Tshidi conceptualize ties created through marriage and maternity as cutting across spatial boundaries as well. Yet FBD marriage creates a situation in which affines and matrikin would also be co-resident agnates, especially if the composition of the local lineage segment conforms to the ideal. Where this occurs, the ideal of matrilateral alliance would appear, to the ethnographer, to confront the problem of agnatic conflict. For Tshidi, however, there is no problem, at least at the theoretical level: if a man is both FB and MB (in each case, real or classificatory), it is the cultural expectations surrounding the latter relationship which must be actualized. When it is pointed out to Tshidi that the conflicting interests characteristic of close agnatic ties do not disappear when an agnate and a matrilateral kinsman are the same individual, they inevitably reply to the effect that an MB and his ZS *never* fight. Agnation becomes affinity and matrilaterality, and conflict gives way to alliance.

2. *The politics of marriage.* Although in the idiomatic context Tshidi, in common with other Tswana, stress the economic advantages of intralineage marriage, their view of the politics of marriage is not quite so simple. In their view, confirmed by marriage statistics that we will discuss later, the royal lineage is bound up in such a complex web of affinal ties that most men are related to their wives in numerous ways. As one royal informant stated, "We all marry each other; we always have done." Indeed, the affinal links created over several generations have led to the development of a network of multistranded relationships. In other words, an intralineage marriage, although always a (real or classificatory) FBD union, is almost never that alone, and the matrilateral relationship between spouses may be closer than the agnatic one. A leading member of the Tshidi ruling lineage could trace kinship links to his wife in seven different ways, and one chiefly wife was the FBD, MBDD, WBD, FFFBSSDD of her husband. Intralineage marriage is both potentially advantageous and dangerous to both parties to it. For the wife-taker, it creates the opportunity, in the indigenous view, to transmute agnatic opposition into affinal support, and to deflect rivalries, at the cost of permitting access to intrasegment affairs. (The mother's brothers are expected to take an active interest in any matters concerning their ZS's.) For the wife-giving group, the marriage legitimizes efforts to exert influence over the husband, to claim the right to say in the affairs of his children, and later to become *bomalome*

(mother's brothers) of his *heir;*[22] the Tshidi model admits the possibility of a descent group being thought of as a permanent *bomalome* category in relation to the ruling line. In other words, the essence of the Tshidi view of the politics of marriage is that it creates support for a husband in return for the *promise* of a relationship to his heir in the next generation.

Marriage as Exchange

Marriage modulates relationships within the ruling lineage and between this lineage and groupings external to it. As we have already pointed out, any marriage involves a series of expectations: the wife-giving group is offered the opportunity to become *bomalome* of the heir and to assume a position of influence in return for allocating political support to the husband. When such political support is withdrawn, the husband may attempt to limit the affinal group's chances of ensuring the accession of its sister's son. For example, soon after he received rumor of his FBS's rebellious intentions, Chief Montshiwa (1849–1896) announced publicly that his heir would be the son of a wife other than his rival's sister, to whom he was married. The action of the Makgetla lineage, a collateral of the ruling line, also demonstrates the importance of the exchange: its leaders refused to permit the marriage of one of their female members to an unsuccessful chief whose chances of removal appeared high at the time. Such a marriage would not have increased the possibility of their becoming *bomalome* to a future chief. The nature of the expected transaction is clear: both parties are making investments; if they fail, or look likely to fail, the alliance may terminate, although the marriage may continue. In this sense, connubium is not, in itself, a political alliance (cf. Barth 1959: 40). Rather, it creates a frame for the negotiation of power relations.

It is clear from the history of marriage among Tshidi royals that segments of the ruling lineage are indeed bound together in a complex web of affinal ties, that most segments have such ties with the Makgetla lineage (universally viewed as a permanent *bomalome* category in relation to the chiefly line), and that some have chosen to marry into commoner groups. If we viewed this ruling lineage as composed of an aggregate of immutable genealogical relationships, then it would be possible to view marriages of FBD's, MBD's, and so forth as objective events. It is true that Tshidi have ideas about the different forms of marriage; we will return to this later. But whether a given marriage is classified as MBD or FBD is an outcome of political competition; the marriage type is not an objective fact based on pre-existing definitions of relationships.

The complexity of the web of affinity within the ruling line may be gathered from the following figures: Of the 163 marriages of this lineage which have been analyzed, 100 involved women with whom the husband had some prior traceable relationship. Of these, 79 had more than one agnatic, matrilateral, or affinal tie which could be definitely established.[23] It should be added that the remaining 21, those in which only one traceable relationship existed, included a large number of men whose ascendants were politically inactive. Most of the 79 were marriages of men of the politically powerful segments.[24] The important point, then, is that the relationships between spouses in intralineage marriages involving powerful men are not single or clear. Nor is it the closest relationship which is necessarily emphasized. Take the following example. The ruling segment of the royal lineage, the Tau segment, took wives from the Makgetla lineage and from the Tawana segment of their own lineage. Makgetla women are spoken of by the Tau wife-taking segment as MBD's, while wives from the Tawana segment are FBD's. While it is true that, today, the Tawana segment is regarded as closer genealogically to the chiefly segment than is the Makgetla lineage, Makgetla women were spoken of as MBD's in 1850, at which time the genealogical distance between the head of the Makgetla descent group and the chief was exactly the same as that between the present chief and the senior member of the Tawana segment. Thus it may be seen that genealogical proximity does not necessarily determine, in any objective fashion, the assignation of relationships. Although it is not possible to demonstrate it here, the very fact that genealogical relationships are constantly being redefined as a result of political competition means that the relationship between spouses may change in the wake of such competition (cf. Comaroff 1973).

What, then, determines whether women are regarded as MBD or FBD? We may begin to answer this question through a further example. Montshiwa (1849–1896), although the genealogical son of Tau, was fathered leviratically by Tawana, the junior half-brother of Tau. Tawana had several houses of which one, the house of Mosela, was particularly powerful, having raised five politically active sons. Montshiwa was aware, throughout his reign, of the possibility of opposition from this source. The first woman he married, Majang, was a daughter of this house. During Montshiwa's reign, the sons of Mosela believed that their sister was the chief's principal wife—an impression that Montshiwa did nothing to alter, although after one of the sons of Mosela was rumored to be planning an attempt to depose Montshiwa, the chief publicly announced that the son of another woman was to be his heir. Throughout his reign, Montshiwa continued to arrange marriages between himself, his sons, and his (full) brothers' sons and women descended of the house of Mosela. These marriages demonstrated Montshiwa's concern with this potentially dangerous source of opposition. His marriage strategy constituted an attempt to convert the proto-factional core into a recognized wife-giving category—his affines, and mother's brothers of his lineal descendants. It should be noted that, by this time, the Makgetla descent group had become established as just such a wife-giving category, bomalome to the ruling segment. For though the descendants of Makgetla were chiefly agnates, the repeated marriage pattern had led to their being perceived by the tribesmen as bomalome; this effectively removed them from the field of competition for office, in return for which they enjoyed continued political influence. (It is necessary to reiterate that, in the Tshidi view, mother's brothers do not compete with their sister's sons for office.) Montshiwa's marriage strategy aimed to convert the recognized status of the Tawana segment to a wife-giving status like that of the

Makgetla. But the Tawana segment resisted all attempts by Montshiwa and his sons to have them spoken of publicly as mother's brothers. In all public contexts, the descendants of Mosela, themselves always regarded as the head of the opposition faction, constantly stressed that the marriages were FBD marriages, "as is Tshidi custom." The Makgetla lineage, on the other hand, accepted the recognized collective status of mother's brother, and never attempted to assert the agnatic dimension of their marriages.

These two responses indicate that it is not biology which determines the assignation of marriage form. Rather, it is political competition for the management of meaning. Throughout this period, the Tawana faction was actively involved in competition for the chiefship. Its members were never prepared to accept elimination from the competitive arena without a struggle. On the other hand, the men of the Makgetla lineage, recognizing the realities of their relative power, were well aware that their chances of capturing the office were remote. Thus they allocated their efforts and resources to establishing for themselves the role of mother's brothers and influential advisers of the chief, and the role of powerful king-makers when the balance of power did not clearly favor any one segment.[25] (It should be noted that the Makgetla lineage contracted the same number of marriages with the Tawana segment as with the Tau segment. In other words, whoever became chief, the Makgetla relationship to the incumbent would have been the same.)

It is not possible to investigate here the full implications of Tshidi marriage strategies, or to enter into any further detail on the complex indigenous connotations of different marriage forms, save to say that MBD marriages and FBD marriages are, in a fundamental sense, cognitive devices. They are labels which describe sets of expectations: MBD marriages imply that the wife-givers are supporters within the lineage, while FBD wife-givers[26] are competitors. The labels "MBD marriage" and "FBD marriage" represent statements of the political relations between the respective parties at a given point in time. As such, they are distinctly mutable. Marriages modulate relations within the ruling lineage, but they do so in a specific way, for they are signifiers of the state of power relations between agnatic segments, the basic constituencies of Tshidi politics. One important function of the forms assigned to Tshidi marriage is to provide a cultural mode for expression of the politics of agnation and, hence, of competition surrounding the chiefship. Competition over the assignation of labels—over the management of meaning—is an integral part of the political process.

We are aware that the brevity of this account has made it impossible to place this aspect of marriage in a broader processual paradigm, or to compare our description with other analyses of the politics of marriage. However, we have sought to make a rather simple point: the meaning assigned to marriage is not immutably predetermined, and marriage does not necessarily establish alliance or, for that matter, transactional relationships of a predetermined order. Rather, the meaning given to marriage is a means by which actors attempt either to (1) influence the course of transaction, or (2) publicize its outcome. Marriage in itself is not a political transaction: it provides one conceptual arena within which actors compete to manage and impose meanings.

CONCLUSION

It is becoming widely accepted in sociological discourse that social reality is constructed through social process; the meanings which people attach to elements in their universe are products of their social and cultural circumstances. One might elaborate on this by suggesting that a crucial variable in the construction of reality lies in the *management* of meaning: actors compete to contrive and propagate interpretations of social behavior and relationships. In this regard, the construction of social reality and the management of meaning are appropriately analyzed through the notion of political process which we set out at the beginning of this chapter. The management of meaning is an expression of power, and the meanings so managed a crucial aspect of political relations.[27]

Brokerage and marriage have typically been treated in the literature as transactions. The analysis has generally assumed the organization of interaction *within* given "boundaries" of meaning. Our argument goes further by suggesting that political relationships are underpinned by the attempt to *create* or mediate boundaries of meaning. This may perhaps be made clearer by applying the logic of our argument to that implicit in transactional analysis. The models of transaction and exchange suggest that actors engage in strategic interaction to acquire values as items of currency. Some analysts, employing these models, have recognized the importance of the competition through which values are defined; as Kapferer (1972) has shown, transactions should be seen as outcomes of prior strategies. We argue that it is to this competition, rather than to the "substantive" transaction itself, that *analytical* primacy should be given. The processes to which we would draw attention are those through which values are imputed to items—those which determine the entire interpretation of an interaction as exchange. To define an interaction by stipulating those values which are *apparently* exchanged may be misleading. Rather, these values must be looked at as strategic components of attempts to contrive an image of the interaction. Values, then, are not always given; nor are they just the vehicles of interaction. They may, rather, be an expression of the terms within which one party wishes the interaction to be viewed.

The transactional game should not be seen as consisting just of the competition to acquire values; it involves strategic attempts to attach meanings to the relationship within which it takes place. In the case of the Focaltown broker, the broker must contrive meanings for the relationship between client and patron to render it intelligible and thereby to render his own intervention both necessary and legitimate. Indeed, his role is contingent upon the construction of these meanings. The ethnography of Tshidi royal marriage shows that the political implications of particular marriage forms do not reside *in*trinsically within the contractual relationship of marriage, but are attached *ex*trinsically to marriage forms as outcomes of the competition to manage their meanings. An FBD or MBD marriage exists by virtue of the meaning which one party manages to impose on it.

The meanings contrived by brokerage, and by the assignation of forms to marriage relationships, speak of the power of those who contrive them. They may be taken as indicative of the political relationships which inform their milieux. They may also be regarded as exemplars of the fundamental attribute of power— the capacity of *ego* to impose, implicitly or explicitly, constructions of reality upon *alter*. Politics, we have suggested, is behavior associated with the unequal distribution of valued social resources. The capacity to manage meaning is, perhaps, the most valued and the most valuable resource structuring political life.

ACKNOWLEDGMENTS

This chapter is based on field work carried out by Cohen in Newfoundland (1968–1970) and Comaroff in South Africa (1969–1970). Cohen's research was conducted under a Fellowship of the Institute of Social and Economic Research, Memorial University of Newfoundland, and supported by a grant from the Department of Community and Social Development, Government of Newfoundland and Labrador. Comaroff's research was assisted by a grant from the Esperanza Trust. The authors thank the following for their constructive criticisms and advice on an earlier draft of this essay: Ken Brown, Roy Fitzhenry, Keith Hart, Bruce Kapferer, Jean La Fontaine, Chris Pickvance, Bryan Roberts, and Basil Sansom.

NOTES

1. The fact that the processual trend originates within *African Political Systems* itself has often been overlooked in histories of political anthropology. For a discussion of this, and a critical review of the development of processual analyses of politics, see Cohen 1973.

2. We do not enter into discussion here of the desirability of this trend. The argument is lucidly made by Worsley (1968).

3. For the application of such critical evaluations of transactional analysis to political behavior, see especially Asad 1972 and Paine 1974.

4. This is essentially the view of power presented in the theories of "post-Liberal democracy" (MacPherson 1964) and "psychological" embourgeoisement (Speier 1969).

5. The notion of cognitive management, only hinted at in the early seminal statements of transactionalism and exchange theory, is now being increasingly developed by transactional analysts, largely as a consequence of the influence of the interactionist sociology epitomized by the work of Goffman. For example, it has been recently employed in the analysis of interaction within a work milieu by Kapferer (1972). What we emphasize here is the desirability of seeing "management" as a resource, *sui generis*, which is fundamental to the exercise of power. Therefore it should not be treated as a mere adjunct to more tangible and substantive resources.

6. While not ascriptive in the "true" sociological sense of the word, these roles were imbued with ascriptive ethos in a way deliberately rejected by the self-conscious meritocracy of modern entrepreneurial leaders.

7. There is a tendency to religious homogeneity in different regions of Newfoundland; Herring Bay is almost exclusively Protestant. Even in multidenominational communities, the various groups are often territorially discrete.

8. Thus, in a sample of 391 respondents, 47 percent of those who could name four leading members of the provincial Liberal party did *not* name Smallwood.

9. The directness of the relationship between leader and followers which characterizes populist movements is discussed by Worsley (1970: 244 ff.). In the Newfoundland context, it is lucidly captured in the following quotation describing the *modus operandi* of Joseph Smallwood, Premier of Newfoundland from 1949 to 1972: "At his office, or in his home, federal ministers or corporate vice-presidents still found themselves upstaged in mid-interview by a fisherman determinedly demanding instant action on a job, a misplaced pension, or an unemployment insurance claim" (Gwyn 1968: 233–234; see also Smallwood 1973).

10. *Report of the Newfoundland Royal Commission*, cmd. 4480 (London: HMSO, 1933).

11. An exemplary ethnographic picture of the "welfare community" on this coast of Newfoundland is to be found in Wadel 1973.

12. The inability to organize appears to characterize even routine aspects of community life. For example, Faris shows how so customary a procedure as the annual lottery for trap berths in Cat Harbour becomes a crisis: "the annual cod trap berth drawing is . . . a long and agonising affair, for hours are spent on decisions about just who is to draw for the crew and what berth the person drawing will choose" (Faris 1972: 103).

13. Writing about Cat Harbour, on Newfoundland's east coast, Faris says: "Local leadership and the exercise of power are logically viewed as socially aggressive and persons who submit to this behaviour place themselves in potential danger of exploitation" (1972: 103).

14. Smallwood's prime-ministerial longevity was largely built on his overcommunication of his affinity to the *baymen* rather than to the *townies*. He called his administration "Her Majesty's Outport Government." See Smallwood 1973: 509.

15. For comparable, if differently ordered, accounts of Tswana marriage, see Schapera 1938, 1940, 1950, 1957, and 1963. The present description represents only a partial consideration of the data, and is drawn specifically from the Barolong boo Ratshidi rather than from the Tswana in general.

16. The Barolong boo Ratshidi, inhabitants of a chiefdom situated in the South Africa-Botswana borderland, are also known in the literature as Tshidi-Barolong, or more simply as the Tshidi.

17. The dynamics of faction structure, although clearly important, are beyond the scope of the present paper. They are explored in detail in Comaroff 1973.

18. It follows that the rank of these units in relation to each other may itself become a matter of conflict. However, it is beyond the scope of this account to pursue this problem. In addition, the ideal of residential contiguity is not always achieved in practice, but it is specifically with the Tshidi model that we are here concerned.

19. Tshidi often point out that a dispute between a man and his father's brother may also be caused by the fact that, when a man dies, one of his brothers may—if the dead man's children are still young—act as a guardian over their property and position. Dispute frequently arises when the dead man's sons believe themselves old enough to manage their own affairs, only to find their father's brother reluctant to relinquish his position.

20. In one case, which occurred in 1970, the disputants both blamed their father's brother, despite the fact that he had been away as a migrant laborer since their infancy. When

questioned about this, one said: "Yes, but there are ways," referring to mystical techniques of extending malevolent influence in spite of physical separation.

21. One aspect of the transmission of property among the Tswana is that household heads divide certain of their resources among their houses. This property is eventually divided among the members of those houses, so that a man inherits some property via his mother.

22. In Tshidi theory, *bomalome* are always powerful chiefly advisers; indeed, in practice, they may become the most powerful men in the government of the chiefdom.

23. It was not possible to collect full marriage histories for every case. Those in which definite relationships could not be traced are not included in this figure, even when informants said that the spouses were remote agnates. Hence the figure of 79 is, if anything, an underestimate.

24. It is through involvement in the web of affinal ties that segments continue to be regarded as close agnates of the chief and remain influential in the chiefly lineage. For example, the descendants of Matsheka, whose direct lineal descendant is an FFFBSSS of the present chief, were for many decades a politically inactive collateral segment and gradually became regarded as remote agnates of the ruling line, "not really royals." During the last chief's reign, their leaders began to emerge as a politically powerful grouping. The chief married the sister of their senior man. When he asked about leading Matsheka men, the ethnographer was told that they are *bomalome* of the chief—but that they are also close agnatic kin. In this case, the marriage signified their re-entry into the political arena.

25. We appreciate that the problem of competition between the affines of one man is not dealt with in this chapter. See Comaroff 1973: Chaps. 6 and 7.

26. In the case of marriage between a man and his father's *full* brother's daughter, the wife-giving and wife-receiving groups are, of course, coterminous. In marriage between a man and his father's half-brother's daughter, the groups involved are different houses fathered by one man. Although both forms fall under the heading of "real" FBD marriage, their political implications are somewhat different. Father's-full-brother's-daughter marriage is rare in the case of the Tshidi ruling lineage. Where it occurs, it is clearly more appropriate to speak of a wife-giver than of a wife-giving group. Because this form of marriage has occurred very rarely, we will not discuss it further. "Real" FBD marriage should be taken to imply F½BD marriage, where the wife-giving group is composed of a set of full siblings.

27. Indeed, it seems to us that, in this regard, the anthropology of political life is generically integral to the sociology of knowledge.

REFERENCES

Asad, T. 1972. Market model, class structure and consent: a reconsideration of Swat political organisation. *Man*, N.S., 7 (1): 74–94.
Bailey, F. 1969. *Stratagems and Spoils: A Social Anthropology of Politics*. Oxford: Blackwell.
Barth, F. 1959. *Political Leadership Among the Swat Pathans*. London: Athlone Press.
―――. 1966. *Models of Social Organization*. Royal Anthropological Institute Occasional Paper No. 23. London.
Blau, P. 1964. *Exchange and Power in Social Life*. New York: Wiley.
Boissevain, J. 1966. Patronage in Sicily. Man, N.S., 1 (1): 18–33.

Cohen, A. P. 1973. The management of myths: an essay in the grounded theory of politics. Ph.D. dissertation, University of Southampton.

Comaroff, J. L. 1973. Competition for office and political process among the Barolong boo Ratshidi of the South Africa-Botswana borderland. Ph.D. dissertation, University of London.

Cunnison, I. 1959. *The Luapula Peoples of Northern Rhodesia: Custom and History in Tribal Politics*. Manchester: Manchester University Press, for the Rhodes-Livingstone Institute.

Faris, J. C. 1972. *Cat Harbour: A Newfoundland Fishing Settlement*. 2d ed. St. John's: Institute of Social and Economic Research, Memorial University.

Foster, G. M. 1963. The dyadic contract in Tzintzuntzan: patron-client relationship. *American Anthropologist*, 65: 1280–1294.

Gwyn, R. 1968. *Smallwood: The Unlikely Revolutionary*. Toronto: McClelland and Stewart.

Kapferer, B. 1972. *Strategy and Transaction in an African Factory: African Workers and Indian Management in a Zambian Town*. Manchester: Manchester University Press.

MacPherson, C. B. 1964. Post-Liberal democracy? *Canadian Journal of Economics and Political Science*, 30 (4): 485–498.

Mayer, A. 1967. Patrons and brokers: rural leadership in four overseas Indian communities. In M. Freedman, ed., *Social Organisation: Essays Presented to Raymond Firth*. London: Frank Cass.

Newfoundland Royal Commission. 1933. *Report of the Newfoundland Royal Commission*. Cmd. 4480. London: HMSO.

Noel, S. J. R. 1971. *Politics in Newfoundland*. Toronto: University of Toronto Press.

Paine, R. B. P. 1971. A theory of patronage and brokerage. In R. Paine, ed., *Patrons and Brokers in the East Arctic*. St. John's: Institute of Social and Economic Research, Memorial University.

———. 1973. Transactions as communicative events. Paper presented to the Decennial Meeting of the Association of Social Anthropologists. Oxford.

———. 1974. *Second Thoughts About Barth's "Models."* Royal Anthropological Institute Occasional Paper No. 32. London.

Perlin, G. 1971. Patronage and paternalism: politics in Newfoundland. In I. Davies and K. Herman, eds., *Social Space: Canadian Perspectives*. Toronto: New Press.

Schapera, I. 1938. *A Handbook of Tswana Law and Custom*. London: International Institute of African Languages and Cultures.

———. 1940. *Married Life in an African Tribe*. London: Faber.

———. 1950. Kinship and marriage among the Tswana. In A. R. Radcliffe-Brown and C. D. Forde, eds., *African Systems of Kinship and Marriage*. London: International African Institute.

———. 1957. Marriage of near kin among the Tswana. *Africa*, 27 (2): 139–159.

———. 1963. Agnatic marriage in Tswana royal families. In I. Schapera, ed., *Studies in Kinship and Marriage*. Royal Anthropological Institute Occasional Paper No. 16. London.

Silverman, S. F. 1965. Patronage and community-nation relationships in central Italy. *Ethnology*, 4 (2): 172–189.

Smallwood, J. R. 1973. *I Chose Canada: The Memoirs of the Hon. Joseph R. "Joey" Smallwood*. Toronto: Macmillan.

Speier, H. 1969. The worker turning bourgeois. In H. Speier, ed., *Social Order and the Risks of War: Papers in Political Sociology*. Cambridge, Mass.: M.I.T. Press.

Wadel, C. 1973. *Now, Whose Fault Is That? The Struggle for Self-Esteem in the Face of*

Chronic Unemployment. Newfoundland Social and Economic Studies, No. 11. St. John's: Institute of Social and Economic Research, Memorial University.

Worsley, P. M. 1968. Review of *Political Anthropology*. *British Journal of Sociology,* 19 (1): 100–103.

————. 1970. The concept of populism. In G. Ionescu and E. Gellner, eds., *Populism: Its Meanings and National Characteristics*. London: Weidenfeld and Nicolson.

Hindu Transactions:
Diversity Without Dualism

McKIM MARRIOTT

Hindu and in general Indian, South Asian society has developed transactional thinking perhaps further than has any other. It exhibits an elaborate transactional culture, characterized by explicit, institutionalized concern for givings and receivings of many kinds in kinship, work, and worship. Hindu thinking about social transactions viewed from the modern West may seem peculiar for the biological substantialism on which it builds, and for its special orientation to questions of rank. Nevertheless, the systematic monism and particularism that pervade Hindu sociology may help us to envisage what a theory of transactions might be if relieved of the peculiar Western philosophic burdens of dualism, universalism, and individualism.

This essay proceeds from the axiom that the pervasive indigenous assumptions of any society, such as Indian notions of the identity of actor and action and of the divisibility of the person, provide bases on which an anthropologist may construct his models of cultural behavior in that society. It applies that axiom by constructing a monistic, dividualistic general model of Indian transactions, fitting this model first to the most accessible data, which are on the interrelations and ranking of castes. It then proceeds to a wider review of the typical transactional tactics and strategies of groups and persons in India's varied moral, instrumental, and affective systems of action. This review leads to the finding that a culturally adapted two-dimensional transactional model, apparently simple and uniform, can nevertheless generate some of the Indian civilization's fabled diversity. "Transactional culture" and internal diversity appear as connected facts here, and could be so elsewhere.

ASSUMPTIONS: DIVIDUAL ACTORS AND SUBSTANTIAL ACTION

Indian thought about transactions differs from much of Western sociological and psychological thought in not presuming the separability of actors from actions. By Indian modes of thought, what goes on *between* actors are the same connected processes of mixing and separation that go on *within* actors. Actors' particular natures are thought to be results as well as causes of their particular actions (*karma*). Varied codes of action or codes for conduct (*dharma*) are thought to be

109

naturally embodied in actors and otherwise substantialized in the flow of things that pass among actors. Thus the assumption of the easy, proper separability of action from actor, of code from substance (similar to the assumption of the separability of law from nature, norm from behavior, mind from body, spirit or energy from matter), that pervades both Western philosophy and Western common sense (see, for example, the analysis of American kinship by Schneider 1968) is generally absent: code and substance (Sanskrit *puruśa* and *prakriti, dharma* and *śarira,* and so on) cannot have separate existences in this world of constituted things as conceived by most South Asians (Marriott and Inden 1973). Before one begins to think of Hindu transactions, one thus needs firmly to understand that those who transact as well as what and how they transact are thought to be inseparably "code-substance" or "substance-code." The latter term will be used in this essay to stand, perforce awkwardly, for belief in the nonduality of all such pairs.

The media of Hindu transactions are substance-codes that may be scaled from the relatively "gross" (*sthula*) to the relatively "subtle" (*sukṣma*). "Gross"— that is, lower, less refined, more tangible, and less widely transformable substance-codes—are contrasted with higher, less tangible, more refined substance-codes that are "subtler," more capable of transformation, and therefore imbued with greater power and value. For example, knowledge may be considered subtler than money, and money subtler than grain or land, but grain or land not so gross as cooked food or garbage, which have less power of generation. Such a scale may be understood as resembling the distinctions among communications codes capable of generating more and fewer messages; but Indian thought understands subtler substance-codes as emerging through processes of maturation or (what is considered to be the same thing) cooking. Thus subtler essences may sometimes be ripened, extracted, or distilled out of grosser ones (as fruit comes from plants, nectar from flowers, butter from milk); and grosser substance-codes may be generated or precipitated out of subtler ones (as plants come from seed, feces from food).

Facilitating the elaboration of Indian transactional thought are its further assumptions as to (a) the particulate and therefore divisible, highly diverse nature of substance-codes, (b) the constant circulation of particles of substance-code, and (c) the inevitable transformation of all natural entities by combinations and separations of their substance-codes. Such ancient and widely held Indian assumptions, if abstractly stated, seem compatible with the theories of modern natural scientists, although they conflict with common Western popular beliefs in standard, stable entities and in the normally impermeable, autonomous person.

Much but not all of Indian reflective thought also explicitly assumes (d) that substance-codes have one ultimate origin or one ultimate destination, usually both.

All schools of Indian thought tend to agree that substance-codes are necessarily found in mixed conditions in this world and that the making of perfect separations, or purifications, is an almost insuperable problem. As Tambiah has written (1974), "boundary overflows" are taken by Hindu thought to be inevitable and prevailing conditions, rather than the anomalies that they are taken to be in the boundary-oriented theories of Mary Douglas (1960), which are typical of thought in the dualistic West. Consequently, South Asian categorizations of humans and other genera start, but rarely stop, with neatly branching taxonomies; instead, they run, as Tambiah points out, to complex paradigm- and key-like arrangements (defined by Kay and Conklin in Tyler 1969) and often, more flexibly, to lattice-like cognitive structures (Dubisch 1964) that provide for all manner of intersections among taxonomic categories through remixtures of previously differentiated substance-codes.

Correspondingly, persons—single actors—are not thought in South Asia to be "individual," that is, indivisible, bounded units, as they are in much of Western social and psychological theory as well as in common sense. Instead, it appears that persons are generally thought by South Asians to be "dividual" or divisible. To exist, dividual persons absorb heterogeneous material influences. They must also give out from themselves particles of their own coded substances—essences, residues, or other active influences—that may then reproduce in others something of the nature of the persons in whom they have originated. Persons engage in transfers of bodily substance-codes through parentage, through marriage (Nicholas and Inden 1970; David 1973b), and through services and other kinds of interpersonal contacts. They transfer coded food substances by way of trade, payments, alms, feasts, or other prestations. Persons also cannot help exchanging certain other coded influences that are thought of as subtler, but still substantial and powerful forms, such as perceived words, ideas, appearances, and so forth. Dividual persons, who must exchange in such ways, are therefore always composites of the substance-codes that they take in (Inden 1972: 33).

Persons, like beings of all other categories, may preserve their particular composite natures and powers by stabilizing (typically by "cooling," removing heat from) their constituents, and by admitting into themselves only what is homogeneous and compatible; or they may transform their bodies with their inherent codes by mixing and/or separating their particulate constituents, sometimes with the help of catalytic heat, or by heterogeneous inputs.

The elaborate transactional and transformational culture of India is well represented in reflective thought on such topics as marriage and gifting in the books of *dharmaśāstra* and epic history (see Kane 1941), as it is in the actual tournament-like forms of weddings (Inden 1972; Vatuk 1973), feasts (Marriott 1968a; Beck 1973a: 155–181; Khare 1974), services, trade (David 1973a, n.d.), and child management (Beals 1962: 15–22). It is equally represented in the classical medical texts of Caraka and Suśruta and in popular ideas of health and diet (see Beck 1969; Babb 1973; Carstairs 1957; Obeyesekere 1963). One can show that the *varṇas* in textual accounts of Vedic sacrifice (Inden 1969a), or the castes in an Indian village (Marriott 1968a), are partly scored by indigenous opinion, and are ascribed natures, qualities, ranks, and powers that correspond to the castes' relative dominance in the normal round-robin of transactions in substance-codes, such as foods.

Of course, what are here called "transformations" within actors consist also of transactions among parts of actors, while "transactions" among actors may constitute transformations of the actors transacting and sometimes of the system of transactions. Thus transformations and transactions may be understood as a single set of processes, considered in two ways, internally and externally (E. V. Daniel, personal communication).

South Asian cultural understandings of how social differentiation and power rankings arise out of transactions and transformations may be stated in three formulas: (1) In the absence of reciprocation in the same or an inferior medium of substance-code, those who give are to be recognized as differing from and as standing in rank, power, and quality of substance-code above those who take; the takers are thereby recognized as inferior, but are also made partly like the givers. (2) Those who reciprocate in the same medium are regarded as being made much the same as each other and are therefore to be reckoned as equal. (3) Those who do not exchange with each other at all, even indirectly, are considered to be different in substance-code and to be potential antagonists; but since they lack asymmetrical relations, they must be scored as not unequal (Marriott 1968a: 149; Marriott and Inden 1974). (Conversely, an exchange in any medium is itself transvalued according to the ranks of the actors between whom the exchange occurs.) These three scoring formulas are called "asymmetrical exchange," "symmetrical exchange," and "symmetrical nonexchange" by David (n.d.).

The tournament-like "total prestational" models of exchange suggested by Mauss (1954: 10–12, 37–41), and systematized by Homans (1961: 316–335) and by Blau, like the redundant, competitive peck-orderings of action observed in the ethologist's chicken yard (see Allee 1958: 129–153), can all be shown to depict part of Indian talk and action concerning rank fairly well. However, any scorings of Indian competitive actions would remain insufficient if, in Western style, the scorer attended only to the game-like actional displays (as in Marriott 1959 and 1968a) and failed to note that the players have at stake also the preservation or transformation of their own natures. Transactions, notably nonreceivings and receivings as well as initiations of action, both demonstrate and bring about natural or substantial rankings through what are thought to be the actors' biomoral losses and gains. A pattern of distributions or communications is thus also implied. Such communicative, distributive events are assumed to be general: one actor and his action are never for long quite like another actor and his action, and they all change constantly through recombinations of their parts. But actors and their interactions are never to be separated from each other; they change together.

While much of Indian thought is emphatically monistic and dynamic in these respects, it is also, of course, highly particularistic: each actor and action is unique. Actors and actions, as matters of both natural and moral fact, are thought to be of infinitely varied and unstable kinds, since circulations and combinations of particles of substance-code are continuously occurring.

Hindu macrosociology is consistent with these microbiological ideas. It presents explicit cosmogonic theories (for instance, Manu 9: 3–5, 14–18, 32–35) in which the gods, the Brahman *varṇa*, and the king, divinity, morality (*dharma*), and royal power (*ksatra*), the power to give punishment (*daṇḍa*) subtly with speech or grossly with weapons—all are seen as transformations of each other and of the original undifferentiated cosmic energy or protoplasm (*brahman*). In the cosmic *brahman* there inheres both power or energy and an embracing code (*puruśa*) for transactions among the differentiated genera of beings whose substances, codes, and powers emanate from the *brahman*.

Recent ethnography tells of the same sorts of cognitions among Hindus in rural areas, where the categories of gods and men are thought to be mutually continuous, uninterrupted by distinctions such as "sacred" and "profane," "spirit" and "matter" (Aiyappan 1973; Hiebert 1971: 131–132, 138–139). All beings are gradable by "power" (*śakti,* etc.), and power is understood to be synonymous with both religious virtue and effective worldly dominance (Davis 1974; Wadley 1975). Divine power is graded, mainly according to its unrestricted applicability, in at least six declining degrees: salvation, shelter, rescue, help, nonmaleficence, departure. The prayers, stories, and tangible transactions used in worshipping divinities having these powers distinguish means by which an actor may suitably influence a king, a patron, an employer, a kinsman, a petty official, and a low servant or child, respectively (Wadley 1975). Power is thought to be variously present in persons, in bodies, in castes, in gods, in land, in education, in ritual action, and so on, and may be manifest in style of life and interpersonal influence (Sengupta 1973). It circulates and moves everywhere (Abbott 1932).

Transfixed by South Asia's appearance of cultural and social diversity, and preoccupied with sociologies (like Weber's) that are built upon such historical European issues as church versus state, tradition versus rationality, rank versus equality, and autocracy versus individual rights, most sociologists have not fully recognized the predominant monism of Hindu thought. Weber himself (for instance, 1968: 545, 552–553, 590) and sometimes Dumont (1962: 49–50) are exceptional in recognizing that Indian thought joins certain ideas that are in the West regarded as ultimately dual. However, most sociologists have anticipated Dumont's preferred practice of postulating for India dichotomies equivalent to the familiar European dualities. "Religious" asceticism is regarded as opposed to worldly social structure (Dumont 1960); the ritual status or "purity" of castes is distinguished from their secular power and wealth; and the sacred "wholism" of the caste system is seen as opposed to the atomistic cult of "individualism" (Dumont 1970).

Such direct translations of differently structured cultural data into the dualistic patterns of Western thought are the ordinarily unexamined, standard procedure of social science. But one must ask whether the mistranslations that may result have not often hindered our comprehension of South Asian society. The following analyses will attempt to reduce some of the misunderstanding by constructing transactional models closer to what we know of South Asian actors' pervasively monistic cognitions of reality.

Given nonduality, the problem will be to discover how diversity develops. Discovering how diverse caste substance-codes develop out of transactions in one relatively gross medium—cooked food—is a first step that existing data permit us to take.

INTERCASTE TRANSACTIONS OBSERVED

Occupational castes are conceived in South Asia as natural genera, and these genera are, like dividual persons, conceived as composites of various substance-codes. The differing natures of castes are thought to be owed (1) partly to their origins in differently ranked bodily parts of the original Code Man (Puruśa), and to the generations of cross-breedings among the original genera and their mixed descendants (Rg Veda 10: 90; Manu 10: 9–72; Tambiah 1974). The offspring are ranked so that genera originating from more homogeneous ancestry and from more consistent or harmonic (sexually and occupationally) acts of mixture stand higher (Marriott and Inden 1973, 1974). Castes also owe their natures (2) partly to the transformations that their substance-codes undergo through certain ceremonial transactions (saṃskāra, mangala, etc.), which involve subtractions from and additions to their natures; and (3) partly to their incorporation of diverse other substance-codes, bodily and nonbodily, through the transactions involving services, food, and so on, that make up their respective means of subsistence, and through the differing times and places of their residence (Marriott and Inden 1973, 1974).

Small-community life requires that there be many transactions among members of the various castes. Frequent transactions can occur only when they are agreed to be appropriate to the ranks of the castes, or when they are carefully neutralized (David n.d.). The ranks attributed to the castes are evaluations of their natures according to the donor and recipient relationships in the transactions that are believed to have formed those natures. "Attributional" rankings according to the natures of the castes and "interactional" rankings according to their relationships of exchange thus amount in South Asian theory to two aspects of the same thing (Marriott 1959: 106). Still, ranked judgments of castes' natures are difficult for actors to establish only from the castes' claimed or reputed origins, or from what might be inferred about their natures using the possibly deceptive evidence of their currently visible attributes. Persons trying to decide about rank tend therefore to rely primarily on the evidence provided by current or recent transactions (Marriott 1968a).

One-Dimensional Analysis

In Figure 1, a condensed example from "Konduru" village in Andhra Pradesh (Hiebert 1971: 57–62), the asterisks indicate permitted transfers of cooked food and water occasionally occurring among members of some of the local caste groups. The cells shown as blank indicate pairs for which no intercaste transaction of this kind is accepted. Six types from among the thirty-two castes in the village,

FIGURE 1

Castes in Konduru:
Net Food Transactions and Opinion Rank

Food Received By

Castes	Brahman	Carpenter	Vaiṣṇava	Farmer	Tribal	Leather-worker	(+)	(-)	Net	Opinion Rank
Brahman	4		*	*	*	*	4	0	4	5
Carpenter		2			*	*	2	0	2	4
Vaiṣṇava			2			*	1	1	0	3
Farmer				4	*	*	2	2	0	3
Tribal				*	5	*	2	3	-1	2
Leather-worker						5	0	5	-5	1
(-)	0	0	1	2	3	5				

Food Given By (left margin label)

Data from Hiebert 1971: 57, 60-61.

those castes presenting the most varied transactional patterns, are here selected for attention. The total of the permitted giving transactions of each caste is the sum of the asterisks in its row; this is recorded under the positive sign just to the right of the matrix. The total of permitted receivings—the transfers coming in to each caste—is the sum of the caste's column, which is recorded in the row beneath the matrix. This bottom row is given a minus sign, since received values are believed to have negative effects on caste rank. The numbers within the "identity boxes" along the main diagonal—where the row and column of each caste intersect—are the totals of all transactions going to and from each caste, here added without regard to positive or negative sign. In the "Net" column, however, the algebraic signs have been taken into account, and the figures represent the number of "giving" transactions *minus* the number of "receiving" transactions.

In Konduru, as in most other localities where parallel studies of both transactions and opinions have been made (Marriott 1968a; Freed 1970; Barnett 1970; David n.d.; Davis 1974), caste ranking according to local opinion appears to correlate closely with the order of the castes' net numbers of transactions. The opinion ranks shown in the figure are derived from a separate large sampling of public opinion (Hiebert 1971: 58–62). Among the castes shown, the ordering of transactional net scores and the ranking by the sample of opinions correlate perfectly. The Brahman castes (Smartha and Ayyavaru), whose members can give cooked food and water to almost all other castes and who will receive these things from members of no other caste, attain the highest net number of transactions— four out of a possible five. Because the Brahman castes are almost perfect "winners" in the food tournament, they are ranked at the top by local opinion. By contrast, the Madiga Leatherworker caste, whose members give to none and receive from all five of the other castes, is a perfect "loser" and thus stands at the bottom in opinion.

The other four selected castes of Konduru are ranged between Brahman and Leatherworker. The Vaiṣṇava Temple Attendant caste (Nambi) here ranks second to the Brahmans as a receiver, since its members take food only from Brahmans, but ranks next to lowest as a giver, since it can give food only to Leatherworkers. The Vaiṣṇavas' position may seem ambiguous because their total number of transactions is only two, but their net transactional score of zero puts them precisely in the middle of the rank list. The Farmer (Reddi and Munnuru) castes, on the other hand, transact more vigorously than the Vaiṣṇavas, totalling twice as many pair relationships; but the Farmers are clearly bracketed with the relatively isolated Vaiṣṇava caste at the midmost rank, since the net value of the Farmers' transactions is also zero. This demonstrates the variety of transactional strategies that are available to castes competing for rank or power within the complex but precisely ranked system of exchange.

Some conclusions about these transactional data from Konduru are mathematically evident, but visually not very apparent, from their arrangement in Figure 1. The reason is that this matrix, like most previous representations, makes its horizontal, vertical, and diagonal axes out of a single ordering of the castes by their net scores. Such an effectively one-dimensional arrangement of data would be quite suitable for representing transactional situations in which all relevant acts are completed, such as a peck order in which all pecks hit their mark, or a communications network in which all messages are received. It may still be fairly suitable for representing situations in which the completion of an act, such as a challenge or a transfer of food, is subject not only to the intention of the initiator but also to acceptance by the recipient—provided that the resulting rank orders of initiators and recipients do not greatly differ. But in Konduru, as in most other localities where Hindu transactions have been studied, refusals to receive are numerous and sometimes discrepant with the rank order of giving, and are felt to be highly significant. Consequently, Figure 1 seems somewhat disordered, especially along its vertical axis. Here more successful givers (Farmer and Tribal) are placed below the less successful Vaiṣṇava. Some intransitivities are present. Vaiṣṇava appears higher than Farmer and Tribal, but cannot give to either; Carpenter can give to Tribal and Tribal can give to Farmer, but Carpenter cannot give to Farmer; and so on. The data along the main diagonal axis are obviously disordered, since the numbers representing total transactions fluctuate without obvious pattern.

Faced with similar apparent disorders or anomalies in the middle of a competitive set of supposedly well-ordered Hindu transactions, most analysts (e.g., Gough 1959; Bailey 1957: 266–267, 1964: 59; Dumont 1970: 75–79, 83–89, 251; Beck 1973a: 15–17, 267; Barnett 1970: 132–172; Orans 1974) have attempted dualistic explanations, invoking a disruptive contrast between ultimately disparate values or "criteria"—"status" or "purity," "blood" or "ritual" versus "power," "dominance," "work," or "instrumentality." Faced with less precise, but no less obvious signs of disorder, others (e.g., Pocock 1955; Cohn 1961; Srinivas 1962: 10, 42–69, 1966: 6–10, 14–27; Marriott 1955a, 1968b; Lynch 1968) have looked for explanations in the plurality of valued Hindu styles of life, or in various remote standards or audiences differing from the immediate and the local. A finding of greater disorder and diversity in behavior at the middle rather than at the top and bottom would be especially surprising, since it would be contrary to the usual finding of greater conformity of behavior in the middle ranks of any stratified system (e.g., Homans 1961: 336–358). It would also be contrary to the finding of sharp consensus on rank throughout Hindu caste systems (Hiebert 1971: 60–61; Freed 1963; Marriott 1968b). Before we credit any such explanation of alleged disorder, however, there is a prior question as to whether more complete ordering cannot be found within the transactional data themselves, even at the middle ranks.

Two-Dimensional Analysis

A culturally informed rearrangement of the Konduru data of Figure 1 can in fact reveal a clearer transactional picture, one that is simultaneously ordered in at least two ways. Figure 2 takes into account the major distinction of meaning and action between the giving and the receiving of substance-code. The effect is the same as that of rearranging the data in the form of a two-dimensional graph or Guttman scale (e.g., Goodenough 1965; Barnett 1970: 97–107). Since the present data on giving and receiving are not actually dual, or separate, but represent one set viewed in different aspects, a single two-dimensional matrix seems simpler and preferable to separate giving and receiving scalograms (used in similar circumstances by Beck 1973a: 154–181).

The vertical axis of the matrix in Figure 2 rearranges the castes of Figure 1 in the order of their local standings as *givers* of substance-code, while the horizontal axis keeps the castes in the order of their ranks as *receivers*. The castes' overall transactional ranks are not explicitly recorded here; but since their net transactional scores are arithmetic sums of values along the giving and receiving axes, their ranks will correspond approximately to the locations of their "identity boxes" along the main diagonal (dotted line). A slightly more exact graphing of the castes' overall ranks could be achieved by projecting the values of the giving and receiving axes as spatial measures on equal-interval scales. But a rough idea of the castes' net transactional ranks may be gained from the matrix, without such graphing, by rotating Figure 2 clockwise until the main diagonal is approximately vertical (as is done in Figures 3, 4, and 5).

FIGURE 2

Caste Rank in Konduru:
Two Orders from Food Transactions

Food Received By

Food Given By	Brahman	Carpenter	Vaisnava	Farmer	Tribal	Leather-worker	(+)
Brahman	[4]		*	*	*	*	4
Farmer		·		[4]	*	*	2
Tribal			·	*	[5]	*	2
Carpenter		[2]		·	*	*	2
Vaisnava			[2]		·	*	1
Leather-worker						[5]	0
(-)	0	0	1	2	3	5	

Data from Hiebert 1971: 57.

Figure 2 has the effect of putting all the data on completed transactions together in the upper right half of the matrix, revealing a two-dimensionally transitive pattern. It separates widely the castes linked by positive transactions (Farmer, Tribal) from those characterized by much nontransaction (Carpenter, Vaiṣṇava), and exposes the differences between castes that are placed in the same or adjacent ranks.

Differences of transactional strategy are highlighted here. The castes on the right side (Farmer, Tribal) are those that give in so many relationships and refuse in so few that their ranks as givers are higher than their ranks as nonreceivers. The castes of the left side (Carpenter, Vaiṣṇava) are those that refuse in so many relationships and give in so few that their ranks as nonreceivers are higher than their ranks as givers.

The overall transactional scores (in boxes) that index these differences of strategy are now spatially sorted out: higher scores, marking the castes that transact in more pairs, are on one side of the dotted diagonal (and also on the diagonal at the highest and lowest ranks); lower scores, marking the castes that transact in fewer pairs, are on the other side of the diagonal.

A GENERALIZED MODEL OF TACTICS AND STRATEGIES

Simple numerical tables (Figure 3, *B* and *C*) can project more fully the kinds of rankings and strategies observed among certain castes in Konduru. Figure 3 illustrates hypothetically, in one medium and on a small scale, all the combinations of givings and receivings that can occur for any actor. In part *A* enough transactions (ten) are postulated for five actors to transact mutually with perfect asymmetry. Then in parts *B* and *C* all twenty other potential combinations of exchange and nonexchange are displayed for the same number of transactions. The transactions are assumed to be transitive and redundant throughout, conditions regularly postulated among Hindu actors and approximated in the actual sets of castes shown in Figure 5.

The values in Figure 3 are ordered in two obvious ways: in part *C* rank values (net transactions) are ordered from greater at the top to lesser at the bottom, as in a dominance matrix or peck order of asymmetrical exchanges; in part *B* overall strategic values (total transactions) are ordered from lesser at the left to greater at the right, as in a communication matrix for situations where symmetrical action may occur (Kemeny et al. 1966: 384–391). Imagined in superposition, as they should be, these two parts of the figure together inform the viewer that each transaction of any actor is necessarily oriented in several directions at once.

The net transactional rank (row total less column total) of an actor in any position of giving and taking may be read from the body of part *C*. The overall transactional strategy (row total plus column total) of the same actor may be read by referring to the corresponding cell of part *B*. For example, an actor who gives in only one pair relationship and receives in four will be found in both parts of the figure at the intersection of "Give 1" and "Receive 4"—in the vertical line of "5" boxes in part *B* and in the horizontal line of "−3" in part *C*.

An actor whose overall strategy resembles that of a sociometric isolate stands at the left-hand corner of part *B*. This actor is evidently self-sufficient and unchanging in substance-code, since the total flow of his transactions is minimized to no output and no input, for a perfect total of zero transactions. Such a strategy might be characterized as reclusive and introverted. Yet an actor following such a strategy in the South Asian scheme enjoys a net transactional rank at the median point (zero)—halfway up and halfway down—as one can see from the corresponding left corner cell of part *C*.

At the right-hand corner of part *B* is located the identity box of the kind of actor who maximizes his total transactions to four givings and four receivings, for a total of eight—the largest possible total of symmetrical (i.e., two-way) transactions. Such an actor's exchanges have the form of the receiving "star" of a popularity sociogram, and also the radial pattern of a switchboard operator. This maximal transactor's role resembles that of a leading member of one of Bales's (1970: 81–83) groups who has influence over others through the sheer breadth of his reciprocal communications. He resembles the reciprocating chief who can pool

FIGURE 3

Actors' Overall Strategies and Ranks, Using Ten Transactions

(A) Asymmetrical transactions.   (B) Strategies
(total transactions).   (C) Ranks (net transactions).

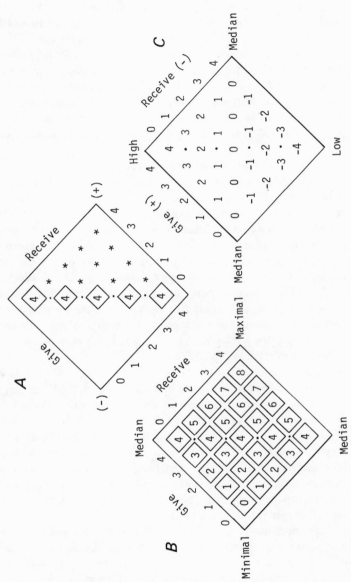

and allocate what he receives in a redistributive manner (Sahlins 1965: 141). In the South Asian context postulated here, he is also a reconstitutor and redistributor of substance-codes—his own and others'.

The net transactional rank of such a maximal transactor appears at the corresponding right-hand corner of part *C*, where it is shown to be zero (four givings less four receivings). The rank of the maximal transactor is thus the same as the rank of his opposite, the minimally transacting actor, according to this South Asian model.

One notices from Figures 2 and 3*B* that actors tending in this right-hand direction—those seeking higher ranks as givers than they hold as nonreceivers—like members of the Farmer and Tribal castes in Konduru, complete overall numbers of transactions that exceed the median. Actors seeking higher ranks as nonreceivers—those on the left-hand side, like members of the Carpenter and Vaiṣṇava castes in Konduru—complete fewer than the median number of transactions. What these opposites have in common with each other and with the whole central row of Figure 3*C* is their balanced reciprocity, the perfect symmetry of their givings and receivings.

Such overall maximizing and minimizing—opposite transactional strategies—are both means of rising above or avoiding a fall into the lower ranks of the system. However, minimizing and maximizing strategies inevitably also prevent access to the highest rank. Their perfect symmetry suits them only to the middle rank.

All symmetrical strategies tend toward averaging the natures of the actors. One cannot maximize the total number of one's transactions without increasing one's own acceptances of substance-code, which half of the time will be lowering; and one cannot give maximally without distributing some of one's better substance-code, which will also be lowering to one's nature. One cannot minimize the total number of one's transactions without reducing the outputs of one's inferior substance-code, outputs that would be elevating to oneself; and one cannot reduce one's total intake beyond midpoint without failing to obtain some substance-code of superior value.

Only complete strategic asymmetry or imbalance—giving to all and taking from none (at the top), or taking from all and giving to none (at the bottom)—can lead to placement at the extremes of rank. The most highly and most lowly regarded actors in such a system can be neither isolates nor stars, neither independents nor redistributors. Instead, the highest and lowest ranks must be filled by actors who are linked with all other actors, transacting with each in just one, not both, of the possible directions.

To transact asymmetrically with all and symmetrically with none is to maintain the median number of total transactions (four in the ten-transaction model of Figure 3*B*). This perfect asymmetrical posture is shared not only by the highest and lowest actors, but also by all other actors along the central line (of boxed fours) between the highest and lowest positions.

The overall strategies and rankings are compounded out of just four tactical elements that are available to any actor vis-à-vis any other within the postulated Hindu scheme of transactions. These four dyadic tactics—here termed *optimal* and *pessimal* (higher and lower in asymmetrical exchange), *maximal* (symmetrical exchange), and *minimal* (symmetrical nonexchange)—are displayed algebraically in Figure 4. Each of these tactics is used consistently and exclusively in all relationships only by actors at the corresponding extreme corners of Figure 3, parts *B* and *C*. All other actors build up their strategies by combining two or more of the four tactics, using one tactic in some relationships, another tactic in other relationships—typically optimal toward inferiors, pessimal toward superiors, maximal toward allies, minimal toward rivals. Only when the set of his tactics is completely perceived can one characterize an actor's overall strategy and rank.

The relative simplicity of this generalized model of the strategies and tactics of Hindu transactions is complicated in actuality by the multiplicity of different media in which the same actors usually transact. A transaction initiated in one medium is often answered in another, as when gifts of fresh food from men to gods, apparently subordinating the gods, are answered by the gods' far more powerful "blessings" in the form of garbage. Such action may seem to occur in a single medium, but the substance-code that is exchanged must be re-evaluated according to the ranked natures of the transactors: the food bestowed by gods upon

FIGURE 4

Four Tactics in Ranked Transactions

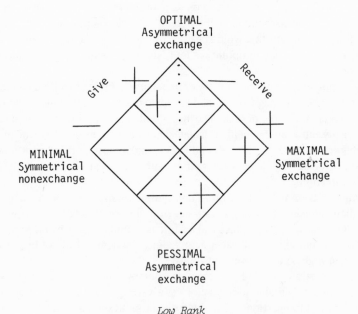

men is transformed so that it becomes superior to the same food previously offered by men to gods. Since the scales of actors, media, and tactics are all mutually defined, highly consistent calculations are felt to be possible, despite such complexities.

Since actors and their actions are held to be aspects of each other, actors having certain strategies and ranks should have predictable characteristics, and vice versa. In the following section are empirical samplings of data on the characteristics imputed to actual groups and persons in relation to their transactions. These are offered as tests of the abstract models we have constructed.

THE VARNA STRATEGIES OF CASTES

The four food transactional tactics of Figure 4 approximate the strategies of what Indians conceive to be the four elemental genera (*varnas*) of their classical society—Brahman (optimal strategy), Kṣatriya (maximal strategy), Vaiśya (minimal strategy), and Śudra (pessimal strategy). The essentials of the *varna* strategies may be found outlined in the classical moral code books, but scarcely need texts or teachers for their propagation, or governmental action for their control (*pace* Srinivas 1966: 5). These strategies are thought to be inborn codes in each *varna*, in each derivative caste in the present, and in each person. They recur inevitably through cooperation and competition among actors at any level in any South Asian locality. All four strategies mingle what Western analysts understand as the values of "purity" and "power" in differently defined strivings toward higher rank, toward what Das has demonstrated as the explicit object of classical domestic ritual—a superior quality of life on a scale extending from life to death.

Transactions in ordinary cooked food among occupational caste groups have been recorded in detail in at least a dozen villages. Extracts from such recordings are given from one of these villages in Figures 1 and 2, and from seven more in Figure 5. (Further recordings are available in David n.d., Davis 1974, and Freed 1970.) For clarity of presentation, each of these extracts shows the strategies of just five to seven castes—of comparable occupations, as far as possible—selected out of larger local sets of from fourteen to twenty-eight castes.

Since ranks and tactics are adjusted multilaterally, any selection of a certain combination of castes, like the historical accidents of migration and co-residence, can affect the relations of all. Figure 5 is slightly biased toward inclusion of castes that exhibit either maximizing or minimizing strategies. Consequently it underrepresents the majority of castes in these villages that follow more nearly central, asymmetrical strategies. Since minimizers in the selection outnumber maximizers, and since these minimizers go to greater extremes in their strategies than do the maximizers, the numbers of transactions in the examples (except part *D*) will be found to be less than the full set of ten transactions that is postulated in the generalized models of Figure 3. The total transactions of each actual caste thus also tend to be reduced by one or two points below the values projected in Figure 3.

FIGURE 5

Strategies of Some Castes in Seven Villages:
Transactions in Ordinary Cooked Food

(A) Kishan Garhi, U.P. (Marriott 1968a: 152.)   (B) Rasulpur, U.P. (Imtiaz Ahmad, personal communication).   (C) Ram Kheri, M.P. (Mayer 1960: 36–40), and Potlod, M.P. (Mathur 1964: 130).   (D) Devapuram, A.P. (Subrahmanyam 1969).   (E) Olappalaiyam, Tam. (Beck 1973a: 163).   (F) Nallapakam, Tam. (Barnett 1970).

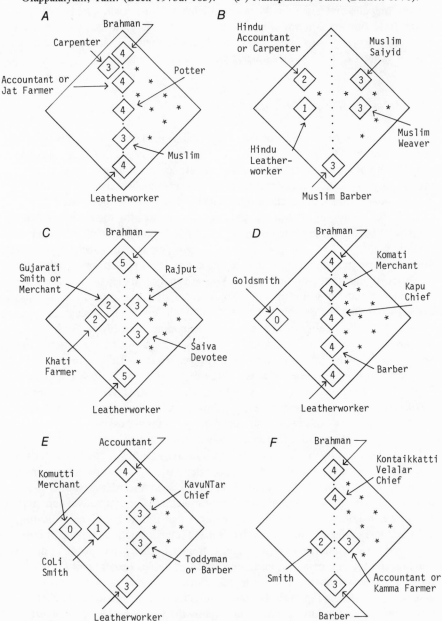

Relative positions are approximately maintained, however, and the examples are otherwise representative of transactions among the larger sets of castes from which they are drawn.

Maximal (Kṣatriya) Strategy

Castes that follow some maximal tactics and thus appear on the right side of the diagrams in Figure 5 include Rajputs and their allies in the Madhya Pradesh villages (part C) and other landed, dominant, or ruling groups and their allies, like KavuNTar Chiefs and Kamma Farmers in Tamilnadu (parts E and F). Also notable among the maximizers are Muslim elites in eastern Uttar Pradesh (part B) and landed tribals in Konduru, Andhra Pradesh (Figure 2). Among the allies of these groups and sharing somewhat in the symmetrical, maximal strategy is a broad spectrum of farming, laboring, and serving groups not shown in the examples, in addition to the Muslim Weaver, Śaiva Devotee, Toddyman, and Barber—typical members of a dominant alliance—that are shown. In parts of Southeastern India (represented by examples D, E, and F), some of these allies once formed a set known as the "Right-hand castes" (Beck 1973b; Hiebert 1971: 59, 62).

The control of land and labor is a common power of all these dominant, maximizing groups. The substantive connections among landedness, long-term labor arrangements, and a reciprocal or redistributive strategy of food transactions are obvious. Land can yield taxes, or rent, or crops, but requires for these yields some dependable organization of manpower. The widespread taking in and giving out of food is one powerful way of organizing many men for conquest, defense, or agricultural production. Most extreme in this symmetrical strategy, emphasizing mutual cooperation and equalization of substance, are the tribal peoples (Sinha 1965: 58–66).

Less obvious is the consistency between the maximizing forms of symmetrical exchange in land control, labor, or food distribution, and the maximizing strategies of marriage, descent, worship, diet, and temperament. Larger, more open networks of marriage are typical of landed groups, both peasant and tribal, as has often been noted (e.g., Beck 1973a: 232; Gupta 1974: 68–69; Plunkett 1973; Sinha 1965: 66), and so are polygyny and concubinage. Remote ties of descent may also be cultivated (Beck 1973a: 97–99). Males of the same groups may also practice the widest diets (sometimes including wild meats and alcohol—all "heating" substances), and may be thought able to transform their heterogeneous intakes with this greater "heat" into outputs of greater gifts, payments, sexual power, and violence (Carstairs 1957: 84, 188; Mayer 1960: 44–45). The high turnover in all these gross and varied media is designed to extract more essences, to achieve the greatest quality and potency in subsistence, action, and group substance-code.

Goddesses and demons who are the special icons of such Hindu groups enjoy similar "hot" diets and temperaments (Carstairs 1957: 165) and may be worshipped by congregations, through choral dance, collections, public sacrifices, and distributions of meat (e.g., Blank 1973; Mayer 1960: 99–103). All these are celebrations of maximal exchange. The transactional forms of popular Islamic festivals are also highly compatible with this mixing and maximizing style (e.g., Aggarwal 1971: 154–155, 159–164).

Most dominant landed groups qualify their symmetrical strategies by asymmetrical tactics. While preserving broad, reciprocal relations with some other castes, they also raise themselves above the maximal extreme, with its consequences of equality and a middle rank. Asymmetry only slightly qualified by reciprocity is the classical strategy of aristocrats in the Kṣatriya *varṇa* as sacrificers and givers of gifts, and of the Aryan king as collector of taxes and dispenser of punishments (Manu 7; 10: 74–77, 113, 119). The Jat Farmers of Kishan Garhi (Figure 5A) and the Kapu Chiefs of Devapuram (5D) approximate this nearly optimal, royal strategy, as do the KV Chiefs of Nallapakam (5F). With changes in transactions go changes in actors: both Jat and KV are in these villages vegetarian groups, given to Brahman-like styles of life, and the conservative KV are characterized as more likely to withdraw than to seek alliances or risk violence (Barnett 1973). A single farming group, the Khatis, appears on the minimizing left in the two M.P. villages (Figure 5C), apparently for the reasons discussed in the next section.

Asymmetrical deviations in a pessimal direction may occur when groups otherwise likely to pursue a maximizing strategy—here certain Muslims, servants, and lesser allies of the leading maximizers—lack a quantity of resources sufficient for making valuable transfers to many others. These castes appear near the main vertical line at lower ranks.

Minimal (Vaiśya) Strategy

Most groups on the left sides of the diagrams—those whose tactics include minimizing the number of relationships in which they exchange cooked food—are identifiable as skilled artisans (carpenter, blacksmith, goldsmith) and merchants. Artisans and merchants are two main components of what in parts of South India are called the "Left-hand castes." These are usually nonlanded, nonagricultural groups, having relatively small populations. Their subsistence is based on their internalized technical or commercial capacities, and on their manipulation of tools, goods, or money, rather than on their management of manpower (Beck 1973a: 262–275). Either symmetrical alliances, with reciprocal exchange of food, as on the right hand, or involvement in the asymmetrical feedings of long-term patronage and services exchanged upward and downward would tend to restrict their economic mobility as skilled contractual workers, or as traders bargaining on the market. These castes all consciously keep substantial degrees of independence, and are thus deliberate participants in what David (1973a, n.d.) calls the "nonbound" mode of symmetrical, minimal relations of exchange.

Groups of quite different occupations, neither artisans nor merchants, also appear on the minimally transacting left in four villages (Figures 2, 5B, 5C). These other groups are sectarian minorities, such as Vaiṣṇavas in predominantly Śaiva,

Śākta, or Smārta villages (Vaiṣṇava Temple Attendants in Konduru; Khati Farmers and others in Ram Kheri and Potlod), later immigrants from other regions (Gujaratis in the M.P. villages; Left-hand castes in the southern villages), and the "conquered" local minority castes (the Hindu Carpenter and others) of a predominantly Muslim village in Bara Banki District, U.P. (Figure 5*B*). What all these groups have in common with each other and also with skilled artisans and merchants in general is that, while each has some resources and putative higher standing elsewhere, all are felt to be weaker elements in their respective present localities. Since such castes are less likely to win rank or power at the local tournaments of exchange in cooked food, they are not surprisingly found pursuing tactics of symmetrical nonexchange. Their denial of any enduring local connectedness is not without its costs—for lacking long-term alliances and a dependable income of food and related aid, these groups must rely more on their own substance-codes, on their capacities to maneuver and negotiate profitably by their wits from day to day. Among such minimizing food transactors of a North Indian market town, snacks and private picnics take the place of the large feasts of landlords, and general mistrust replaces the rural blocks of substantial solidarity (Fox 1968: 97–100, 114–115). According to observations in northern Sri Lanka by David (1973a, n.d.), fishermen or artisans endeavor to equalize each transaction in order to allay the hostility of their customers.

Similar tactics become evident in other transactions of the minimizing castes. Obligations are limited to the joint family, and possibilities for deep lineage development are usually ignored (Fox 1968: 59–61). Marriage networks are possibly narrower, as would follow both from the smaller average size of these groups and from their "concern with a tight-knit marriage community" (Beck 1973a: 233; Morrison 1972: 59–60). More textual, Sanskritic, and internally "ritualized" styles of worship are said to separate—even isolate—smiths, merchants, Left-hand castes, and the Jain or Vaiṣṇava sectarians of some localities (Beck 1973a; Mathur 1964: 163, 167–168, 191–192 n. 7; Srinivas 1955: 22–25). This of course applies as well to minority Hindus in Muslim areas.

The diets of the minimizing strategists are limited in comparison with those of the omniverous maximizers. Their food regime is usually vegetarian and characterized by both fasting and extreme selectivity; they avoid "hot" and favor "cool" foods. While avoiding transfers of any sort of cooked food, they are of course active in transfers of other, subtler media less intimately involved with gross bodily substance-code—preferably grain, metals, and money.

Symmetrical concomitants of the policies of controlled intake are cautious disbursements and a reputation for miserliness (Fox 1968: 60). Similarly, the merchants in Carstairs' samples exhibit the greatest degree of anxiety over sexual laxity or loss. In transactional terms, the power of these groups is felt to be conserved in the self-contained integrity of their substance-code, and in their power thereby to generate wealth (e.g., Carstairs 1957: 119–123).

The minimizing transactional strategy is plainly that of the trader—the social category designated by the classical name Vaiśya. In older texts (e.g., Manu 1:

90), the term refers broadly to the tactically mixed strategies of the residual (after Brahman and Kṣatriya) category of common people—those with productive power (*viś*) who grow grain, rear cattle, trade, supply their betters, and pay taxes; the Komati Merchant in Devapuram (Figure 5*D*) and some of the farmer castes would be examples of this strategic type. Today, however, a concept of the Vaiśya as a tight-fisted transactor is well developed.

Pessimal (Śudra) Strategy

The groups with more ''receiving'' than ''giving'' relationships in Figures 2 and 5 fall into two occupational categories: Barbers take food as well as bodily substance-codes directly from patrons of many castes; and Leatherworkers do the same, usually from more castes, and in a still lower medium—animal carcasses. Intakes in such low media have their values, especially coming as they do from superior castes, and so does the cooked food taken in payment. But relative rank and power are surrendered in return for these valuable receipts. The receivers cannot reciprocate in the same media or with things of the same value. They are bound to return their masters only deferential services. These pessimal strategists employ a combination of parts of the symmetrical tactics, maximal and minimal, that seems to them the best available—and seems to others the worst.

Pessimal strategists also take much and give less in matters other than food. They typically receive brideprice payments for their daughters, unlike either maximal or minimal transactors. They may serve as priests and exorcists for lower gods and demons, and in these capacities transmit on behalf of higher castes offerings that the donors would themselves shun (Hiebert 1971: 133, 135). Dietarily they are likely to be even more omniverous than the maximal transactors, since they can neither select much among the foods that are their income, nor redistribute much of what they receive. The bodily substance-codes of these low castes are necessarily expected to become the most unselectively heterogeneous, their powers diluted and restricted, their temperaments gross and animal-like. As removers also of what the higher castes conceive as ''pollution'' (Harper 1964), the lowest among them are masters of negative transformations—of destruction by contrast with the Brahman's creation.

Optimal (Brahman) Strategy

As possessors of the greatest power (*śakti*) to make transformations between grosser and subtler substance-codes, and as the leading purveyors of such power and its results to others, the Brahman castes exemplify the optimal transactional tactic of Figure 4. They therefore take the top rank of any set of castes in which they appear. The Brahman castes appear in no matrix as receivers of any lower forms of substance-code, such as ordinary payments for services, or wives from lower castes, or ordinary cooked food. As the most selective, epicurean-like receivers, Brahmans typically accept substance-code only of very perfect form, such as gifts of land, money, and whole grain. All these are goods that can be transformed and applied toward the leisure necessary for gains in still subtler substance-code, and they can yield still higher power and rank. Brahmans take the highest place through their own divinity, through their exclusive pessimal exchanges with still higher, more generous gods, and through their great gifts to other terrestrial men—cosmic knowledge in the form of substance-transformative ceremonies, teaching, and advice.

Thus Brahmans earn, through refusal or controlled acceptance, the minimal transactor's gain of nonmixture and integrity for their own substance-code. They also earn, through their wide distributions, the maximal transactor's gain of universal domination. Their tactic thus may be considered an asymmetrical compromise made up of the more rewarding parts of those two opposite symmetrical tactics.

The Brahmans, writes Beck (1973b: 392), "were considered above the division" between Left- and Right-hand castes. Carstairs (like Gough 1956 and Vidyarthi 1961: 146–203) finds Brahmans calculating a depersonalized regime of asymmetrical exchange (1957: 115–119), involving the enjoyment of wealth, a rich diet, vegetarian or otherwise, and a complex, formal familial and sexual life. Brahmans' special concerns are with cultivating their subtler powers through maintaining a favorable balance in mental transactions of potent thoughts and words (see especially pp. 216–259). Not austerity but the perfection of living power is their aim.

Among the typical occupations of Brahmans are those of scholar, teacher, reciter, ritualist, and mystic. These imply varied transactions, which have long involved the dilemma of the lowering effect of accepting gifts offered by others (Heesterman 1964). The strategies of the Brahman castes appear to vary in their strategic emphasis according to the transactional environment. Brahmans in general practice some symmetrical exchange of feast foods where they have large, landed, farming populations in parts of the North (Figure 5A) and symmetrical nonexchange where they form a less favored, competing minority (e.g., Beck 1973a: 11, 266).

Other local caste groups approximating the Brahman's typical optimal strategy are certain Accountants (Figure 5, A and E), Carpenters (5A), and Merchants (5D), and as noted before, certain Farmers (5A) and Chiefs (5D, 5F). All these groups resemble Brahmans in many traits. Here along the central path, as elsewhere in the left and right regions of the matrices, castes may be seen to move by altering their transactions, and in so doing, to alter the natures that are theirs by birth.

ACTION SYSTEMS AS TRANSACTIONAL STRUCTURES

Exchanges like those shown in the matrices of Figures 3 and 5 are simultaneously relevant to each of the Indian classical types of "end"-oriented action. The ends can be distinguished (anticipating Weber and Parsons) as *dharma* (moral), *artha* (instrumental), *kāma* (affective), and *mokṣa* (ultimate). That all these theoretical ends may be relevant to analyzing any behavior of any actor is clearly the view of the classical Indian moralists (e.g., Manu 1: 79–84, 87–91; 2: 2–5, 8–9; 7: 17–26—as recognized by Dumont 1960: 41), as well as of Weber and Parsons. Thus a caste group or actor described as following a certain strategy in cooked food may be regarded as carrying on exchanges that ipso facto affect rank, power, wealth, mind-body metabolism, and so on. Thus also no one of these types of action can be allocated exclusively to any one genus of men. (Dumont translates into historical Western dualities, rather than following either Indian or Western analytical thought, when he personifies "religious" functions in the Brahman "priest" and secular, "political" functions in the Kṣatriya king. See 1962: 51; 1970.)

The moral, instrumental, and affective aspects of some transactions have been noted in the examples above. Transactional overviews of the matrices oriented to each of these broader ends of action may now be given by way of summary.

Moral Action (Dharma)

Cults and sects, and communities. In pursuit of the highest moral values, the strategies of most castes have been noted to cluster along the central, vertical line of pure asymmetry. Those are strategies characteristic both of ancient Brahmanistic sacrifices and of the continuing main tradition of ranked Hindu worship known as *puja*. On the right side, practicing maximal, symmetrical transactions, are the blood-sacrificing Tantrik cults: the more extreme of these would reverse the usual asymmetries of exchange, and confuse all substance-codes, making untenable any further distinctions of high and low (e.g., Carstairs 1957: 102–104, 118). In this transactional position, too, are some features of Sikh and Islamic practice. On the extreme left are the Jain sects, concentrating value by the most controlled transactions (Sangave 1959). Ranged between these extremes from left to right are the Hindu devotional cults of Viṣṇu, Śiva, and the Goddess. Among Vaiṣṇava cults, that of the chaste Rām generally stands to the left in its methods, and that of the amorous Kṛṣṇa further right. Among worshippers of the Devi, those who follow the cult of Durgā may stand less far right than the worshippers of Kālī and her servant, Bhairava. Animal-sacrificing *śākta* cultists more often make transactions in gross bodily substance while vegetarian Vaiṣṇavas tend to favor media such as words and music. Balanced at the center, but swinging pendulum-like toward both right and left in its mythology, is the ambiguous cult of Śiva, the "erotic ascetic" (O'Flaherty 1969).

Within all these cults transactionally one can identify the pessimal, receptor strategies of the majority of Hindu worshippers, who take whatever the many gods may choose to give. The annual religious cycle of a town or village includes special observances for many gods, some of them associated with the *varṇas* and their typical transactional forms. Thus Dasera may be seen as a redistribution by the

Kṣatriya, ruler or farmer; Dīvālī, as an accumulative display by the Vaiśya; Holī, as a universal abasement, Śudra-style; and other festivals as educative performances by Brahmans (Singh 1970: 261–262).

One may question whether actors in such diverse cults, sects, and communities do not differ in the total transactional structure that they assume, or at least reorient that structure to exalt their own respective strategic values—Tantrik sectarians perhaps putting the maximal transactor at the top, Jains the minimal transactor, and so forth. Both Jains and extreme Hindu Tantriks are small minorities; but, like the majority of Hindus who stress the pessimal tactic of devotion, they seem to derive their *raison d'être* from their distinctive ways of maneuvering within a structure that they share with the whole society. The large minority populations of Sikhs and Lingayats, having established separate, divinized moral orders beyond their birth groups, appear to replicate within themselves features of the general transactional structure, with the religious preceptor at the apex (Marriott and Inden 1974).

Buddhist communities in South Asia build upon the tradition that Gautama was both prince and ascetic. Fusing parts of both maximal and minimal transactional strategies, he rose above both by a Brahman-like tactic to become the universal enlightener (Reynolds 1972). Mendicant monks of Sri Lanka similarly retain certain royal ceremonial prerogatives at death (Kemper 1973: 208–209), and the truly enlightened and rare *arhat* can achieve in life a Brahman-like supremacy over both monk and king.

Only in Muslim parts of South Asia do greater departures appear sometimes to occur from this general transactional structure (Marriott and Inden 1974). For example, a one-dimensional structure, lacking the maximal and minimal strategies, is suggested by the finding in Rasulpur village (Figure 5B) that opinions of caste rank correlate with the order of the castes' food-giving alone better than with the order of receiving or the order of net scores. This finding suggests that only pious giving matters, and that the natures of the receivers are not altered by what they receive. Rank in that village could therefore be represented better by returning the matrix in Figure 5B to a horizontal position, and perhaps better still by eliminating the dimension of receiving, whose ordering seems irrelevant.

Life stages (āśramas). The widespread two-dimensional, four-tactical transactional structure that we have approached through the relations of *varṇas,* castes, and sects is implied in Indian thought on marriage, family, and sexual roles, and is explicitly evident also in classical moral texts on the passage of persons through the stages (*āśramas*) of life (e.g., Manu 2: 26 through 6: 86, as noted by Ronald Inden in a personal communication).

The first stage, studentship, requires a pessimal tactic like that of the Śudra: the student must serve, and should absorb, the teacher's superior substance-code, while living on alms begged from a plurality of others.

The second stage, that of householder, requires the maximal transactional tactics typified by the Kṣatriya or farmer. To complete his duties, the householder must throw himself into getting and giving, must become, as a result, a heterogeneous person, and must constantly divide and distribute his own substance-code for the provision of sons, sacrifices, and alms.

The third, brief stage of forest-dwelling entered by the householder on his retirement is marked by an extreme version of the optimal Brahman tactic: the forest-dweller should take nothing produced by others, and dispose of all that he possesses.

Having thus gained moral perfection and learned self-discipline, the retiree may shift to the fourth stage, that of *samnyāsa,* or renunciation. This stage requires the tactic of minimal transaction in gross substance that typifies the Vaiśya. As a mendicant, the *samnyāsin* can no longer gain by gross and lavish giving. He sinks from the moral perfection of the forest-dweller by accepting alms in low-ranking media from all persons, but uses this tactic to reduce his attachment to any intake. He thus increases his actual independence, his freedom from external influence. To the extent that the living renouncer succeeds in minimizing his transactions, especially through developing inner powers of thought, he achieves a subtler, thus more perfect substance-code. His exudations, if any, have very concentrated power (O'Flaherty 1969: 315–316). Contrasting with the highly heteronomous student, the highly heterogeneous householder, and the highly dividual forest-dweller, the renouncer becomes that rarity for Indian social thought—a relatively autonomous, homogeneous, individual person (cf. Dumont 1965: 99).

If the actual *samnyāsin*'s rank is sometimes uncertain, complicated by doubts and ambivalences (e.g., Carstairs 1957: 55–56, 102), one may refer to his position in Figure 3, where his strategy of symmetrical nonexchange gives him a median rank. If he is sometimes respected much more than his current minimal transactions would justify—more than the comparable Vaiśya among the *varṇas*—this seems due to an assumption of a cumulative effect, explicit in the texts: the renouncer should have achieved the virtues not of a single strategic position alone, but of each previous stage that he has visited in sequence.

Honor (izzat, mārta, and so on).   Personal prestige or honor, apart from caste or stage of life, may be won and lost through tournaments in various media that presume the same sort of two-dimensional structure of four transactional tactics.

Honor is perhaps most widely conceived as arising out of verbal competition for influence (e.g., Hiebert 1971: 62–68; Steed 1955: 115, 131–135). In Kishan Garhi, a "big man" is "one whose talk is heard" or "heeded." Some men are said to try to gain in honor by maximizing their verbal transactions, that is, by speaking with many others. These are said to make themselves heard, but to suffer from too much speaking—their many words begin to lose effect. Speaking frequently with others also means listening to others, and that brings a man down to the common level. Other persons, like those of the Left-hand castes, are self-consciously withdrawn from too much give-and-take, here of verbal substance. These may develop an honorable reputation for accumulated wisdom, and for the good sense of keeping aloof from petty discourse, but if a restrained man is never forthcoming he cannot gain great honor. When his words are respectfully requested by others, only then should the man of most honor speak, and then the influence of his few words will be great.

A homologous sort of competition may take place in feasting on an interpersonal scale within a local caste group, as among the Brahmans of Kishan Garhi. Feast encounters among sixty men, all potentially hosts and guests, yield ranked categorizations of the actors as "refined men" (those who are feeders but not fed), "men" (those who are sometimes feeders, sometimes fed), "their own men" (neither feeders nor fed), and "dogs" (fed, but not feeders).

Mutual violence is another common medium in which competition for honor goes on among persons, families, and larger kin groups. Attacks upon persons seem to be most exactly computed in Muslim villages of West Panjab, Pakistan, where the ranks of local caste groups as well as persons are said to be scored according to previous unreciprocated acts of murder, assault, and marriage (conceived as a coup for the taker and a misdemeanor for the giver when a woman moves outside her original kinship circle). Whether self-restrained, minimal violence is to be credited as highly as manifest, maximal violence is not evident in this area (Ullah 1958). The usage of honorable violence clearly is thought to have both minimal and maximal varieties in India, however, according to several reports (Hitchcock 1959, 1960; Morrison 1965: 116–145; Steed 1955: 131–135).

Given simultaneous competition by the same persons in two or more media, and at different levels of particularity, the opportunities for ambiguity and for divergences of personal rank from group rank are numerous (Srinivas 1962: 68–69). Indian particulate theories of persons and groups readily accommodate such divergences, however, and offer no grounds for surprise—unlike simpler Western theories of stratification (e.g., Bouglé 1971: 9, 12, 19; Bailey 1957: 271, 1963; Barth 1960; Dumont 1970: 183, 257)—at persistent ethnographic reports that personal rank in rural South Asia conforms only partly, usually less than halfway, to caste rank (Marriott 1955b; Bopegamage and Veeraraghavan 1967: 56, 151–152; Hiebert 1971: 62–67). The dualistic analyses previously offered with such findings have attributed the disjunctions or "deviations" to intrusions of the conflicting "economic" or "political" situation into the ritual order of the castes (interpretations summarized by Barber 1968). Degrees of verbal influence and effectiveness in feasting and applying violence may indeed be correlated with differences in personal wealth, command of different numbers of supporters, and so on. However, the divergences cannot be considered as products of heterogeneous factors in conflict. Rather the structures that appear to "deviate" are in fact homologous and connected, capable of additive treatment since they are generated from the same monistic premises by the same transactional logics.

Instrumental Action (Artha)

Self-interested rational action regarding people and goods is directly described by the forms of exchange that have just been considered for moral action.

Political transactions. Putting exchange in a political context, one sees that those aggressive householders who are willing to give and take in solidary relations and communicate most widely are the natural builders of alliances—the active leaders of factions, parties, kingdoms. Others who are withdrawn from aggressive action and from verbal communication, who are independent in subsistence and solidary with no others, will be neutral, and potentially either enemies or allies. Those senior persons who are retired from active struggle, restrained in their aggressive action, free from external influence themselves, but directive toward others and generously disposed, are likely to be cast in the role of arbitrators, parent-figures for the whole community, heads of state. Those who are listeners, dependents for their subsistence, passively directed by others, are followers, "progeny," pawns.

The four political roles just described are transparently those of maximal, minimal, optimal, and pessimal transactors. Each role has its classically associated transformation of power, or energy (*śakti*): *kṣatra* and *daṇḍa* (force and punishment), *viś* and *tapas* (productivity and austerity), *brahman* (totality), and *seva* (servitude, help), respectively (Dumézil 1948: 25; Inden 1969b). Each of the first three roles has been approximated ethnographically in descriptions of the styles of leadership in South Asia (Hitchcock 1958, 1959; Morrison 1965: 116–145, 1972: 60–63; Orenstein 1965: 168–197; Steed 1955: 108–109, 115), styles far more varied than Blau's single unilateral definition of power (1964: 312–313) would seem to allow.

Leaders heavily involved in reciprocal transactions, friendly or unfriendly, are portrayed in Orenstein's discussion of "active" and "unsanctioned" leaders, in Morrison's analysis of the "dominant" type, and in Hitchcock's and Steed's work on the martial Rajput. Mandelbaum summarizes other descriptions of the "alliance" strategy of such rural leaders (1970: 253–264, 468, 627). In Java, the Tantrik Bhairavist warrior-king is of an extreme but similar type (Anderson 1972: 10). Organization-builders of the cut of Sardar Vallabhbhai Patel are examples of the maximal transactor on the Indian national scene: these may be formidable figures, but are generally not the most powerful and respected of all leaders, as their rank in the model in Figures 3 and 4 predicts.

The opposite, minimally transacting leader, often a puzzling figure for the non-Indianist, appears frequently enough in ethnographic accounts: Orenstein's "passive" leaders and Morrison's selfless "service" type are examples that find their apotheosis in M. K. Gandhi (Rudolph and Rudolph 1967: 192–216, 247–249), and among the innumerable other hermits and anchorites of Indian political history. Their degree of respectability and influence should vary from moderate to supreme, depending on whether their tactics are considered at the instant or cumulatively, as noted in the discussion of life stages.

Many accounts show the topmost leaders as persons of a third, compromise type whose strategies combine minimal receiving with maximal giving. In Konduru the arbitrating temple priest (Hiebert 1971: 64–65); in Rajput Khalapur, the judge and high-school principal (Hitchcock 1959, 1960); in Kasandra, the complex Indra-singh, alternately retiring and participating (Steed 1955); in rural Panjab, the village arbitrator and the gentle but frowning Sikh guru (Morrison 1965: 128–129); and in the Indian nation, Jawaharlal Nehru, philosopher of struggle—each of these exemplifies an approximation of the optimal strategy.

Economic transactions. The matrices of transactions derived above from transfers in the relatively gross substance-code of ordinary cooked food (Figures 3 and 4) describe main features of an economy that is isomorphous and coordinated with the moral and political systems of action that we have just discussed.

Generation of gross substance-code evidently occurs at the top of this economy, from within the highest actors themselves or from their transactions with the gods above them, since without getting it from lower actors they nevertheless give it. Conservation of substance-code, at least continued self-possession and perhaps accumulation, occurs at the left of the matrices, since these actors both take from and give to few others. Collection and distribution of substance-code are the characteristic activities of those at the right, who seem to subsist on the traffic itself. Consumption alone, the destruction of substance-code, is an activity permitted only to those at the bottom, who receive but do not give ordinary cooked food.

A matrix of gross labor or service would tend to have the same form as the matrix of food transfer. The complementarity of these two matrices arises from the fact that the foods and services are commonly exchanged for each other.

A matrix of exchange in subtler substance-codes, such as grain or money, would be more nearly filled with transfers; and a matrix of grosser substance-codes, such as garbage or feces, would be less filled, since these are transferred only from much higher to much lower castes (Marriott 1968a). Other media await research.

The economy described here seems logically complete, circular, and therefore capable of sustaining itself. The actors' strategies appear to supply them with the resources they need to continue to follow those strategies.

The valuation of each actor and activity may be read, like rank and power, from the matrix of Figure 3C. The relative value of any particular exchange of substance-code within one medium is the difference between the values of the two positions between which it moves. The media, as noted earlier, are valued according to their ranges of transformability.

This economy is thus a peculiarly relativistic and particularistic one, in which givers and receivers are not generally substitutable for each other. A diversity of actors' choices, including opposite choices, is built into the matrix; this diversity would exist entirely apart from differences of choice arising out of quantitative variations in the supplies of a given kind of substance-code. Furthermore, the choosing transactors, unlike "economic men" in the standard marketplace, are not independent of each other: the presence or absence of each affects the situation of the others (George Rosen, personal communication).

A hypothetical sketch of the distribution of land and labor implied by a perfect specimen of such an economy is given by Beck (1973a: 15–17). The debatable results of such empirical explorations as have occurred to date are summarized by Orans (1974). Further transactionally informed research is needed.

Affective Action (Kāma)

Transactional strategies are believed to constitute affective temperaments through the ways in which they cause substance-codes to enter and leave, or not to enter and leave, the person. Diet, body-mind activity, and social tactics are thought to have mutual effects. Indian assumptions about the person here resemble the many-faceted theories of Erikson, and particularly agree with his attention to the bodily sphincters as providing general modalities of personal style (1963: 72–108). Indian theorists (Caraka, Suśruta) have much to say also about internal transformations of substance-codes, their channels and flow, their mixtures and separations.

The catalytic "heat" of the maximal transactor is thought to be both a product and a cause of his high intake and output in gross substance-code. Anger, aggressiveness, eroticism, openness, and liberality are effects of the inclusive diet followed, while choice of such a diet is logically determined by the inborn affective disposition, by moral demands and instrumental necessities (Carstairs 1957; Hitchcock 1958; Steed 1955). Conversely, the stabilizing "coolness" of the minimal transactor, whether in worship, business, politics, or sex, is thought to be partly an effect of a "cool," restricted intake in foods, words, and original bodily substance-code. Coolness likewise capacitates the minimal transactor for a restricted output.

None of the psychiatric categories of the West fit well, but homologies have been suggested between what is called "psychopathic personality" and the functioning of the maximal transactor, and between an "anal" complex (Spratt 1966: 205–224, 300–313), if not obsessive-compulsive character (Carstairs 1957: 163–164), and the mental make-up of the minimal transactor. Maximal and minimal tactics are logically complementary and may alternate in the same persons (O'Flaherty 1969; Anderson 1972: 27, n. 54), often according to age and state of health (Steed 1955: 123–124).

Optimal transactors, whether moral, political, or economic, are necessarily concerned with their powers to effect transformations in both directions between gross and subtle substance-code, and thus with the particular mixtures of "hot" and "cold," or catalysis and stability, in their own persons. The ethic of the Bhagavad-Gita, combining instrumental action with emotional detachment, can be understood as one compromise typical of many required by the tactic of optimal exchange. Transactionally defined as powerful originators, preferably in subtler verbal and mental media, optimal transactors are pushed inevitably toward fantasy. Their pathology should be typically schizoid (e.g., Carstairs 1957: 225–259).

Pessimal exchangers, at the opposite pole of asymmetry, must give gross effort for gross intake; they receive subtle substance-code from their betters but do not give any. Affective concomitants of pessimal exchange are dependency and depression (Miller and Kale 1972), relieved by excitations and hysteria.

The affective dispositions of the sexual genera must be seen as variable across this whole matrix. Males, believed to have greater capacities for control of their exchanges and transformations of substance-code, therefore have greater opportunity for optimizing their transactional tactics and personal temperaments. Females, believed to have less controllable propensities toward maximal exchange, may counterstrive toward minimal exchange through restrictions, and thereby oscillate between these two poles; but since more of their transfers are receivings and are necessarily in gross or bodily substance, they tend always to adopt pessimal strategies (Minturn and Hitchcock 1966: 99; Obeyesekere 1963).

CONCLUSION

Starting from Hindu cosmology and the ethnography of intercaste relations, this chapter has formulated part of a general model of South Asian transactions and deduced from it some properties of diverse occupational castes, cults, communities, economic interest groups, political styles, sexual genera, psychological types, and so on. Giving and receiving, two dimensions of a unitary exchange relationship, order transactors distinctly and yield four elemental codes or tactics: two asymmetrical ones (optimal, pessimal) and two symmetrical ones (maximal, minimal). These four tactics can define both the fourfold positional system of Hindu society and the four stages of personal life (*varṇāśrama dharma*). In combinations, they constitute transactional codes or strategies typical of the diverse castes, cults, and other categories having apparently opposed or disparate values. Transactors and transactions are oriented ultimately neither toward "purity" nor toward "power" as usually understood in social science, but toward a unitary Indian concept of superior value—power understood as vital energy, substance-code of subtle, homogeneous quality, and high, consistent transactional status or rank. All of these are regarded as naturally coincidental or synonymous.

Since this transactional model attempts to follow Hindu cognitions of monism, particularism, and dividualism, it necessarily ignores some assumptions as to ultimate dualities that are explicit or implicit in the Western sociological tradition—sacred versus secular, status versus power, action versus actor, code versus substance, norm versus disorder, society versus individual, and so forth. It analyzes the strategies of ascetic renouncers and economic accumulators as displaying the same minimizing tactic. It analyzes dividualistic competition among persons and ranked interchanges among castes as culturally nondisjunctive enactments that assume at different levels the same meanings of relationships. Overriding the distinctions of conventional social science and treating civilizational structure as a continuous, natural emergent of relationships, this expansion of a Hindu ethnosociology of transactions resembles recent developments in general sociological systems theory (e.g., Buckley 1967: 40). It may suggest some potentialities for the development of diverse and productive ethnosociologies elsewhere, and for an expansion of the social sciences that have arisen in the West.

ACKNOWLEDGMENTS

Thanks are due for their comments on earlier drafts to D. W. Attwood, Kenneth A. David, Mary Douglas, Bruce Kapferer, Charles M. Leslie, T. N. Madan, Manning Nash, Lee I. Schlesinger, Michael Silverstein, and Stanley J. Tambiah. For his instigation of and collaboration in the larger ethnosociological enterprise of which this essay is a part, I am obliged to Ronald Inden, who is not, however, responsible for all the interpretations here set forth.

REFERENCES

Abbott, John. 1932. *The Keys of Power*. New York: Dutton.
Aggarwal, Partap C. 1971. *Caste, Religion and Power*. New Delhi: Shri Ram Centre for Industrial Relations.
Aiyappan, A. 1973. Deified men and humanised gods: some folk bases of Hindu theology. 9th International Congress of Anthropological and Ethnological Sciences, Chicago. Paper no. 0393.
Allee, Warder Clyde. 1958. *The Social Life of Animals*. Rev. ed. Boston: Beacon Press.
Anderson, Benedict R. O'G. 1972. The idea of power in Javanese culture. In Claire Holt, ed., *Culture and Politics in Indonesia*. Ithaca, N.Y.: Cornell University Press.
Babb, Lawrence A. 1973. Heat and control in Chhattisgarhi ritual. *Eastern Anthropologist*, 26: 11–28.
Bailey, Frederick G. 1957. *Caste and the Economic Frontier*. Manchester: Manchester University Press.
———. 1963. Closed social stratification in India. *European Journal of Sociology*, 4: 107–124.
———. 1964. Politics in village India. Brighton: School of African and Asian Studies, University of Sussex. Mimeographed.
Bales, Robert F. 1970. *Personality and Interpersonal Behavior*. New York: Holt, Rinehart and Winston.
Barber, Bernard. 1968. Social mobility in Hindu India. In James Silverberg, ed., *Social Mobility in the Caste System in India*. The Hague: Mouton.
Barnett, Stephen A. 1970. The structural position of a South Indian caste. Ph.D. dissertation, University of Chicago.
———. 1973. The process of withdrawal in a South Indian caste. In Milton Singer, ed., *Entrepreneurship and Modernization of Occupational Cultures in South Asia*. Durham, N.C.: Duke University Program in Comparative Studies on South Asia.
Barth, Fredrik. 1960. The system of stratification in Swat, North Pakistan. In E. R. Leach, ed., *Aspects of Caste in South India, Ceylon, and North-west Pakistan*. Cambridge: Cambridge University Press.
Beals, Alan R. 1962. *Gopalpur, a South Indian Village*. New York: Holt, Rinehart and Winston.
Beck, Brenda E. F. 1969. Colour and heat in South Indian ritual. *Man*, n.s., 4: 553–572.
———. 1973a. *Peasant Society in Koṅku: A Study of Right and Left Subcastes in South India*. Vancouver: University of British Columbia Press.

————. 1973b. The right-left division of South Indian society. In Rodney Needham, ed., *Right and Left*. Chicago: University of Chicago Press.

Béteille, André. 1969. *Caste, Class and Power*. Berkeley: University of California Press.

Blank, Judith. 1973. The story of the Chou dance of the former Mayurbhanj State, Orissa. Ph.D. dissertation, University of Chicago.

Blau, Peter M. 1964. *Exchange and Power in Social Life*. New York: John Wiley.

Bopegamage, Albert, and P. V. Veeraraghavan. 1967. *Status Images in Changing India*. Bombay: Manaktalas.

Bouglé, Célestin. 1971. *Essays on the Caste System*. Trans. D. F. Pocock. Cambridge: Cambridge University Press.

Buckley, Walter. 1967. *Sociology and Modern Systems Theory*. Englewood Cliffs, N.J.: Prentice-Hall.

Caraka. 1949. *The Caraka Samhita*. 6 vols. Jamnagar: Shree Gulabkunverba Ayurvedic Society.

Carstairs, G. Morris. 1957. *The Twice-Born*. London: Hogarth Press.

Cohn, Bernard S. 1961. The pasts of an Indian village. *Comparative Studies in Society and History*, 3: 241–249.

Das, Veena. n.d. On the categorization of space in Hindu ritual. In Ravindra K. Jain, ed., *Text and Context: The Social Anthropology of Tradition*. Philadelphia: Institute for the Study of Human Issues. (In press.)

David, Kenneth A. 1973a. Hierarchy and equivalence in Jaffna, North Ceylon: normative codes as mediator. 9th International Congress of Anthropological and Ethnological Sciences, Chicago. Paper no. 0584.

————. 1973b. Until marriage do us part: a cultural account of Jaffna Tamil categories for kinsmen. *Man,* n.s., 8: 521–535.

————. n.d. And never the twain shall meet? Mediating the structural approaches to caste ranking. In Harry Buck, ed., *Structural Approaches to South Indian Studies*. Chambersburg, Pa.: Wilson College Press. (In press.)

Davis, Marvin G. 1974. Rank and rivalry in rural Bengal. Ph.D. dissertation, University of Chicago.

Douglas, Mary. 1960. *Purity and Danger*. Harmondsworth, Middlesex: Pelican.

Dubisch, Roy. 1964. *Lattices to Logic*. New York: Blaisdell.

Dumézil, Georges. 1948. *Mitra-Varuna: essai sur deux représentations indoeuropéenes de la souveraineté*. 2d ed. Paris: Gallimard.

Dumont, Louis. 1960. World renunciation in Indian religions. *Contributions to Indian Sociology*, 4: 33–62.

————. 1962. The conception of kingship in ancient India. *Contributions to Indian Sociology*, 6: 48–77.

————. 1965. The functional equivalents of the individual in caste society. *Contributions to Indian Sociology*, 8: 85–99.

————. 1966. A fundamental problem in the sociology of caste. *Contributions to Indian Sociology*, 9: 17–32.

————. 1970. *Homo Hierarchicus*. Chicago: University of Chicago Press.

Erikson, Erik H. 1963. *Childhood and Society*. 2d ed. New York: W. W. Norton.

Fox, Richard G. 1968. *From Zamindar to Ballot Box: Community Change in a North Indian Market Town*. Ithaca: Cornell University Press.

Freed, Stanley A. 1963. An objective method for determining the collective caste hierarchy of an Indian village. *American Anthropologist*, 65: 879–891.

————. 1970. Caste ranking and the exchange of food and water in a north Indian village. *Anthropological Quarterly*, 43: 1–13.

Goodenough, Ward. 1965. Rethinking "status" and "role": toward a general model of the cultural organization of social relationships. In Max Gluckman and Fred Eggan, eds., *The Relevance of Models for Social Anthropology.* ASA Monograph No. 1. London: Tavistock.

Gough, E. Kathleen. 1956. Brahmin kinship in a Tamil village. *American Anthropologist,* 58: 826–853.

———. 1959. Criteria of caste ranking in South India. *Man in India,* 39: 115–126.

Gupta, Giri Raj. 1974. *Marriage, Religion and Society.* Delhi: Vikas.

Harper, Edward B. 1964. Ritual pollution as an integrator of caste and religion. In E. B. Harper, ed., *Religion in South Asia.* Seattle: University of Washington Press.

Heesterman, J. C. 1964. Brahmin, ritual and renouncer. *Wiener Zeitschrift für die Kunde Süd- und Ostasiens,* 8: 1–31.

Hiebert, Paul G. 1971. *Konduru: Structure and Integration in a South Indian Village.* Minneapolis: University of Minnesota Press.

Hitchcock, John T. 1958. The idea of the martial Rajput. In Milton Singer, ed., *Traditional India: Structure and Change.* Philadelphia: American Folklore Society.

———. 1959. Leadership in a North Indian village: two case studies. In Richard L. Park and Irene Tinker, eds., *Leadership and Political Institutions in India.* Princeton: Princeton University Press.

———. 1960. Surat Singh, Head Judge. In Joseph B. Casagrande, ed., *The Company of Man.* New York: Harper and Row.

Homans, George C. 1961. *Social Behaviour: Its Elementary Forms.* London: Routledge and Kegan Paul.

Inden, Ronald. 1969a. Exchange, sacrifice and hierarchy in early India. Mimeographed.

———. 1969b. Social mobility in pre-modern Bengal. Center for South Asian Studies, University of London. Mimeographed.

———. 1972. Marriage and rank in Bengali culture: a social history of the Brahmans and Kayasthas in Middle Period Bengal. Ph.D. dissertation, University of Chicago.

Kane, Pandurang Vaman. 1941. *History of Dharmaśāstra.* Poona, Bhandarkar: Oriental Research Institute.

Kemeny, John G., J. Laurie Snell, and Gerald L. Thompson. 1966. *Introduction to Finite Mathematics.* 2d ed. Englewood Cliffs, N.J.: Prentice-Hall.

Kemper, Steven E. G. 1973. The social order of the Sinhalese Buddhist sangha. Ph.D. dissertation, University of Chicago.

Khare, Ravindra S. 1974. The contemporary Hindu hearth and home. Manuscript.

Lynch, Owen M. 1968. The politics of untouchability: a case from Agra, India. In Milton Singer and B. S. Cohn, eds., *Structure and Change in Indian Society.* Chicago: Aldine.

Mandelbaum, David G. 1970. *Society in India.* 2 vols. Berkeley: University of California Press.

Manu. 1886. *The Laws of Manu.* Trans. G. Bühler. *Sacred Books of the East,* vol. 25. Oxford: Clarendon Press.

Marriott, McKim. 1955a. Little communities in an indigenous civilization. In M. Marriott, ed., *Village India.* Chicago: University of Chicago Press.

———. 1955b. Social structure and change in a U.P. village. *Economic Weekly,* 4: 869–874.

———. 1959. Interactional and attributional theories of caste rank. *Man in India,* 39: 92–107.

———. 1968a. Caste ranking and food transactions: a matrix analysis. In Milton Singer and B. S. Cohn, eds., *Structure and Change in Indian Society.* Chicago: Aldine.

———. 1968b. Multiple reference in Hindu caste systems. In James Silverberg, ed., *Social Mobility in the Caste System in India.* The Hague: Mouton.

Marriott, McKim, and Ronald Inden. 1973. Towards an ethnosociology of Hindu caste systems. 9th International Congress of Anthropological and Ethnological Sciences, Chicago. Paper no. 2206.

_____. 1974. Caste systems. *Encyclopaedia Britannica,* Vol. 3, 982–991.

Mathur, Kirpa Shankar. 1964. *Caste and Ritual in a Malwa Village.* Bombay: Asia Publishing House.

Mauss, Marcel. 1954. *The Gift.* Trans. I. Cunnison. London: Cohen and West.

Mayer, Adrian C. 1960. *Caste and Kinship in Central India: A Village and Its Region.* Berkeley: University of California Press.

Miller, Robert J., and Pramodh Kale. 1972. The burden on the head is always there. In J. M. Mahar, ed., *The Untouchables in Contemporary India.* Tucson: University of Arizona Press.

Minturn, Leigh, and John T. Hitchcock. 1966. *The Rājpūts of Khalapur.* Six Cultures Series, vol. 3. New York: John Wiley.

Morrison, Charles. 1965. Dispute in Dhara: a study of village politics in eastern Panjab. Ph.D. dissertation, University of Chicago.

_____. 1972. A comparative study of urban castes: Ahluwalias and Saralias in Ambala city. *Journal of the Indian Anthropological Society,* 7: 47–63.

Nicholas, Ralph W., and Ronald Inden. 1970. The defining features of kinship in Bengali culture. Mimeographed.

Obeyesekere, Ganath. 1963. Pregnancy cravings (dola-duka) in relation to social structure and personality in a Sinhalese village. *American Anthropologist,* 65: 323–342.

O'Flaherty, Wendy Doniger. 1969. Asceticism and sexuality in the mythology of śiva. *History of Religions,* 8: 300–337, 9: 1–41.

Orans, Martin. 1974. Caste ranking: sacred-secular, tails, and dogs. In Edwin Gerow and Margery D. Lang, eds., *Studies in the Language and Culture of South Asia.* Seattle: University of Washington Press.

Orenstein, Henry. 1965. *Gaon: Conflict and Cohesion in an Indian Village.* Princeton: Princeton University Press.

Plunkett, Frances Taft. 1973. Royal marriages in Rajasthan. *Contributions to Indian Sociology,* n.s., 7: 64–80.

Pocock, David F. 1955. The movement of castes. *Man,* 71–72.

_____. 1972. *Kanbi and Patidar.* Oxford: Clarendon.

Reynolds, Frank. 1972. The two wheels of dhamma. In G. Obeyesekere et al., *The Two Wheels of Dhamma.* Chambersburg, Pa.: American Academy of Religion.

Rudolph, Lloyd I., and Susanne Hoeber Rudolph. 1967. *The Modernity of Tradition.* Chicago: University of Chicago Press.

Sahlins, Marshall. 1965. On the sociology of primitive exchange. In Max Gluckman and Fred Eggan, eds., *The Relevance of Models for Social Anthropology.* ASA Monograph No. 1. London: Tavistock.

Sangave, Vilas Adinath. 1959. *Jaina Community: A Social Survey.* Bombay: Popular Book Depot.

Schneider, David M. 1968. *American Kinship: A Cultural Account.* Englewood Cliffs, N.J.: Prentice-Hall.

Sengupta, Syamalkanti. 1973. Aspects of stratifications in West Bengal villages. 9th International Congress of Anthropological and Ethnological Sciences, Chicago. Paper no. 1253.

Sharma, K. N. 1961. Hindu sects and food patterns in North India. *Journal of Social Research,* 4: 45–58.

Singh, Yogendra. 1970. Chanukhera: cultural change in eastern Uttar Pradesh. In K. Ishwaran, ed., *Change and Continuity in India's Villages.* New York: Columbia University Press.

Sinha, Surajit C. 1965. Tribe-caste and tribe-peasant continua in Central India. *Man in India,* 45: 57–83.

Spratt, Philip. 1966. *Hindu Culture and Personality: A Psycho-analytic Study.* Bombay: Manaktalas.

Srinivas, M. N. 1955. The social system of a Mysore village. In McKim Marriott, ed., *Village India.* Chicago: University of Chicago Press.

_____. 1962. *Caste in Modern India and Other Essays.* London: Asia Publishing House.

_____. 1966. *Social Change in Modern India.* Berkeley: University of California Press.

Steed, Gitel P. 1955. Notes on an approach to a study of personality formation in a Hindu village in Gujarat. In M. Marriott, ed., *Village India.* Chicago: University of Chicago Press.

Subrahmanyam, Y. Subhashini. 1969. Some aspects of social change in a fringe village in Andhra Pradesh. Ph.D. dissertation, University of Delhi.

Suśruta. 1907. *Suśruta: An English Translation of the Suśruta Samhita.* Trans. K. I. Bhishagratna. 4 vols. Varanasi: Chowkhamba Sanskrit Series.

Tambiah, S. J. 1974. From varna to caste through mixed unions. In Jack Goody, ed., *Character of Kinship.* Cambridge: Cambridge University Press.

Tyler, Stephen A., ed. 1969. *Cognitive Anthropology.* New York: Holt, Rinehart and Winston.

Ullah, Inayat. 1958. Caste, patti and faction in the life of a Punjab village. *Sociologus,* 8: 170–180.

Vatuk, Sylvia. 1973. Gifts and affines in North India. 29th International Congress of Orientalists, Paris.

Vidyarthi, Lalita P. 1961. *The Sacred Complex in Hindu Gaya.* New York: Asia Publishing House.

Wadley, Susan S. 1975. *Shakti: Power in the Conceptual Structure of Karimpur Religion.* University of Chicago Studies in Anthropology. Department of Anthropology, University of Chicago.

Weber, Max. 1958. *The Religion of India.* Trans. H. H. Gerth and D. Martindale. Glencoe, Ill.: Free Press.

_____. 1968. Religious groups. In Guenther Roth and Claus Wittich, eds., *Economy and Society: An Outline of Interpretive Sociology.* New York: Bedminster.

A Signal Transaction
and Its Currency

BASIL SANSOM

Let us suppose a sale where the price is paid in real or
imaginary cattle.

MARCEL MAUSS, The Gift

This chapter is about conventions that govern talk about the topic of bridewealth
among the Pedi tribespeople of Sekhukhuneland, South Africa. I have to begin by
framing an announcement with a frankness that the Pedi themselves would decry.
In Sekhukhuneland, Pedi suitors give cash in partial payment for their brides.

Though Pedi find it disquieting, this development is hardly surprising. A
hundred years ago Aylward (1870: 188) saw Pedi labor migrants returning from
the diamond diggings at Kimberley. These first Pedi wage earners wore breeches
and carried breechloaders bought with their earnings. Long ago, money ousted
livestock in Sekhukhuneland as the standard of wealth and as the dominant
medium of economic exchange. The puzzle is that Pedi still conscientiously
conceal the monetization of bridewealth. Though a payment of bridewealth is
nowadays largely made up of cash, Pedi describe it as if it were made up of so many
cattle, sheep, and goats, and this is no minor quirk of metaphor. Pedi insist that the
valuables of bridewealth should always be given their proper animal designation.
To speak of "money for brides" is not merely out of order, it is a breach of taboo.
Why should a people who pay cash for brides still persistently assert that they
exchange the cattle, goats, and sheep of marriage?

In refusing to call the cash of bridewealth cash (*chêletê*), the Pedi put a further
construction on an event which, by its nature, is already crammed with significance. One of the clichés of Sekhukhuneland is that, in return for bridewealth, "a
man gets more than a bride." In the drawn-out and spectacular ceremonial
attendant on marriage, a great deal is said and done to provide a commentary on the
multiple significance of the event. Manifold transactions are entered into and
completed by a range of persons. At one point rebellious women, transvestite for
the occasion, bring the bride to the home of the groom, exchanging blows with any
men they encounter en route. In their interchanges with men, the transvestites
express female resentment against the presumptuousness of males, and their
attacks must be bought off by the men they belabor. These women are mentioned

143

here only to indicate that a Pedi marriage is characterized by a series of exchanges and episodes, each of which contributes its charge of meaning to the total event. The passing of bridewealth and the removal of the bride are central episodes, but they are set within an entire complex of exchange. Calling cash "cattle" or "livestock" adds further complications to already complex procedures of exchange that are all regarded by Pedi as essential to the making of a marriage.

To make sense of the oddly persistent nominal animals of bridewealth, I treat Pedi formulations about the constitution of marriage payments as a cultural commentary that elaborates the significance of a complex exchange. By special designation, the valuables of bridewealth are set apart and their transfer is made unlike those dealings in which money can be frankly mentioned. In short, the items of Pedi bridewealth are marked by special nomenclature, and this marking removes their formal transfer from the realm of mundane economic exchange. My task is to show what is achieved by the removal, to show why the exercise is necessary, and, finally, to explain why the practice takes its particular form. I argue that, by turning cash into livestock, the Pedi make the transfer of bridewealth a *signal* transaction, dissociating the signal value of things from their economic worth.

The distinctions between signal value and economic exchange value, between signal transactions and market dealings, are thus germane to my analysis. The Pedi themselves rely on the validity of these distinctions, which they express in their own idiom. They are able to argue their own case to resolve an issue that, for anthropologists concerned with Africa, has taken the form of a debate on the suggestion that the passing of bridewealth does not, for Africans, represent the purchase of a wife (e.g., Gray 1960). In Sekhukhuneland, it is no paradox to assert that, though bridewealth is made up largely of cash, no man ever buys a wife. The logic that gives validity to this statement has implications for social exchanges that occur beyond the confines of Sekhukhuneland. Wherever complex exchanges have standard forms and also entail transfer of economically valuable commodities, the locals provide a commentary to put the economic significance of the exchange in its proper perspective. People must work against the defeating possibility that economic value could supervene and turn a complex social exchange into a simple market deal. This is an essay about the way in which a currency of signal value has retained its integrity despite the introduction of money, its inimical competitor.

WHEN CASH BECOMES CATTLE

The Pedi supply rules for turning cash into a currency of bridewealth in nominal units of livestock. In constituting bridewealth, let 10/- stand for either "a goat" or "a sheep" and count £5 as "a cow." The nominal cows, sheep, and goats of bridewealth stand in transitive relationship: small stock can be changed into cows just as money can become animals. The use of fractions, "part animals," is ruled out, and the equation of cash and kinds of livestock can be expressed in whole numbers thus:

$$£5 = 10 \text{ goats/sheep} = 1 \text{ cow.}$$

One should remember that this device is used to turn cash into livestock, not vice versa. In fact, once an amount of bridewealth is finally constituted as so many (nominal) cattle, sheep, and goats, it is impossible, without further information, to work back and discover what tangible items made up the bridewealth.[1]

The irreducibility of nominal amounts of bridewealth is ensured by another rule. No Pedi will ever pay bridewealth wholly in cash. In tribute to tradition, some animal(s) will always be included in the bridewealth to "walk the path" between the natal homes of groom and bride. While inclusion of at least one beast is mandatory, no rule prescribes the ratio of cash to live animals. Thus some people pay more in cash than in livestock, others give goats rather than a cow, and so on. (Nonetheless, in a country of depleted flocks and herds, it is prestigious to transfer as many live animals as possible. There is thus some incentive to make up bridewealth in animals rather than cash, though only the richer Pedi chiefs are able to render payments wholly in living animals.) What, in the final accounting of a payment, is represented as "a cow" could indeed reflect the living reality of a cow. Or one of the so-called cows of bridewealth could derive from an original contribution of 10 goats, or 7 goats and 3 sheep, or £5. Such mixing of cash and livestock robs each nominal unit of any concrete referent. One knows that any declared unit of bridewealth originated in things, but the substantial nature of the original item is always obscured. Just how far nominal "amounts" of bridewealth are removed from any market calculations of value can be shown by referring to prices that animals command in ordinary economic transactions.

Along the borders of Sekhukhuneland, which is a tribal Reserve set apart from surrounding tracts of white-owned farms and state lands, stand several auction pens at which occasional stock fairs are held. At the fairs, all dealing in stock is limited to one-way traffic between tribesmen and whites. Only Africans from the Reserve present cattle for sale. The buyers without exception are whites, and a white auctioneer is in control. The interracial structure of trading reinforces the impersonality inherent in sales by auction, and naked market forces quite clearly determine price. Anyone watching sales can gain a fair idea of going rates for cattle. But a going rate is a generalized notion. Something more particular is required to resolve the disputes that often arise when, in dealings between tribesmen, the price of a particular beast is at issue. Appreciating this, Pedi tribesmen not only sell cattle at auction; they also make use of the auctioneer and white buyers as cattle valuers.

Cattle owners will take an animal to auction to put a price on its head. When cattle destined for valuation but not for sale are presented at auction, the auctioneer is unaware of the owner's intentions and the bidding proceeds in the usual way. When the highest bid is reached, the auctioneer, following a rule of normal practice, will refer to the owner, who must consent to sell at the price reached in the bidding. The owner then declares his dissatisfaction with the price and withdraws his beast; and far from having made an unsatisfactory trip to market, this owner has fulfilled his purpose. He leaves the sale with an unsold beast, but the animal has been valued. Selling at border auctions is dogged by high rates of withdrawal, for about one-third of the animals presented are taken away before the hammer falls. Some withdrawals are the "genuine" withholding of animals by owners who intended to sell only at the right price. Most are not. Appeal to auction is the accepted tribal mode for putting a cash value on a beast.

Valuation of cattle is especially relevant to those engaged in the negotiations that lead to marriage. However Pedi choose to designate the payments, bridewealth is, among other things, a price. Bargaining through an intermediary who acts as marriage broker, a girl's father or guardian will indicate that he will not let her go for less than a minimum sum (normally £70–£80) which he stipulates in cash. Since a suitor will hand over a mixed fund of both animals and cash, it is always necessary to decide the cash value of the animals he proposes to transfer. The difference between the guardian's stipulated price (S) and the cash value of the animal contribution (A) will have to be made up in cash (C), since $A + C$ must equal S. Obviously, C is an arguable amount when $C = S - A$ and A is an estimated value. Thus an appeal to auction can put an end to haggling by providing prices for beasts whose value is at issue.

The profound irrelevance of economic valuation to the formula for turning cash into the nominal animals of bridewealth is made ludicrously apparent at the stock fairs. At sales I witnessed in 1960, the worst scrub cattle never sold for less than £14. The maximum price I recorded (£48) was given for a fine bull, while £23 represents the median price. Unlike cattle, sheep and goats are seldom sold to whites; but, in everyday trade within the Reserve in 1960, full-grown small stock changed hands for prices that ranged between £2 and £3. I was unable to determine when Pedi began to substitute cash for the live animals of bridewealth. However, older informants confirmed that substitution had been in vogue and based on the same money equivalents for animals for as long as they could remember. Over years of inflation the disparity between the price of livestock and its nominal value as bridewealth has increased steadily. Clearly the values of a formula that counts 10/- as a goat/sheep and £5 as a cow make economic nonsense.

The discrepancy between bridewealth as a price and bridewealth as a number of nominal animals affects social action in a number of ways. To appreciate these, due weight must be given to the nature and the strength of the prohibition on straight talking about the valuables of bridewealth. As I have mentioned, such talk is taboo.

To break taboo (*goila*) is to "spoil" (*gosenya*) both social relationships and relationships between mystical powers and men. With a weight of meaning, the notion of "spoiling" is used to categorize acts such as the seduction of minors, incest, or the fouling of ponds and streams with human excrement. Improper talk about bridewealth thus keeps company with a wide range of forbidden acts that are both humanly checked and mystically punished. To use words that imply that any man's wife has been bought is classed as an insult, akin to the attribution of bastardy to her children. The voicing of such an insult readily leads to violence and the court cases that follow on assaults. However, the rules do not dictate that the "realities" of bridewealth can never be discussed. In appropriate contexts one can employ circumlocutions (described below) to discuss the nominal as opposed to the cash value of things given as bridewealth. In this talk, careful verbal formulations ensure that a front is assiduously preserved. Bridewealth, even when its cash value is at issue, is always described as if unspoiled by monetary intrusion.

Leaving bridewealth unspoiled reflects a certain delicacy and restraint; but, more positively, the economically irrelevant designation of a payment of bridewealth encourages a form of boasting that is culturally approved. Boasting of bridewealth amounts to an unreserved vaunting of legitimate position and marital status.

Pedi compose praises (*serêto*) of chiefs, of lineages, and of famous men. Poems composed by men and women in praise of self are also common. Women's praises often include mention of bridewealth. Thus one woman included these assertions in her personal poem of praise:

> My marriage feast was big,
> The bridewealth five cattle
> And many-colored goats.

I have indicated that a bridewealth payment which starts off as, say, a live cow plus cash can be given its nominal designation in a variety of ways. Will the cash be turned into goats or cows or sheep, and in what proportions? However, once the work of turning bridewealth into nominal animals is done, the "amount" arrived at is finally established. This amount cannot be reconstituted, and this means that each bridewealth payment is personalized or tailored to a marriage. Announcing the form a payment took is like waving one's marriage lines. Hence the occurrence of boasts about bridewealth in praise poems which, above all, are declarations of the worth of specific groups or persons. Less studiedly and especially among women, there are many occasions when remarks about who is who include mention of amounts of bridewealth: "That is Dora who married Matenge from Tsopaneng. Bridewealth was six cattle." As long as money is left out, vaunt or announcement of bridewealth is unabashed. Women know the formal details of each other's marriage payments as well as they know each other's names and origins. Name, place of origin, and amount of bridewealth are all recited together as marks of personal identity. Further, the announcements of personalized amounts are harmless because they do not vulgarly discriminate between persons on grounds of wealth. Praise poems vaunt feats, including the feat of marriage; but they seldom include boasts about property.

In its limited way the evidence so far presented is conclusive. Patently the Pedi set up two realms of discourse and meaning that are distinguished by wholly disparate grounds for evaluating the items that are transferred as bridewealth. Hence bridewealth is given dual significance. It is both a price counted in cash and a consolidated "amount" made up of nominal units. By appeal to the logic of contraposition and contrast that is germane to functional analysis, a number of inferences about the effects or consequences of this opposition can be drawn. If we accept that two modes of evaluation (one grounded in economic rationality, the other not) exist side by side, we can summarize the effects as follows:

1. Crass verbal expression of the cash cost of brides is superseded and, to a degree, suppressed by a respect for the nominal designation of the "amounts." The nominal overlies the real.

2. The triumph of nominalism neutralizes bridewealth by removing the sting of invidious comparison. This is true because the relative worth of bridewealth payments is inexpressible unless nominal amounts are somehow broken down and described anew. This point is well illustrated if one considers that an expensive and prestigious payment of chiefly bridewealth that begins as ten cows will be called "ten (nominal) cows." At average prices, its cash value would be about £250. But a commoner could make up bridewealth described as "ten cows" by offering a single live animal plus nine five-pound notes, at a cost of about £70.

3. Awareness of the divide that separates the cash from the nominal value of bridewealth is well established in social consciousness, for people must either adopt special procedures to differentiate between an economic and a nominal reality or break taboo.

4. The nominal designation of each bridewealth payment is fixed and can thus supplement proper names, place of origin, and so on, as a mark of individual identity.

EXCHANGE AND COMMENTARY

To take my interpretation further, I posit that the big events of social exchange—especially those complex exchanges that approximate Mauss's ideal of a total prestation—should be treated as multiple transactions. In complex exchanges a series of issues are resolved when separate things are presented, purposefully defined, and then transferred. This is a departure from Mauss's position, for he posits both the combination and the confusion or confounding of the things and the persons that are joined in any total prestation. My proposal is akin to Gluckman's appreciation of tribal ritual which, he argues, segregates the roles that typically combine and overlap in persons whenever social relationships have many strands.

Gluckman's key thesis about roles and ritual is that "the greater the multiplicity of undifferentiated and overlapping roles, the more ritual to separate them"

(Gluckman 1962: 34). After advancing this idea, Gluckman goes on to apply it to more minute and mundane observances in the conduct of social relations. Formal rituals apart, "most roles and relationships in tribal life have considerable ceremonial attached to them, in the form of at least a highly marked code of special etiquette, the observance of social distance, *and/or the avoiding of subjects in conversation*" (Gluckman 1962: 33; my emphasis). In this formulation, the standard acts that serve to segregate roles are coextensive with accepted means that actors employ to signal social differentiation when they are engaged in communicative work. One could say that, where typical social relationships are multiplex, ritual, ceremonial, and etiquette can be "read" as a "commentary" on the segregation of the items included in an individual's repertoire of roles. Modified thus, the thesis about ritual and overlapping roles can yield a proposition that applies to commentaries and complex exchanges. The greater the number of transactions that combine in the standard form of a complex social exchange, the more a commentary is required to separate them. The commentary in question is, of course, one that is supplied by the social actors themselves, whether as explicit verbal expression or as patterns of action in which meaning is implicit.

What such commentaries achieve, whether they differentiate between roles or transactions, is clarification, through more precise and elaborated definition of situations and events. People can come to terms with the complexities of social life because they are given the means to think about the manifold aspects of relevant situations. Separating roles in thought entails recognition of the specific capacities that inhere in persons, and such capacity is ceded in role designation itself. When particular transactions that combine in a complex social exchange are separated, there is, however, a further difficulty. One can recognize a distinct transaction and be quite clear about the identities of the transacting parties and the general nature of the things transferred; even so, the significance of the transaction is not fully apparent until appeal can be made to criteria for evaluation. To comprehend the force of a transaction, it is necessary to evaluate the extent to which its occurrence modifies social relationships or individual capacities. In consequence, a commentary on a complex exchange must not only be an analysis that distinguishes one transaction from another; it must also provide the various grounds for evaluating the import of exchanges. Thus the greater the number of transactions that are combined in the form of a complex social exchange, the more a commentary is required both to announce their peculiar values and to distinguish their separate significances.

Before returning to the Pedi and their bridewealth a further point about separation and commentary should be made. Several transactions can coincide in one major transfer between donor and recipient. Where the identity of the parties to the exchange remains constant and whatever is exchanged is transferred entire, a commentary can point to the plural significances of the act. In such cases, different grounds for evaluating the actions are highlighted as criteria for distinguishing the coincident transactions from one another.

CONSTITUTING BRIDEWEALTH

In Sekhukhuneland, a standard event is enacted on the eve of each marriage feast to publicize the making up of bridewealth. At this juncture the serious business of marriage negotiation is over. Haggling is now only a memory, for the cash value of bridewealth has been agreed; the suitor's ability to pay has been established; and there is no longer any chance that the proposed marriage will not take place. What remains is the proper labelling of bridewealth items, largely a matter of making money masquerade as cattle, sheep, and goats. In the event, action proceeds on the false premise that the marriage is, in fact, at risk, and this fiction makes the affair an entertainment. Nonetheless, set rules govern the entertainment and give it a typical form. First, there are the questions of the identity of the main performers and the composition of the audience before whom they will act.

Those eligible to attend the gathering are kinsmen or associates either of the groom or of his father, and when they attend the marriage feast next day they will again be in evidence as the groom's party. There are certain essential actors. The groom is either present or attends by proxy—an arrangement that allows migrant laborers to marry while away from home. The groom's father attends together with the head of his minor patrilineage. The mother's brother of the groom (or his heir) must also be present. These actors apart, there is a general obligation on any male kin and friends of the groom's family to attend, though only the absence of an essential actor or his delegate could invalidate the proceedings. The location is a courtyard lent for the occasion and generally removed from the houses where women are busy preparing for the feast to be held the next day. The man who owns the courtyard generally acts as master of ceremonies.[2]

Redundantly, the master of ceremonies explains why the assembly has foregathered. He is allowed to talk for as long as his speech is entertaining, but when the audience grows restive the business of the meeting begins. The bridewealth must be collected from contributors, and this is done item by item in a series of rounds. Those I have described as essential actors must attend because they must all give something toward bridewealth. Every Pedi payment of bridewealth should contain:

1. A contribution that the groom's father supplies from his personal estate.
2. A contribution from the house into which the groom was born. Pedi are patrilineal and permit polygamy. In polygamous households each wife is given a separate house with associated property, a feature of organization in Southern Africa that Gluckman (1950) has called "the house-property complex." Ideally, the contribution from the house should be supplied from income derived from the bridewealth that accrued to the house through the marriage of the groom's full sister. Brothers and sisters thus linked through bridewealth stand in special relationship—they are "cattle-linked" (Krige and Krige 1943).

3. A contribution from the groom's mother's brother (ideally, a "cattle-linked" brother). Without this gift the marriage cannot take place. Incidentally, the mother's brother's obligatory contribution reflects a preference for marriage with the mother's brother's daughter.
4. The senior male of the groom's minor lineage similarly assents to the marriage by making his contribution to the bridewealth.

Once, these obligatory contributions emphasized the importance of kinship in social organization. Today the obligatory contributions are still made but, typically, the kinsmen concerned hand over only token amounts. Young men making first marriages do not rely on their fathers, agnates, or mother's brothers for their bridewealth. Instead, they earn bridewealth themselves by saving money gained as wages in South African towns. Anyone present can mark and claim special relationship with the groom by proferring a contribution and assisting the groom into marriage. Although the groom's father presents the first and second contributions listed above, these often, in fact, have originated as his son's wages. This procedure maintains the appearance that a bridewealth fund is accumulated by group rather than by individual effort. Today, in typical payments of bridewealth, the groom contributes at least three-quarters and usually more.

Collecting the bridewealth takes time, for there are rounds of announcements and men step forward in turn to pledge contributions to the fund. The groom's father, who presents the bulk of bridewealth, releases the main contributions bit by bit. It takes four or five rounds to realize the target sum which, though known in advance to most participants, is not mentioned in this setting. Throughout, the groom's father, the master of ceremonies, and others gamely pretend to squeeze potential contributors on the groom's behalf. They play on obligations of friendship and on family ties. Men in the audience posit the existence of obligations (often hilariously conceived) where there are none. The excitement of the event is in the style and flair that actors bring to their performances. The only thing at stake is a reputation for social performance.

My interest in this scenario is in the form of words used when contributions are presented and defined. Remember that Pedi bridewealth is paid in both money and livestock and that the cash component normally outstrips the live component in economic worth. Most contributions will thus be made in cash. Yet, in all the announcements, cash contributions are initially declared as unqualified cattle, sheep, or goats. Such initial descriptions are inherently ambiguous. A pledge of "a goat" could refer either to a ten-shilling note or to a live animal worth three pounds.

Even though the meeting is an entertainment, its purpose is to provide witnesses who could testify to the constitution of bridewealth in any subsequent dispute. Ambiguity about the substantial nature of the bridewealth cannot persist, and the nominal animals must be identified as contributions of cash or livestock. Each contributor is subjected to cross-examination: is his pledge one of livestock or of cash? The questions are posed and the answers supplied without using the words that, in sePedi, refer unambiguously to cash. The determination must be made, but it is not made quickly.

The donor of a cow is asked whether his cow has horns; if it walks home at night; if it is one of those that sleep and never waken. If a goat is pledged there are queries too: does it eat grass? has it slept under a mattress for years? is its tongue green? These questions are coupled with quips and remarks about the donor's character and demeanor as members of the audience make the occasion memorable by attaching aphorisms to persons. Some of the phrases used in questioning are time-worn, others are novel. In a deluge of verbal expression, the distinction between money and animal contributions is established on the basis of a simple rule. A five-pound note is "merely a cow" (*kgomo fêêla*); smaller sums are counted as "mere" goats or sheep. Real animals are something more. They are complimented and lauded by citing their attributes as living things—they eat, drink, sleep, walk, yield milk, and mate. The meeting builds to a climax when the bridewealth is finally made up and announced as an "amount." The contributions, live or inert, have been added up to produce a figure of so many nominal cattle, sheep, and goats. The next day this amount (bridewealth in its nominal mode) will be announced at the wedding feast. The nominal amount of bridewealth paid will also be registered with the local chief. The bride will be "married with" the formally constituted amount which will, henceforth, be associated with her. Its designation as a consolidated amount of nominal units will live on.

I have explained how "mere cows" and living cows can be told apart so long as proper forms of words are used in the telling. If one wishes to estimate the total cash value of bridewealth, a further step is necessary. Live animals that are pledged or presented must be priced. There is no difficulty in identifying the relevant beasts, for the contributors have ostentatiously described them. Talking about their monetary worth need offend no one as long as the question of price is raised outside the context of discussion about bridewealth. Even at the gathering itself, it is no solecism to address a private aside to a fellow witness and, speaking as if the question were detached from the concerns of the gathering, ask how much the brown cow in X's kraal is worth.

The distinctiveness of bridewealth as a created entity that is made a thing in itself could hardly be more patent. There are compelling similarities between what happens to bridewealth items at the gathering just described and what happens to persons in rites of passage or to things that are blessed in acts of consecration. Bridewealth, though secularly made up, is dedicated to a purpose. The valuables change their status as they are named anew. As the Pedi say, once the meeting is over, these valuables *are* the "cattle/sheep/goats of marriage." The significance of making up bridewealth can be pointed in another way, by distinguishing the procedure as an activity governed by constitutive rather than regulative rules.

As Searle (1972: 135) explains, "constitutive rules do not merely regulate but create or define new forms of behaviour." They can be contrasted with regulative rules, for instance the rules of etiquette which apply to interpersonal relationships that "exist independently of the rules of etiquette" (p. 138). Because "constitutive rules constitute (and also regulate) an activity the existence of which is logically dependent on the rules" (p. 139), it is clear that the activity has no existence without these rules. If a constitutive rule is altered or disregarded, the activity dependent on it is subverted. The making up of Pedi bridewealth is a separate and creative activity, each phase of which is essential if the proper construction is to be put upon the passing of these valuables. The passing of bridewealth properly described as nominal animals is an act quite distinct from a market exchange or from other transactions attendant on marriage.

As I remarked earlier, commentaries on complex exchange not only separate transactions but also present and contain grounds for evaluating the effect of each transaction that is distinguished. The Pedi bridewealth scenario is a distinct activity and its outcome is the announcement of an "amount" of bridewealth distinctively formulated in nominal animal units. What do such "amounts" express with regard to the worth of the payment? What do they indicate that is different from the formulation that "bridewealth was worth eighty pounds"? These questions can be answered by relating bridewealth to other types of transaction in Sekhukhuneland in which nominal animals are transferred.

All fines paid into the courts of Pedi chiefs and certain payments of damages are described and made over in the idiom of nominal animal currency. Again, when a Pedi youth is initiated into manhood, a cow (always, today, a "mere cow" or five pounds) is paid to the chief. Thus in fines, damages, bridewealth, and in the fee of initiation, there is parallel use of the same special currency. As it happens, the Pedi keep these payments in the "coin" of nominal animals distinct from each other as "the cows/goats/sheep of bridewealth," "the cow of initiation," "the cow of seduction," "the goat of insult," and so on. They supply no abstract term for grouping these payments together as members of a class. I argue, however, that the analytic grounds for providing such a term are evident. Like the payment of bridewealth, the cow of initiation unambiguously signals a change of status. Fines in court as well as the standard payments of damages that are associated with specific wrongs also work to modify status. Gluckman (1965: Chap. VII) has argued that, in African jurisprudence, the committing of a wrong by one person against another puts injurer and injured into a relationship of quasi-familial status which accretes other elements than the wrong itself. Payment of damages therefore repairs the injury done to the relationship as well as to the individual, while any fines paid into court repair wrongs to the relationship of wrongdoers with the community or the chief. All Pedi payments of nominal animals thus signal and effect modification to status formally conceived in terms of rights. To capture the significance of its transfer, we need to recognize the nominal animal currency of Sekhukhuneland as jural tender.

In Sekhukhuneland, jural tender is part of the vocabulary of everyday speech, not merely a creature of the courts or a wrought formality of important exchanges. Sums or amounts made up in jural tender are essential terms in conversations when people try to define the measure of a man or the nature of a situation. Thus jural tender has currency in a running commentary on social relations. Its utility in commentary derives from the detail and precision with which rights and subsets of rights are linked to constituted amounts of the jural currency. To know what is in payment is to know precisely what is in a contract. This point may be briefly illustrated.

What is transferred in a woman who is destined to be married is a set or "bundle" of rights. This bundle is divisible into distinct subsets of rights. In Sekhukhuneland, rights to sexual access, rights to domestic service, and rights in genetricem are conventionally distinguished as subsets. Each of these subsets is subject to a distinct act of transfer. It is, of course, moved from one holder to another by payment of a sum of nominal animals. When people make exchanges, the transfer of one subset of rights may or may not coincide with the transfer of other distinguishable parts of the bundle.

The amount of bridewealth that, in my account, was constituted on the eve of marriage was a compound sum. In it there were animals by whose transfer the groom secured rights to the domestic services of his wife. Other animals secured rights in genetricem. Typically, the groom would have gained sexual access to his future bride years or months before completion of the marriage negotiations. He would then have handed over the "cow of betrothal." Though it rarely happens today in Pedi country, rights in genetricem and rights to domestic service would be separately transferred if a debt of bridewealth were to be negotiated. A bridewealth debtor only gains full legal rights to his offspring once he has rendered bridewealth in full. Thus payments in jural tender can be broken down or built up to correspond with the analysis or synthesis of rights in persons. In effect, people can be taken apart and put together again by commenting on their status in relation to the transfers that subtend it. I have given only indicative details, but Pedi bridewealth is constituted so that the most wide-ranging discussions on relationships of marriage and affinity can be conducted in its idiom. Hence the statement of an amount of bridewealth that has been transferred to legitimize a particular marriage is cryptic. What Pedi isolate and comprehend in their formal statements concerning amounts of bridewealth is the signal value of the exchange. Imbued with signal value, any transfer of nominal animals in Sekhukhuneland is made a signal transaction.

MARKET VERSUS SIGNAL VALUE IN SOCIAL EXCHANGE

By now it should be clear that the transfer of Pedi bridewealth is doubly instrumental. Cash and jural tender are discrete currencies that serve as instrumentalities for the achievement of disparate ends. However, the contrast between cash and jural tender, though crucial, is unsatisfactory because it is culture-bound. Jural tender is something that belongs to Sekhukhuneland. The next step is to show that jural tender, while peculiarly Pedi, represents a general class of goods transferred in special types of social exchange. Here I am hampered by the relative underdevelopment of general notions of transactional types under the rubric of symbolic interaction.

In their market aspect, bridewealth deals in Sekhukhuneland yield readily to economic analysis. It is, for instance, no taxing task to account for one economic aspect of the deal. In Sekhukhuneland the terms for the payment of bridewealth have been shortened so that suitors must pay cash down to get their brides. While still a legal possibility, bridewealth debts are seldom negotiated. Further, the denial of credit facilities to suitors makes sound economic sense. Bridewealth has cash value and, by local standards, represents a large capital sum. Most suitors are bachelors, and Pedi bachelors are generally given a low credit rating, on grounds which are shrewdly assessed. The legal procedures for the recovery of bridewealth debts favor the continuance of a marriage and work in the debtor's rather than the creditor's favor. It can, in short, be shown that there is a general probability that any bridewealth debt will become a bad debt and the subject of dispute. On these grounds, with outspoken rationality, the guardians of Pedi brides justify their refusal to risk bad bridewealth debts. Economically, the payment of bridewealth comes into focus as the transfer of a large capital sum in a local economy where money is in short supply and where the payment of full bridewealth is itself regarded as an economic achievement that establishes the creditworthiness of the man. By achieving a marriage, a husband has demonstrated his ability to save. Precisely because of their prior investment and added responsibilities, married men can raise loans while bachelors are treated with suspicion.

While I have not sought to demonstrate the validity of these assertions about bridewealth debt, there has been no difficulty in presenting a summary characterization of the economic predicament. This is because the notions employed in the characterization are given. In contrast, a vocabulary for discussing the general character of Pedi bridewealth in its other aspect—that of a noneconomic but instrumental exchange—must be provided. This is surprising, because what Pedi jural tender represents is a mode of evaluation of the significance of things that is as general and familiar as the derivation of currencies that express economic worth.

The crux of the matter lies in the difference between formulations about the market value and the signal value of things. Here market value stands for what, in economics, is sweepingly referred to as the exchange value of an item. The market value of an item is simply the price it would realize at going rates if it were offered for sale on a local market. In a fully monetized economy, market value is the cash equivalent of an item. Wherever money is not the sole or dominant medium of economic exchange, the market value of an item can be expressed in terms of equivalents in goods or services for which it is customarily transferred in local barter or trade. To have market value, an item must be saleable or ordinarily the object of trade.

Signal value, in contrast, is the capacity of a standard item, introduced into a recognized form of exchange, to evoke the acceptance of grounds for the ascription of social potential to persons. Just as market value is contingent on the existence of a market and the possibility of sale, so signal value requires both a transacting public and recognized transactional forms. Thus while market value is dependent on economic exchange, signal value inheres in signal transactions—a highly conditional form of social exchange. A signal transaction is a standard and specialized act of social exchange whose completion establishes (or reasserts) grounds for ascribing particular capacities to relevant persons and/or for designating the social relationships into which, by virtue of the ascribed capacities, those persons are enabled or constrained to enter. A crucial difference between market and signal transactions is in the derivation of their currencies. Transfer of *the* proper items of signal value effects a signal transaction, while passing *an* appropriate sum of money effects a sale. The difference is in the relative restriction of the currencies of signal transactions, which are particularistically defined as exchange items that work highly specific ends. The particularization of the currency of signal transactions is further relevant as a source of limitation on negotiation between parties in social exchange. Parties to signal transactions must respect the form of the exchange. Their dealings must not only be mutually acceptable, they must also satisfy canons of propriety—or the dealings will fail to qualify as acts of signal value. What the parties cannot amend by mutual negotiation are any standard stipulations that specify the currency of a signal transaction. Signal transactions are interesting as a class both for the certainty of the outcomes they are designed to bring about and the inherent limitations to interpersonal negotiations that they impose.

There is, in any particular setting, an inevitable opposition between signal and market valuation. This opposition is most evident when, as in the case of Pedi bridewealth, signal valuation and market value are inherent in the same substantial objects of exchange. Faced with this contingency, Pedi reassert the signal value of bridewealth by placing a rarefied construction on the objects of exchange. Their taboo on the mention of cash puts primary public emphasis on the signal value of the items transferred. In any economy of social exchange, the signal value of things must be dissociated from market valuation. The distinction between market value and signal import is a general necessity.

This is well illustrated in Marriott's (1968) treatment of caste ranking and food transactions in Kishan Garhi, a village in Uttar Pradesh. Before showing how multiple transactions in the village serve to establish and assert the detailed discrimination entailed in ranking twenty-four castes, Marriott discusses the local ideology that assigns value to the range of objects that can be included in exchange. Marriott's aim is to distinguish socially discriminatory transactions from those that may be freely entered into without compromising the caste status of donor or recipient. To this end he establishes a hierarchy or graded series of types of food. Gifts of food that carry little or no discriminatory import are "honorific" because the recipient may use them at will. "Such a gift earns diffuse spiritual merit (*pun*) for the donor" (Marriott 1968: 143). At the other end of the scale are "inferior foods," so described because their acceptance establishes the inferiority of the recipient's caste rank relative to that of the donor. The discriminatory import of the transaction can be neutralized by symmetrical transfers—when individuals both give to, and receive from, one another inferior foodstuff. The burden of caste discrimination is carried by inferior grades of foodstuff that feature in asymmetrical transactions.

In Kishan Garhi "the best state of food is raw (*sidha*)" (Marriott 1968: 143). Then follows a superior category of cooked food that is "somewhat less freely convertible than raw foodstuffs" (*ibid.*). Most discriminatory is inferior cooked food (*kacca*). The acceptance of *kacca* food is most damaging in its social implications: "To accept inferior food is to accept one's lack of honour, one's more intimate, routine dependence on the food provider" (p. 144).

What clearly establishes exchanges of food in Kishan Garhi as signal transactions is the way they were adduced by Marriott's informants as the grounds for establishing the relative ranks of village castes. When required to determine the relative ranks of castes, the "villagers in almost every difficult case referred to ranked transactions in food and sometimes also to ranked relationships of service as bases for their decisions" (p. 141). Exchanges of food in Kishan Garhi fulfilled the requirements of signal transactions in that they supplied the grounds for ascription of capacities to persons and, further, designated the relationships into which, by virtue of caste position, people were enabled or constrained to enter. The arrangement of foods in a graded series is instructive. Uncompromising foods are also the most convertible; socially invidious prestations are not convertible. The most durable types of food generally fall into the honorific category (though this also includes less durable examples), while inferior foods are prepared foods and therefore perishable. Honorific exchanges are thus more like money, while the medium of a socially implicating transaction contributes to its ascriptive character. An important point for the village economy is that the raw foodstuffs that are the product of agriculture are released for economic as well as honorific exchange. Truck in raw foodstuffs is not in itself socially compromising. Caste rank is therefore not at issue in a wide range of dealing. It is, on the other hand, *the* issue when exchanges particularized by their currency are completed. No community can afford an economy in which there is no limitation to the number of transactions that carry signal values, for signal value is as much the enemy of free trade as market value is the opponent of signal import. One of the peculiarities of the Pedi situation was that the assertion of market value over and against signal value seemed to be the more threatening.

The contrast between market and signal value can be construed as a principled opposition. In principle, the usefulness of money both as a standard of value and a medium of exchange is that it opens up possibilities for conversion. In contrast, the assertion of signal value depends on the restriction, particularization, and dedication of transactional forms to specific ends.

The logic of ascription combines with the requirements for successful communication to dictate that the articulation of any signal transaction must characteristically be unequivocal and free of any redundancies or "noise." Here we can appeal to the form of the Pedi bridewealth transactions, in which ambiguities are eliminated on two fronts. In the first place, I noted that the constitution of bridewealth did not occur in an arena where serious negotiations about the real issue took place. Pedi tribesmen took time off to mark an end to the hard bargaining and to establish its culmination as a celebrated fact. Men negotiate toward the completion of signal transactions. Again, they may base their negotiations on the previously accomplished exchanges, which serve as grounds for their legitimate pretensions. Unlike an act of sale which enriches the vendor (or, at least, supplies him with cash), a signal transaction establishes facts. If these are contestable or if they can easily be denied, a signal transaction loses its force. Signal transactions are for a transacting public to recognize. If recognition is denied, a signal transaction reverts to a less implicating form of exchange. Signal transactions, therefore, mark the beginnings and the ends of negotiation and supply grounds for the conduct of further dealing, and in this respect they reflect the all-or-none character of ascriptive acts. If a social capacity is ascribed, it must be unstintingly ascribed: a man either is or is not married, either is or is not a member of a certain ranked caste. Signal transactions are reference points; they are completed in unique moments of time. Since they express outcomes, they cannot entertain uncertainty.

In the graded series of food transactions in Kishan Garhi, there was a commentary on convertibility which served to point the distinction between cash and the currencies peculiar to signal transactions. In the 1930s Nadel (1937) noted the emergence of what he called "a ritual currency" in Nupe country. The Nupe currency is cited here not because it furthers my analysis but because it shows a West African people faced with a problem that parallels the Pedi case.[3] Before the monetization of their economy, Nupe used cowries as a medium of exchange. Nadel (1942: 314) found that "Certain standardized amounts, e.g. brideprice, certain traditional gifts and payments, are expressed more often in cowrie shells than in modern money." Again, this was a manner of speaking, for the actual transfers were made not in cowries but in sums of cash. However, there were certain transfers—the payment of soothsayers, gifts given to mourners to signal their attendance at funerals, payments of musicians at rituals—in which those who performed a service had to be paid in real cowries. Each of these transactions served as a ground for establishing relationships of status between donor and recipient. Finally, Nadel described how cowries together with lengths of cloth were conspicuously wasted when thrown into the grave of a dead person to serve as a farewell gift: "this 'gift to the dead,' a public display and sacrifice at the same time of wealth, had the meaning of an index of social status and ambition" (Nadel 1937: 490). The farewell gift was, in other words, a declaration of signal intent. In general, when money coexists with traditional currency, the traditional currency, less used and no longer convertible, becomes appropriate to the expression of signal rather than market value. As Nadel (1937: 491) remarks of Nupe, "it looks as if the negligible trade which is still done in cowries, the last survival from an economic system smashed by 'culture contact,' were kept alive not so much by economic necessity as such as by the necessity to provide that special 'ritual currency' which in itself is nothing but a result of the same impact of culture contact." The Nupe mark signal transactions in two ways. Either they expend economically valueless but signally potent cowries or, like the Pedi, they gloss the transfer of money by describing monetary transactions as if these were still paid in a defunct coin. Either way, signal import is conveyed.

Two further points about Pedi practice can be clarified. Throughout my account I have emphasized the way in which, by invoking the notion of "spoiling" or "breaking taboo," the Pedi suppress formulations that frankly admit the monetization of bridewealth. The purpose of signal transactions is to communicate ascriptive grounds; the cash or market interpretation of the transfer could interfere with this communication. More precisely, the Pedi taboo ensures that the signal import of bridewealth is overcommunicated while, in public utterance, the market implications of bridewealth are undercommunicated. The point is that the Pedi do not deny the substantive nature of bridewealth—they ensure that the market value is soft-pedalled. Undercommunication and overcommunication have been proved to be useful ideas in discussing the presentation of self. The individual who is forced to make what is generally considered to be a less favored choice can, nonetheless, preserve his self-esteem by overcommunicating the pros and undercommunicating the cons of his decision (cf. Wadel 1973: 41). Pedi taboo here serves as a device for the institutionalized overcommunication of the more honorable and signal force of bridewealth transactions.

My final point concerns the seriousness of purpose and the levity of expression that curiously combine in the Pedi bridewealth scenario. How should this apparent combination of opposites be explained?

In Sekhukhuneland it is artifice that provides a currency to assert that bridewealth is a signal transaction. There is a contraposition between realms of discourse that is contrived and wholly owes its maintenance to a studied regard for constitutive rules. Contraposition of this kind provides the ideal circumstances for joking and the hilarious assertion of vital social truths. Tribesmen march off to constitute bridewealth on the basis that £5 counts as one cow or ten sheep or ten goats. This is fair enough. But they also know that, while £5 can count as a cow, it takes about £20 to buy a cow and that, to buy a good cow, even £20 will not suffice. I have referred to the formula that equates £5 with a cow as "economic nonsense." The formula, while signally important, is an absurdity. But then: "An absurd formula may, for instance, be used to highlight the solemnity of an occasion. A translation which emptied it of its absurdity, treating it, for instance, simply as the announcement of impending solemnity, would miss the fact that the absurdity is used as a means of conveying that something special is happening, and hence must be present, *as* absurdity" (Gellner 1973: 70).

I would like to say, in conclusion, that I have tried only to solve a puzzle that was of my own making. For the Pedi the contrast between money and the cash that becomes nominal animals is something given and unproblematic. *Chêlête* (the white man's money) and units of jural tender are items in the Pedi lexicon, part of every tribesman's vocabulary. Their use is governed by rules of lexical selection, and to understand the effects of these rules is only a beginning if one's aim is to understand the meaning of a text or commentary in which the words occur. In the end, my analysis is simply designed to give substance to the assertion that, when someone speaking in sePedi utters remarks that include mention of nominal sheep or goats or cattle, his predications will have signal import.

ACKNOWLEDGMENTS

I would like to thank Dr. P. T. W. Baxter, Professor M. Gluckman, and Professor B. Kapferer for their detailed and helpful comments on an earlier draft of this essay.

NOTES

1. Field work was carried out in Sekhukhuneland in 1960–1961 just as the South African currency was decimalized, rands and cents replacing pounds, shillings, and pence. Here I have quoted amounts in "old" rather than "new" money. I have previously discussed some aspects of the local economy of Sekhukhuneland (Sansom 1972).

2. The number of people who attend the making up of bridewealth is an indication of the popularity and social standing of the groom and members of his family. I witnessed the making up of bridewealth on six occasions, and my experience yields a lower limit of thirty and an upper limit of about fifty congregants at such events.

3. It should be evident that I regard signal transactions and signal value as notions of general applicability and their formulation as a proposed solution to a particular problem that is manifest in many guises in anthropological writings. I have noted that I depart from Mauss, for whom total prestations were inherently undifferentiated. Of particular relevance is Mauss's treatment of situations in which there has been a departure from original forms, when special symbolic exchanges accompany the "brute" exchange of items of economic worth (e.g., Mauss 1954: 47–53, 118–119). Recent publications that, like Nadel's Nupe material, provide discussion about cash and dilemmas concerning social value include the work of Davenport (1961) and Burridge (1971). In his "Filthy Lucre" Zakuta (1970) deals with such dilemmas in the contemporary United States.

REFERENCES

Aylward, A. 1870. *The Transvaal of Today*. Edinburgh: William Blackwood.

Burridge, Kenelm. 1971. *New Heaven, New Earth*. Oxford: Blackwell.

Davenport, W. 1961. When a primitive and civilised money meet. In Viola E. Garfield, ed., *Proceedings of the 1961 Annual Spring Meeting of the American Ethnological Society. Symposium: Patterns of Land Utilization and Other Papers*.

Gellner, E. 1973. *Cause and Meaning in the Social Sciences*. London: Routledge and Kegan Paul.

Gluckman, Max. 1950. Kinship and marriage among the Lozi of Rhodesia and the Zulu of Natal. In A. R. Radcliffe-Brown and Daryll Forde, eds., *African Systems of Kinship and Marriage*. London: Oxford University Press, for the International African Institute.

———. 1962. Les rites de passage. In Max Gluckman, ed., *Essays on the Ritual of Social Relations*. Manchester: Manchester University Press.

———. 1965. *The Ideas in Barotse Jurisprudence*. New Haven: Yale University Press.

Gray, Robert F. 1960. Sonjo bride-price and the question of African "wife-purchase." *American Anthropologist*, 62: 34–57.

Krige, E. J., and J. D. Krige. 1943. *The Realm of a Rain Queen*. London: Oxford University Press, for the International African Institute.

Marriott, McKim. 1968. Caste ranking and food transactions: a matrix analysis. In Milton Singer and Bernard S. Cohn, eds., *Structure and Change in Indian Society*. Chicago: Aldine.

Mauss, M. 1954. *The Gift*. Trans. Ian Cunnison. London: Cohen and West.

Nadel, S. F. 1937. A ritual currency in Nigeria—a result of culture contact. *Africa*, 10: 488–491.

———. 1942. *A Black Byzantium*. London: Oxford University Press, for the International African Institute.

Sansom, Basil. 1972. When witches are not named. In Max Gluckman, ed., *The Allocation of Responsibility*. Manchester: Manchester University Press.

Searle, J. 1972. What is a speech act? In Pier Paolo Giglioli, ed., *Language and Social Context*. Harmondsworth, Middlesex: Penguin.

Wadel, Cato. 1973. *Now, Whose Fault Is That?* Newfoundland Social and Economic Studies, No. 11. Toronto: Toronto University Press.

Zakuta, Leo. 1970. Filthy lucre. In Tamotsu Shibutani, ed., *Human Nature and Collective Behavior*. Englewood Cliffs, N.J.: Prentice-Hall.

Exchanging Words

DAVID PARKIN

THE AIM

The concept of exchange has two broad referents in anthropology. On the one hand the reference is to a universal and fundamental principle by which society and culture are organized. The principle is expressed in Malinowski's identification of the binding obligations of reciprocity, in Mauss's notion of the gift, and, at its most comprehensive, in Lévi-Strauss's view of the systems of cultural exchange involving women (and, one should add, men), goods and services, and messages, and in his view of the underlying rules regulating the interrelationships of these "surface" exchange systems (Lévi-Strauss 1963: 296).

On the other hand the concept of social exchange may refer microscopically to a process by which individuals' actions, beyond and apart from normative constraints, are governed by their personal perceptions of the most rewarding ends of relationships and the means by which such ends may be attained. The two partners to the relationship are engaged in a constant process of exchanging or withholding deference, affection, information, or material goods, of making concessions or securing recognition, all of which may alter their positions of dominance or power with regard to each other. Such processes are frequently referred to as transactions and, for consistency, I refer to their study as transactional analysis.

Transactional analysis draws its metaphors from familiar economic concepts and from game theory. Here it is interesting to note that, in a paper presented in 1952, Lévi-Strauss conceptually links together the rules underlying his systems of exchange and communication and those underlying the economic maximizing game theory of Von Neuman and Morgenstern (1944). The latter are quoted approvingly as contributing to a consolidation of social anthropology, economics, and linguistics into one great field (Lévi-Strauss 1963: 297–300). In referring to their work Lévi-Strauss uses such terms as "maximizing . . . to advantage" and "play, move, choice, and strategy" (*ibid.*, 298). He claims that the "formal" rules of marriage and the rules underlying individual or group strategies aimed at acquiring, for instance, the most or the best wives are susceptible to the same methods of investigation and, indeed, we dare interpret, are fundamentally of the same order.

And yet, in spite of this early conceptualization, the spirit of intellectual unity can hardly be said to be reflected in the influential transactional analyses of such

163

scholars as Bailey (1969), Barth (1966), Blau (1964), Homans (1958 and 1961), Kapferer (1972), Paine (1967 and elsewhere), and others, to say nothing of the numerous mathematically minded game theorists usually labelled as economists, sociologists, or political scientists.

To confine ourselves to anthropology colleagues, why have they rejected the search for common factors linking the two kinds of rules? Is it because they believe that the two kinds are simply not of the same explanatory order? Or because their intensive focus on the individual, or on the group acting as an individual, technically precludes a more comprehensive analysis of socially more extensive rule systems? Though rarely explicit, both of these may be found as reasons.

Bailey, it is true, does formulate an important distinction between normative and pragmatic rules (1969: 4ff.), which has echoes of Firth's normative asymmetry of ideals, expectations, and action (1951), as well as of Lévi-Strauss's mechanical and statistical models (1963: 283–289). But Bailey's rules are, as he frankly points out (p. 17f.), at a more "concrete" level of abstraction than those mathematically formulated by Von Neuman and Morgenstern, and, it is reasonable to assume, than those more general rules of communication proposed by Lévi-Strauss.

On the one hand, then, Lévi-Strauss and, in his own view, Von Neuman and Morgenstern deal with rules of exchange which are products (or "ends") of logical systems, whether the system be mathematics, marriage, mythology, or language. On the other hand, the transactional analysts are dealing with rules which indicate *means* to ends and arise from the condition of man as a maximizing and economizing animal able to choose for himself independent courses of action. This chapter is an attempt to relate the latter to the former: I want to show that individual strategizing does indeed operate within areas of choice and "rational" means-to-end relationships but that, at a more inclusive level, the choices are set in ordered categories of social and personal meaning over which the individual per se has little if any control. These larger categories are themselves governed systematically by rules. The distinction is essentially (and not merely analogously) the classical Saussurian one between *parole,* by which individual creativeness is manifested in unique utterances, and *langue,* which paradoxically directs this creativeness by requiring it to be expressed by reference to, though not necessarily in slavish imitation of, an existing body of grammatical rules. In short, the constraints on choice are the limitations of any grammar of communication, in both its positive and negative aspects.

My starting point is to consider the methodological assumptions of transactional analysis. I go on to suggest that while transactional analysis looks for the points of disjunction in human relations, that related branch of anthropology also focused on interpersonal relationships, symbolic interactionism, tends to emphasize the points of conjunction, mutual satisfaction, and harmony. From this I then argue that, both in the anthropologists' methodological assumptions and in the cultures of the people they study, we can distinguish the operation of two conceptually opposed ideologies: of negotiable (i.e., disjunctive) and altruistic (i.e., conjunctive) exchange. The ideologies are examples of the ordered sets of social and personal meaning mentioned above whose logical relationship to each other is governed by more general rules of communication. These in turn provide a kind of underlying cultural blueprint for the specific (e.g., normative and pragmatic) rules of interaction obtaining within a particular culture.

THE METHODOLOGICAL ASSUMPTIONS
OF TRANSACTIONAL ANALYSIS

Enough has been written about transactional analysis for us to agree on a number of immediately obvious defining characteristics. The field is concerned with actors consciously or nonconsciously taking decisions and making choices. These decisions and choices are based on a notion of rationality in the terms of the particular culture. The notion of rationality assumes the existence of material and nonmaterial objects of value. It further assumes that men are generally impelled to possess or have access to these valued objects and that they do so at what they perceive to be the minimum cost to themselves. But the very existence of *valued* objects implies that the objects are technically limited in quantity, or conversely that they are relatively scarce, and that, therefore, men are engaged in a zero-sum game necessarily predicating competition.

These are some of the distinctive properties of the approach. They are assumptions about human behavior and cognitive orientation. Provided that you start with the notion of actor, any of the other four or five assumptions can follow and the explanatory paradigm falls logically into order. For example, the actor is capable of selecting between alternative courses of action; he does so while playing in a zero-sum game; this assumes that he is competing for valued objects; the game further implies consensus among the combatants about the rules of competition; the agreement about rules implies a common conception of rationality within the terms of the game (i.e., within the terms of a given culture); rationality, as a cultural conception of the most *efficient* organization of means to ends in social action, assumes that men are likely to maximize their chances of attaining desired goals at least cost, or certainly not at greatest cost, to themselves. And so on.

Leaving aside the question of whether this kind of tautology is justified if it can be used as a heuristic device (see Kapferer 1972: 5 on Blau 1964), I wish to consider three issues arising from it: the concepts of value and of rationality, and the extent to which individuals can operate freely beyond and apart from the wider institutional and normative constraints of society.

Regarding the first issue, I think that Kapferer puts his finger on what is important when he asks us to discover "the circumstances which may lead individuals to value the activity in which they are engaged for the intrinsic qualities of the activity itself rather than for the benefits it may typically bring" (1972: 6). I regard this as referring to the process by which certain kinds of activities may achieve a state of unquestionable legitimacy or sanctity, and so become imbued with symbolic justification. We move closer here to the familiar view that all kinds of transaction, material and nonmaterial, are to be understood as a process of symbolic communication.

With regard to the second issue, Kapferer also asks us to discover "the conditions under which an individual or group may display one kind of rationality rather than another" (1972: 6). Though the jargon is clumsy, I think it may be preferable to refer to the different kinds of rationality as different emic *sets* of classification and explanation within a culture. That is to say, I am interested in the way in which people within a culture may "switch" from one mode to another of classifying, explaining, and justifying events and behavior as "rational." The etic rationality of the external observer—for example, the view that man is fundamentally an economizing animal—is assumed to be over and above these folk rationalities and to be based on universal rather than particular cultural rules, an assumption which ignores ethnocentric intellectual bias. The distinction between emic and etic modes of explanation suffers the stigma of once fashionable concepts. But the distinction does enable us to ask whether, for example, the "values," "roles," and "statuses" being newly generated by social interaction fit logically into the actor's views of his culture (emic), or whether they can be identified as part of "our," the outside observer's, analytic categories (etic).

The third issue, the extent to which individuals may manipulate social relationships independently of normative and institutional constraints, is complex. Kapferer approvingly contrasts Blau with Homans and Barth: Blau "does not view individuals as independent social actors and he attempts to avoid the dangers of psychological reductionism"; through his concept of "emergent property," Blau "recognizes that wider structural and institutional processes influence individual action" (Kapferer 1972: 6–7).

Barth and Homans certainly suggest a kind of individualistic reductionism. Homans announces himself frankly as an "ultimate psychological reductionist" (1958: 597); and Barth suggests that though roles (i.e., actual performance) may be generated by statuses (i.e., sets of rules of interaction) we can only understand the ways in which these latter are generated by starting "on a more elementary level" (1966: 3). It is true that Barth explicitly excludes a "psychological" explanation (p. 5) of this elementary level, which he sees as based on transactional or reciprocal evaluations of behavior. But when we look at the one empirical context in which his ideas are applied, that of a fishing vessel off the coast of Norway, we find him claiming that a consistent pattern of the fishermen's behavior "can only be explained in terms of *their* transactional obligation, involving prestations of willingness or eagerness and constant readiness to work, as well as their interest in observing, evaluating, and controlling the dispositions of the skipper" (p. 8). Not quite a psychological explanation perhaps, but one that leaves us in no doubt as to the emphasis placed on the individual in the explanation. Nevertheless, Barth has constant need of the concept of role in the section of his paper that deals with this one empirical context, a point of some significance as I shall indicate below.

That said, I do not really see a significant difference between Blau's concept of emergent property and Barth's notion of a generative model, or even between these and Homans' description of an exchange paradigm in his 1958 essay (pp. 598–599). Perhaps the difference for Kapferer is one of intention, for Blau does "attempt to bridge the gap between abstract institutional and normative explanations of social behaviour and the psychological reductionism exemplified in Homans' theory of social exchange" (Kapferer 1972: 7). More generally, this relates to the now rather worn debate about the relative merits of methodological individualism and holism (for recent examples see Boissevain 1968, Cohen 1969, Gluckman 1968, Kennedy 1967, and Paine 1967). Mitchell states succinctly that the analysis of social relationships in terms of social networks anchored on individuals is not a substitute for an analysis in terms of social institutions, that the two involve different levels of abstraction, and that they in fact complement one another (1969: 14–15, 48–49). At first sight this would seem to imply that the debate referred to above centers on a false problem—that there is in fact nothing to debate, since both analytical dimensions are necessary and we cannot therefore prefer one to the other.

This invites two comments. First, the two dimensions are indeed complementary, in the way that any social analysis must comprehend the organization of interpersonal as well as collective relationships and activities. But there is still considerable room for debate as to (a) how much *emphasis* may be placed on either in the interpretation of data and, most important, (b) how much "change" (however this is defined) in either dimension is determined by change in the other. The answer to (a) may indeed be a matter of preference between micro and macro: wife beating may be explained as a product of a particular correlation of personal networks and conjugal expectations, but may also be explained as a product of a combination of institutional and historical factors characterizing the development of specific social and economic strata. The answer to (b) is commonly that the idea of a feedback mechanism ensures that both institutional and personal influences can be accommodated within a single analysis. But this is something of a blind, since it is clear that the feedback is not seen as evenly flowing; moreover, the very *raison d'être* of transactional analysis, with its concepts of "emergent property" and "generative model," is to demonstrate the creation of new social forms ("institutional change") out of the processes of personal interaction—with historical, institutional, and wider economic and political forces as little more than environments exercising short-term restraint and offering manipulable resources. There remains much to debate.

The second comment, however, is that Mitchell himself, while repudiating an exclusively structural-functional holistic approach, is not by any means an individual reductionist. Whatever the varying views of his fellow contributors to *Social Networks in Urban Situations,* Mitchell turns to the concept of role to link the explanations of institutional normative processes on the one hand and processes of personal interaction on the other (1969: 45–46). The concept of role is given only a few paragraphs' attention (and, of the three orders of relationships identified by Mitchell, the structural, categorical, and egocentric, relates very closely to the structural), but they are illuminating and important. From different theoretical standpoints, then, both Barth and Mitchell make use of the concept of role.

Let me do some recapping. I have reconsidered three issues, arising from methodological assumptions in transactional analysis, which may now be stated as simple propositions. First, the most familiar one: material and nonmaterial transactions can be regarded as aspects of a more general process of symbolic communication. Second, we may usefully incorporate in our analyses the distinction between emic and etic categories and explanations of social process. And third, the concept of role, and by implication role theory generally, emerges as an important descriptive and analytical "bridge" linking institutional and ego-centered explanations of social process.

These three propositions overlap. (1) Symbolic communication by definition has its own grammar or system of rules which (2) can be analyzed (phon)emically as well as (phon)etically, while (3) the concept of role itself refers to a main component of symbolic communication which can be explored at a "subjective" level, in terms of a culture's emic categories, or at an "objective" level, in terms of an inferred universal or etic set of categories. In either case, role is ultimately a verbal symbol. I do not want to become bogged down in this chapter in the emic/etic distinction, and do no more than use it as a piece of shorthand methodological notation.

Bearing in mind the overlap, I shall deal with these three propositions. After that I shall attempt to show that, whatever else it may involve, social interaction must be understood as the transaction of symbols and that what we conventionally call social change can be viewed as the transaction of those kinds of verbal symbol which we call roles.

MATERIAL AND NONMATERIAL EXCHANGE AS SYMBOLIC COMMUNICATION

Rewards of Exchange

Analytically we can distinguish between (a) the rewards, goals, or ends of exchange and (b) the items or media of exchange—that is, what is actually transacted. Empirically these are sometimes, though not always, the same. The focus on rewards puts the emphasis on the actor and on economizing or maximizing behavior aimed at the acquisition of material *and* nonmaterial "goods." As Burling puts it, in opposition to the view that economic anthropology is primarily and even exclusively concerned with material goods, "we must repeatedly economize *between* material and non-material ends. We must make repeated choices between goals, some of which are material while some are not. We must decide whether added leisure is more important to us than the extra money we could earn by working overtime. Would I rather have a new car or a trip to Europe?'' (1962: 803).

A logical extension of this view, as all transactional analysts seem to agree, is that it is the satisfaction of cultural ''values'' which is the reward of all successful transactions, whether the value is in the possession of a material good or in some intangible item like ''the symbols of approval or prestige'' (Homans 1958: 606). But of course a cultural value is itself symbolic: whatever the personal intentions of the new-car buyer, his choice of car, and his own genuine protestations that the car is for purely ''practical'' rather than, say, prestige purposes, he is by his very purchase of the vehicle slotted into one of a number of categories of car owners and so is, to a lesser or greater degree, likely to be accredited with particular social characteristics. Apart from being distinguished from persons who do not own cars, he is distinguished by year, size, condition, color, and make of car. This is not to say that, like turbans on ''chiefly'' Kachin, these distinctions necessarily make statements about his status, as car insurance firms feel obliged to assume. They may indeed do so, though frequently wrongly and inconsistently. They constitute some of the forms of the everyday cosmology of an industrial society, in which persons are identified by and with consumer goods and thus classified. The totemic parallel may be spurious, but it is clear that many people do have crude stereotypes of a Volkswagen owner as distinct from a Morris Minor or Jaguar owner. Their stereotypes are constructed no doubt out of the more specific exegesis of the car dealer and mass media experts, but are also formed by currents of public opinion arising from observation and rumor. Whether we intend or like it or not, then, the material rewards of exchange locate us in a system of social classification and ''stand for'' or symbolize popular conceptions (or, if you like, misconceptions) of social and personality types pertinent to our particular culture or subculture.

The example is extreme, but it demonstrates an analytical shift from the actor to the environment in which he acts. The parties to a relationship may indeed control much of the way in which transactions are conducted between them, but settlement of the deal and due apportionment of the rewards of exchange place them in a classificatory frame over which they have little, if any, control. In this respect it is irrelevant whether the rewards of exchange are material cars or the nonmaterial ''symbols of approval or prestige'' to which Homans refers, since both place the actor controlling the transaction in a more general cultural scheme of symbolic classification. The nonmaterial is by definition conceptual and so subsumes the material, the value of which can only be interpreted by the actor within a scheme of intellectual and verbal classification.

Gift Exchange

When we turn to the items and not just the rewards of exchange, we encounter an analytical distinction which is difficult to substantiate empirically. A strict interpretation of the distinction would imply that some transactional media (material and nonmaterial) are unambiguously means to ends. Transactional analysis, in its emphasis on the rationality of actors, and implicitly on a distinction between means and ends, takes a subjective starting point: the means and ends of an exchange relationship are what the analyst interprets as its costs and rewards in the minds of the actors. Moreover, what may be a reward of exchange now (say, the acquisition of wealth or some "symbols of approval") may at a later stage be bartered in a "new" (or continuation of the "old") relationship. Or, the means of exchange may be ends in themselves at one point in time (i.e., they are "expressive" in that they produce short-term gratification, as Parsons would say) but may be means to further ends at a later point in time (i.e., they are "instrumental" in that they produce long-term gratification). Goods which are transacted, therefore, may be either means or ends of exchange, depending on the actor's perception of the use to which they are being put within a specific time sequence. This is itself open to the analyst's interpretation.

It follows that the only transactional medium which can be identified in the actor's mind as unambiguously both a means and end of exchange is Malinowski's "pure" gift. Like true love, with all its pains and pleasures, the "pure" gift is both cost and reward. Now, as outside analysts we know well that the "expressive" exchange of gifts can have the unintended consequence of eventually securing nonaltruistic interests. Looked at from the outside, the expressive is thus seen to be instrumentally effective. But the very use of the word "gift," the meaning of which I assume to have universal semantic identification of one kind or another, indicates that we see the actor as concerned primarily with the altruistic interpretation. However, culturally approved altruistic exchange, when carried on in more than simply ephemeral contexts, frequently and perhaps always establishes accumulated and even corporately held material and nonmaterial interests. This being the case, the actor who voluntarily engages in altruistic exchange, yet is unaware of the growing web of utilitarian interests enveloping him, thereby subscribes unquestioningly to whatever moral dictates buttress the altruism.

Put in a more familiar vein, then, institutionalized gift exchange is loaded with moral content: the morality proclaims altruism, or such similar ethoses as egalitarianism, while concealing the development of a range of personal and group interests which are unlikely, in "reality," to be distributed equally. But we know that a system of morality is rarely communicated to an interacting population in the form of rational argument. Symbols do the job more effectively. What are the symbols in institutionalized gift exchange? Do they emanate from the gift itself or from the relationship in which the transactions occur? In fact they come from both. To argue that it is the social relationship alone out of which the symbolism arises is tautological, for this is tantamount to saying that a morally binding relationship is symbolized only by itself. The communicative power of a symbol has its initial locus in either a concrete object, a gesture, or a word, and ultimately in an abstract idea. What better in gift exchange than that the initial locus be the gift itself? The gift may assume a variety of forms, material and nonmaterial, and may be said to release symbolic "meaning" in the context of the relationship. The symbol itself may be regarded as de Saussure's "sign," which can be broken down into two components: the "signifying," in other words the locus or gift itself; and the "signified," or the social relationship. The general "meaning" of the symbol is then the social implications and consequences of the perpetuation of this particular culturally recognized relationship of gift exchange as distinct from other such relationships.

If the gift can be regarded as the signifying component of the sign, then we are attributing an active rather than passive role to it: we are claiming that, like the form of a word, it is an inanimate material object, yet that, in conjunction with whatever is signified, it can exert sufficient force to stimulate our perceptions and evoke an intellectual response. I find this view close to the first part of Mauss's largely intuitive belief that "The thing given is not inert. It is alive and often personified, and strives to bring to its original clan and homeland some equivalent to take its place" (Mauss 1970: 8). And if we accept the likelihood, as anthropologists seem to, that a gift triggers reciprocal obligations to repay, then we surely accept the second part of the statement. I do not mean that we accept it literally in its form as an ethnographic metaphor, any more than we accept that a gift among Maori necessarily has a "magical and religious hold over the recipient" (*ibid.*). May I speculate that Mauss was here expressing his intuition through what he regarded as correct ethnography—or perhaps he unintentionally fitted the ethnography to his intuition?

On the basis of his own extensive field work in the area, Firth has questioned the validity of Mauss's ethnography (1967: 9–10), and we must accept this objection. But even if the ethnographic examples were correct, they would still be no more than particular cultural realizations of a presumably universal mutual responsiveness of the consciences of donors and receivers which keeps the exchange of gifts going until honor is satisfied or enmity expressed and conscience therefore made redundant. In short, not only the process of transacting gifts, but the very choice of which gift to transact, locates the donor and receiver in a wider scheme of symbolic classification. I once witnessed an anthropologist of upper-class origin commenting on the alleged tendency of working-class people to give each other sweet (rather than dry or medium) sherry for Christmas. Whether or not this is true, it is clear that here the "thing," sweet as opposed to medium or dry sherry, had classified not only working-class gift exchange but, by its negative innuendo, a perception by the upper class of its own rules of gift exchange. I instance this genuine if trivial case concerning an anthropologist to illustrate how all of us are frequently unaware of how, in our choices, we are ourselves classified by the objects of our evaluation. Examples abound in everyday speech.

NEGOTIABLE AND ALTRUISTIC IDEOLOGIES OF EXCHANGE

I have examined the analytical distinction between the means and ends of exchange. Transactional analysts impute rationality to actors who strive to ensure that the rewards of exchange (the ends) are worth more than the costs (the means).

The attainment of the reward goes beyond satisfying the actor's drive toward maximization of self-interest. Whether material or nonmaterial, it locates him in a symbolic system which, at its most significant, classifies whole social categories, and at its most trivial invokes elementary personal stereotypes. Taking culturally recognized gift exchange as the one example in which the actor minimizes his perception of differences between costs and rewards, we find that here too the choice and nature of the gift (whether material or nonmaterial) locate the donor and receiver in the same overall symbolic system of classification.

Transactional analysts have concentrated on the more "rational" kind of transactions rather than on gift exchange, because they have seen the former as fundamental in generating new forms of social organization. But I would hypothesize that patterns of gift exchange can be at least as potent, if not more potent, forces for change. Their high moral content facilitates the symbolic and therefore unquestioned ideal of altruism which may act as an unintended cover for the development of utilitarian interests between donor and receiver. Where the development of these interests becomes increasingly biased in favor of one of the two parties, then the discrepancy between the altruistic ideal and the utilitarian content of the relationship is particularly marked. As a general process characterizing exchange spheres other than that of gifts, this is at the heart of many examples of emerging social inequality: in a recent publication (1972) I showed how two custom-hallowed exchange spheres centering respectively on bridewealth and funerary expenditure symbolized a supposedly "egalitarian" order of relations, yet in the long term actually facilitated the economic differentiation of social categories in an African farming community.

The two types of exchange, altruistic and nonaltruistic, are of course familiar anthropological fodder. To take a recent and important example, Sahlins has proposed a spectrum of reciprocities which extends from altruistic ("pure gift") generalized reciprocity at one end, through balanced reciprocity in the middle (nonexploitative and overlapping with gift exchange), to negative reciprocity at the other end. Negative reciprocity includes "transactions opened and conducted toward net utilitarian advantage.... The participants confront each other as opposed interests, each looking to maximize utility at the other's expense" (1965: 148).

The spectrum can be reduced to the two poles of altruistic and negotiable (or exploitative) exchange to correspond with the distinction with which I have been dealing. Sahlins associates movements along the spectrum with large-scale, morphological, and partially evolutionary developments of society. This is the level of abstraction and generalization at which he has chosen to operate and, as far as I can judge, it is both legitimate and borne out by the admirably detailed evidence he presents. But Sahlins obviously does not deny the coexistence of the different modes of exchange in a society at one point in time, and indeed I think his findings can be used to suggest a range of possible combinations of this coexistence.

In an essay concerned with interpersonal exchange, I am clearly dealing with a level of abstraction which is much more limited in time and space and in its range of types of society. I am concerned with the coexistence of the two idioms of exchange and their covariant relationship, a matter to which Davis (1973: 166) draws our attention. Transactional analysts, by focusing on the rationality and the maximization of self-interest of actors, have obliged themselves to consider negotiable exchange as a fundamental fact of all human behavior rather than as one of two principal modes by which actors may interpret the forms of exchange in interaction. I argue, however, that as ideologies the two modes can be treated as independent, covariant social facts.

Let me try to elaborate on this. Transactional analysts require that the most significant social relationships be regarded as transactions between parties. So far, so good. They impute rationality and the maximization of self-interest to the actors. That is to say, they climb into the minds of the actors and see them managing their relationships according to a personal, but socially universal, program which urges them to achieve profit at minimal cost. But, unlike what is implicit in Sahlins' scheme, the transactional approach does not appear to be concerned with whether or not this is a culturally valued process. The maximization of self-interest *can* be recognized by a part or the whole of a society, as a cultural ideology. As examples we have the Dionysian ethos, the "get-ahead-quick" ideals in many Western commercial career contexts, and the local acceptance of the institution of *chakari* and other forms of institutional exchange as "bribery" in Nepal (Caplan 1971). In a complementary but opposite manner, institutionalized gift exchange is based on an ideology of altruism. In referring to "ideologies," anthropologists have tended to focus their analyses on those which emphasize the altruistic "goodness" of man; and when they focus on "negative" ideologies, like beliefs in witchcraft, they frequently place them apart from altruism. But, of course, an ideology of witchcraft is of the same analytical order as an ideology of altruism or ennobling morality.

There are, then, ideologies of negotiation just as there are altruistic ones; they may coexist in the same social situation and, in variable combinations, in the same society.

The central tenet of transactional analysis, however, appears to be that the maximization of self-interest is an axiomatic and universal feature of the human condition that underlies the exchange nature of social relations. Transactional analysis does not attempt to identify and analyze those social circumstances in which this supposed axiom of human behavior is raised to a level of cultural consciousness and identification. This is surely incomplete: it is like recognizing as an axiom the human propensity to symbolize and impose intellectual order on man's physical environment but neglecting to consider also the recognizable cultural manifestations of this propensity.

In summary I suggest that the transactional nature of relationships obliges us to take into account not only the actor's view of means and ends as costs and profits, but also the fact that these means and ends, as "goods" transacted and acquired, are "things" which, because they fall into cultural systems of classification, locate the actor in these systems. Where the perceived relationship between the "thing" and the actor is very close and even "intimate," as in Mauss's view of the gift, then the "thing" may be said to provide the primary locus for the symbolic expression of the social relationship. This is most obvious in institutionalized gift exchange but is surely embryonic in all individual cases of "pure gift" giving.

Similarly, there can be a perceived close relationship between the actor and the goals or rewards of an exchange relationship: goals and rewards valued by the actor are also culturally valued; and so the actor's social fortunes are tied up with the more general cultural evaluations of these "things." To my mind, the most important contribution of Barth is his emphasis on changing ecological conditions as constituting variable environments of opportunity. Ultimately it is ecological (and we might also add, technological) conditions which govern the availability of valued goods; and, though cultural evaluations of the rewards of exchange are not strictly *determined* by techno-ecological conditions, these conditions impose limits on the intensity of such cultural evaluations. If diamonds were discovered and produced in uncontrollable abundance, or if an unprecedentedly large number of persons in a society assumed saintly dispositions, there would surely follow some cultural redefinition of the places of these "things" in the system of values. Diamonds might even cease to be regarded as rewards of negotiable exchange relationships; they might assume the status of "cheap" and therefore more frequently transacted gifts. Saintliness might cease to be bestowed through an ideologically "pure gift" relationship with a god, spirit, or prophet, and instead be legitimately regarded as the prize of successful bargain and negotiation with these agencies. Thus the two ideologies of negotiable and altruistic exchange would be preserved as coexisting spheres of cultural evaluation, but with some transposition of the "goods" transacted in them.

ROLE TERMS AS SYMBOLS OF EXCHANGE

To say that actors' choices of rewards and gifts locate them in a wider environment of cultural and symbolic classification is to raise again the issue of the relationship between the micro and macro levels of analysis—between individuals making strategic choices in interaction and normatively defined institutional frameworks. I repeat that I agree with Mitchell, whom I do not regard as a transactional analyst, in viewing these two levels of analytical abstraction as complementary rather than as alternatives, though I think also that one may be emphasized much more than the other, to the latter's possible detriment. The concept which seems to lock these two levels in flexible but balanced complementarity is that of "role."

Have we really recognized Nadel's contribution here? As well as viewing role as an intermediary between society and the individual, he recognized it as operating "in that strategic area where individual *behaviour* becomes social conduct." Even more importantly, he argued that the concept of role was based as much on systems of "linguistic" (meaning "verbal") classification as on observation of "constancies of behaviour" (1956: 20). In other words, "roles" are more than consistent ways in which people carry out tasks; they are above all verbally identifiable. The distinction is akin to the etic/emic one. The question is: With whose verbal identifications do we start our analysis of other societies? With our own semantic labels or with those of the society under study?

This is not quite the simple methodological question it seems. Though in our distinction between "society" and "culture" we always attempt not to confuse our "subjective" with our "objective" criteria, we tend to use the concept of role "objectively," superimposing a seemingly agreed set of terms for distinct types of social conduct. At the most general level we talk of ritual experts, political representatives, jural spokesmen, economic managers, homestead heads, and so on; and at the most specific we identify witches, doctors, priests, warriors, elders, chiefs, plaintiffs, defendants, litigants, entrepreneurs, and others. Such concepts as role differentiation, role reinforcement, role conflict, and role deviance are also used in this "objective" manner.

Now it is precisely through the use of such agreed "etic" concepts that social anthropology and sociology are able to formulate hypotheses and test them cross-culturally. They are part of our common language of discourse without which communication becomes impossible. They may sometimes reflect the dispositions and prejudices of centuries of Judeo-Christian thought, but they are all we have.

Nevertheless, though with Berreman (1966) I balk at the extreme formalism of much ethnoscience, I share the concern expressed by Sturtevant (1964) and others at the continuing tendency in much anthropology to omit any systematic discussion of how these imposed classifications relate to classifications of the same activities in the particular culture (see Whiteley 1966). Does the culture have a specific term for plaintiff, for defendant, or for witness? Does it have many such terms for what we would identify as one role? Or are some of our roles expressed only by phrases (i.e., *paroles*) in the culture's language, phrases which have to be created anew every time the person's activity is described? There is, in other words, an emic as well as an etic classification of forms of social conduct, and the relationship between them is essentially that between what we commonly call "subjective" and "objective" criteria. But whereas the description "subjective" suggests "ideal" or "imagined" phenomena, supposedly observed by us in the minds of our informants and distinct from the "factual objectivity" solely dependent on our own observations and judgments, the emic/etic distinction places both views of culture within a verbal and ultimately linguistic framework. Is this an advantage? It supposedly is, for that kind of study in which one wishes on the one hand to place systematic emphasis upon the cultural meanings which actors attach to events and on the other hand to avoid exaggerating the uniqueness of a particular culture. The etic, if the linguistic analogy is correct, represents a theoretically limited range of "roles," only some of which are socially significant in a particular culture and only some of which are given consistent semantic identification.

In practice it is neither possible nor necessarily fruitful to attempt an etic classification of all the roles (even assuming agreement on the definition of this concept) identified in human cultures. For American society alone, Klapp (1962) is reported to have identified a folk classification of over 800 roles (Sturtevant 1964). It may be here that the analogy with phonetics, concerned as it is with a technically limited human physical capacity for making communicable sounds, breaks down. For role, as a concept, cannot be reduced to physical features. Moreover, it is an element of man's symbolic creativity which, by definition, is unlimited. Our "etic" classification of roles is, in the end, no more than the somewhat arbitrary collection of concepts which we use in sociological discourse.

So, to return to my question, do we start our field work by fitting this collection of concepts to our observations? Or do we start with a folk classification of "social types"—that is, roles operated by members of the particular society in which we are working? Though the two must constantly be kept in mind and seen against each other, I find persuasive the case for explicitly and systematically starting with the people's own classification. Indeed, I suspect that, less systematically, this is what we always do, but then we slip from the vernacular terms and phrases to our neater analytical ones. In the process of translation from folk concepts to "scientific" ones, we not only distort emic features to fit them to our own way of thinking (cf. Douglas 1973: 27), we also miss the opportunity of tracing *changes* going on within the folk classifications. Consider, for example, the gradual adoption of loan words in place of an earlier variety of phrases, many formed on the spot, to describe "new" or innovatory roles and objects. This movement from the use of a wide and potentially infinite variety of phrases to the use of a single word or limited number of words represents not only a transition to phonemic economy and specificity, but also the development of formal terminological categories out of more wordy functional ones (Bruner et al. 1956, in Spradley 1972: 173). From a psychological perspective, Bruner illustrates the development thus: "From 'things I can drive this tent stake with' we move to the concept 'hammer' and from there to 'mechanical force.' "

The Giriama of Kenya, among whom I worked, seem not to have a single vernacular term for "entrepreneur." Since the Second World War, entrepreneurs in their current, "capitalist" form (defined in Parkin 1972: 8) have emerged in numbers in the area in which I worked. The "traditional" term *shaha*,[1] which refers to a person of wealth *and* authority, could conveniently be used to refer to entrepreneurs. Elders do use it, but less often than such phrases as *atumia enye mali* (literally, "elders having property") or simply *enye mali* ("having property") and other, less common phrases. The Swahili-Arabic loan term *mtajiri* ("rich merchant") and sometimes even the abstract term *utajiri* ("wealth") tend to be used by younger men, though all age categories of men (not women) appear to be equally competent in Swahili. The apparent partial eclipse of the more traditional term *shaha* by the Swahili root term *-tajiri,* conceptually mediated by intervening phrases, tells us something of the ideological conflict going on in Giriama. Elders by no means fully accept the customary legitimacy of modern capitalistic entrepreneurship and, it may be speculated, are reluctant to attach the term *shaha,* with its sense of wealth incurred through *legitimate* authority, to this new phenomenon.

It is almost inevitable that, as in other languages, both types of reference, the variable phrase (the "functional" or descriptive category) and the invariable word (the formal category), will continue to coexist, the former perhaps increasingly the euphemism or circumlocution for the latter. It is precisely this coexistence of the two types of signification that permits the fitting of new concepts to existing lexicons, for varying phrases can smuggle in modifications of "meaning" beneath the single term to which the phrases are perceived to be attached. We can speculate that the changes in connotation of such well-known anthropological terms as "native," "primitive," and "tribe" have been mediated through innumerable attached phrases of this kind. The loan word, by contrast, may represent a terminological abridgment of concepts which challenge too fundamentally and rapidly some key cultural rules and ideologies. This goes counter to the conventional view that loan terms are adopted because they already depict a particular practice. Sometimes this is indeed the case. But often the borrowed term by no means replicates the original "meaning"; consider the famous pan-Indian and African example of *hoteli,* which refers to a cafe/eating house/shop rather than to a place offering accommodation—for what sense would there be in paying for accommodation when there are likely to be "relatives" nearby to provide it? In the Giriama example, the Swahili-Arabic root term *-tajiri,* insofar as it is used more by young than by older men, parallels a growing cleavage in the society between young farmers who are accumulating property and those who are losing it (the latter conceptualized as "elders"). In other words, this "drastic" adoption of a loan word corresponds with a recent economic cleavage which is itself associated with cognitive dissonance—in the sense that disputes about appropriate and inappropriate behavior center on a perceived conflict between what I earlier called altruistic and negotiable ideologies, associated respectively with property-losing elders and entrepreneurial younger men. I shall return to this ethnography later.

It is not the adoption of loan words with which I am specially concerned. I used the loan word as an extreme example of the formalization of diffuse modes of classification in single words rather than phrases. A folk concept of "role" or "social type" (like that of "policeman" or the Nuer *kuaar muon/kuaar twac,* meaning "leopard-skin chief") is of course a formalized abridgment of the same kind: like Turner's symbol it condenses a fan of meanings around a core,[2] within a single acoustic form. Put simply, then, the verbal concept of a role is a symbol. This is hardly surprising for, as Sapir noted long ago, the word is the symbol of all symbols. But the verbalization of social type, which we call a culturally recognized role, contains within its particular symbolic configuration specific information about the expectations, aims, and qualities of actors, and even about some of the rules for interaction.

The wheel is coming full circle and we can talk again about the analysis of exchange. The idea that verbalized roles are symbols, the information from which is constantly and selectively exchanged by persons in interaction, is surely central to that general field which, after Blumer's original coining of the term, we call symbolic interactionism. Consider, for example, Blumer's and Mead's discussion of role taking (Blumer 1969, in Spradley 1972: 76). The overlap between symbolic interactionism and the work of Homans, Barth, Kapferer, Blau, and other transactional analysts has become increasingly obvious to anthropologists. The difference can be crudely stated thus: Symbolic interactionism focuses on the exchange of ideas or concepts, on the assumption that the individual in interaction uses them to direct his behavior in such a way that the result will be what he interprets as a harmonic fit between his own and other people's views of his role;[3] there is no explicit use of the notions of maximization and rationality. Transactional analysis is centered on such notions and is concerned with the exchange of "values" (both conceptual and material) without respect for and commonly in the face of any consideration of a harmonic fit between the actor's and other persons' perceptions of his role. Transactional analysis emphasizes the points of disjunction and negotiation in a relationship, while symbolic interactionism emphasizes the areas of common, even if newly interpreted, conceptual understanding. Both are concerned with the generation of new social forms; these forms are seen on the one hand as resulting from negotiated exchange in which the two partners compete for dominance, and on the other hand as arising from mutual adjustment to a shared interpretation of the meaning of the relationship. My contrast ignores the partial overlap and is of course highly simplified; it might be argued that Blau and Kapferer have at least half a foot in the field of symbolic interactionism. But I believe that the contrast represents the tendencies inherent in the two approaches.

I think that by analyzing interaction (a) as the exchange of verbalized roles and (b) in the context of altruistic and negotiable ideologies as I defined them, we go some way toward accommodating the two approaches within the same analysis. The distinctive feature of my approach, I think, is that I emphasize not just the general exchange of concepts or "values" but more particularly the exchange of folk conceptualizations of roles, expressed in the language of the culture concerned. My methodological starting point is the axiom that in all cultures altruistic and negotiable ideologies coexist, but their respective degrees of legitimacy as normative rules of social conduct covary both with situation or "domain" and with time. I turn now to apply these ideas to my own field data. As always in social anthropology, we begin less by asking our informants preselected questions (for we lack the categories to do so) than by listening to them asking each other, usually through an interpreter. Ideally at least, mastery of the language will eventually enable us to move from the position of an audience to that of a participant.

AN ETHNOGRAPHY

An early vivid introduction to the Giriama of Kenya was a meeting at a local trading center in mid 1966, two and a half years after that country's independence, between government and political party officials and local people, including men and women of all ages and also children. The meeting was conducted almost entirely in Swahili and I had no difficulty in following it, though most later meetings of a more localized kind were conducted in the closely related Giriama vernacular, which I had to learn. From this linguistic point of view, the field work situation was not typical, though I did what most field workers would do and simply listened.

As at many such meetings in this immediate post-independence era, the call was for communal unity and cooperative economic progress. Older men stated that, though economic development was desirable, many men who had achieved great personal wealth returned insufficient wealth to such cooperative enterprises as new school buildings, communal commercial ventures, scholarship funds for bright pupils, and so on. They referred to such entrepreneurial men as *wafanya maendeleo* (Swahili for ''makers of progress''), clearly and publicly indicating respect for the principle of economic development. They also reminded the gathering that the men were nevertheless no more than *watoto wetu* (Swahili for ''our children''), with a style and emphasis that suggested that this alone gave the moral weight to their accusation.

The counter to this accusation came not from anyone identified, either by himself or others, as an enterprising farmer/trader, but from the officials who, after first paying deferential tribute to the wisdom of these elders (*wazee* in Swahili), urged them not to impose their ''old ways'' on the ''young and educated'' lest economic development be jeopardized. Two examples given of such ''old ways'' were (a) allowing relatives and family and close friends (summarized by the Swahili *jamaa*) to ''consume'' individually acquired wealth and (b) ''spending'' time, labor, and money on ''medicines,'' ''curing'' (*dawa* and *uganga*), sorcery (*uchawi*), and ceremonial festivities (the officials used the term *matanga,* ''funerals,'' but seemingly referred to other ceremonies as well).

This is a tight abridgment of many hours of talking. From it we can discern a perceived opposition between ''elders'' and the ''young and educated.'' There is also the suggestion of an alliance between the latter and government officials. Though both sides ostensibly agreed on the value of economic development, the two were spoken of as opposed on the question of which set of normative rules should be followed in distributing the acquired wealth. Reduced still further, the debate concerned the respective moralities of an ideology of individualistic enterprise, only ultimately and indirectly benefiting the wider community, and an ideology of communal contributions. The first justifies the negotiable, entrepreneurial roles of individuals as both the means and end of economic development. The second justifies these features only insofar as they are subsumed in an overriding altruistic obligation.

This familiar twofold division of moral claims occurred at just about every meeting that I attended, and was expressed in both the Giriama vernacular and Swahili. It is presumably universal and occurs in a variety of forms and emphases. It was stressed among Giriama as a result of recent changes which have been compressed within living memories.

The particular cultural emphasis (as illustrated, for example, by the elders' categorization of wealthy, entrepreneurial men as "our children") takes the form of a belief, widely held by all age groups and largely but not completely documented by figures (Parkin 1972: 31), that contemporary Giriama society has seen the emergence of rich young men and poor older men. This situation is stated to be a reversal of the customary expectation that control over such resources as patrimony should be the prerogative of biologically senior men. By drawing on existing cultural terms of address and reference which stress generational distinctiveness, including the use of teknonymy, the speakers can discuss the economic cleavage as an intergenerational one. In other words, the same issue can be talked about in two culturally alternative ways.

We can return at this point to my distinction between the variable phrase (the functional category) and the invariable word (the formal category). When Giriama explain a dispute between the rich young and the poor old as caused by intergenerational conflict, they tend to draw on condensed word formulas for describing such familiar events—that is, they use a kind of ethno-jargon. A witness to the dispute may condemn a young man's "insolence" simply by declaring, "I call that elder my brother, yet I am called father by X," implying that X (possibly a man in his forties) is therefore son to the elder and should heed the rules of generational seniority. A switch in the classification—"I call that elder my brother, yet I am also called brother (or brother-in-law) by X"—implies that in the speaker's view the rules of generational seniority have been misapplied and that perhaps a moot between elders who are "equals" should be held to decide the issue. And so on.

But when Giriama explain the dispute in bald, "exploitative" economic terms, they are much more likely to use variable phrases created more or less on the spot, and such familiar "secondary" elaborations as "He achieved his wealth by ensorcelling/poisoning his kin/neighbors/rivals." More recently, they might say that wealth was achieved by "bribing" (using the Swahili word *ku-honga*) government officials.

Giriama society has always had its wealthy men who could be seen by the outside observer to be every bit as "exploitative" as any contemporary entrepreneur. But the Giriama distinguish between what I translate as the "redistributional" economy and the modern "capitalist" economy. According to the Giriama, the former men of wealth (*shaha*) did not permanently alienate the property but channelled it back into a community of supporters; in the "capitalist" economy, on the other hand, as a result of cash cropping and external market factors, property (i.e., land and trees) is seen as permanently alienated, with no compensatory redistribution. These are, I repeat, folk conceptualizations; as in any other society, "redistributional" and "capitalist" exchange spheres continue to coexist, though the larger economic transactions occur in the latter at present.

The terms "redistributional" and "capitalist" are actually inadequate translations for the two contrasting sets of Giriama concepts or ideologies. The first refers to set terms indicating rules for holding, allocating, and acquiring property on the basis of generational and agnatic seniority. Giriama justify such rules as being at the heart of Giriama "traditional" notions of property. They frequently link the concept of redistribution to specific customs, in particular the agreement among neighboring palm-tree owners not to sell their palm wine to each other at significant profit: a mental tally is kept of such "sales" with a view to ironing out any undue profits made by a neighbor, though large producers may sell with moral impunity at a distance from their neighborhood. This profitless exchange sphere shades into "pure" gift giving among kin, affines, and neighbors, as evidenced by the expectation that people will contribute amply to collective drinking and eating ceremonies and by the demand, described above, that successful entrepreneurial men contribute some of their wealth to communal enterprises. It is this set of "traditional" concepts which is constantly attacked by government officers as a drain on economic development.

The second set of concepts, that of "capitalism," is manifested in the disapproval of *permanent* sales of land to nonagnates for the benefit of young men; this disapproval is expressed particularly by those who are dispossessed yet have some kind of political voice—in other words, poor elders. That is its "negative" side. Its "positive" side is, as we saw from the account of the meeting, the encouragement given it by government officials, who reward successful entrepreneurship with loans and who condemn communal restrictions on individual enterprise. Bearing in mind my earlier definitions, I think we can identify these two respectively as overarching altruistic and negotiable ideologies.

Let me link up much of the foregoing discussion and suggest that the three broad categories of "social types," the poor elders, the entrepreneurial young men, and the government officials, are verbally associated with these two ideologies as shown in Table 1. This schema depicts two contrasting sets of claims not just about how political authority and economic privilege should be exercised but also about how it should be discussed.

Let me focus on the left-hand part of the table and look at the key vernacular terms which denote, in a symbolically condensed way, an altruistic authority system. We start with a Giriama taxonomy of social types (i.e., roles) of authority. In a number of unprompted conversations with Giriama elders the following blueprint emerged: The Giriama "government" is headed by *autumia a kaya* (singular: *mutumia wa kaya*), meaning elders of the *kaya*. The *kaya* is a kind of traditional capital occupied nowadays only by a handful of senior elders and their wives, but it is a symbolic rallying point in anti-government demonstrations. As well as agreeing that these elders head the "government," Giriama of all ages speak of them as the foremost experts on traditional lore and ritual. In addition, they are supposed to have some legitimate supervisory powers not only over local ritual activities but also over a number of secret societies of male elders which were apparently strong sixty years ago (see Champion 1967). They are said to belong to the most senior living age-grade (*rika*). They are contrasted with other elders who are not members of the *kaya* and who are assumed to be of less senior age-grades. The term for such an elder is simply *mutumia*.

Any man beyond the age of about fifty will be called *mutumia,* but only an elder

TABLE 1 *Two Ideologies and the Support Expressed for Them by Various "Social Types" Among the Giriama of Kenya*

Altruistic Ideology	Negotiable Ideology	
Poor Elders	Rich Young Men	Government Officials
Support for the ideology is expressed mainly in the vernacular through the use of key "customary" words, each a symbolic condensation of cultural rules and concepts about the acquisition of property according to generational and agnatic seniority.	Support for the ideology is expressed both in Swahili (mainly loan words) and in the vernacular, mainly through variable phrases, themselves reflecting the still half-defined and partially accepted concepts about acquiring property in the face of generational and agnatic seniority.	Support for the ideology is expressed in Swahili through a possibly equal mixture of formal and functional terms (set words and variable phrases).

who is a homestead head will be called *mwenye mudzi* (literally, "owner of the homestead/village"). In the contemporary period of rapid economic change involving much dispute over rights to land and trees, neighborhood and lineage/clan moots, called *kambi*, are as active as ever. To sit on them as a regular witness-cum-mediator (*mugiriama* or *chodherwa*)—not just as a witness called to give evidence for the occasion only—a man must be not merely a *mutumia* but also a *mwenye mudzi*. In practice the jural sphere overlaps the ritual one, for most local moots use mystical oaths (*viraho*) and, less frequently, a shaman (*muganga wa mburuga*; literally, "doctor of the oracle"). Of all these roles, that of the shaman is the only one filled almost exclusively by either women or young men, not by elders. Giriama also say that most senior elders who regularly attend moots are medicine doctors (singular: *muganga wa mukoba/kombo*).

One term, *mwenyetsi*, which once meant "territorial section head," has lost this meaning nowadays and refers to a Kenya citizen generally (cf. Swahili *mwenyeji*); it is not used to distinguish Giriama from each other. Other terms are *muhongohi* (literally, "the main pole supporting the beams of a house"), applied to the most senior member of the six main *kaya* elders, and *dzumbe*, applied to a government chief or subchief. (Interestingly, *shaha*, with its meaning of authority *with* wealth, was rarely mentioned in discussing authority per se but would sometimes come into other discussions about past or "traditional" men of property.)

I did not carry out word-frequency tests to check the degree of lexical predictability of these terms, but I believe from actual accounts that there is a high probability that most will occur when Giriama elders explain or discuss their "own" authority system. I stress that these are not terms which I have had to dig out, so to speak, from the language; rather, they encountered me frequently and I had to use them in turn. If one were to investigate a particular item of conversation including these terms, one would discover a number of organizational principles by which the terms were related to each other, for instance, neighborhood, kinship, friendship, and religion. As it is, two main principles are apparent from my abstract: authority is dependent on divisions of age and generation, including both agnatic and nonagnatic seniority; and jural authority shades over into ritual authority. Lumping these together in a single summary statement, one might say that elders rule through their command over ritual resources and the redistribution (but not monopolization) of economic resources. This is a familiar sociological definition of authority in subsistence societies with limited movable property, simple technologies, and low rates of role differentiation and specialization. And it is no accident that, by this process of abstraction, we find that the "emic" Giriama and the "etic" sociological definitions of authority converge. For Giriama as much as for the sociologist, the definition represents an ideal type. The cultural expressions of the definition may differ, but within their respective codes these definitions depend on formal terminological categories—that is, invariable words. The words are *mutumia, mwenye mudzi, rika, muganga,* and so on, on the one hand, and "multiplex," "undifferentiated," "unspecialized roles," and so on, on the other hand.

For the reasons I have already given, relating to the use of ascriptive generational rules for acquiring property, the Giriama definition of customary authority does seem to presuppose an altruistic ethic. The ideal that elders, in contrast to government magistrates and doctors, provide their jural and ritual expertise not for personal gain but simply because it is "the custom" actually receives some empirical support. As I have explained elsewhere (1972), proportionately few entrepreneurial men are elders, and of those elders who are ritual specialists few earn incomes which approximate those of enterprising farmers. Most significantly, it is in the name of "custom" that such elders continue to dispose of land and trees, selling them to raise cash for sons' bridewealth, lavish ceremonies, and medicines, even in the face of genuine poverty.

I turn now to consider how the negotiable ideology is expressed by predominantly young, entrepreneurial men who are encouraged by government officials in their policy of economic development based on the individualistic expansion of productive capital. The question now is: what conceptual channel enables enterprising young Giriama farmers to "smuggle in" their own perception of the local-level authority system? After the preceding analysis of economic changes in Giriama society, it should not be surprising to find these young farmers legitimizing their new roles by "qualifying" and elaborating on the normally less variable connotations of such authority terms as those listed above. That is to say, by implicit reference they verbally redefine these key role terms. An alternative though probably less frequently used channel is to employ such loan words as *mtajiri* to provide a focus for a new or modified concept.

The modification of a key role term's meaning is achieved by juxtaposing it with a phrase, the meaning of which is actually at variance with that connoted by the role term when used by, say, an important elder. The result is to introduce an ambivalence or even a semantic contradiction within the key role term. Should the altered meaning catch on, one may then find elders themselves moving toward a usage of the word with this new meaning.

To take an example, it is frequently asserted by both elders and young men (a) that *mutumia* can only be used to refer to an aged man or a man of a senior *rika* (age-grade), and (b) that a *mwenye mudzi* (homestead head) must be a *mutumia*. But on other occasions *mutumia* is used as a term of address and sometimes of reference to the relatively few men who are homestead heads but are not otherwise biologically or genealogically senior. In other words, the explicit rule is that a *mutumia* is necessarily an aged person and that only a *mutumia* may be a *mwenye mudzi*; it is qualified in practice by an implicit rule that a *mwenye mudzi* must be a *mutumia,* even when his age and genealogical status suggest otherwise. This semantic ambiguity of *mutumia* was noted as long ago as 1891 when Taylor (p. 37) pointed out that as "a title of respect" for an old man (or woman) *mutumia* was also "sometimes applied to a young person in a position of authority." We do not know the proportion of such young men or the nature of their authority. Homesteads were very much larger then, but it may have been possible in a few instances for a young man to become head, in the absence of father's brothers or close agnates able or willing to take on the position. The meaning of *mutumia* would here be ambiguous with regard to the man's age but not, as nowadays, with regard to his genealogical seniority and his wealth. Now the few young men (in their thirties and forties) who are homestead heads tend to be well above the average in wealth and entrepreneurial achievements, and they constitute a relatively recent status category resulting from the economic changes described earlier. Their designation as *mwenye mudzi* and therefore as "respected" *mutumia* legitimates not only their status but also the negotiable ideology by which they achieved it, the ideology which is seen to flout an altruistic idealization of custom. That is to say, their designation by these role terms legitimizes their permanent purchase of trees and land and their alienation of this property from agnatic descent groups; their necessarily selective refusals to contribute "generously" to communal enterprises or "needy" individuals, perhaps agnates, other kinsmen, or affines; and their increasing use of government courts and legal facilities in preference to the local-level moots. The old ambiguity contained in the role term *mutumia* which Taylor indicated seems therefore to have undergone a shift which is to the ideological benefit of entrepreneurial young men.

The conferment of legitimacy is not all one way, however. The redistributional-cum-altruistic ideology continues to be legitimized by the recognition of elders' mediatory and ritual roles, which do remain vitally important in a society in which land disputation and a common belief in the mystical cause of such misfortune require these informal sources of adjudication and cure to supplement those of the government courts and hospital. To give an example, it seems very likely, on the basis of an analysis of life histories (cf. Taylor 1891: 82), that twenty-five or thirty years ago the roles of diviner-shaman (*muganga wa mburuga/kitswa/pepo*) and medical doctor (*muganga wa mukoba/kombo*) could and often would be performed by one male elder, with some elders emphasizing one or the other as a specialty. The formal verbal distinction now regularly made between the two roles would not have been expressed so frequently, if at all; a ritual specialist would be called simply *muganga*, with further contextual elaboration needed to indicate which of his special skills was being referred to. Nowadays the two main functions of divination and therapy are performed by separate persons who are thereby designated as distinct social types. More than this, medical doctors are exclusively male elders (genuinely senior) while shamans are either young males (usually under thirty) or women (whose position warrants more discussion than can be attempted here). In the jargon this is what we might call a simple case of role differentiation and specialization. It has paralleled, within the same time period, the development of an economic cleavage, conceptualized as an opposition between a minority of wealthy young homestead heads and the majority of more senior ones. During this period the role of medical doctor appears to have become more profitable while that of diviner-shaman has become relatively much less advantageous (though even the doctors are poor by comparison with the young entrepreneurial farmers, to whom they continue to sell land and trees).

It is striking that this precise differentiation into the two types of *muganga*, the one older and earning more than the other, corresponds inversely with the appearance of a number of young homestead heads who are often much wealthier than their more numerous older counterparts. In noting this inverse homology, I have interpreted it as one of a number of customary concessions nonconsciously given by entrepreneurial young men to elders in exchange for the jural protection and freedom from customary constraints which they need in order to pursue their expansionist aims (1972: 15, 38). That is to say, the young men acknowledge the superior ritual powers of elders not only by paying them medical fees but also by using the precise terminological distinction between the two types of *muganga*. In exchange, their anti-customary entrepreneurial activities are implicitly legitimized by the elders, whose expertise they have sought, under the cover of the elders' "agreement" to redefine such terms as *mutumia* and *mwenye mudzi* in the way I have described. Over the long term, of course, the exchange is unfairly balanced, because few medical doctors enjoy a consistently high rate of success; moreover, doctors can easily, through repeated failure, become subject to accusations that they are against rather than for humanity—in other words, that they practice sorcery. Entrepreneurial farmers, on the other hand, continue to amass their holdings of land and trees. Indeed it can legitimately be argued that the young homestead heads cede ritual potency for economic freedom and that, in doing so, they secure a bargain.

But we must also place equal emphasis on the taxonomy and semantic inter-relatedness of role terms, through which this process of bargain and differentiation is identified in the culture. The system of exchange here described is not only that of individuals formulating strategies to maximize personal benefit by transacting ritual for economic "goods." Each individual exchange relationship runs along the lines of a wider exchange of new, modified, or existing concepts of role, which are made cognitively salient in the culture by being transacted in verbal form. Speakers shift back and forth from formal verbal categories of the conceptually condensed and lexically predictable kind to functionally descriptive ones which are conceptually more diffuse and lexically less predictable. But they do so within channels largely outlined by an underlying homology of ideas.

This homology may be regarded as a kind of "pristine" set of ideal correlations, as the preceding material has demonstrated:

1. Age:youth :: (politico-jural) seniority:juniority
2. Age:youth :: wealth:poverty
3. Age:youth :: ritual power:ritual impotence

The homology could be picked out from just about any "traditional" African ethnography, and possibly from other ethnographies, on the basis of the words and phrases which people in the culture use to compare and contrast and thereby to evaluate social conduct. This chapter provides an example in which the first and third sets remain unchanged: elders are still sought as the most important witnesses and mediators; and supreme ritual power remains a vested attribute of age. But there is also a partial inversion of the second set through the tendency for young homestead heads to be wealthier than older ones. It is also worth noting that a short-lived inversion of the third set occurred among Giriama in 1966 in an anti-sorcery movement in which young men temporarily dispossessed elders of their ritual medicines and in some cases proclaimed their own better methods of cure (Parkin 1968). The more enduring, but by no means permanent, inversion of the second set described in this chapter can be seen in Giriama contemporary modes of explaining disputes and misfortunes; I believe it to be associated with a threatened shift from a primarily altruistic to a negotiable ideology of exchange relations, and with a movement from a primarily redistributional to a capitalist economy.

The attempt to relate an underlying explanatory logic to observable behavior invites the familiar charge of mystifying the analysis. But the analysis does have an empirical starting point, namely the words people use to identify social conduct. The homology of underlying ideas and their partial inversion do seem to reflect a "shadow"[4] in the way in which people speak of social conduct: new "meanings" are attached to role terms, or new role terms are affixed to old "meanings." It is not simply that new relationships are generated by this process; a reordering of concepts and signs is also given legitimation.

CONCLUSION

An analytic and theoretical concern with exchange as the basis of communication is implicit in all anthropology. If we regard one broad category of the theory as focused on actors, then the antithesis is the type of theory that sees actors themselves as also, at a different remove, objects of exchange. The first has as its basic postulate that man's maximization of gains over costs is a fundamental motivating principle in social interaction. The second can be illustrated by a quotation from Ardener (1971: xlv): "The terminology of semiotics can be expressed more mechanistically through communication theory. We have to visualize that the message on one channel becomes itself the channel for meta-messages. Lévi-Strauss (1963: 61) implicitly states the general case, from the particular case of women: *human beings speak, but they are themselves also symbolic elements in a communication system.*"

The second comprises the first. The actors transact valued goods in a zero-sum game; but the valued nature of such goods (both material and nonmaterial) locates the actor himself in a wider system of classification. These systems of classification are themselves not static: the signs and meanings of which they are made up may be transposed; or new concepts may be given meaning through existing signs.

Two such systems of classification which appear universal in human cultures are what I simply call altruistic and negotiable ideologies. That is to say, I see actors legitimizing their social conduct by reference to these two ideologies. An altruistic ideology may be regarded as the cultural expression, writ large, of a notion of the "pure" gift; a negotiable ideology holds, in Calvinist fashion, that everything has its price and must be paid for. A strong tendency in transactional analysis is to view both as manifestations of "maximizing man" and to argue that, in the end, even altruistic ideals may be given or taken as concessions in social relations according to the free play of market forces of supply and demand—in other words, that even the "pure" gift is either a cost, an investment, or a reward. But, as well as being tautologous, this view ignores the extent to which an altruistic ideology, including the notion of the "pure" gift, achieves conceptual and semantic distinctiveness only by standing in an opposed relationship to a negotiable/exploitative ideology. We have to understand the process by which there is a shift in emphasis in a society from one kind of ideology to the other for the legitimation of particular events and activities. To include the actor in this process, we have to look at the culturally designated roles which he is regarded as playing, for folk concepts of roles are crucial elements in any ideology of legitimation. Just as we may say that a system of classification "changes" by transpositions of its constituent signs and meanings, so we may say that an ideology "changes" by transpositions of the cultural meanings of roles and the verbal forms in which they are expressed.

A folk taxonomy of authority roles which achieves a high degree of lexical predictability through the regular use of one or two "words" for each role (e.g., the familiar *kuaar muon/twac* for the Nuer leopard-skin chief) expresses an ideology in a conceptually abridged and condensed form. Changes in a taxonomy may come about by the incorporation of a loan word; but most changes in meaning of the individual "words" regularly used to describe roles seem to result from repeated qualifications or elaborations expressed in accompanying phrases. Thus, through the medium of *paroles* of infinite verbal variety but similar conceptual thrust, the most formalized elements of the taxonomy are altered. To take one example, I have suggested that a partial shift in the meaning of *mwenye mudzi* among Giriama (from "one who rules by dint of age" to "one who rules by virtue of economic self-sufficiency") has come about in this way, in correspondence with an increase in the legitimation of a negotiable rather than altruistic ideology of authority roles.

But I have also suggested that this change in meaning of a key role term within the taxonomy has in turn modified the meaning of some other role terms by virtue of contrastive or homologous relationships to them. Pocock (1961: 76; cited in Ardener 1971: lix) provides a superbly crisp quotation from Adam Ferguson (1767) which illustrates this phonemic character of role terms: "The titles of *fellow citizen* and *countryman* unopposed to those of *alien* and *foreigner*, to which they refer, would fall into disuse and lose their meaning." The exchange of role terms is therefore not random; it generally follows an underlying cultural template of ideas, a kind of *langue,* which is also recognizable in other cultures.

It must be individuals whom we observe in verbal exchanges of role terms, the result of which at one level of abstraction is to affirm a switch in emphasis from one to the other set of legitimizing claims. At the more fundamental level of abstraction is the much more difficult task of finding the principles by which one key role term and not another has been subjected to significant alteration of meaning; or has been supplemented by a loan word; or has been dropped altogether from the folk taxonomy. To do this we need to discover how the concepts behind the taxonomy relate systematically both to each other and to the constituent role terms making up the taxonomy.

NOTES

1. Although this term is in fact of Swahili and Arabic origin, Taylor (1891: 24, 83) regarded it as unquestionably Giriama at the time of his writing.

2. Cf. Nadel's "governing property" of a role (1956: 34ff.).

3. The following is one of the many passages in Blumer's work which aptly summarize these features: "[Symbolic interactionism recognizes that] one has to *fit* one's own line of action in some manner to the actions of others. The actions of others have to be taken into account and cannot be regarded as merely an arena for the expression of what one is disposed to do or sets out to do" (Blumer 1969: 72).

4. E. Ardener, "Some Outstanding Problems in the Analysis of Events" (forthcoming), introduces the concept of the language-shadow. I acknowledge the danger of allowing an attractive metaphor to delude us into crediting it with analytical usefulness. But I do think that this one provides a way to apprehend the relationship among cultural "thought," speech, and action.

REFERENCES

Ardener, E., ed. 1971. *Social Anthropology and Language*. ASA Monograph No. 10. London: Tavistock.
_____. Forthcoming. Some outstanding problems in the analysis of events.
Bailey, F. G. 1969. *Stratagems and Spoils*. Oxford: Blackwell.
Barth, F. 1966. *Models of Social Organization*. Royal Anthropological Institute Occasional Paper No. 23. London.
Berreman, G. D. 1966. Anemic and emetic analyses in social anthropology. *American Anthropologist*, 68 (2): 346–354. Reprinted in Spradley 1972.
Blau, P. M. 1964. *Exchange and Power in Social Life*. New York: John Wiley.
Blumer, H. 1969. *Symbolic Interactionism: Perspective and Method*. Englewood Cliffs, N.J.: Prentice-Hall. Abstracted in Spradley 1972.
Boissevain, J. 1968. The place of non-groups in the social sciences. *Man*, N.S., 3 (4): 542–556.
Bruner, J. S., et al. 1956. *A Study of Thinking*. London: John Wiley. Abstracted in Spradley 1972.
Burling, R. 1962. Maximization theories and the study of economic anthropology. *American Anthropologist*, 64 (4): 802–821.
Caplan, L. 1971. Cash and kind: two media of bribery in Nepal. *Man*, N.S., 6 (4): 266–278.
Champion, A. M. 1967. *The Agiryama of Kenya*. Royal Anthropological Institute Occasional Paper No. 25. London.
Cohen, A. 1969. Political anthropology: the analysis of the symbolism of power relations. *Man*, N.S., 4 (2): 215–235.
Davis, J. 1973. Forms and norms: the economy of social relations. *Man*, N.S., 8 (2): 159–176.
Douglas, M. 1973. Self-evidence. In Royal Anthropological Institute, *Proceedings, 1972*. London.
Ferguson, Adam. 1767. *An Essay in the History of Civil Society*.
Firth, R. 1951. *Elements of Social Organization*. London: Watts.
_____, ed. 1967. *Themes in Economic Anthropology*. ASA Monograph No. 6. London: Tavistock.
Gluckman, M. 1968. Psychological, sociological and anthropological explanations of witchcraft and gossip: a clarification. *Man*, N.S., 3 (1): 20–34.
Homans, G. 1958. Social behaviour as exchange. *American Journal of Sociology*, 63: 597–606.
_____. 1961. *Social Behaviour: Its Elementary Forms*. London: Routledge and Kegan Paul.
Kapferer, B. 1972. *Strategy and Transaction in an African Factory*. Manchester: Manchester University Press.
Kennedy, J. G. 1967. Psychological and social explanations of witchcraft: a comparison of Clyde Kluckhohn and Evans Pritchard. *Man*, N.S., 2 (4): 216–225.
Klapp, O. E. 1962. *Heroes, Villains and Fools: The Changing American Character*. Englewood Cliffs, N.J.: Prentice-Hall.
Lévi-Strauss, C. 1963. *Structural Anthropology*. Trans. C. Jacobson and B. G. Schoepf. New York: Basic Books.
Mauss, M. 1970. *The Gift*. Trans. I. Cunnison. London: Routledge and Kegan Paul.
Mitchell, C., ed. 1969. *Social Networks in Urban Situations*. Manchester: Manchester University Press.
Nadel, S. F. 1956. *The Theory of Social Structure*. London: Cohen and West.
Paine, R. 1967. What is gossip about? An alternative hypothesis. *Man*, N.S., 2 (4): 278–285.

Parkin, D. 1968. Medicines and men of influence. *Man*, N.S., 3 (3): 424–439.
———. 1972. *Palms, Wine and Witnesses*. Scranton, Pa.: Chandler. London: Intertext.
Pocock, D. F. 1961. *Social Anthropology*. London and New York: Sheed and Ward.
Sahlins, M. D. 1965. On the sociology of primitive exchange. In M. Banton, ed., *The Relevance of Models for Social Anthropology*. ASA Monograph No. 1. London: Tavistock.
Spradley, J. P., ed. 1972. *Culture and Cognition: Rules, Maps and Plans*. Scranton, Pa.: Chandler.
Sturtevant, W. C. 1964. Studies in ethnoscience. *American Anthropologist*, 66 (2): 99–131. Reprinted in Spradley 1972.
Taylor, W. E. 1891. *Giriama Vocabulary and Collections*. London: Society for Promoting Christian Knowledge.
Von Neuman, J., and O. Morgenstern. 1944. *Theory of Games and Economic Behavior*. Princeton: Princeton University Press.
Whiteley, W. H. 1966. Social anthropology, meaning, and linguistics. *Man*, N.S., 1 (2): 139–157.

Lying, Honor, and Contradiction

MICHAEL GILSENAN

Sociological structures differ profoundly according to the
measure of lying which operates in them.

GEORG SIMMEL

This essay focuses on the ways in which meaning emerges in the practical reality of
the everyday world rather than on the formal construction of systems of classification and symbolism.[1] With a particular concentration on the manifold practices of
what will be called "lying," I shall try to show the way in which individuals in a
Lebanese village negotiate and transact about the most important area of value in
any culture, social personality and the significance with which behavior is invested. I shall go on to argue that *kizb,* the Arabic word translated here as "lying,"
is a fundamental element not only of specific situations and individual actions, but
of the cultural universe as a whole; and that further it is the product of, and
produces in turn, basic elements and contradictions in the social structure. Instead
of proceeding by the study of taxonomic systems, I shall assume that tacit and
explicit sets of meaning can be examined through everyday activity.

For Simmel the lie is chiefly significant because it "engenders by its very nature
an error concerning the lying subject" (Simmel 1964: 312), and because it
fundamentally affects the reciprocal knowledge which is at the root of all interaction. The lie is a technique for the restriction of the social distribution of knowledge
over time, and is thus ultimately woven into the system of power and control in a
society. How it informs certain kinds of social relations, and in what spheres,
becomes for Simmel the major problem, and this leads into his famous discussion
of secrecy.

His emphasis on the process of manipulation of meaning by the lying subject
highlights the part lying plays in the constitution of the self. A lie by X about X is a
classic instance of "creating the self," of purposely fashioning a social personality
"out there" for one's own contemplation, of making an object of and to the subject
for his own aesthetic self-regard. Knowing *what* he lies about in reference to
himself and *how* he does so gives the key to the innermost realms of the individual.
But lying in the everyday world is also a conscious act directed at another; it is
always part of social meanings and social relations. Indeed, the lie is usually
accessible to the observer, not in its original form in the actor's intention, but as a
judgment made by others (or an other) of certain verbal or behavioral signs.[2] Lying

191

often manifests itself to us socially as an attribution made by others to the actor of a specific intention, whether or not such an intention "in fact" existed. The modes and conditions of such attributions are sociologically as significant as the strategic, purposive use of lying by a subject. It is here, in the examination of the lie in action, that we learn the full meaning of the classification "that is a lie."[3]

Such judgments may be public and discrediting, or they may be privately made by the other who for some reason has no interest in revealing his judgment and is prepared to go along "as if" things are as they seem. There may be tacit cooperation and collaboration, or challenge and social compromise. Moreover, all the while others may be unsure, unable to answer the question whether such and such an act or statement is a lie or not, and they may turn to procedures for testing it when it is relevant that they do so. Such "monitoring" will depend on whether there is information, uniformly or selectively available, for verifying the individual's representation, or whether it is simply unverifiable and a matter of trust. Similarly, the lying subject may have difficulty in discovering if he is believed, and the nonlying subject in realizing that his conduct is labelled by some as a lie. Uncertainty as to the precise degree of lying or truth on both sides will always be present and subject to active assessment in problematic situations. For insofar as falseness undermines our notions of legitimate and right behavior, indeed the certainty of our grasp on the reality of the common-sense world, it constitutes a threat of a serious order to our social reality.[4] The conjunction or disjunction between appearance and reality, shifting and ever critical, is hedged with ambiguity concerning judgment and value, act and intention, what is concealed and what is revealed.

THE CONCEPT OF KIZB

The meanings and range of the word *kizb*[5] will emerge in the course of this essay. Precisely because it is a thematic and constantly used concept in the everyday world, it has a wide span of meaning and reference, and as manifested in behavior it may take a complex range and form. Children rush up to other children in the street and falsely announce the death of a famous singer;[6] a friend says he is going to a particular place and asks if he can do something for you, when in fact he will be somewhere else altogether; another has found 1,000 lire in a field, you can ask X and Y (carefully rehearsed) who were with him; and so on to infinity. Here the lie is simply a matter of tricking another, often by coordinated group effort, and demonstrating in a simple way an ability to fool him. The essence of it consists precisely in the liar's ultimately *revealing* the lie and claiming his victory: I'm lying to you, you ate it! In the laughter there is the sense of superiority, the fleeting dominance of A over B. There is the risk too that it will fall flat, or even backfire on the perpetrator with direct denunciation of the *kizb*. These little scenes are played out constantly by children and young men among themselves, though rarely in this form by socially fully mature males.

In this aspect *kizb* is associated with a rich inventiveness and imagination, a verbal quick-footedness and extemporaneous wit that have strong elements of public entertainment and play about them. Players are not necessarily called to account for the factual basis of their talk, providing that an appropriate setting of banter, camaraderie, and play has been established in interaction. Even so, though the young men may indulge in the (often competitive) verbal fantastic for its own sake, it does not accord with the weight and seriousness of anyone who claims a full social "place," a "station." In such a case it would indicate a certain lightness and lack of self-respect, and a married man of, say, his middle thirties would risk becoming a joke himself if he told too many (a role, incidentally, which some, lacking prestige and social standing, settle for, thus capitalizing on verbal skills where more solid resources are lacking).[7]

This "artificial" quality of word play based on *kizb* brings us to two more general, complementary senses of the term that relate it specifically to judgments on the nature of the world. The first may be illustrated in the words of a taxi-driver friend, twenty-seven years old, married and known for his bravado, cockiness, and putting on the style, who had come back from a job driving people into Beirut for New Year's Eve. He returned from the capital to the quiet impoverishment of the village, and ecstatically rehearsed the extraordinary nature of the scene with vast enthusiasm.

> The streets were all hung in lights, decorations everywhere, people all over the road and pavements and filling the open-air cafés. The girls' dresses, heaven, the girls' dresses were up to here [graphic gestures]!! There were Buicks, Alfas, Mercedes, Porsches, and Jaguars bumper to bumper.[8] People were kissing in the street, it was unbelievable, it would drive you mad, you can't imagine, it was . . . like *kizb* . . . absolutely . . . like *kizb*!

Here is a scene of glitter and artifice, style and fantasy; an ornate, baroque extravagance of wealth, display, and ornament, of gleaming chrome and glittering clothes, that goes beyond reality and is totally divorced from the everyday world of common experience—in short, like *kizb*. My notes are full of accounts of unusually vivid occurrences where people were all over the place, cars, bullets whizzing everywhere (seen in person, or on film or television), that in the end were characterized and summed up by the phrase "absolutely like *kizb*" (*shi mithl al kizb abadan*). Lying therefore is not to be understood only in terms of strategies and judgments in social relations, or as a technique for gaining or showing superiority. It possesses its own aesthetic of baroque invention and is part of a style, of a wide range of variations on the cultural theme of appearance and reality, and it is recognized at once for what it is.

Now the social world in its aspect as part of God's creation, and the Muslim community bound by His revealed imperatives, are part of Truth. Truth indeed is something "pre-eminently real, a living force which is operating in the very process of life and death in the world of existence."[9] But insofar as the world is the place of men's activity and a product of their own constructing without attention to its real underlying principles, it becomes the realm of the apparent, of what is vain and fraudulent. Though the Truth is present in the revelation of the Quran and the religious law, few men know the true, either of themselves, others, or the world. Or perhaps more accurately it should be said that the fact that Truth *is* accessible in Quran and Islamic teaching, could be known, and *yet* men spend their daily lives ignoring it, shows that they are not passively ignorant but actively liars. Moreover, lying is linked in the Revelation, as they well know, with ingratitude and hypocrisy, two other major and salient aspects of unbelief. Lying is thus a blasphemous act, the direct contradiction of the Truth, and the active opposite of the sacred. The sacred creates, its opposite destroys. These are not theological statements only, for they are used to characterize a world view by the villagers themselves, whose sense of the disjunction between apparent and real, born of a system of dominance in which status honor is critical, is very acute. *Kizb* is linked to endless reiteration of a world scepticism, and a pessimistic and detached sense of deception: "the world is a lie my friend, all of it's a lie" (*ad-dunya kizb ya 'ammi, kullu kizb*). Why these elements of the Islamic cultural universe are selected rather than others, and why there exists the particular elective affinity of ideology and social group, can be understood by examining the operations of the lie in the widest and the most limited range of social relations.

LORDS AND STAFF IN NORTH LEBANON

The village in which I worked in North Lebanon was until the late 1960s one of the main centers of an old Bekawat family of Kurdish origin. It is still one of the most important rural foci of the family's interests in terms of olive groves and agriculture, even though most of the lords now live in the cities of Beirut and Tripoli, from where they have easy access to the village. Estimates of the number in the family reach as high as 5,000, and it is a family in name only. Different segments of it are the most significant local-based land-owning groups in the area, the only real material resource of which is land. Though they now live for the most part outside the villages, the family members dominate the political economy of the region almost as effectively as in the days when their horsemen exercised in the fields below their imposing, thick-walled palaces. Up to contemporary times, the "houses" of Muhammad Pasha and Mustafa Pasha ruled this land and much of the mountain and plain across what is now the border with Syria, and their influence and power are by no means dissipated, though the modalities are in the process of transformation.

Members of this stratum are bound by a constellation of interests founded on the direct monopoly of resources. In this situation we do not find a sanctifying tradition and legitimizing myth in the sense familiar to anthropologists. Rather, the historical charter is one of conquest and warrior leadership, backed originally by Ottoman appointment.[10] The ideology is one of status honor, hierarchy, and coercion expressed in an elaborate idiom of respect. (''We kiss their hands in spite of ourselves,'' said one peasant to me, *chasbin 'anna,* ''whether we like it or not.'') This type of domination is personal, domestic, and quasi-manorial, and is also a persistent system of political and judicial authority.

Under the Ottomans the lords were relatively independent of the central government. Powers of taxation and conscription were in their hands, as was control over the various exactions of produce, labor, and personal services which might with greater or lesser arbitrariness be claimed. They built up political connections with the notables of Syria and Mount Lebanon, and they have dominated all regional elections for the national assembly from the time elections were introduced under the French in the 1920s. Their estates were and are still sometimes of considerable size. The most important bey in the village, for example, possessed around 3,000 hectares of land on the plain, most of it in Syria, and passed back and forth with considerably more authority than the police or army of either government could command in the area. The common statement ''He had such and such a number of villages'' is a reflection of a single and simple reality: land, houses, and, in many but not all cases, livestock and all the means of production were in the hands of the beys. Moreover, as I shall note later, the colonial period of the French mandate after the First World War strengthened their political and economic position considerably.

The linchpin of the system as far as the village setting is concerned, and the group on which I shall particularly focus, is what might be called in Weberian terms the staff—those persons who put themselves at the disposal of the ruling order as instruments for ensuring the obedience of, and the production of a surplus by, the peasants and laborers. In the village these persons claim to be of one family, let us call it Beit Ahmad, claim to be Circassian in origin (i.e., from outside, non-Arab peoples), and claim to have established themselves independently as small landowners and horsemen (in the full honorific sense of the term). Their services could not be demanded through contractual or customary right; these services could be obtained only by incorporating Beit Ahmad into the system of domainal rule in a position of privilege and status.

Beit Ahmad were important to the lords perhaps for two major reasons: first, the scale of the land holdings, at least in the case of the real men of power among the beys; and second, the size and nature of the ruled orders. To administer the one and control the other the population of the lords themselves, scattered among their villages of the plains and hills, was insufficient. The staff administered villages (indeed they still act as estate managers and bailiffs) and guarded the lands and honor of their lords against infringement by other lords or by truculent laborers.

Yet despite, or perhaps because of, their common stake in the system of domination, the relationship of lords and staff is marked by constant ambivalence. The former, often divided by the very fact that their monopoly of political and economic power concentrated the struggle and competition for that power among themselves, needed their henchmen against members of other lordly groupings. Therefore the lords might encourage the corporate, family nature of Beit Ahmad as a mobilizable force. But this was hazardous, since this corporate force founded on kinship and a shared sense of status and interest might on occasion be turned against a bey's house (and even drive it from the village when a direct infringement of Beit Ahmad's privilege occurred).[11] And family links might prevent a hench-man from protecting a lord against the "request" of the henchman's cousin for money. Ambiguities in the relationship are recognized privately on both sides, particularly among the young men of the staff. "We made them, not the other way round" is an often-heard statement which, if not totally accurate historically, nonetheless reflects the real sense in which the lords depend on the staff (or *aghawat,* the honorific term by which they are known). Most significantly, the lords have been able for various reasons to buy out much of the staff's own lands around the village, thereby separating the staff from the means of economic independence and administration.

Beit Ahmad are therefore a much more heterogeneous grouping than the local lords. Divided into four major segments with a genealogical charter going back only four generations, they are united less in deeds than in words.[12] Most of the older men were or are attached personally in some way to a bey's service, though some held on to enough land to be free of such ties. Their generation shares a keen sense of the interest of the ranking groups as opposed to the "peasants," though their lifestyles are in fact increasingly similar to those of the persons they regard as the lower strata.[13] They themselves were men of the horse and gun in the interwar period especially and before significant patterns of social change had really impinged on the region. These elders still feel part of a traditional political economy in which beys and aghas are in a symbiotic relationship and committed to the perpetuation of the structure of domination.

In the family as a whole some own a little land, or rent it on favorable terms from a bey; some rely entirely on the lords for employment as bodyguards or chauffeurs; some are mechanics, construction workers, and lorry drivers; others serve coffee and make water pipes for the lord's guests; some are not much more than casual agricultural laborers. Beit Ahmad's position as Beit Ahmad is riddled with contradictions, and I would argue that it is in this gray zone of contradiction that the lie comes into its own. For the family's internal politics are highly fragmented, a series of day-to-day alliances in the context of minute fluctuations of influence and standing. Where low income, limited resources, and irregular work restrict wealth and the opportunities for real autonomy yet men are firmly attached to status honor and hierarchy, personality becomes most critical and the social significance of the individual and his prestige the greatest resource.

This is all the more the case because Beit Ahmad are part of a political and economic system based on monopolistic control of major resources and status honor by ruling groups, a system which produces among the privileged strata a primary stress on what a man *is*, his own individuality, his unique "place" and reputation. You cannot be trained for it in any formal sense; it must be your own creation (providing, that is, that you have been born into the "right" family and station in the first place). Though being of Beit Ahmad and of a certain descent has external reference, what counts within the family is the purely personal standing which a brother's or father's reputation will not make for you. The older men, in whose days the horse and gun were the dominant symbols of chevalier culture and prestige, scorned the idea of work as alien to their ethic and their being. An *qabadi* (a real man) did not *work*—the concept was meaningless. He simply was. To be a lord's companion, to be a hunter, to praise the bey in elaborate courtesies, to be a horseman, to be the administrator of seven villages, was not work. That was left for peasants and had no place in the aristocratic code. You *are* so-and-so and what you can make that statement stand for by your own actions. You observe respect, hierarchy, and etiquette; you sit upright, or lean slightly forward, one hand on knee, legs uncrossed;[14] you walk deliberately and slowly; you speak in a voice that demands attention and that silences others, assertively, emphatically.

Such men, and some of their sons as well, were *murafiqin* (companions, bodyguards, followers) to the lords, a position in which their courage and their capacity to dominate others and deter opponents would in the nature of circumstances be tested. Their position as the *aghawat* could never be legitimated merely by sitting in a certain way and observing the niceties of style, though a lord might happily relax in Tripoli or Beirut with more concern for his inheritance than for his honor. Members of Beit Ahmad depend(ed) far more on day-to-day situations, encounters and performances of honor in which claims and challenges are always possible. The lords were at least in origin Ottoman appointees, men of government, noble rank, beys and pashas, part of the provincial politics of notables. Beit Ahmad has only what it can make of itself and is not able to command the range of alliances of the Bekawat or their economic base. The aghas are locally bound to a particular village and often individually bound to a particular bey. Their greatest deeds are usually on behalf of someone else and in response to someone else's wishes in the idiom of the heroic aesthetic.

Contrast this with Clifford Geertz's analysis of the descriptive taxonomics of a society in which the whole weight is on ritualized anonymity and what Geertz calls a "settled haze of ceremony."

> The anonymization of persons and the immobilisation of time are thus but two sides of the same cultural process: the symbolic de-emphasis, in the everyday life of the Balinese, of the perception of fellow men as consociates, successors, or predecessors, in favour of the perception of them as contemporaries. . . [the] various symbolic orders of person-definition conceal . . . [what] we call personality behind a dense screen of ready-made identities, iconic selves [Geertz 1966: 53].

In our case, in complete contrast, where "weight" and personal prestige are crucial, anonymity is equivalent to relegation to a kind of neutral zone in which personal liking may be present but one would say "he's a good man, poor fellow" with a shrug.[15] He who "has value" and is "not easy" must make claims to that value. Those who do not, or cannot do so, but go about their lives within a restricted sphere of their immediate family lose out at election time or when influence is sought and traded with some lord, as well as in the day-to-day rehearsals of self and place.

Anonymity is a judgment, even an attribution of social nonvaluation. Members of Beit Ahmad often demanded of me why I had been talking with such and such a one. The reply that I was asking him about his life history or descent would always produce roars of sardonic laughter. "*That* has a *sira* [a socially significant biography]? *That* has a *tarikh* [history]?"[16] Such comments are made of a "peasant" by definition, as it were. To say any man is a *fellah* is to locate him in a nonhonorific stratum, to stamp him with anonymity, to label him one for whom questions of prestige and status cannot arise. Why talk to a peasant? Derisory comments of the same order are also made about members of Beit Ahmad by other members, though never in my experience in front of nonmembers. "He has a *sira*? He has a descent? I told the bey yesterday that you were asking about his descent and he said: 'It's well known what his descent is. He's a dog and the son of a dog!' So much for his genealogy! His father had nothing and he has less. He's a liar [*kazzab*], just a liar."

SOCIAL STATUS AND PATTERNS OF KIZB

One does not hide, then, behind various classificatory masking devices as in Bali. Rather one steps forward, differentiates oneself, invites judgment, and strives to establish a significant social biography. It is something to be insisted on, to be claimed as unique, always potentially at issue in the everyday world because circumstances may at any time throw up a crisis in which the self will be challenged and defined. I once upbraided a friend from Beit Ahmad for what I regarded as ridiculous swagger and putting on the style. "Look," he replied, "here, if you don't *fannas* [show off] you are dead. You have to put it on to live here. You think my brother isn't a *fannas* because he never sits outside the shop and doesn't talk much and people in the family think he's weak and sickly? You should see him at the top of the village [where the "peasant" families live], he's the biggest *fannas* in the whole village, talking about how he'll organize these and those votes and who's going to pass exams, etc., etc. Up there he makes himself the lord of the village. Watch him." I did, and it was true.[17]

Most important, these social-status performances take place for the most part before those with whom one is consociate.[18] It is their judgment, rather than that of outsiders or the "peasants," which is significant; it is with those who know one best that transactions over one's social self occur. They are of all people best equipped to monitor one's behavior, and they have the most knowledge of one's biographical situation and life history. In my experience there is a high degree of consensus on readings of individual character in our sense of the term, and on mechanical abilities or skills (e.g., motor repair). I never heard men "lie" on these topics—perhaps there were too many practical and objective tests available. The variation and flexibility and transactions occur with respect to one's social standing and the degree to which one ''counts'' in the everyday world. Your consociates share with you a childhood environment that emphasizes the importance of the fluctuations of individual prestige and a competitive idiom of social relations. Among the children patterns of joking and lying emerge over time between two or more in which one is *mistillim* (taken over) by the other(s); in which verbal ability to outmaneuver another is cultivated and an appreciative eye for the minutiae of personal and general style and strategy is developed. Onlookers would say *istill-mu*, he ''captured him,'' ''got him in his hand,'' ''got a hold over him.'' Idioms of superiority abound to describe the sparring between individuals that is conducted through boasting of oneself or one's father, through display and bravado, through deceiving another in *kizb: akalha* (he ate it, he was beaten), *mawwithu* (I killed him), *māt abadan* (he died).[19]

All the time the question of what lies behind this behavior is present. People ask ''what does he mean by this, what does he intend?'' (*shu biyiqsud*), ''what's he after?'' (*shu biddu*), ''what's the goal?'' (*shu al hadaf*), ''what is his interest?'' (*shu maslahtu*). Narratives about events are full of ''I asked myself what he was really after.'' When the actor particularly wishes to communicate something to another without an ulterior motive and without deception there are very simple cue phrases: *'an jadd* (seriously), *bitsaddiq?* (will you believe me?), *ma mazah* (without joking), *wahyatak, wahyat abuk* (by your life, by your father's life).[20] Many accounts of confrontations or encounters include the question ''how should I make myself out to be?'' (literally, ''how should I make/do my condition; how should I react and appear to him?''). So one often hears ''I pretended that I had never heard of it'' (*'amilt hali ma'indi khabr*, ''had not information on the subject''). How one ''makes oneself'' and ''having information'' go together in lying and judging other's appearances. Even with consociates the field of interpretation is relatively open, incidents can be glossed in many different ways, and the shifting everyday character of practical experience gives plenty of scope for individual style and display.

There are other modes of display and performance: *mazah* (joking), *haki* (idle talk, empty words), and *tafnis* (showing off).[21] All are terms which characterize that world of invention, fantasy, humorous elaboration, artifice, and pretense indicated by the word *kizb*; all focus on display. *Khallina nfannas'aleihum*, a man might say—''let's show off in front of them.'' And so he drives past at high speed, or cuts into a discussion with: ''Politics? No one knows what I know about politics. I'm the lord of politics. I invented it.'' Another wants to borrow a particularly fine set of prayer beads from a friend so that he can walk through the village with it for a few days, ostentatiously flicking it through his fingers in front of everyone. It is all show.

Such are the idioms and styles which men manipulate and in which they work the variations in constituting a social self. The lie occurs throughout as a leitmotif in a constant interaction of judgment on the apparent and the real, what is and what seems. But what happens when the self becomes problematic in a radical way, quite beyond the everyday momentary interchange, so that it is critically threatened or threatens others? What constitutes such a crisis and how is it handled? In the next section I will discuss a series of events or sustained processes of action which demonstrate how crisis and the actors involved are defined, and the different collective and individual strategies that are adopted.

HONOR AND THE DEFINITION OF MAKHLU'

It is characteristic of the principles of this social world to be what I would call highly visible. The basis of politics, the armature of domination, is exposed rather than masked.[22] At least at the general level the code of honorable male social conduct and values is equally articulated and "on the surface." Similarly, status is negotiated in behavior that emphasizes visibility and making claims in the public domain about one's acts and biography. The status honor ethic sets the terms of relevance and provides what I shall call situations of ultimate reference within which and in the light of which men transact their socially significant selves. These ultimate situations are familiar from practical experience.[23] When they occur, or more precisely, when they are defined as having occurred, loss of face or even social degradation is threatened.[24]

Once an act or series of events is defined as radically undermining the whole social ground of an individual or group, the responses become increasingly limited and prescribed on a kind of all-or-nothing basis. The question is how we reach that point. Such definition takes place over intervals of varying spans; the situation *becomes* critical as certain options are closed off or fail, as their failure narrows the alternative viable and socially reasonable definitions. In other cases the precipitating circumstances may be defined *by their very nature* as critical, as in a public killing or direct challenge. But for a killing the relevant time span may be open-ended, and the response may remain merely "potential" for years.[25] For a face-to-face insult or blow, instant retaliation may be demanded, at least when an audience whose judgment is significant for the one challenged is present. Either the test is met at some proper point, or the individual is socially compromised, devalued in some degree, or even, in extreme circumstances, destroyed as a moral and social being. But even here the successful maintenance or degradation of self takes place as a process of definition over time, and in this process interest and strategies such as the lie are vital. It rarely involves a denunciation of an accuser by a perpetrator, but it becomes defined as socially visible at the terminal point of crisis, when room for maneuver and redefinition has vanished and persons can no longer agree on procedures for defining what has happened, or keep it socially invisible.[26]

The disruptive nature of the demands of honor is only too real in men's experience.[27] To define a situation publicly in terms of honor and to have that definition endorsed as socially authentic by the relevant performers rules out alternative choices to a large extent and entails serious risk and disruption. Within Beit Ahmad, therefore, much effort goes into preventing an event's being categorized in these ultimate terms. Any one of the family who insists on such definitions and who presses every fine point of personal honor produces a kind of social *reductio ad absurdum,* pushing the code into chaos. Individualism and fearlessness then threaten the social value of others in the family by making what should be socially masked and invisible, public and visible. How can a counterdefinition be achieved? Such persons, ever likely to see an insult or a slight and ready to go for a gun, are "anonymized," despite their emphatic egoism. They are defined in such a way that their conduct, however provocative, does not demand a response, causes no infringement on another's place, but in fact socially validates that other's nonresponse. Such men are *makhlu'* , reckless, mad, asocial, dislocated.[28] Their talk and conduct can therefore be received without reaction, and no social devaluation is suffered. The shame, indeed, lies in making a response or setting them off. Their individuality is neutralized by tacit social collaboration and classification.

One of the two men classified by this term in Beit Ahmad had in fact killed a member of a *fellah* family because the latter had wounded a cousin in a fight. The seventeen-year-old went up the hill a few days after to the *fellah* quarter of the village and fired six bullets into the offender. He ran out of the shop in which the shooting had occurred and was halfway down the hill when he realized he had left his sandals in the shop in his haste. He returned through the crowd of *fellahin,* gun in hand, and then walked slowly down the long hill with his back to them. Members of Beit Ahmad fired off their rifles in acclamation and a senior man (brother of the wounded cousin) shouted to him: "You went up the hill a boy and came down a man!" He was jailed for seven years and since his return has been regarded as *makhlu'* . (By the complex dialectic of self and others his behavior is in fact of this type. It is said that he was always fearless but that since his sentence he has become unstable and *makhlu'* .) While I was there he was shot and robbed by an ex-colleague in a gang from outside the village. The family's only concern in the internal meetings which followed was whether one of the other families of the village had done it. Had it been so, there would have been little choice but to continue the cycle of revenge, since his being *makhlu'* defined him as socially anonymous within the defining group but not vis-à-vis outsiders, to whom he remained "visible" and a member of Beit Ahmad.

The second case hinges on the process of individualizing rather than on anonymizing. A member of Beit Ahmad, also now said to have been known before his death as *makhlu'* and famous for a whole series of robberies and extortions (from the lords and outside the village), was killed by another member of the family. The murdered man's father, an elder of high prestige, defined his son as *makhlu'* . The boy had been violent-tempered, an outlaw, reckless and unfearing. He had persistently sought to get 10,000 lire from the great lord of the village, and it was because of this that his cousin, who was the lord's bodyguard, had finally shot him in ambush. The father insisted that it was not "a killing that called for revenge," that his son was fundamentally asocial and that therefore revenge would be "out of order."[29] Peace should and must be made.

The victim had two brothers. In terms of the code, as long as a brother is unavenged one is, in a basic sense, in a state of social pollution. No one expects immediate revenge, but the situation of ultimate reference has occurred. Now here the killing is within the family, the victim is defined as *makhlu'*, peace has been made, and there is a collective interest in maintaining it.[30] And yet. . . . How the two brothers cope with this situation is important. The elder always carries a gun very openly and is treated with great courtesy and etiquette of social "place"; much complimentary phrasing is directed to him by the young men, his peers, and the elders. He sits at the shop where members of Beit Ahmad often gather, goes on deputations to ask favors from local leaders, is full of the verbal performances of honor, and behaves very much like the man of position he is treated as. The younger brother, an army corporal who is seldom in the village, is quiet and much respected as a man of character. It is of him that men say the killer is frightened: "Why? Because he says nothing and silence frightens.[31] The other's a liar [i.e., the other brother]. That's our family for you, we're all *kazzabin* and there isn't one who is worth a franc." These remarks, which could be made publicly within the family only at the cost of confrontation, were kept for an outsider.[32]

In these cases the category of *makhlu'* has been used to devalue a social personality within the family. On the one hand the actor's capacity for forcing the issue is neutralized. His behavior is defined as not requiring action in terms of the scheme of ultimate reference, which is the criterion he constantly and threateningly invokes. On the other hand, where the *victim* is classified as *makhlu'* (and is now said to have been so regarded before the killing occurred, which may or may not be accurate), his death is defined as one for which revenge is "out of order." He does not count. Yet ambiguity remains, and members cooperate to maintain and vigorously enact appropriate definitions of the relevant persons placed in this situation of ambiguity; men interact with them in the everyday world as full social, moral personalities. In both cases, the definition as *makhlu'* was operative within the family only. In the second case, had the victim been killed by a villager from outside the family, a very different course would probably have been followed. For then the social position of Beit Ahmad as a whole, and its claim to corporate status honor, would have been radically challenged.

COPING WITH THE LOSS OF HONOR

How does one who has in fact lost out in the competition for prestige and regard cope with his devalued situation when the code retains its social power and importance for him? The speaker who commented sourly on the family being worth no more than a franc is a man who had sold his inherited land and had been prodigal in spending money on his friends until the money, and the friends, ran out. He had gone abroad following a local altercation and on his return drifted around, finishing up as an impoverished *marafiq*/servant at a lord's house and as an outlaw. Apart from the memory of his father, who had been a celebrated hero of

Beit Ahmad, he has no weight or prestige and is regarded as something of a joker (which indeed he is, or has become). He is on the fringe of the family in terms of social significance. He constantly attacked what he called the *kizb* of Beit Ahmad to me,[33] and his definition and use of lying form our third case.

What follows is direct from notes, and I have interpolated relevant additional information in brackets.

I had a row with Muhammad [a distant relative] in the shop. He insulted me, and I didn't return the insult because he's always drunk. A fight started and he called out Mustafa [another relative], "my brother," and Mustafa came and clouted me with his staff on the head. I grabbed the staff and then he got me with a spanner as well. People finally separated us; you should have heard the screaming and shouting. I went off to my quarter of the village to those who are most closely related, and they wouldn't do anything or go near it. My cousin even greeted Muhammad the next day!

So I let my beard grow and said I wouldn't go into the village but would sell all I had. Everyone thought, "By heaven, he's going to kill someone." Up came several of the men saying that they'd bring Muhammad to kiss my hand in atonement. So I said I wouldn't have anything to do with them. But I knew what was going on and my heart was really happy. All the senior men came [and he proudly listed them] and Muhammad swore he meant nothing by it and there was much performance of respect behavior and he kissed my hand, etc., etc. They begged me to shave my beard, we ceremonially smoked a water pipe and drank coffee together, and off they went. But I knew I was all alone.

No, I wanted to make a road for Muhammad on which he would die while he was still alive [i.e., force him to endure his own social death]. So I set out to become big friends with him. We drank arak together and became the best of friends. One day he came to me and said there's a bit of thieving we could do, so we did a few jobs in that line.

Then one of the young lords I now work for came to me and suggested a theft at the expense of another section of the *behavat*. So I said to myself, "Here's the chance." The boy gave me 150 lire and I went off to Muhammad and told him that they wanted us to burn the house and had given 150 each, and put the money straight into his hand. At night off he went, and I stood fifty yards off with a rifle while Muhammad stole the stuff. Muhammad fled, because he was already wanted for causing a car accident some months before and for robbery. I stayed in the village and they arrested me, though the family told me to run.

So I told them that Muhammad had set up the whole thing, because I knew the lords would get me off with a year or so and pay me no money in jail. I got out on bail before sentence after seven months and the senior men brought Muhammad and me together. I said that I had been beaten up, so what could I do but talk? And within a few days we were close friends again. The village went crazy when they saw us together again.

At the trial Muhammad was sentenced *in absentia* to fifteen years, and I to ten, but I wasn't bothered because I knew the lord could fix it.[34] That's Muhammad settled. I've finished off his children's future as well. But I keep up a show of friendship and sincerity. Yet in my heart, that's another thing. Now he's an outlaw and has no way out. That's what I call real vengeance. If he surrenders and goes to jail the kids will die of hunger. *Rujula* [manliness] does not lie in clouting someone who has clouted you

[referring to his nonresponse to the blow in the first quarrel]; that is merely self-
defense.

Look at the family. They're all my relatives, though I have no paternal uncle or
brothers [closest in cases of honor]. I did the whole thing myself, and it all started from
a blow with a staff. The rest of the family just fight and have no respect for
themselves—all noise and *kizb*. That's the way of the village. Real manliness is
destroying your enemy without all the talk and lies, doing it in secret.

Here is a man who is faced with the fact that his social biography, formed by
others' judgments and his changing life situation, has become devalued over time.
His father is cited as the acme of courage and honor while he, now married and of
an age when men claim full social status, is virtually a servant and unable to
mobilize support when threatened with a crisis. As a teenager he sold the olive
groves of his inheritance and threw away the money in reckless generosity. Such
generosity at that age gains him no social place, since teenagers are still dependent
and not full members of the group; he also has no brothers or paternal uncles. Left
with nothing, and publicly without position, he has constructed a valued self "that
no one knows" which he defines as his *real* self. This self is constituted out of a
manipulation of what is secret, not by a public performance of place-claiming, for
this is denied him by his social biography and the monitoring of his consociates.
Everything that passes for etiquette, respect, manliness, and so forth is for him
interpreted as "all *kizb.*" It is not that he pretends to the superiority of a different
code of honor. Quite the contrary: in his perspective it is he who has the greater
sense of what the code of honor *really* is, since he understands just how far the talk
and bravado of appearance is from the reality. Reality is concealed; therefore his
conduct is in the same mode of concealment. The lie which destroys—pretense of
friendship based on a full intention and not mere empty form—is for him true
manliness.

His self is founded not merely on something not revealed, but on something
hidden deliberately, on the secret as a stratagem of aggression. It is a product of his
manipulation of the lie to destroy another.[35] (Muhammad is indeed spoken of as
"dead," *meyyit,* in the family.) But at the same time that the secret is his weapon
and as it were frames his sense of personal distinctiveness, he has been *forced* into
secrecy. He still has no way to status and social significance in his public
biography. He cannot make claims on the basis of his view of the code, since that
would involve a radical criticism of the dominant interpretation of others, and his
strategies could lead to complete disgrace if made public as intentional acts. He
cannot even say "I have a secret," and indulge in the hint of superiority and
guarded knowledge. He has constructed a private rationalizing ideology, based on
what he sees as the contradiction between others' codified standards of honor and
their actual practice. The real contradiction, however, is found in his attempt to
create and legitimate his social biography by those same criteria of significance by
which his social status will, in fact, be judged marginal and insignificant. Given
the terms of the code, which he himself accepts and is forced by the system to

accept, the contradiction can only be mediated by concealment and the lie. As Simmel has put it: "We may think . . . of the *'lebenslüge'* (the 'vital lie') of the individual who is so often in need of deceiving himself in regard to his capacities, even in regard to his feelings, and who cannot do without superstition about gods and men, in order to maintain his life and his potentialities" (1964: 310). Out of such a contradiction, generated in a specific set of social relations and meanings, is born an ideology, a "superstition" about self and others, at once individual and social, secret and public; an ideology which inevitably reflects the contradictions that generated and maintain it, and of which it has itself become an active element.

Infringement of sexual honor poses similar crucial problems for the man who lacks social status and social support. One individual of Beit Ahmad, on his return from working abroad, gathered enough by intuition or hints to know that his wife might have been illicitly involved with another member of the family. This latter is a highly regarded and very forceful, assertive personality of almost the classic type. The situation was loaded, the choices limited and largely in the returning husband's hands, though they depended also on the anticipation of likely collaboration and behavior. To acknowledge infidelity would be desecration of his total social self unless he killed the wife and challenged the alleged offender. The latter is a member of a large family of brothers and his nearest male kin are from a numerous segment of the family. Either way the husband's existence within the family would have become impossible, though he could have simply left the village altogether and his social world with it. He chose instead to make a point of going regularly to the house of the supposed seducer, going around with him, praising him publicly, and acting the part of the friend and companion with enthusiasm. To my knowledge other family members extended the same collaboration as in our second case, and the matter never reached any form of public doubt. The husband and wife are treated "as though nothing has happened." However, one day a relative who had a grudge against the husband, when drunk and complaining to me about our subject's behavior over some matter, went on: "Why does he do this to me of all people? When he came back from abroad it was I who told him there was absolutely nothing to the talk about his wife and X. I pushed him off to X's house, told him nothing had happened, and supported him." I interpreted this as a way of assuring me that the husband's status was in fact compromised and his honor destroyed; as a way also, under the guise of showing how great a friend he had been to the other, of making sure that I knew of the affair. Two of the younger men of the family who were with me, both close friends, said not a word and I joined their tacit pretense that nothing had been said or heard by making no reply or sign of reaction, though I was in fact shocked by this breach of collective performance. No one mentioned the outburst after we had left the relative's house; we continued the vital lie of "as if" and avoided the definition of the situation that our host had almost thrust upon us.

In a less dramatic setting, many of the younger men and those who had no social place also treasured the notion of the secret self hidden from the public gaze, unknown by all yet knowing all. The secret and the sense of knowing others' secrets are the two sides of this complex process of individuation of the self in a society where you as an individual personality are at issue, when for various reasons you may not "count." Time and again, words to this effect would be said: "Look, you are here to write a book. Ah, if you knew about my life you could write three books or make a film! No one knows my life. But I keep a diary and write everything in it. I don't say anything, but I *know*." One man, asked to tell about his life history, said: "I used to be a bodyguard for such and such a bey and now I drive the car to transport laborers morning and evening." After my suggestion that there might be more to his life than that, he suddenly added: "Oh, you want to know my *real* life, the truth. That would take days to tell. If you knew all my life you would never stop writing. No one knows me."

Now the point is not that this sense of self refers to what is "in fact" the ultimate individual reality. We should note rather that, for many, only this form of giving significance and uniqueness to the individual biography is available. The sole expression of the secret may be in a diary and in the satisfaction of *really* knowing what one's self is, while the world sees only the appearances of a bodyguard and taxi driver. The world of interpretations is devalued, the self exalted. At the same time, the fact that the mode in which the self is exalted is one of secrecy bears witness to the public, pervasive dominance of the code of status honor. Only in the sanctuary of the private domain is the self free from running the gauntlet that public claims or definitions must face—the possibilities of challenge, of circumstances arising which reveal that what one claims for oneself is unfounded or *kizb*, the revelation of a gap between appearance and reality as others judge it. Our final illustration will be of a situation, very precisely bounded in space and time, in which claims were made and falsified without the claimant being aware of the true extent of the disaster.

A RELIGIOUS CASE:
A LIAR AS THE INSTRUMENT OF TRUTH

There is one social identity in which the relation of the hidden and the revealed is particularly important, and that is the role of the religious specialist. Perhaps *the* type case of the basis of authority in most societies is one concerning the control of significant knowledge. The questions are: what constitutes this knowledge (i.e., the culturally recognized components)? how is it constituted in practice in social situations? and how is access to it governed or achieved? Claims to such access have to be authenticated and given warranty by signs which other members accept as valid.

"Knowledge" in Islamic teaching, and in the everyday world of the village, falls into two major categories, *'ilm* and *ma'rifa*. The first is essentially the knowledge of the religious sciences, such as is acquired by *training* in one of the religious colleges, and by familiarity with the Quran and theological texts. *'Ilm* is, as it were, external, existing independently of any individual. To become a specialist one goes through a formal process of passing examinations in a religious college and graduates as an *'alim. Ma'rifa,* however, might be crudely defined as knowledge which derives from illumination, or knowledge of God's concealed purposes, of the *batin* which lies behind the apparent world or *zahir. Ma'rifa* is an internal quality of a person, recognized by specific culturally authenticated signs and performances.[36]

An identity as *sheikh* (as a man with *ma'rifa* is called) must therefore be attributed to the individual by others on a different basis from that of *'alim.* If he is to achieve authentication he must be credited with illumination, with knowledge of the *secret,* of the concealed *batin.*[37] The problem is how men come to credit the subject with knowledge of what by definition is hidden from them. How do *they* dress the individual in the mantle of holiness, award him sanctity—or, to put it another way, make his miracles for him? How do they grant holiness to or withhold it from those who claim it, and in what terms may it be claimed or demonstrated?

One evening a *sheikh* from Syria and one of his followers appeared in the village and went to the reception room of the *ra'is belediya* (the mayor) for their right of hospitality. It happened that another *sheikh* who is well known to this section of the family and often visits it was also present, and it was decided to hold a *zikr* (ritual of chanting the names of God in unison) with the guests. The room was crowded, mostly with young men of Beit Ahmad, but with some senior men as well. Our *sheikh* opened the ritual as we all sat around the room by asking the local singer to sing some of the hymns in praise of the Prophet Muhammad. The singer has what are commonly regarded as a beautiful voice and phrasing. He began, and the audience shouted out with pleasure at certain finely sung phrases, rocked back and forth, and sang the refrains. Our *sheikh* began to murmur prayers, until his face screwed up in an expression almost of pain and he began to weep copiously, occasionally giving a huge shout of "Allah" and shuddering violently. In this sea of movement the Syrian *sheikh* sat motionless and evinced no particular reaction. The singer stopped, and the guest's follower was invited to take his turn.

As soon as he did so, the visiting *sheikh* was seized with convulsions of the right shoulder and an agonized weeping. His murmurs of ecstasy continued throughout the singing. When it ended everyone stood in the crowded room for the *zikr* proper. Our *sheikh* led the proceedings until the visitor interrupted him to change the form and tempo of the chanting and movement. He substituted a far more rapid and complex rhythm and swirled round, darting at different points in the circle with great violence and much shouting of the names of God. One boy of about ten collapsed, jerking and moaning; the mayor himself jumped up and down shouting and twitching, and rounded furiously on those who tried to restrain him; and the ritual eventually collapsed in chaos because the performers could not follow the visitor's conducting. After a short rest and a sermon on religious values, our *sheikh* left the room.

The visitor then started a long speech to the effect that our *sheikh* was now an old man and not up to the task of leading and teaching the young men. Were it not for him (the guest) there would have been no *zikr.* People should follow his way and

take the path to him as members of his *tariqa* (religious fellowship). At this point
one man stepped forward with an expression of immense piety and asked to take
the oath. This caused suppressed amusement and exchanged glances, since he is
one of the most disreputable members of the family, known for the very opposite of
piety and for being a great joker and liar. The visitor instructed him to go off and
make the ritual ablutions and then to pray the prescribed prayers of prostration
twice. He disappeared into the next room and we heard a series of pious
ejaculations. Meanwhile the guest enlarged on how he had knowledge of the *batin*
and could see into the heart of a man, where others saw only the *zahir* of
appearances. He was asked his opinion of the would-be disciple and he replied that
as soon as he had seen him he had known that he was ready for admission to his
fellowship. But should there not be some investigation first? "Nonsense," he
said. "If he has committed any sins or has not prayed and fasted, he will do so after
taking the oath, whether he likes it or not" (in other words, he would be compelled
by his new *sheikh*'s power). The acolyte returned and went through the oath
ceremony and was exhorted to bring many new members for the fellowship. The
sheikh then told many stories of his miracles. He also explained that his violent
shuddering during the chanting was because the spirit of the Prophet Muhammad
had descended on him, while the waving of his arms was to clear away the evil
spirits.

The "disciple," as soon as his master had left to sleep, exploded with laughter
and said that all the pious ejaculations we had heard from the next room were
between mouthfuls of food; that he had not ritually washed, just splashed water
over his head and hands; moreover, that he was not even in a state of ritual purity
(meaning he had had sexual intercourse with his wife that day and not carried out
the prescribed ablutions afterwards). This liar, meaning the guest, had not even
known that; it was a blessing our *sheikh* had gone off to sleep for he always knew
(and he cited examples of other *sheikhs* who had this power of insight into the
hidden). The visitor left the next day without succeeding in gathering any money
from those he approached.

Here the lie was used to unmask the claims of an individual to a specific social
identity and to attribute to him the opposite of those socially valued powers of
which he gave all the signs. How was it done? We should note that the visitor came
as a stranger. He was not in his own community, where knowledge of his
biography might have worked against or for him. He presented all the repertory of
signs and behavior referring to and demonstrating religious power. He wore a
beard, the green-banded turban, and long flowing outer garment, all assumed only
by *sheikhs*; moreover, he appealed to the shared symbols and interpretations of the
religious province of meaning. But at the crucial point of *knowing,* of discerning
the apparent from the true, he was discredited. His stranger status, far from being
an advantage, became a handicap, since it meant that he lacked knowledge of the
life histories and personalities of those to whom the claims were made, although
those claims had to be authenticated by means of such knowledge. Had he *not*
spoken of the age of our *sheikh* and his own superiority as teacher and ritual

specialist, and gone on to attribute miracles to himself, such a discrediting would not have taken place. As it was, he made the members' own biographies relevant, without himself having access to them. Of all men a *sheikh* deserves close monitoring, for "any fool can grow a beard," and this above all others is the identity in which appearance and reality must be socially accepted as one. The *mabruk* may turn out to be the *mal'un*.

Our own *sheikh* had been a regular visitor for two years before making any attempt to adopt followers. He had come to the one house of the family which has a kinship relation with his own, a relation of whose great prestige the house's members are highly conscious. In appearance, manner, tone of voice, and display of religious knowledge he was exemplary. Gradually he met more and more of the family and acquired great understanding through careful observation of the individuals' conduct. He never claimed miraculous powers, invoking only the tradition of religious standing of his own family, which was celebrated throughout the region. By the time of this incident it was being said that our *sheikh* knew what you thought and felt; how you would not dare go before him in a state of ritual impurity, because he would send you away without a word. His little personal queries, backed by his long observation, were interpreted as evidence of personal insight into men's inner, secret selves. (I knew one or two individuals who kept away from him because they were engaged in illicit affairs they were sure he knew of, and so avoided facing his anger, nervously looking for any sign that he really did know.)

Indeed, it once happened that the man who featured as the unmasker and the *kazzab* in the incident with the Syrian was asked by the *sheikh* before they made the prayers whether he had made the ablutions or not. He had not, and at once attributed insight in secret things to the *sheikh*. This was the man who said to me after his performance to the unsuspecting Syrian that it was a blessing our *sheikh* had gone off to sleep, since he could never have behaved in that way in front of him. As it was, he was free to play on the shared knowledge of his own discreditable character and history and his capacity as a liar to expose the visitor as a "liar," without the visitor realizing that his authenticity had been denied. The cues, glances, long looks of apparent piety with only a hint of eye movement—and the massive collaboration by others in this piece of theater—went past the guest. The guest claimed knowledge, and therefore authority, but the signs he gave of it were discredited. The signs and meanings in themselves are socially part of a shared attitude toward the religious domain and the nature of human reality. The unmasker carried out his devaluing with reference to them, and presented himself, by means of a lie, as the defender of their authenticity against a "liar." The miracles were withheld.

To say miracles were withheld is to repeat that miracles, knowledge of the secret, and therefore authority depend by their nature on the judgments and attributions made by relevant others. Clearly this process may be relatively independent of the acts of the person being judged or of face-to-face situations in which that person is participating, once initial interaction has established the socially valid nature of the person.[38] Our *sheikh*'s credit was built up through accounts of him, through interpretation of his conduct which drew on the socially accepted paradigm of what "real" *sheikhs* are and what defines them.[39] Men refer then to their own biographies, to the common stock of knowledge at hand about what *sheikhs* in essence are, and to conduct. Out of these three elements emerges a man's social significance. These attributions are made over time in social situations in which very often the person at issue is not present at all. Warrants and authentications are presented in individual accounts and in what men generally say. Authoritative sanctity, more perhaps than anything else in social life, is in the eye of the beholder.

Let us shift the emphasis in Goffman's description of the cardinal social sin—"the sin of defining oneself in terms of a status while lacking the qualifications which an incumbent of that status is supposed to possess" (1962: 505)—and say rather that others withhold the qualifications from one. Though the visitor presented all the outward typical signs of *sheikh*liness, he placed them in a context of challenge to our *sheikh* and explicit verbal claims to knowledge of the secret. Yet he provided no focus of interest which might incline people to accept his assertions and no reasons for such an acceptance. Without knowledge acquired over time of the particular social world, specific self-attributions have no interactional basis for validation (unless water is to be turned into wine, of course). It is not self-destruction and self-compromise that is at issue, so much as compromise by what might be termed others' interpretative manipulations of your behavior. The visitor made the common-enough mistake of assuming that the transmitter of messages and culturally endorsed signs is in control of their meaning, and forgetting that meaning is also given to messages in social life by others.

The stranger was thus led from claim to claim by our performer,[40] without realizing the way in which he was being defined by his audience. The point of the whole performance was to show that our secret, or shared knowledge of the performer's biography, which enabled us to interpret his elaborate piety as *kizb*, *was a secret* to one who should "know." The liar used the lie to uncover the "truth"; that is, to make an attribution of meaning to the visitor's behavior which was validated by our shared secret. Every typical mark of holiness became an additional mark of *kizb*. The liar became the instrument of truth and revealed/created the lie of the unwitting subject.

CONCLUSION

Lying in its various forms is clearly important in all societies, yet few detailed studies of lying practices and the social distribution of knowledge have been done.[41] There are many tantalizing hints as to what a study of lying in everyday interaction might reveal to the anthropologist. Gombrich notes that in a Sinhalese village the truth, exalted in theory as a major value, is in fact endlessly sabotaged by lying, which "is bound to be frequent in a culture much concerned with the preservation of status and dignity"; Burridge says that the relations between

Kanakas and whites are characterized by both sides as relations of habitual lying and hypocrisy; Talal Asad offers the interesting observation that the Kababish of the Sudan represent themselves as "liars, thieves and deceivers," each man recognizing "that the only resistance his fellows can offer to the absolute power of their rulers consists in varying degrees of evasion."[42]

All these authors show lying as a generalized element within sets of social relations in which, in different ways and for different reasons, mutual knowledge and power or status are individually and structurally crucial.[43] In all these accounts, the main problem for actors is one of controlling certain kinds of information, and this also remains basic outside systems of domination and status containing separate social groupings of unequal rank and power. Robert Murphy has referred to the example of the Mehinacu Indians of Brazil, who are forced to live in close proximity to one another and have such an inordinate stock of knowledge of each other that achieving *non*relations is vital if social life is to persist. Such nonrelations are attained by scrambling the messages with an excess of information and by employing enormous skills in mendacity, thus producing a setting in which "nobody really knows . . . what is true and what is false; they are given ample doubts and few convictions." Lying is vital to the life of this society— indeed, lying *makes it possible*.[44]

This question of doubt leads us back to our case study. The importance of the ambiguity of native categories has been stressed by Leach in his work on Kachin social structure.[45] I would argue that the Lebanese example shows us the other side of the same sociological coin. Here, it seems to me, people have to deal with a normative social order regarded as primary in the sphere of politics, prestige, and rank—the status honor code. This code is distinguished by its public nature, relative simplicity, prescriptive-imperative character, and apparent precision of reference; if certain acts are performed, certain others should follow, and the line between honor and dishonor is absolute and clear, a kind of all-or-nothing proposition. But people actually live by secrecy and *kizb*, in complex situations, by tacit collaboration and flexibility, and by blurred definitions. They exist by *creating* ambiguities out of the unambiguous exigencies of status honor, the private out of the public, the invisible out of the visible. And they do so in ways that must at the same time appear to others to satisfy the demands of the normative code, all the while conscious that situations may arise which pose critical challenges of violence or shame.

In the setting of the village the ideology of honor, in terms of which prestige transactions are apparently conducted, gives rise to certain central ambiguities and contradictions—particularly so because it is an integral part of a historical context in which honor as a mark of group status ranking has been "oversanctified" as an instrument in the use and legitimation of power. So on the one hand honor is crucial to the status position of Beit Ahmad and each individual, while on the other it is only in fact by *kizb* that social life can go on at all and the group's fragile corporateness be preserved. Hence, for example, those who are most fearless in defining situations in terms of the code of challenge and response, and who should be the most prestigious, do most to threaten the common interests of the consociate group and are defined as *makhlu'*, "asocial." The ideology itself produces *kizb* out of the tensions between it and the demands of the everyday world. Still, in this aspect, lying, along with the ambiguity which it reflects and produces, acts as a positive, "enabling" element in the everyday world. It makes the coexistence of code and social life possible.

If we relate ideology and social structure more concretely, however, *kizb* appears as an image and a source of alienation. For in the overall social setting the terms of exchange in which status is negotiated are changing. The lords have, over the years, bought up most of the independent landowners of Beit Ahmad. They have, at the same time, increased the local dependence of many of the staff by tying them to personal service and encouraging them to insist on the hierarchy of status honor. (They have also exacerbated peasant-staff relations by using Beit Ahmad where necessary against the *fellahin*.) Honor has become more and more a primary value and resource over which men transact, while it less and less reflects the realities of power and structural position. Its real economic and political base has been undercut, since the family has been progressively separated by the lords from the independent means of administration and autonomy.

This has entailed significant transformations in the social position of the family and its different segments, transformations that are masked by *kizb* as well as by the public performances of claim making and honor. The younger men are acutely aware that there is one major difference between their own and their fathers' generation. The cars, tractors, and harvesters that they drive and the guns that they carry belong to others, not to them. The young men are separated, in terms of the ethic of Beit Ahmad, from what gives them significance. The boasting, talk, bravado, and *kizb* are now, so to say, at one remove and on a secondhand basis. Men argue about the various qualities of "their" cars, but the knowledge that they drive them for other people, that they are to be hired and fired, and that outside the village the boast of being from the family would be an insignificant claim, is a source of bitterness. The sense of everyday reality, the practice of the everyday social world, has become problematic in its relations to those values that give the social world and the self their meaning.

It is noticeable that the young men work mainly in family groups and in specific kinds of occupations. Twenty-three of them worked on the new airport runway in Beirut; five go to Syria in the summer to man a combine harvester and thresher; others travel to different areas of Lebanon in threes or fours. Wherever they go they go as members of Beit Ahmad, and only in very few cases does one take employment on his own. Furthermore, they work in a very particular kind of occupation: tractor driver, bulldozer driver, harvester driver, taxi driver, and so on. They do not go to Tripoli or Beirut to jobs in light industry or services or trades.[46] Now the notion of "work," as I have mentioned, is alien to the chevalier ethic of status honor. Work is a reality of the life situation of many of the family and they have become specialists in the semiskilled field of driving heavy vehicles. But in the village a man is not a driver, he is a "chauffeur." Indeed it does not seem to me fanciful to designate them "horsemen on tractors." The young men swing a tractor up the hill, roar past those sitting outside the shop, spin it three times on its axis (to the ruin of tires they can scarcely afford), and display their driving in much the same way as their fathers did their horsemanship. Horse and tractor alike are vehicles for display. It is driving style about which one boasts; it is the make and power of the tractor or lord's car that you drive (and the make of revolver that goes with it too) that you discuss with immense technical expertise. A "peasant" once told me that Beit Ahmad were "all mechanics," which is true. But among themselves they *are* "chauffeurs," as their fathers *are qabidiyat* (men of valor). Yet at the same time the complex contradictions between ethos and reality are ever present. One friend said sardonically to me: "Look, you saw what I was saying over there and all the showing off about the Buick and being a chauffeur? *Kizb*, my friend. What am I? I'm a taxi driver, that's what I am." *Kizb* bridges the gap between form and substance, ethos and the actualities of the political economy, but at the same time men directly experience and *know* that it is a false "solution" to the problem.

It is this complex situation which explains the elective affinity between this stratum and a view of the world (the world as constituted by men's actions, divorced from what is religiously right) as itself *kizb*. If we move beyond the narrower definition of the term "ideology" into the realm of religion and belief, "lying" emerges as a principle opposed to, and actively in the world opposing, the truth and the sacred. "Knowing" the interior, "real" world of the *batin* becomes the supreme mark of authority for the man of religion (the *mabruk* or blessed); but it also, in the profane dimension, is the mark of the dangerous, manipulative skills of the liar (the *mal'un* or cursed). The latter is dangerous precisely because the everyday life men live is a domain of lying, both theologically and in practice. Both *mal'un* and *mabruk* can see behind the veil of men's acts, and they present mirror images of each other.

Kizb thus is a vital theme in ideology and the code of honor, in social practice and social structure, and in the world view and belief system.[47] The last sphere in which it is also thematic is that of dramaturgy, situational interaction, and the creating/performing of a self. It can be argued that exactly because honor is increasingly separated from a base in political relations much behavior described as *kizb* takes on the appearance of a kind of game. Men play at and with lying, and it has its own generalized aesthetic and styles. It might seem, therefore, that nothing is "really" at stake, that it is "only" a game, and that statuses are not actually changed. For any given encounter or performance this may be quite true. But encounters and making claims are part of processes over time participated in by your consociates, not one-time events before different audiences. They become part of you, of your style, of what you *are*. The aesthetics of honor are crucial; ritualism and individualism go together.

The honor code forms what C. Wright Mills (1940) has called a "vocabulary of motives" with its own societal controls. Lying is important because it is part of the language by which men set up what they hope are socially authentic and legitimate grounds for conduct. The adequacy of their claims may at any time be tested, as we saw in the example of the Syrian *sheikh*. One has always to think in terms of the long perspective, of anticipated consequences for one's "name" and "place," for one's performance is expected to be relevant to future phases of social action. Games are deadly serious after all, and none more so than those concerning honor and the significance of the person in his social world. For the ultimate stake, when all the bravado, joking, talk, swagger, word play, and *kizb* are over, is your self.

ACKNOWLEDGMENTS

I am most grateful for the comments and suggestions of Drs. Ken Brown, Ernest Gellner, Bruce Kapferer, and Basil Sansom. Professor Leo Kuper very kindly performed a detailed critical reading of the paper in its first draft. The research was carried out between April 1971 and July 1972 for the Manchester University anthropology department project on politics in the Lebanon, directed by Professor Emrys Peters and financed by the SSRC. I am very grateful for their support and for the unending cooperation and hospitality of those with whom I worked in the Lebanon.

NOTES

1. The work of Mary Douglas on purity and pollution, of V. W. Turner on symbolism, and of Cl. Lévi-Strauss on *la pensée sauvage* and the structure of myth, has a different focus. I would hope that the approach here complements their theoretical perspectives.

2. I exclude of course situations in which the observer knows as a matter of fact that such and such a statement is untrue—for example, that X was not in his house when he claimed to have been.

3. "Lying" is to be understood in the rest of this essay in this double sense of intentional act and/or attributional judgment by others.

4. See Goffman 1959, pp. 58–70, for a discussion of misrepresentation in social performances and its threatening aspects.

5. Properly, in classical Arabic, it is *kidhb,* defined in Wehr's Arabic dictionary as "lie; deceit, falsehood, untruth."

6. Hamid Ammar (1954: 138–139) describes deception and lying by children in an Egyptian village: among other children in games and in attempts to triumph by showing another's credulity; by the children to parents, because punishment is administered inconsistently and capriciously with no chance for the child to explain or justify his acts. About the latter type of lie Ammar writes: "the effects of these techniques of fear as forcing children to resort to lies and deception are reflected in the prevailing atmosphere of adult life which is charged with suspicion, secrecy and apprehension . . . it is not surprising to find the common saying that 'fear is a blissful thing.' " The connection here between lies and dominance and control, though it takes different forms in the Lebanon, is of the greatest importance for this discussion, not least with respect to the pervasiveness of lying and secrecy in interaction and at the broader level of culture and social relations.

7. Pierre Bourdieu, writing of a Berber society in which honor and appearance are crucial,

also notes the limitation on joking and verbal extravagance for the restrained and self-effacing man of honor (Bourdieu 1965: 210–211).

8. Nothing, save a rifle, is the object of more knowledge and discussion than the car. Why this is so will become clear later.

9. Izutsu 1966: 98. This book gives a valuable account of the place of lying (*takdhib*) in the Quran, and a suggestive analysis of its semantic field. He points out that lying is the opposite of truth both as an objective property and as the subjective property of a particular speaker whose language conforms to reality (p. 89).

10. The Ottoman state ruled the region until the end of World War I.

11. There are instances of individual and group pressure on a lord arising from some clash of issue or personality, and one family of lords does appear to have been driven from the village some eighty years ago. Now acts of personal intimidation or extortion are by no means infrequent.

12. There are some fifty-six family households of Beit Ahmad in the village, most of them concentrated in the same area. The overall general pattern is for brothers as they marry to build rooms on to their father's house and share a common courtyard, though as these rooms are added to they also become referred to as houses. I have reckoned them here as separate units. The basic pattern of agnatic compound households is still dominant, though some of the young men now save for long enough to build a separate house that does not share the courtyard of the father's house.

13. As will become clear, the term "peasant" has multiple meanings, mostly pejorative and referring to those of no social standing. The topic is briefly explored later in this chapter.

14. People talk with some discrimination about X's way of sitting in the reception room and on public occasions and about general modes of sitting posture.

15. *Adami*, "a good man," is a term of moral approval but not of prestige. It relates to personal characteristics but not to social rank, save insofar as it is frequently followed by *miskin*, "poor chap."

16. The view from the other side I shall describe later when discussing notions of the self and secrecy in the village.

17. Unable by physique and temperament to compete in the family, he wore his learning like a banner among the "peasants." No other member of Beit Ahmad, it might be noted, had ever reached his level of education.

18. I use the term "consociate," derived from Alfred Schutz's work, to mean those with whose personal biographies one is intimately linked and with whom one has grown up and/or is in daily face-to-face interaction; the community with whom one shares a history and stock of common knowledge about the world; and so on. (See Schutz 1962: 16–17.)

19. The last phrase is applied to one to whom, under the guise of innocence and perhaps in collaboration with others, you have delivered a telling verbal blow or innuendo to which he cannot reply and which forces him involuntarily to *show* his hurt.

20. I once refused to believe that a friend had been shot and killed until the young men who rushed to my house swore *wahyatak*. These cue words are particularly important among the young men, who carry on so much joking in their relations that without sign phrases it would be difficult to indicate the boundary between the authentic/real and the inauthentic/invented-apparent. These cues establish a different domain of relevance and reference. I never heard them used otherwise (to my knowledge!).

21. A distinguished Lebanese scholar suggested to me that *fannas* as a Lebanese colloquial

Arabic verb and the noun *tafnis* come from the French *finesse*. The etymology is certainly plausible, not to say appropriate.

22. As Bottomore puts it: "Neither the slave nor the serf can be in any doubt that he works in whole or in part for the benefit of another man" (in Mészáros 1971: 51). It is quite clear in this society who is dominating whom, particularly at the lords' and peasants' levels. Perhaps the middle is more uncertain and ambiguous.

23. These situations include, for example, infringements on family sexual honor (*sharaf*), which desecrate the family; and attacks on individual honor (*karama*), such as serious insults or armed confrontation, or the murder of a relative, when a man may be thought by others to be a coward or timid.

24. The term "social degradation" is Harold Garfinkel's (1956). The main difference between our approaches is that he proposes a framework for analyzing how a specific ceremony of social degradation takes place, succeeds or fails. Rather than with direct confrontation, I am concerned here with degradation as emerging or becoming potential through processes of definition and transaction.

25. One man I knew was walking down the street in town with a distant relative when the latter suddenly indicated an old man walking ahead of them and said that that was the man who forty years ago had shot my friend's paternal uncle. My friend drew his revolver and killed the old man on the spot. What motivated the relative I do not know. The point is that he forced a definition of the situation on my friend, who had to recognize that his total social identity was at issue. His identity would be degraded if he did not maintain it by wiping out the old blood debt. He was jailed but is now free again, and is himself a potential victim.

26. The little boy may cry "The Emperor has no clothes"; the question is whether anyone will pay attention.

27. In a killing, for example, time is open-ended, and even when blood money is paid the exchange remains ambiguous. Though there is Quranic and traditional warrant for blood price, the convertibility of blood to money is problematic: "a brother is not sold," and who knows what member of the victim's family may take it on himself, or be egged on, to seize an opportunity for revenge years later? The open-ended time span gives the situation flexibility from the revengers' point of view and allows for the maintenance of self without compromise. But it generates its own uncertainties.

28. From a verb root meaning to renounce, cast off, disown, repudiate, depose, have done with (see Wehr's Arabic dictionary).

29. However critical a circumstance killing may be, it is still of course subject to processes of social definition and transaction.

30. In one small family of the village that has no significant collective interest or collective social identity, there have been four murders of close relatives since 1935. The latest killer is in jail, and the one on whom the new duty of revenge falls is now of such an age that he is said to be waiting for the other's release. The grim cycle is expected to continue. There is no conflicting definition by which to restructure the situation so that peace may be made. Everything is visible, and each event has generated a new momentum. One man I knew well had one brother killed, and the other is the one currently in jail for seeking revenge.

31. Silence is of all signs the one regarded as most indicative of full intention. It was often said to me of different individuals that they would not do anything about an event, just produce a lot of talk and threatening while friends rushed forward and pleaded and restrained. It is the one who makes no fuss of protest who is really *nawi shi*, intending something, and who may take revenge. That is when the offender keeps to his house or even leaves the village. The public declaration of sacred intention used on occasions of death or wounding is growing the beard, which is also a claim on other support in a sacred duty of

revenge. As an act of self-degradation it places the person in the category of polluted until "right" in blood has been taken. It is an insistence on a very specific and narrow definition of the situation.

32. It is noteworthy that the brother of the man killed in the shop (the case discussed earlier) also makes much of carrying a gun and a staff, talks very emphatically, and is a very "public" personality in his own quarter of the village. Beit Ahmad describe him in the main as "a good man, poor fellow." The killer "respects" (avoids) the quarter altogether.

33. For example, when the young man defined as *makhlu'* in the first case described earlier insulted someone of the family who did not reply, this man used to turn to me on the quiet and tell me that when it came to a crunch all the family's bravado and status honor were lies and show: "When this fellow goes for them, then it's mouths closed and eyes down and not a sound. Liars!" He is also, ironically, something of an expert on points of honor, the subtleties of the code, and proper behavior. He invokes the Bedouin heroes as "real men," can quote much classical Arabic poetry concerning them, and is a stringent and sarcastic judge of others' actions.

34. In fact our friend jumped bail on the lord's advice and was sentenced to ten years in jail. He is now an outlaw and even more dependent on the lord, whose level of trickery exceeds his own. He does not sleep in his own house any more than does Muhammad, though he lives perpetually in the hope that the lord will arrange clemency for him. The young lord involved came out of jail after a few months.

35. Simmel's discussion of secrecy and individualization is of considerable relevance here: "The measure in which the dispositions and complications of personalities form secrets depends . . . on the social structure in which their lives are placed . . . the secret is a first-rate element of individualisation . . . social conditions of strong personal differentiation permit and *require* [my emphasis] secrecy in a high degree; and conversely, the secret embodies and intensifies such differentiation" (1964: 334–335).

36. I must add here a further gloss, though there is no space in which to develop the point as it deserves. This division of the world has enormous resonance in the village *Weltanschauung,* and is often referred to in discussions of religion, the meaning of Islam, and men's place in the world. People often gloss the *zāhir* (apparent) as *kizb* and the *bātin* (concealed, inward meaning) as truth. He who has knowledge of the *bātin* is *mabrūk* (blessed), one of sacred status. But on the other hand he who has knowledge of the secrets of the everyday world, and can manipulate others because of his cunning, deceit, and *kizb,* is spoken of as *mal'ūn* (literally, cursed). This too is insight into the hidden, but of men's, not God's, purposes. Such understanding and manipulation through penetration into others' *kizb,* used as a foundation for one's own *kizb,* is authoritative knowledge, but diametrically opposed to that of the *sheikh.* It is destructive, profane in a profane world; for where all is *kizb,* as I have already pointed out, the man best able to know others' lies is in a powerful and dangerous position. Furthermore, given the nature of things, one meets up with the *mal'ūn* a great deal more than with the *mabrūk* and he has far more daily, practical relevance.

37. It might be properly called *the* secret, since the *bātin* of God's purpose is of illimitable range and significance. It is the ground of all that is hidden and all that is revealed. Its signs are the verses of the Divine Revelation.

38. The validity may be established through a number of means: for instance, past history, a performance "to type," personality and character, or selection of an audience who may have an elective affinity for the call or message.

39. Even in our *sheikh*'s case there were some who were rivals of the house to which the *sheikh* regularly came, and some who were simply skeptical, who said of him that "the only reason he comes to our village is that here they kiss his hand and in his own they don't. There they know him."

40. The unmasker, for example, piously asked how he would get the *sheikh*'s aid when the latter left the village, and the *sheikh* replied that his follower should simply shout his (the *sheikh*'s) name from the hilltop and he would appear.

41. The extent to which anthropologists themselves are caught up in patterns of concealment and secrecy, a rich field for research, is analyzed by Berreman (1972: xvii–lvii).

42. Gombrich 1971: 262–263; Burridge 1970: 37; Asad 1970: 242. None of these works centers on interaction patterns.

43. Cf. Bohannan (1957: 48–49), Kiefer (1972: 101), and Gulliver (1963: 229). These authors are concerned with lying as an expected part of specific, highly formalized situations of legal dispute. They are not immediately concerned with its patterns in other areas of social interaction. J. K. Campbell shows that in the highly competitive world of the Sarakatsani shepherds of Northern Greece, also characterized by an elaborated honor code, it is a virtue to lie to and cheat non-kin in the bitter fight for scarce resources (1964: 279–283, 316).

44. Murphy 1972: 227–228. He refers to a thesis by Thomas Gregor of Cornell University, 1969.

45. Leach 1965: 106. "The ambiguity of native categories is absolutely fundamental to the operation of the Kachin social system. . . . It is only because the meaning of his sundry structural categories is, for a Kachin, extremely elastic that he is able to interpret the actuality of his social life as conforming to the formal pattern of the traditional, mythically defined, structural system." In usage, Arabic terms such as *beit* (house) and *'ailat* (family) are every bit as vague and flexible as Kachin categories of village and other groupings. In both societies the ideal structure is elaborate and rigid. I am stressing the importance of the *practices* through which ambiguity is produced, not only the conceptual-categorical elasticity.

46. It might be noted, though I shall not discuss the matter in detail, that there are very few marriages with women from outside the family, and that endogamy here is not only ideology but actuality for Beit Ahmad.

47. Max Weber long ago pointed out the implications inherent in the utilitarian ethic which, like the ethic discussed here, has its own logic and breeds its own lies: "Honesty is useful, because it assures credit; so are punctuality, industry, frugality, and that is the reason they are virtues. A logical deduction from this would be that where, for instance, the appearance of honesty serves the same purpose, that would suffice. . ." (1958: 52).

REFERENCES

Ammar, H. 1954. *Growing Up in an Egyptian Village*. London: Routledge and Kegan Paul.
Asad, T. 1970. *The Kababish Arabs*. London: C. Hurst.
Berreman, G. 1972. *Hindus of the Himalayas*. Berkeley: University of California Press.
Bohannan, P. 1957. *Justice and Judgment Among the Tiv*. London: Oxford University Press.
Bourdieu, P. 1965. The sentiment of honour in Kabyle society. In J. G. Peristiany, ed., *Honour and Shame*. London: Weidenfeld and Nicolson.
Burridge, K. 1970. *Mambu*. New York: Harper and Row.
Campbell, J. K. 1964. *Honour, Family and Patronage*. Oxford: Clarendon Press.
Garfinkel, H. 1956. Conditions of successful degradation ceremonies. *American Journal of Sociology*, 61: 420–424.
Geertz, C. 1966. *Person, Time, and Conduct in Bali*. New Haven: Yale University Press.

Goffman, E. 1959. *The Presentation of Self in Everyday Life*. New York: Doubleday.
————. 1962. On cooling the mark out. In A. Rose, ed., *Human Behaviour and Social Processes*. London: Routledge and Kegan Paul.
Gombrich, R. 1971. *Precept and Practice*. Oxford: Clarendon Press.
Gulliver, P. 1963. *Social Control in an African Society*. London: Routledge and Kegan Paul.
Izutsu, T. 1966. *Ethico-Religious Concepts in the Quran*. Montreal: McGill University Press.
Kiefer, T. 1972. *The Tausug*. New York: Holt, Rinehart and Winston.
Leach, E. R. 1965. *Political Systems of Highland Burma*. Boston: Beacon Press.
Mészáros, I. 1971. *Aspects of History and Class Consciousness*. London: Routledge and Kegan Paul.
Mills, C. Wright. 1940. Situated actions and vocabularies of motive. *American Sociological Review*, 5 (December).
Murphy, R. 1972. *The Dialectics of Social Life*. London: George Allen and Unwin.
Schutz, A. 1962. *Collected Papers*. Vol. 1. The Hague: Martinus Nijhoff.
————. 1964. *Collected Papers*. Vol. 2. The Hague: Martinus Nijhoff.
Simmel, G. 1964. *The Sociology of Georg Simmel*. Trans., ed., and with an introduction by Kurt H. Wolff. New York: Free Press.
Weber, M. 1958. *The Protestant Ethic and the Spirit of Capitalism*. New York: Charles Scribner's Sons.

Part Three

EMERGENT PROPERTIES AND TRANSACTIONAL ACTIVITY: CONTINUITY AND CHANGE

Bureaucratic Transactions: The Development of Official-Client Relationships in Israel

DON HANDELMAN

By and large the study of contacts between officials and their clients has proceeded according to assumptions of efficiency, role specificity, and universalistic criteria in decision making postulated by the Weberian ideal-type construct of bureaucracy. In this vein a recent study notes: "According to the ideal model of Western bureaucracy, all role relations, including those with clients, should be highly specific in orientation. Individuals should bring into interaction only those segments of their selves which are officially relevant to communication in a bureaucratic setting and to the particular problem at hand" (Danet and Gurevitch 1972: 1167). According to this construct it is immaterial whether an official receives a particular client only once or many times in succession, for each occasion of contact will be treated by both according to the assumptions noted above; each contact will therefore be resolved according to bureaucratic procedure, and will have little or no cumulative effect on subsequent contacts. Behavioral variations from the ideal-type construct, as for example the emergence of social relationships between officials and clients, have on occasion been termed "de-bureaucratization" (see Blau and Scott 1962: 232–234; Katz and Eisenstadt 1965: 255–259), a form which connotes deviance more readily than variance. This major approach to the study of bureaucracy is relatively uninformative about official-client relationships, since these relationships remain largely an aspect of deviant phenomena like de-bureaucratization.

However, Weber's conception of the social relationship can readily be considered as one potential outcome of contacts between officials in service bureaucracies and their clients. According to Weber, the social relationship requires "at least a minimum of mutual orientation of the action of each to that of the others"; the meaning attributed to the relevant actors is contextually or indexically understood rather than "normatively 'correct,' " and there is "a probability that there will be, in some meaningfully understandable sense, a course of social action" (1964: 118).[1] For this chapter the above criteria can be rephrased to read as follows: Officials and clients attend to the presentations, offers, and responses of one another. They evaluate and attribute meanings to the content of all perceived behaviors within the context of their encounter, as it is jointly constituted by the

223

officials and clients present; and to their contact they attribute the possibility or probability of subsequent contacts. The social contact is differentiated from the social relationship by the probability that there will be subsequent contacts between the same sets of persons, who will continue to attend to one another and to evaluate their actions indexically. The social relationship is therefore constructed through the cumulative actions and effects of a series of social contacts; and the relationship is an emergent property of the history of social contacts between particular persons, regardless of the more formal or clearly specified attributes of status which they present to one another.

As anthropologists increasingly turn to the study of complex societies and their attendant bureaucratic apparatus, they may well find that social relationships do operate as substantive factors in contacts between officials and clients; one of their tasks will be to specify the conditions under which such relationships develop, the manner of their development, and the social consequences of such affiliations for persons so linked. In the approach to such questions a transactional perspective will have analytic strength.

The subject of this chapter is the development of relational links between a welfare department and client household in Jerusalem during a span of some fifteen years.[2] The foci of this study are the transactions which were effected between clients and the department, and the effects of these contacts on what I term the welfare career-line. Put more simply for the moment, the problem is this: given a bureaucratic agency which is oriented toward terminating the affiliations of clients as speedily as possible, and given clients who are more or less also interested in terminating their welfare affiliation, at least at the outset of their contacts with the agency, how is it that their affiliation becomes more complex and endures for a lengthy period of time? From the perspective of formal organization theory such a question should not be problematic, or this question might be treated in terms of phenomena like de-bureaucratization. If we take the transactional approach, such a question directs our attention to the negotiated properties of social order, and to the resources, means, and forums which persons may attempt to mobilize and realize in order to further their interests of the moment.

In order for a person legitimately to receive unspecified benefits from a service bureaucracy, he must be screened, accepted into the category of "client," and in turn accept this categorization, at least in contacts with bureaucratic personnel (see Zimmerman 1969, 1971; Jerry Jacobs 1968–1969). This arrangement is what I term bureaucratic "affiliation." In the context of a welfare office this arrangement is composed of rights and expectations, with relatively unspecified boundaries, which permit welfare caseworkers and clients to come into interpersonal contact with one another. In such contacts interaction follows a pattern of offer/request/demand and response.[3] Since the object of the contact is for the client to be extended advice, aid, or material benefits, the kinds of offers and demands made by either side (at least in the Israeli context) are not specified by the initial affiliation. Since the parameters of the content of offer-response can be quite vague, and since the pattern of offer-response is a sequential one, each of the parties to the contact is in effect exerting some control on their joint activity, its outcome, and its subsequent effect on their affiliation. Burns (1958: 138) has noted that

> The essential feature of control is that it limits the possibilities of action for the next agent, whether self or other. The first consequence of this viewpoint is that the agent is involved in a process. No social act is self-starting; when we act, we deal with a situation set up for us by the actions of others and ourselves in the past, and the result is another situation in which we and the others will have to act further. When we act, we aim so to control that future situation that the next actor will be led more easily in the way we want.

The sequence of offer and response is what I term transaction or exchange, and the "controls" such transactions introduce into subsequent contacts between the parties are the initial emergent properties of the affiliation.[4] Since the terms of affiliation are variable, and since either party can choose to make an offer as well as to accept or reject the offers of the other, transactions are integral to a process of negotiation in which the terms and duration of affiliation are open to bargaining.

While Blau correctly identifies the dual strain toward reciprocity and imbalance in social contacts, as persons attempt to stay out of debt to others while trying to attain status superiority (Blau 1964: 26), the evaluation of relative power in social contacts and social relationships depends more specifically upon the identification of the resources which either party can introduce to obtain benefits from the other. As the social situations of both parties alter through time, not only relative to one another but relative also to other parties and factors, their resource capacities also change, affecting their attempts to achieve or maintain reciprocal or differential contacts, and therefore affecting the power balance between them. In the context of this study, resources are considered to be attributes of person or social situation which, when introduced into social contacts, have the capacity to elicit responses from alter that accord with the apparent momentary interests of ego, whether ego perceives the operation of such attributes or not.[5] "Realized resources" are those which indeed do elicit responses that accord with the momentary interests of ego on given occasions. However, if resources are to affect interpersonal negotiations in social contacts, they must be presented in some way in order to be evaluated.[6]

I have suggested that affiliation is an emergent property of contacts between service officials and prospective clients, and that the realization of resources in the transactional process of negotiation may result in the emergence of social relationships between officials and clients, viz. the probability of subsequent contacts between the same sets of persons, which in turn may affect the nature of their affiliation. A useful way of organizing these sequential activities and processes is through the ideas of "career" and "career-line." Goffman (1970: 119) writes:

> Traditionally the term career has been reserved for those who expect to enjoy the rises laid out within a respectable profession. The term is coming to be used, however, in a broadened sense to refer to any social strand of any person's course through life. The perspective of natural history is taken: unique outcomes are neglected in favour of

such changes over time as are basic and common to the members of a social category, although occurring independently to each of them. So a career is not a thing that can be brilliant or disappointing; it can no more be a success than a failure.[7]

While "career" may be utilized only to delineate stages of living through which a person moves, and the ways in which stage transitions are accomplished, the idea of emergence is inherent in the notion of career-line. The development of a "social strand" is, as I have suggested, the substance of a transactional process of negotiation between relevant parties. The substance of this process is the resolution of patterns of offer and response, and the directional implications for the kinds of offers and responses which may subsequently materialize. Thus subsequent offers and responses are contingent upon previous resolutions and the directional implications contained within these patterns. So the resolutions of transactions are not necessarily identical to or identified with the interests or intentions of either party, but are products of the parties' conjoint activities which constrain and guide the content and directionality of subsequent contacts. Transactions, their effects, and their directional implications are elements in and of an emerging story line which is neither the attribute nor the product of any single person, but derives from the developmental operating structure of relationship between relevant persons.[8] "Career-line," metaphorically and processually, signifies the emergent directional line of negotiated resolution which is the social relationship; and which, as it develops, can affect and alter conceptions of affiliation held by the relevant parties. This in turn may affect the goals, resources, and opportunities which parties to the relationship have, and thereby affect the nature of transactions in which they engage, the kinds of negotiated resolutions that can materialize, and, again, the conceptions of affiliation which the parties hold.[9]

I will return to these general considerations of transaction in the light of the case study to be discussed below. Prior to this analysis, however, the reader should be introduced to aspects of welfare in Israel—more specifically, to department and client orientations to affiliation, and to the resources each party may be able to realize in transactions to influence the form of the affiliation.

ORIENTATIONS OF THE WELFARE DEPARTMENT
AND CLIENTS TO AFFILIATION[10]

The welfare career has often been considered in terms of stigma and associated negative moral constructs, as have other deviant careers (cf. Edgerton 1967; Goffman 1970; Becker 1967). In a cogent analysis of conceptions of welfare in the United States, Beck (1966–1967: 266–267) writes:

> Whether the welfare label is applied to a population of users, a program of activities, an organization, or a set of issues, it immediately signals an area of special phenomena, outside the normal scope of business. As such, it generates reputational disadvantages for everything so labelled, in the eyes of ordinary committed people. These

disadvantages need not arouse high feeling or even criticism. The mere attribution of doubt to the moral character of the labelled persons . . . can have far-reaching . . . consequences.

And the social costs paid by clients labelled in this way can be great indeed in societies which mobilize elaborate bureaucratic procedures to define, process, and in a sense punish such persons (cf. Kay 1969).

The welfare career is also stigmatized in Israel, but less so, I think, than in many other Western nations. As a Zionist nation with a Law of Return, Israel was pledged to care for the basic wants of all those Jewish immigrants who came to settle. The commitment to care for non-Western immigrants within a Western bureaucratic framework inevitably involved a multitude of service and welfare agencies, public and private. Their need to deal with persons of different cultures forced experts to reconsider conceptions of stigma (cf. Palgi 1963); and many aspects of what would be termed "welfare" in Western societies were part of the immigrant absorption process in Israel (cf. Kushner 1968; Shokeid 1971a, 1971b; Weingrod 1966). Overtaxed Israeli public welfare agencies have not developed elaborate investigative procedures to test the eligibility of candidates; and public welfare caseworkers are largely desk-bound, relying for information about clients on the presentations of the clients themselves.[11] While welfare aid is generally not considered desirable, it is acceptable to request such support to meet immediate needs. In this study of a small town in western Galilee, Marx (1972: 284) noted:

> many people feel they fare best by staying in regular relief work and supplementing it by welfare assistance. This applies particularly to middle-aged men supporting large families, most of whose children still attend school. In families such as these, relationships are affected by the dependence on bureaucratic agencies: the number of primary relationships is reduced; relationships among even close kinsmen, such as brothers, become dormant and ineffective; even the obligations between parents and children are limited.

In 1965–1966, 17.7 percent of all families in Israel applied for some form of welfare assistance. Of these families, 85 percent received "guidance and care" while 22 percent received monthly welfare payments (Kanev 1968: 94). Israeli public welfare offices are accessible to applicants who live on the economic margin, and for whom assistance of any kind can be a significant boon.

The Welfare Department orientation toward clients is a short-term one, with the ideal welfare career conceived of in much the same way as Beck has described: "the welfare user experiences the need of special facilities, goes into a residual welfare institution to receive them . . . and in fact leaves the aegis of the welfare world as quickly as he can" (Beck 1966–1967: 273).[12] While the department is a public service bureaucracy ideologically committed to dispensing services to persons who qualify, it is also concerned with terminating the affiliations of clients by removing them from the welfare rolls as soon as their resources rise above the minimum. This is usually accomplished by finding employment or some other

source of income for the client. Termination of affiliation is termed "rehabilitation,"[13] and a high turnover of clients is a major criterion of department success.
By erasing the rolls the department combines aid and "rehabilitation," and is able
to divert its benefits to other applicants and clients.

As a bureaucratic organization, the department is also concerned to expand its
budget, and to add personnel to manage expanded services. While the department
must compete for scarce funds with a series of other departments, there are strong
ideological rationales for this activity: that there are always more needy clients
than funds or personnel to care for them, and that the current level of benefits to
clients does not meet their needs. It is probable that the larger the number of clients
affiliated with the Welfare Department, the larger are budgetary allocations
received by the department, and the greater the strength of the department becomes
in the competition for additional allocations (cf. Sjoberg et al. 1966: 327).[14] This
presumes that size and need of clientele are given as indicators of the significance
of department functions. Is it then more profitable for the Welfare Department to
follow an orientation of long-term client affiliation or one of short-term client
affiliation? Long-term affiliation gives the department greater control over a
narrower span of clients. Short-term affiliation allows for less control, but permits
it to be exerted over a wider span of clients. Since short-term affiliation is closely
related to criteria of department "success," this is the orientation which tends to be
followed, at least with the clients whose records I examined.[15]

There is a further reason for the short-term orientation of the department. If the
department fails to rehabilitate a client (that is, erase him from the welfare rolls),
transactions between the parties will continue, and the client may be able to realize
additional resources with which to induce allocations from the department. Then
the very transactions through which the department seeks to terminate affiliation
operate to upset its timetable and to extend the welfare career-line of the client.
Furthermore, the responsibility for failure to "rehabilitate" rests primarily with
the department, and not with its clients. By accepting a person into a "morally
suspect category of activity" (Beck 1966–1967: 274), namely that of "welfare
client," the department defines the person as "less responsible," and by contrast
defines itself as "more responsible." As the more responsible party with benefits
to allocate, the department attempts to "rehabilitate" the client by offering various
avenues to termination of affiliation, through which the client will again be defined
as "responsible." It is in the interests of the department to overcome what it has
perceived and defined as deficiencies in a client, or to provide inducements for him
to overcome these. If the department can persuade the client to accept an offer of
employment, and thereby become "responsible" once again, any further lack of
success will be attributed to the failure of the ex-client, regardless of whether such
employment met his needs, since he will have competed in the marketplace like all
other "responsible" working people who experience their advances and re-
gressions.[16] If the ex-client fails in his work, he can be legitimately re-entered on
the welfare rolls as a chronic social case whose failure was solely his own

responsibility, since his "rehabilitation" had already taken place. The client may then achieve a belated long-term relationship with the department (see also Jerry Jacobs 1968–1969: 420).

Operating with the short-term orientation outlined above, the Welfare Department attempts to control, limit, and terminate the affiliations of clients while proferring needed benefits. To accomplish these purposes the department can realize various resources, which will be mentioned here only briefly. In order to establish the kind of client that the department is dealing with, the latter must construct a composite "client-identity" from the information it has gathered (see Goffman 1963: 2). On the basis of such constructs the department decides about client eligibility and the extent of services which will be offered the client. Becker (1969: 342) writes that members of service occupations

> typically have some image of their "ideal" client, and it is in terms of this fiction that they fashion their conceptions of how their work ought to be performed and their actual work techniques. To the degree that actual clients approximate this ideal the worker will have no "client problem." In a highly differentiated urban society, however, clients will vary greatly, and ordinarily only some fraction of the total of potential clients will be "good" ones.

Then the department teaches the client how to behave and what to request if benefits are to be forthcoming (cf. Jerry Jacobs 1968–1969: 419; Glenn Jacobs 1970: 258). By teaching clients what demeanor is expected of them and what they can request, the department also defines for clients the interests they should have or can have (see W. Richard Scott 1969: 127).[17] The client's acceptance or nonacceptance of the field of relevance implied in the department's conception of the affiliation becomes a matter of transaction and negotiation.[18] Closely linked to the construction of composite client-identities are labels of stigmatization which the department can introduce in phases of the welfare career-line to simplify the complexities of affiliation and to provide legitimation for a different approach to the client.[19] I will go into this in more detail in the case study to follow.

While the department is formally bound by assemblies of regulations which define the nature and content of affiliations with clients, in practice "formal organizational designs are schemes of interpretation that competent and entitled users can invoke in yet unknown ways whenever it suits their purposes" (Bittner 1965: 249–250; see also Zimmerman 1969, 1971). Caseworkers have a good deal of leeway in interpreting which regulations apply to a client in a particular instance, and how they apply. In turn, such interpretations will affect offers made to clients.

Given the conception of an "ideal" welfare career to which the Welfare Department holds, transactions between officials and clients should follow a simply prescribed course. The applicant comes to the department as supplicant, is screened, and begins his bureaucratic affiliation. Understood within the terms of affiliation is the commitment of the department to make unilateral allocations to the client, allocations that will be of value to the client. On the basis of its control of valued benefits and services, and its preparedness to make allocations, the department should have power over the client,[20] and the client should be obligated to pay his debts by complying with department directives.[21] Such compliance results ultimately in termination of affiliation and loss of further benefits for the client. While contacts and transactions last, there is unilaterality of allocations and an imbalance in obligations between the two parties (see Kapferer 1972: 165), and the client reciprocates by accepting the allocations and termination of affiliation. In so doing he reduces the power which the department has over him and regains his full social independence (see Blau 1964: 98). This model does in fact hold for many instances of affiliation, and where it does, the ideas discussed in the first section of this chapter, relating to negotiation, relationship, and emergence, are essentially irrelevant. More interesting for our purposes are the instances in which this scheme does not hold. It does not hold for cases in which the *client* begins affiliation with a short-term orientation, as in the case to be discussed, or for cases in which the client begins affiliation with the intention of maximizing his link to welfare benefits.

There appear to be two major factors which operate to steer transactions and affiliation into a long-term career-line. One is the issue of what is perceived to constitute a "fair exchange" and the other concerns the resources clients can realize to influence affiliation. For the Welfare Department a fair exchange for termination of affiliation consists of the benefits which it has available at the moment.[22] For the client with a short-term orientation to affiliation a fair exchange for termination would appear to be benefits which meet his perceived needs. In many cases what is available cannot be equated with what is needed. The client then attempts to realize resources which will induce the department to provide him with what he sees as a fair exchange for termination of affiliation. In the process he is allocated other benefits which derive solely from welfare sources. He then may become more interested in obtaining these and other benefits, and he will attempt to realize further resources to maintain the supply. By this time his welfare affiliation has become more valuable to him than it was at the outset, and his price for termination becomes more than what the department considers termination to be worth. What happens then may depend upon the kinds of inducements which the client can offer the department to continue allocations.[23] On the other hand, the client who begins affiliation with a long-term orientation will attempt to resist all offers of termination while providing inducements for the department to increase allocations to him. Being uninterested in a fair exchange, he will nevertheless try to maintain the appearance of a "good" client in order to obtain further services. The extent to which either type of client is successful will depend on the resources the client can realize to influence the department, but with time will also depend on certain emergent properties of past and ongoing transactions with the department and on the changing life-situation of the client. It is to a preliminary discussion of client resources that I now turn.

CLIENT RESOURCES FOR INFLUENCING AFFILIATION

While the Welfare Department is geared to assist clients who qualify, the kind and extent of benefits given, as well as the schedule of assistance (see Roth 1963: 107–114), are negotiable. Prospective clients come to the department from various life-situations, and with different personal and social attributes which can be realized to induce allocations. Such inducement is not inherent in attributes; the client must present himself properly in order to "reduce the anonymity of the client categories, to make oneself more visible and thus to win special attention and treatment" (Weiss Bar-Yosef 1968: 38). One attribute which may require little effort to present to the department is the state of health or physical incapacity of the applicant; this, if certified by medical documentation (see Zimmerman 1969), may require the department to adopt a long-term orientation toward the applicant. However, while such client resources may elicit major commitments from the department, client disability will in turn cause the client to be greatly dependent, in a structural sense, upon the department. Such dependency will greatly limit the capacity of the client to dispute department proposals (see Handelman 1971: 191–195). Where such attributes are the major resources to be realized, the converse of department commitment will be client dependence and relative powerlessness to influence the nature of affiliation.

Another attribute for inducing allocations, one that varies in strength during different phases of the individual life cycle, is the age of the applicant. As a child his parents will elicit support for him, and he in turn will be dependent upon them for these benefits. As a young adult the client will elicit less support, but in turn he will be more independent of the department and so able to realize other resources which can affect affiliation. As an older adult the client will again, on the basis of age, be able to elicit department support, but at the cost of greater dependence and lesser influence on affiliation.

Attributes which vary with the domestic cycle are size and composition of the client household. For example, if the household should consist of an unskilled client, an unemployable spouse, and a large number of children below the age of employment, it will be likely to receive more welfare support than a smaller household or one which contains employable persons. However, while a head of household with numerous dependents may be able to elicit extensive support, as his children grow, marry, and leave the household, support will correspondingly decrease.

I previously noted that welfare agencies have stereotypic conceptions of what constitutes a "deserving" client (see Robert Scott 1970; Mayer and Timms 1970: 131); when client attributes can be matched with elements of such conceptions benefits will be forthcoming. In the Israeli context ethnicity of clients or aspects of their family history may function in this way. As well, reductionist labels of stigmatization applied by agencies to legitimize their treatment of clients may be seen as resources of the client at this point. For while the application of such labels may increase client dependency and compliance, it may justify the continuation of welfare benefits.

Possibly the most significant resource which clients can realize to manipulate their contacts with the department is the alternative economic opportunities open to them at that time. The other client resources I have outlined stem from the ways in which the department perceives clients; and their realization depends upon frequent contacts between clients and caseworkers so that the department will have sufficient information to construct composite client-identities. In terms of such composites the department may see clients as dependent and powerless; but as perceived by the client the situation may be quite different, if he has sources of economic reward apart from the department. If these economic rewards do not stem from sources connected to the department, and if they can be concealed from caseworkers, the client may perceive himself as quite independent of the will of the department, and he will then be able to postpone or avoid compliance with department decisions and directives, for as Blau (1964: 32) writes: "The power of an individual over another depends entirely on the social alternatives or lack of alternatives of the subjected individual...." Moreover, the durational significance of alternative opportunities is quite different for clients and for officials. If a client succeeds in opening such an alternative for a period of six months or a year, this can be of profound significance for himself and his household. However, for officials who work in terms of "bureaucratic time" such a period may be quite insignificant. This is so partly because the client daily perceives himself as a full human being with manifold responsibilities, while the department perceives him as a client with a more limited set of obligations which focus on his bureaucratic affiliation.

Other resources which clients can realize in contacts with caseworkers are primarily interactional, and these I term "tactics of self-presentation." Since, in the Israeli context, the public welfare caseworker is largely desk-bound, the ways in which information is communicated by clients to the department have a crucial bearing on the bureaucratic affiliations which develop. From other evidence that I have, it is clear that if a client presents himself only infrequently to the caseworker, and if the department has not yet developed a major commitment to the client, the resulting relationship will be weak and the client will receive only limited benefits. Therefore the tactics clients employ to make the department aware of the extent and variety of their needs are crucial to the strength of any emergent relationship.

One major client tactic is what I term "diversification of demand." In the Israeli context the client household provides "loci" and "areas" for welfare investment. Benefits may be allocated to particular persons or relationships within the household, and the persons involved are what I term the "loci" of investment. The department also allocates benefits to "areas" of household living (for instance, employment, child care, education, housing), and these areas of living may vary along a continuum somewhat different from that of the loci of investment. Thus a household may be represented by a single client locus who demands benefits for a single area of living, or by a single locus whose demands cover many areas of household living. On the other hand, a household may contain a number of client loci who all request benefits for a single area of living, or a number of loci who want benefits for many areas of living. The client who initially has, or who develops, a long-term orientation to welfare aid will try to involve the department in many different areas of household living (cf. Glenn Jacobs 1970: 257–258); and each household member, as well as each relationship between members, will become a potential locus of welfare investments. In this process multiple links are established between department and household; and the extent to which welfare allocations are diversified among household loci and areas of living will in large part determine the future capacity of the department to sever the relationship and terminate affiliation. In my view, the establishment of such multiple links constitutes a process of structural "involvement" which replaces the need for "trust" in the continuation and development of official-client relationships. For, given the ideology of the department, once household needs are properly presented and communicated they can be ignored by the department only with difficulty. Moreover, the needs of household loci and areas of living do not decline at the same rate. The variable rates at which, for example, employment, housing, child care, health care, and education are being rendered unproblematic for various household loci ensure that at any given time the department remains linked to the household: some problems are solved, others continue, and still others begin to emerge. I suggest, then, that the "commitment" of the department to a client household is a function of its structural "involvement" in the household, while such involvement in turn is a function of the diversity of allocations to the household. And, as suggested, allocations (that is, investments) depend upon the kinds of resources realized in transactions between caseworkers and clients. I will return to this point later in this chapter. I will only note here that as multiple links are established between department and client household through ongoing negotiated transactions, clients are further encouraged to provide inducements to elicit diverse allocations (see Blau 1964: 100). While the department's initial commitment to affiliation may have been connected to a single client, with time the unit of affiliation changes and becomes the household. Then severing contacts with a single client does not terminate affiliation.

A second tactic, which I term "complication and contradiction," is primarily interactional and supportive. If a client always behaves in the same way before a caseworker, he will "maintain face" because "the line he effectively takes presents an image of him that is internally consistent, that is supported by judgments and evidence conveyed by other participants, and that is confirmed by evidence conveyed through impersonal agencies in the situation" (Goffman 1967: 6–7). Furthermore, client and caseworker will be in a "state of talk—that is, they have declared themselves officially open to one another for purposes of spoken communication and guarantee together to maintain a flow of words" (Goffman 1967: 34).[24] At times this is opposed to the interests of the client. If his "presentation of self" is consistent over a number of contacts, the caseworker can more easily categorize him and then set allocations accordingly. So at times it is in the interests of the client to present himself to the department in different and con-tradictory ways.[25] Unless he has other sources of information about the client, the caseworker cannot easily know which "face" to treat with, and he tends to treat with all identities the client presents. The client's various behaviors may be encapsulated within a single contact or within a series of contacts, in which the potential for confusing the caseworker is great indeed.[26] Complication and con-tradiction are especially apt when the caseworker calls for a state of talk to present department proposals which the client wishes to avoid without outright rejection. At a minimum, confusion in such contacts requires the allocation of personnel and time to sort out the complications introduced by the client; and at times casework-ers appear to adopt a shotgun approach in treating with all the "faces" which the client presents, thereby further complicating the categorical conceptions of the client which the department attempts to construct.

A third tactic is the coercion of caseworkers by clients.[27] This may take the form of a direct threat to an official or the form of symbolic violation of the official's territory through physical intrusion or verbal abuse. As Marx (1972: 293, 298) describes, such coercive behavior may well be efficacious. My view is that coercion may be effective because its moral evaluation is connected to the status of the welfare client. As indicated previously, when the Welfare Department accepts an applicant as a client the latter undergoes a change in moral status (see Robert Scott 1970). Persons go on welfare when they can no longer completely cope for themselves. If they can no longer cope, their responsibility to look after themselves is somewhat diminished, and the agency which issues aid also assumes some responsibility for the "incompetence" of the client. If a client is a less competent person, with diminished self-responsibility, he is then more entitled to behave in a manner consistent with this redefinition; and he can abuse an official or threaten violence to dramatize the seriousness of his situation without being as severely sanctioned for such behavior as would a nonclient.[28]

While the welfare client may be able to realize various combinations of the resources I have outlined to induce allocations and prolong the schedule of welfare assistance, there are often inherent limitations to the kinds of alternatives which the client can open and exploit. Certain of these limitations are bureaucratic, for in a society in which clients often deal with a variety of service agencies their chances to obtain economic benefits simultaneously from a number of such organizations are limited. So a client's chances of finding work through the labor exchange and continuing to collect welfare monies are minimal. For limited periods of time the client may manage to hold open two or more contradictory sources of income, since communication between organizations may well be slow and incomplete. However, eventually closure of information is completed, because communica-tion flows through channels over which the client has no influence. While the client will often assume that he can continue to keep his alternatives open, they in fact move, over time, more toward closure than toward openness.

As the composition of the client's household changes, so too do his economic opportunities. Children below working age drain household assets, but such liabilities can become economically rewarding if the department can be induced to invest in them. As children grow older they cost more, but their value as an economic asset also increases if the department continues to invest in them. Until children are of working age the internal redistribution of welfare allocations will be the function of one or both parents, who can distribute these benefits to areas of greatest felt need, not necessarily in accord with the bureaucratic purpose of the allocations. As children come of working age they may themselves make direct demands of the department, and allocations to them need no longer pass through the head of the household. Since these children then have sources of benefits alternative to those which derive from the household head, the power of the latter within the household will be weakened. As children marry and leave the household the position of the head is further weakened. While the parents may still receive aid commensurate with their needs, overall allocations to the household will appreciably diminish. In this way diminishing household size closes economic alternatives previously available to the head of the household.

With increasing age and deteriorating physical condition, the capacity of the welfare client to open alternative economic opportunities also diminishes, since most opportunities for unskilled or semiskilled persons require much physical exertion. While waning physical powers can elicit increased welfare aid, the client is driven into a stance of increased dependence on the department, which often becomes his sole alternative (see Blau 1964: 118–120).

When bureaucratic, household, and physiological opportunities diminish and close, the power of the department correspondingly increases. Then previously successful client tactics will have limited utility, since the risk of a reduction in support will threaten the client's sole remaining source of income. The client who exists on the economic margin will always have such problems, and his dependence and compliance will increase.

A CASE STUDY

In the analysis of developing relationships between a particular household and the Welfare Department I have had to rely heavily upon welfare records, supplemented by information I received during field work. I recognize the danger, which Garfinkel (1967: 198) has pointed to, of reading files as "actuarial" rather than "contractual" records. However, Israeli welfare files are meant to be read in both ways, for a file must contain an actuarial record of financial and other welfare allocations which enables officials to formulate accounts of their treatment of the client. Actuarial entries of welfare allocations are a baseline for the interpretation of contractual entries, in which a caseworker expresses opinions and sentiments about clients. My account of the Sasson household accepts actuarial entries as having happened, and accepts other entries as amenable to analytic interpretation in terms of certain suppositions.

This leads us to a second serious problem in the interpretation of records: the imputation of motivations to persons who appear in the files.[29] In this regard I have made three assumptions: (a) that there are persons who come to desire a long-term affiliation with the Welfare Department for the sake of the benefits entailed in such a relationship; (b) that, faced with a situation of choice, such persons attempt to elaborate their sources of benefits within the limitations of incomplete information; and (c) that the department, having accepted a person as a client, attempts to terminate affiliation as soon as this is feasible. While the validity of these assumptions will vary from case to case, my account of the Sasson household assumes that such factors underlie a "typical biography" (Garfinkel 1967: 201) for clients who come to desire long-term affiliation; and it further assumes that the consequences are reproduced in both the actuarial and contractual entries of the welfare files. These entries are not necessarily "what actually happened"; they are what caseworkers understood to have happened. What the client understood to have happened is more problematic to interpret, since the entries are those of the department. Nevertheless, I think we can formulate an account of what the client "wanted to happen" if file entries are seen as bureaucratic reactions to client presentations, and presentations are interpreted in terms of the first two assumptions given above.[30]

I will present the extended case of Zackaria Sasson and his household chronologically, through seven phases of contact with the Welfare Department.[31] Phase I concerns the arrival of the Sassons in Israel and their first abortive contacts with the department. Phase II deals with Zackaria's acceptance as a welfare client, with preliminary transactions about what constitutes a fair exchange for termination of affiliation, with the beginnings of department allocations to diverse household loci and areas of living, and with Zackaria's attempts to develop economic alternatives to department support. Phase III begins with the investment of monthly welfare payments by the department in the household; the department's involvement intensifies, and this has consequences for the emerging welfare career-line. In Phase IV Zackaria loses his economic alternatives, and his dependence on the department becomes known to the officials. The account of Phase V details the increasing attempts of the department to terminate affiliation and concomitantly the lessening value of its conception of a fair exchange for termination. Phase VI involves the attempts of the department to disengage from the household; but as Phase VII demonstrates, the development of the welfare career, paralleled by the emergent process of department involvement in and commitment to diverse household loci and areas of living, militates against termination of affiliation.

Phase I: First Contacts with Bureaucracy (1950–1955)

Zackaria Sasson and his family arrived in Israel in 1950 during a period of peak immigration and few national assets. He was then forty-three years old and his wife, Sima, was thirty-four; they had five children under the age of twelve. Born in Tunis in 1907, Zackaria apparently received no formal schooling, but was apprenticed to a cabinet maker and built furniture for a number of years. Later, with the aid of his father, a goldsmith, he opened a small vegetable shop which he operated until leaving with his family for France in 1949. At this time Zackaria's brothers left for Israel. While Zackaria was penniless, he had relatives in France from whom he expected aid. When this was not forthcoming, and the Sassons were sent to a refugee camp near Marseilles, Zackaria tried to work as a middleman. He would go into Marseilles to buy empty boxes, beer, cigarettes, and slightly spoiled foods, which he would take back to the camp and sell. By the end of 1949 he had decided to follow his brothers to Israel. He exchanged his savings for soap, snuff, and tinned goods to sell in Israel.

Like all new immigrants the Sassons came into contact with the Jewish Agency, which sent them to a transit camp in Pardess Hana.[32] Zackaria asked to be transferred to Jerusalem, but the Jewish Agency representative rejected his request. According to his dossier, Zackaria reacted violently in the agency office, and the police were called to evict him. But, according to Zackaria, the police spent two hours trying to convince him that his request was unreasonable. Zackaria replied that he had only one answer, that Jerusalem was the holy city in which he had always dreamed of living.[33] After eight months in the Pardess Hana camp (*ma'abara*) the Sassons were moved to Jerusalem.

In his confrontation with the agency representative Zackaria struck upon a tactic for coercing the individual bureaucrat—the threat of violence. There are two principal components to this tactic. One is the perception of potential violence by an official whose position is built upon the acceptance and application of supposedly rational rules of conduct. The legitimacy and authority of the official stem from written and unwritten assemblies of rules; and his ability to deal successfully with clients requires that they accept these attributes of his position. The threat of coercion denies the legitimacy of the official's position, and cuts through the trappings of office to strike the official, whose position and territory may be disrupted and desecrated. The other component is the client's perception of violence as a tool which is not actually to be used, except as a bluff to dramatize the extent and extremity of his needs.[34] Such a bluff must be sufficiently sincere in presentation; but its purpose lies just in the presentation, since neither party desires actual violence. And if both behave properly they cooperate to cool the confrontation.[35]

In this instance the official called the police, who evicted the client—a move which reinforced the legitimacy of the official. But it must be stressed that the police were not requested to arrest Zackaria, and he did not threaten them. The police cooled the encounter by ending the presentation; and this opened the way for further negotiations during which the police tried to convince Zackaria that his request was unreasonable. In turn, Zackaria was pacific, stressing his desire to dwell in the holy city of Jerusalem, a stereotype which many Jews would accept as an ideal; and the encounter ended amicably.

Zackaria learned that the tactics of coercion could be rewarding, since he was in fact sent to Jerusalem.[36] But it is probable that he did not employ this tactic lightly.

His position was onerous. He had a wife and five children to support; they had spent eight months living in a transit camp; and given his previous occupations, no good opportunities for earning a living were available. Hence his resort to a tactic which, if misinterpreted, could result in serious consequences for him.

In Jerusalem the Sassons were sent to the Talpiot transit camp, where they received a hut of one large room which contained beds, a table, a food cupboard, and a few chairs. Zackaria registered at the local labor exchange (*lishkat ha' avoda*), joined the Histadrut (the Labor Federation of Israel), and was offered a job as an unskilled laborer (*poel dahak*) with Solel Boneh (the National Construction Company). He accepted but later maintained that his aspirations at the time were to operate as a middleman in Jerusalem: "I thought in every city, in every country, there are markets; then I could always earn enough money. But when I came I saw there are no markets here. In Israel the prices are the same all over. Go from one seller to another, no big difference in the prices, maybe four or five pennies. The prices in Mahane Yehuda (the central market of West Jerusalem) are the same as in Ramle. I can't buy in Jerusalem and sell in Ramle; the prices are all the same. There was no work for me here. I tried but the work wasn't good. Here a man has to be a peddler. I'm not a peddler, I'm a middleman. Nothing to do here." At the time, because of an economic recession, Zackaria was receiving only ten to fifteen days of work a month.

However, he was already testing his bureaucratic supports. By the end of 1950 he owed I£ 15 for six months' back rent in the camp. His earnings were minimal, and in managing his finances he cut expenditures in that area in which he was connected to government bureaucracy. This I consider to be of particular significance. Although I have no knowledge of private debts he may have incurred, his debt to the government was only noted, and he was not pressed to meet his debt or to begin paying rent. He therefore began to discover areas of living in which he could minimize costs and maximize credit to reduce financial stress. In choosing not to pay rent he utilized a bureaucratic reward which he was to elaborate in the future.[37]

In August of 1951 Zackaria was treated for an unspecified ailment in a local health insurance institute clinic (Kupat Holim). While there, he complained to the doctor that he had been unfairly placed in work; that he was really a carpenter; and that the labor exchange offered him only limited employment as an unskilled laborer. The doctor wrote to the Welfare Department, with whom Zackaria had no contact, and described the case.[38] Three months later this bureaucratic intercession bore fruit when the department agreed to allocate to Zackaria funds with which to purchase carpentry tools. Five more months elapsed before he was offered I£ 30 to do so. There were three lessons to be discovered here: bureaucratic intercession could be rewarding, and might require only minimum effort; the Welfare Department was prepared to make an allocation to Zackaria; and the reward could take a long time to materialize, in this instance eight months. By making this investment the department could expect him to earn a higher wage, and ideally he would make no further requests. This attempt to practice preventive welfare did not work out.[39]

Zackaria accepted the offer and returned to the labor exchange with the support of the department. The exchange tested his skill in carpentry in order to place him in appropriate work. Zackaria failed the test and was classified as completely unsuitable for employment in carpentry. Then the Welfare Department withdrew its offer to purchase tools for him.

Zackaria, who was illiterate, then hired a scribe to compose a letter which was sent to the Welfare Department, the minister of social welfare, the prime minister, and Parliament (the Knesset). I view this letter as a further request for bureaucratic intercession, as Zackaria attempted to bypass those officials who had stymied his previous attempt to gain skilled employment. I reproduce the letter since it contains themes which should be examined more closely.[40]

> Very Respectable Minister,
>
> The concerning matter, a request for big success in Israel. At the beginning of my words I will ask you to forgive me for my mistakes and unpleasant expressions written in this letter. I came to ask your face for my luck. To a family of eight people without mentioning the foetus inside the woman, let God help that it will come out successfully. And here is what I ask completely. I, Zackaria Sasson, the son of Gago Sasson, a father of six children, and the above-mentioned foetus, and the oldest of the children is twelve years old. I am today two years in Israel with the biggest family, let God help us that we will be many like this in Israel. I want to let you know that until this day I did not succeed to support my family as a citizen of the country for two reasons. A. In the "exchange" they give me only three or four days a month, and I really cannot understand the justification for it. B. I am not a man of property who can live a life like this. It is true that we are quiet people and we do not want to know our young state ["know" in this context means "demand of"], and rightly so. That is why a man like this should be helped and supported in some way that will insure him at least minimal support in some kind of permanent hired labor or a grocery store, or anything that your eyes will find right.
>
> So in this form that I live now, I, I had to sell everything that comes to me in rations as a citizen of the state. So instead of adding strength to children, that this is the time they grow up, it is not enough that what we receive is so limited, but even that I give my rations to others for bread and water. And if I will continue like this you will be to blame for anything that will happen. Be it the will of our Father in heaven that nothing unpleasant will happen. In addition and to the contradictory, in this I let the government know what is happening in the country, and it will find some way for the successful support of social cases. I will ask you to see my situation as very serious and time short as Passover is coming on us to a good life and peace, give me a pleasant answer, and I will have my pleasant Passover with the help of God, and thank you in advance. I hope you will fulfill what I ask. . . .

It is clear that the author of this letter had no understanding of Western bureaucratic procedure with its stress on communication through appropriate channels (see Marx 1972: 297–298). Zackaria received no reply. In this appeal Zackaria stressed his commitment to work by requesting permanent employment, due to him because he was a citizen of the state, not because he was occupationally competent. However, he indirectly alluded to competence by implying that he had been *rendered* incapable of supporting his family, that if he received the right opportunities he would contribute to the welfare of his family and the nation. So he criticized the labor exchange's lack of concern for his welfare, and pointed out that the rations received were insufficient to feed his household. Rationing allocations, set by the state, were introduced to make certain that all citizens would have staples under conditions of want. By stating that he had to exchange his rations for bread and water, Zackaria criticized the state for its insufficient allotments. Since rationing was a constant in the sense that everyone received the same amount to eat, it represented a legacy of every citizen. Thus Zackaria's statement that he was selling his legacy implied that it was worth less than the state supposed. The letter contained a further warning: if the state failed to find him permanent employment he would become a "social case";[41] the state would be to blame for any untoward consequences, and would also become responsible for the Sasson household.

Four months later Zackaria sent another letter to the Welfare Department and prime minister; again he received no reply, and thereafter he abandoned this approach. The Sassons continued to dwell in their one-room hut in Talpiot camp, and Zackaria continued to work as a part-time unskilled construction laborer. Although unsuccessful in obtaining aid from the labor exchange or Welfare Department, he did strike an alternative source of assistance. In 1953 he came to the attention of a representative of an American-sponsored charitable organization which was attempting to succor the residents of Talpiot camp. I have no information about how this link was forged. Zackaria referred to this representative, a Mrs. Zap, as "the woman from America," and stated that he considered her to be "another kind of social worker." Mrs. Zap committed her time and used her contacts on behalf of the Sassons, and over the next five years she was able to negotiate a number of loans for the household, as well as find jobs for some of the Sasson children. Neither Mrs. Zap nor Zackaria brought their relationship to the attention of the Welfare Department.

By 1955 the economic situation of the Sassons had drastically changed for the worse. During their six years in Israel four more offspring had been born (Table 1), and Zackaria now had a wife and nine children to support. He was forty-eight years old and still employed as a part-time unskilled laborer. Five of his children studied in schools, while the remainder were below school age. Despite the exigencies of the situation, Phase I was essentially a period of the testing of sources of benefits by a man who, if he earned little, still provided for his household without becoming structurally dependent on a particular source of bureaucratic aid. Furthermore, his contacts with the Jewish Agency, the clinic doctor, the Welfare Department, and the volunteer worker indicated that if conditions were right benefits might well be forthcoming; and his failure to press his case with the Welfare Department after its refusal to grant him funds for tools exemplified his independent stance. But Phase II began with an event which deprived him of the capacity to earn a living as he did in Phase I.

TABLE 1   *The Composition of the Sasson Household*

Name	Date of Birth	Position in Household
Zackaria	1907	husband, father
Sima	1916	wife, mother
Isaac	1939	son
Varda	1941	daughter
Lea	1946	daughter
Victor	1947	son
Aharon	1948	son
Rachel	1950	daughter
Sarah	1952	daughter
Benno	1954	son
David	1955	son
Zafrira	1957	daughter
Dalia	1958	daughter

Phase II: The Affiliation of a Welfare Client (1955–1957)

In 1955 Zackaria fell from a bicycle, injured his back, and was unable to continue working. Treatment of his injury led to a comprehensive medical examination which uncovered a series of ailments: myocarditis (a defect, possibly genetic, in the heart muscle), hypertension, high blood pressure, arthritis, diabetes, emphysema pulmonaris, a hernia, and some permanent damage to his back. He was issued a medical certificate which emphasized that he was unsuitable for the heavy physical labor he had been doing, and was referred to the Welfare Department.

I previously mentioned that the department does not conduct extensive investigations into the personal situations of applicants to determine their eligibility for welfare assistance, but instead relies on information about the client which is brought to the welfare office, usually by the applicant. In evaluating this information, high priority is given to labels which emanate from official sources and which designate incapacity. In the absence of other well-defined criteria for welfare assistance, an official label of incapacity is treated as "proof" of the needs of the applicant; and it is around such official labels that caseworkers and applicants cooperate to construct the beginning of client affiliation. Medical certificates are most valuable in this respect because they tend to specify clearly that the applicant is unsuitable for certain kinds of activity, while the issuance of such labels falls outside the caseworker's area of competence and therefore outside her area of responsibility. The caseworker is therefore placed in a position in which she must treat with the applicant. Once proof of need at the time of application is available, the caseworker can then formulate an account of the applicant's past history to legitimate the affiliation and the offering of assistance (see Robert Scott 1970: 282).[42]

Zackaria was assigned a caseworker with whom he had not had previous dealings. From the contact which followed it is apparent that Zackaria was able to impress the caseworker with the extent of his moral commitment to work and family, qualified by all his difficulties and need for assistance—in other words, convince her that his difficulties were endangering his proper commitments. In turn the caseworker began to select attributes of Zackaria's presentation which were compatible with affiliation and the subsequent proffering of assistance. The caseworker noted:

1. Zackaria's attitude to work "was very positive and aware," and "he never complained that his laborer's work was too difficult."
2. "He has very strong identification with positive values in spite of his low position," and "up to this day he gives a lot of charity to poor people on Fridays and holidays as he did in the past."
3. "He keeps his position as head of the family," and "he has very warm and understanding feelings toward his wife. He is sorry about her difficulties as a housewife and mother in their difficult situation."
4. "He is trying to help his children with any difficulties."

Thus Zackaria's general values, and his attitude to work and family, were all positively evaluated by the caseworker, with the implication that he would be a good candidate for clientship and speedy "rehabilitation." I should also note that the negative attributes which the caseworker selected from Zackaria's presentation centered on his relationships with his children, and their classification as "negative" was based on commonly held stereotypes for which Zackaria could not be held responsible.[43]

The materials I examined suggest that, at the time Zackaria was accepted as a welfare client, both he and the department were oriented toward a speedy termination of affiliation. Zackaria couched his requests in terms of employment suitable to his health, and the department was prepared to pay attention to his occupational problems, not because his household had almost doubled in size, but because he was "officially" unable to continue in his part-time work, and because as a good worker and upright family man he was considered to deserve other employment. However, Zackaria appeared to desire employment which was commensurate with the perceived needs of his household, while the department expected him to accept any job as a substitute for the unskilled work he had been doing. While both parties at this point were prepared to accept termination of affiliation, the conditions of termination, the definition of what constituted a fair exchange for termination, remained to be negotiated. Moreover, the department was not sufficiently involved in the household to offer Zackaria the most lucrative form of employment which it could hypothetically allocate.

The department immediately tried to terminate affiliation by offering Zackaria less arduous employment. His caseworker suggested that he take a refresher course in carpentry, and then work as a carpenter. Zackaria refused this schedule of termination, stating that his health was too poor for him to manage such a course.

He was told to consult his doctor about the course, and again he refused. The caseworker then suggested that a social worker consult the doctor. After an initial refusal Zackaria agreed. The doctor stated that Zackaria could manage the course. Zackaria refused to accept the doctor's decision. The Welfare Department then offered to equip a workshop for Zackaria after he completed the course. He in turn proposed that the department give him a store. The caseworker did not consider Zackaria's physical condition sufficiently impaired to warrant the greater allocation of a store, although Zackaria had previously been more of a shopkeeper than a carpenter.[44]

Through this series of transactions the field of relevance of the affiliation and the terms of a fair exchange for termination began to be negotiated. Zackaria was offered a chance to become a carpenter without guarantee of employment. Four years before he had been prepared to accept part-time carpentry, but the recession was still in force, the labor force underemployed, and there were four more Sasson children to feed and clothe. Zackaria lived in a transit camp whose presence proved that a fully employed construction industry did not exist; and he could probably estimate his potential earnings as a carpenter, since he had been employed by a construction firm. Furthermore, his health was poor and carpentry could be taxing. Zackaria did not refuse to work—he refused to take the carpentry course. Thus Zackaria was still a "good" client for whom the conditions of termination could be adjusted. So when Zackaria refused to accept the decision of the doctor, the department raised the value of its offer by proposing to equip a workshop for Zackaria. From Zackaria's viewpoint this offer may well have been even less desirable. As an independent craftsman of little ability competing with skilled craftsmen, he might well earn less than he did as an unskilled laborer. In his former job he was paid when he came to work, while in the new one he would have to compete for clients. Instead Zackaria proposed that he be allocated a means of livelihood with which he was more familiar, in a field in which he was presumably more skilled. But the offer of a store required an investment which the department was not prepared to make, and negotiations were suspended. Zackaria was still considered to be a client who was concerned to find employment in order to support his household.

The following month Zackaria and Sima came together to the department and demanded that their eldest son, Isaac, leave school and work to support the household.[45] Up to this point the department had dealt directly only with Zackaria, over the issue of employment. In a sense, then, Zackaria was equated with the needs of the household, and these needs had centered only on the area of employment. Now the caseworker was faced with the presentations of Zackaria and Sima together, a household locus different from Zackaria alone. Furthermore, husband and wife presented themselves as a coalition opposed to their eldest son, and the department was thereby drawn into a further area of living in the household, that of relationships between parents and child. Department response to this attempt at diversification was very limited. If Isaac were coerced into leaving school and accepting employment, the department could terminate the welfare affiliation of the household, but only at the expense of the education and future of a young man. Therefore the caseworker rejected the parents' demand. In so doing the caseworker attempted to limit the department involvement to the locus of Zackaria and to the area of employment.

Zackaria continued to request a store as his price for termination of affiliation, and his request continued to be rejected by the department. However, in relation to these requests for particular employment he again began to bring other areas of household living to the attention of the caseworker. For example, he requested that two of his younger children be placed in institutions. Note that such requests have multiple implications. While asking for the institutionalization of a child relates most specifically to the area of child care, it also has economic implications in the sense that the removal of a child from the household will leave one less person to be fed; and it may have a spatial implication, that there is insufficient dwelling space to care properly for children. Above all, such requests imply that as long as the head of household is not employed in a worthwhile job, his family will continue to suffer. In this instance the caseworker rejected Zackaria's request, but countered with an offer of baby clothes as an interim measure to reduce household expenditures, without making an explicit financial commitment to the children concerned.

In addition to being drawn into the area of child care, the department was exposed to requests concerning housing. Zackaria requested that the department pay his accumulated debt of five years' back rent for his transit camp hut. This the caseworker rejected, but instead arranged to have the rent reduced. Each instance of negotiation and transaction in which a client request was met by a related counteroffer served to increase department involvement in various areas of household living. Since the responsibility which the department can assume with regard to a particular affiliation is quite diffuse (cf. W. Richard Scott 1969: 124–125), this was not simply a matter of the caseworker's accommodating the client, but a matter of the department's being induced, through proper presentations, to allocate benefits to client needs which could legitimately be considered as its responsibility. But because the department was also continually concerned to terminate the affiliation, it was loath to meet fully the terms of the requests. This in turn induced the client to bring other needs to the attention of the department, in the hope of receiving additional allocations, and perhaps induced the client to request more than he expected to receive in order to be allocated benefits which accorded with his minimum expectations (cf. Glenn Jacobs 1970: 258). Moreover, the original affiliation between the department and Zackaria was being transformed as the department began to become involved in employment, household relationships, child care, and housing; and the wider field of relevance of the affiliation also opened up further areas of negotiation and transaction, as the client brought further needs to the attention of the department. From the client's perspective, the widening field of relevance of affiliation and its associated benefits also increased the cost of a fair termination of affiliation.

During the remaining four months of 1955 Zackaria came to the department office at least once a week to reiterate past requests and to make new ones. In these transactions the central issue of employment for Zackaria was not resolved. However, there were three important consequences of these contacts for the emergence of a relationship between client and department: (a) the subsidiary allocations made by the department further involved it in diverse areas of household life; (b) the fact that such benefits were forthcoming encouraged the Sassons to continue tactics of diversification of demand, not only to dramatize Zackaria's need for a good job, but also for the sake of the rewards themselves; (c) the protracted negotiations over conditions of termination of affiliation upset the department's schedule of short-term client contact, and began to produce a longer-term relationship, in which multiple department involvements in the household ensured the continuance of contacts between caseworker and client.

Zackaria had not worked officially for over a year, and the household subsisted on I£ 20 a month, paid by Mishan, the workers' unemployment fund of the Histadrut. The Welfare Department then met Zackaria's conditions for termination of affiliation by finding a foodstuffs store for him. This, I think, was a clear indication of the value for clients in engaging in extended negotiation and transaction with the department. As in the instance of the carpentry course, the department raised the value of its offer in exchange for termination. Zackaria accepted the offer, but the provisional arrangement collapsed when a third party, a bureaucratic organization over which neither department nor client had any control, sponsored a more suitable candidate for the store. As I previously stated, what the department offers in exchange for termination are the benefits it has available at the time. Having failed to obtain the store for Zackaria, the department substituted the offer of a vegetable-peddling permit. This Zackaria refused, possibly because of the disparity between the two offers in terms of his perceived needs. The effect of this event was to upset once again the department's schedule of affiliation.

Given the inability of the department to allocate the benefits which it had offered, Zackaria began to develop his own economic activities by "renting" a fish-peddling permit from a holder who was unable to use it. Zackaria bought fish in Jerusalem, transported his load by bus to a Negev *moshav* (small-holder's cooperative), of which a brother was a member, and stored the fish there in facilities which his brother had procured. This then became his base for peddling fish to other *moshavim* in the area. Profits were apparently split between the brothers. Zackaria did not inform the Welfare Department about his peddling activities; his telling the department might have formed the basis for making his peddling legitimate, which would have terminated his affiliation.

The department was still searching for employment which would meet Zackaria's needs, and it found a permanent position for him in an olivewood factory if he was prepared to be retrained for the job. In addition, the caseworker offered him a loan to cover the period of retraining, after which he would earn I£ 3 per day. Apart from the store, this was probably the best offer he had received, since his income would be stable and the work not taxing. Zackaria accepted the offer and visited the factory with the caseworker. A few days later he refused to return, stating that the work was too difficult and the pay insufficient. He added that he would have to consult his doctor. A few days later he changed his mind once more, but by this time the factory had found another candidate to fill the vacancy.

Zackaria had been placed in a serious dilemma. He had begun to peddle fish only a few months before. This activity required his absence from Jerusalem for lengthy periods in order for him to operate on a small cost margin. He could not both accept a steady job in Jerusalem and peddle fish in the Negev, since his absence from the factory would be reported to the Welfare Department, which would question his previously assumed commitment to work and reduce the value of future offers, or else would discover his illegal peddling activities and pressure him into accepting peddling as the condition for termination of affiliation. By complicating his presentations to the caseworker, Zackaria made it impossible to categorize him easily as someone interested in work or not, and when the vacancy was filled Zackaria continued with his peddling.

These tactics, intended or not, were successful in that the department still considered Zackaria as a good candidate for "rehabilitation" and continued to make him valuable offers to terminate affiliation. A few weeks later he was informed that a new market, the South Market, would shortly be opened, and that he stood a very good chance of receiving a store there. Zackaria announced his acceptance of this offer, and both he and the department seemed to have agreed once again on the conditions of termination. Again, because of factors beyond their control, their efforts were stymied. There were extensive delays in constructing the South Market, and two months later, in November 1956, his caseworker offered Zackaria a less costly vegetable stall in the Mahane Yehuda market. Zackaria held out for the store and continued to peddle fish. But he did not refuse the offer of the stall outright. At first he was agreeable, then over a number of weeks he complicated and contradicted his stand, and he ended by stating that he desired only the South Market store. The South Market was not to be opened for another two years.

Zackaria apparently spread his rejection of the stall over a lengthy period because he was then engaged in other important negotiations with the department. In 1956 a three-room flat became available for the Sasson family. This was a boon of some magnitude to a family which had lived for seven years in a one-room hut. Zackaria was required to purchase the flat from Amidar, the national housing corporation, in monthly installments over a period of thirty years, and he was at first required to make a down payment of I£ 250. By representing Zackaria as a welfare client to Amidar, the caseworker arranged for a total down payment of only I£ 20. Zackaria refused, maintaining that he did not possess I£ 20. Since the department knew only that he was subsisting on I£ 20 a month from Mishan, his argument was accepted, and it was then agreed that he would pay the amount in four monthly installments. In addition, Zackaria was required to make monthly mortgage payments of I£ 13. He accepted these conditions, and the Sasson family left the Talpiot transit camp. But he met neither the down payment nor his mortgage payments; and not long after the Sassons moved, he informed the caseworker that he wanted to wait for a store in the South Market.

Meanwhile the field of relevance of affiliation continued to diversify and expand. In January 1957 Sima Sasson came to the department office and demanded a divorce, stating the futility of living with Zackaria and ''bringing another child every year.'' Sima then became a distinct locus of department involvement; the caseworker had to begin to process separate demands from both Zackaria and Sima; and the area of the marital relationship was included within the boundaries of affiliation. The caseworker stated that the Sassons would have to reconcile their differences. It is significant that Sima did not (at this time) take her case to the rabbinical court which is competent in matters of personal status. Sima's plaint appeared to be a further inducement for increased welfare support. This is evident in her reference to ''bringing another child every year,'' which has clear economic implications. That she was pregnant at the time emphasized her plea. The caseworker also, at least for the record, did not suggest that the Sassons take their differences to the rabbinical court, for the threat of divorce was taken most seriously. If the couple divorced, the department might well become responsible for the support of two households, and all the children concerned; and this would require major allocations of assistance.[46] The ease with which the caseworker effected a ''reconciliation'' suggests that the estrangement was not serious but instead represented a further diversification to pressure the department for a secure livelihood.

The department further reacted to the threat of divorce by trying to locate employment for Zackaria, on the assumption that steady work would stabilize the marital relationship. Since no openings were available, Zackaria was sent back to the labor exchange, where he refused to accept a work permit.

Tables 2 and 3 present the overall pattern of department responses to requests of clients (109), and of client responses to requests or offers of the department (59), as these were noted in the file entries I examined. As indicated in these tables, Phase II is a period of balance in contacts: in comparison to most other phases, clients accept a high proportion of department suggestions and the department accepts a high proportion of client requests. The spirit of transaction in this phase is, on the whole, one of active cooperation in search of conditions within which termination of affiliation can occur. That these conditions are not finalized is at crucial points a function of happenstance rather than of the designs of either party. Yet the fact that the right conditions cannot be finalized apparently leads Zackaria, and later Sima, to practice tactics which induce the department to expand allocations to diverse household loci and areas of living, and pushes Zackaria to explore alternative sources of economic reward, which in turn cause him to be more resistant to comparatively valuable offers made by the department. His rejection of these offers extends the duration of welfare assistance and, in turn, causes the department to seek other measures of lower value to terminate affiliation, as I will describe in discussing Phase III. Offers of lesser value in exchange for termination cause the Sassons to intensify inducements to obtain allocations, more for the sake of the benefits entailed than for the sake of acquiring remunerative employment commensurate with perceived household needs.

TABLE 2   *Department Responses to Requests of Clients*

Phase	Zackaria			Sima			Zackaria and Sima			Isaac			Varda		
	A	C	R	A	C	R	A	C	R	A	C	R	A	C	R
I	0	0	2												
II	4	0	6	0	0	2	0	0	3						
III	3	2	3	3	2	9	0	0	1	0	2	3	0	1	2
IV	0	2	2	0	0	1	1	0	1						
V	2	0	5	0	0	1	0	1	5	0	1	1	1	0	0
VI	1	1	11	1	0	6	1	2	4				1	0	0
VII	1	0	1	4	0	1	1	0	1						
Totals	11	5	30	8	2	20	3	3	15	0	3	4	2	1	2
		46			30			21			7			5	

A means "accept," *C* means "consider," and *R* means "reject."

Phase III: The Legitimation of a "Social Case" (1957–1958)

Unable to erase the Sasson household from the welfare rolls, the department referred Zackaria to its Rehabilitation Office. The task of the office is to find employment and provide other services for clients whom local welfare offices have been unable to "rehabilitate." Therefore the office tends to deal with hard-core "social cases": persons who are largely unsuitable to regular employment because of physical handicaps, ill health, lack of skills, or advanced age. Offers of employment which the Rehabilitation Office makes in return for termination of affiliation tend to be of less value than those made by the Welfare Department. In other words, by referring Zackaria to the office the Welfare Department was reducing the price it was prepared to pay for termination, while Zackaria's needs remained at their previous level, partially induced by subsidiary welfare allocations.

Zackaria did not appear for his appointment with the office. His wife informed the caseworker that he had abandoned the household, when he was off peddling fish in the Negev. The caseworker interpreted his absence as an indication of severe marital estrangement. A few weeks later Zackaria appeared at the Welfare Department and stated that because his back pained him he was no longer prepared to accept any employment offers which required strenuous physical effort. The department capitulated and began to allocate to Zackaria monthly welfare payments of I£ 29. Previous welfare allocations had built up the value of affiliation; the new monthly payments provided him with the income of a welfare career and firmly defined him as a "social case," one who could not easily or reasonably be "rehabilitated." Although such payments were meant to tide him over until employment could be found for him, they were the firmest evidence of the rewards

TABLE 3 *Responses of Clients to Department Requests/Offers*

	Responses by														
							Zackaria								
Phase	Zackaria			Sima			and Sima			Isaac			Varda		
	A	C	R	A	C	R	A	C	R	A	C	R	A	C	R
I	1	0	0												
II	8	0	10												
III	0	0	5				2	0	0	1	0	3	2	0	0
IV	0	0	1												
V	1	1	5	0	0	1	2	0	0	1	0	2			
VI	3	1	2	2	0	0	1	0	1						
VII	3	0	0												
Totals	16	2	23	2	0	1	5	0	1	2	0	5	2	0	0
		41			3			6			7			2	

A means "accept," *C* means "consider," and *R* means "reject."

which could be obtained by following the welfare career-line. While unskilled or semiskilled employment provided only a static salary, not adjusted according to factors like the number of children in the household, ill health, or situational difficulties, welfare payments represented a sliding scale of income which the client could attempt to manipulate to meet his perceived economic needs. Zackaria had previously been interested more in obtaining rewarding employment than in obtaining a welfare income, but the initiation of monthly payments began to steer him onto the welfare career-line.

The department was further drawn into the area of housing when Amidar threatened to sue Zackaria for back mortgage payments. The caseworker proposed using a welfare incentive to induce Zackaria to meet his financial obligations. If Zackaria would agree to pay 50 percent of his monthly mortgage payments, the department would pay the remaining 50 percent and would raise his monthly welfare payments to I£ 40. Zackaria treated this increase as a welcome adjustment to his welfare payments, and he continued not to meet his mortgage payments. Here the use of welfare incentives appeared to have the effect of encouraging the client to exploit the welfare career-line, for Zackaria had gained a substantial reward for never having made housing payments during his time in Israel. Moreover, this reward in fact reduced pressure on him to begin making such payments; for as long as Amidar received a portion of Zackaria's mortgage payments, it would take longer for his debt to grow to the size at which Amidar would again try to collect.

The field of relevance of the affiliation was further expanded during the next few months when two other household members established themselves as quasi-independent welfare loci within the household. Isaac, aged eighteen, had just completed elementary school and had registered with an evening high school.

Varda, the eldest daughter, aged sixteen, also registered with an evening high school. Varda worked as a maid for a few hours daily, and earned I£ 50–60 a month, most of which she gave her mother. Isaac had refused to work, stating that all his strength had to be devoted to his studies. Both Isaac and Varda asked the department to pay their school fees of I£ 120 per year, and were referred to the Youth Office of the department. The Youth Office consented to pay 30 percent of Varda's fees and a portion of Isaac's fees on condition that he work during the day to support the household. However, the department arranged to have Isaac's fees deferred until he began to work. Coalitions between parents and children within the household functioned to complicate the situation. Sima Sasson supported Varda's request to the department. Zackaria and Sima opposed Isaac's request and demanded that he work, while Zackaria also demanded that Isaac be ejected from the family flat. Isaac, in turn, demanded that his father be made to work to support the household, arguing that he was under no obligation to support the household as long as his father lived. Zackaria and Sima both demanded that their second-eldest son, Victor, aged ten, be removed from the flat because he was continually in trouble with the police. Isaac was at first prepared to register with the labor exchange to be placed in work, but later reversed himself. He then stated that he was prepared to accept "easy work," but rejected a job as a delivery boy, and cried during his meetings with the caseworker. Neither Zackaria nor Isaac accepted employment, and the department began to finance Varda's education.

The department was also drawn into relationships between the Sassons and a neighboring family. During quarrels in which windows were smashed, the Sassons called the police, who refused to process their complaints and instead referred them back to the Welfare Department.[47] The caseworker took no action.[48] In February 1958 Mrs. Sasson suffered a miscarriage in one of these quarrels. She placed a complaint with the police, who again referred her back to the Welfare Department.[49] Both police and social workers agreed that the only solution to these disputes was to move the Sassons to another flat.

Zackaria was summoned to the welfare office. There his caseworker accused him of not working, of "wrecking" his family, and of becoming a "degenerate." In moving from the official category of client to the category of "social case" and then to that of "degenerate," Zackaria had been supplied with two major components of a welfare career: monthly welfare support and the label which justified such support. Note that the caseworker referred to Zackaria as a degenerate not because he had committed a degrading act, but because of the double bind in which the department was placed. On the one hand the police, refusing to process the ongoing series of violent disputes between the Sassons and their neighbors, suggested a change of flat as the solution. This dovetailed with demands the Sassons themselves had been making. On the other hand the department was not prepared to countenance the investment which a change of flat entailed. Instead the caseworker formulated an account of events in which Zackaria would be held responsible for the sorry state of affairs; and she had much leeway in introducing into this account elements relevant to its purpose (cf. Lyman and Scott 1970: 113).

Zackaria appeared to give way and intimated that on occasion he had worked as a night watchman (in other words, that he was prepared to work), and that he had not worked in the past because he was ashamed to accept "women's work." By this time Zackaria was under pressure from the Rehabilitation Office to accept employment in a public works program cleaning and washing stairwells, halls, and courtyards. Aside from being physically taxing, such work returned only a small salary, not commensurate with his perceived needs. By calling this "women's work," unsuited for a mature male because it would undermine his status as head of household, Zackaria offered the caseworker an account that dovetailed with commonly accepted stereotypes, which stressed that such loss of status imperiled marital relationships and hampered the correct socialization of children.

The caseworker, accepting Zackaria's objection, began to speak of other employment possibilities, and Zackaria complicated their meeting by complaining that his wife did not understand him; that Isaac wanted only to study and was "no good"; and that he admired his *moshav* brother who did not work but who was supported by his wife and daughter. Zackaria ended by shouting that he refused to work and that it was Isaac's duty to support the household. Note that, given the extensive involvement of the department in the household, all of these issues were relevant to one or another aspect of the relationship between the department and its clients. Deflected from her aim of discussing employment by the complications Zackaria had introduced, the caseworker reacted by stating that she would speak with Sima and Isaac; and the meeting ended inconclusively.

By the end of Phase III Zackaria peddled fish, and he received both unemployment insurance payments and welfare payments, as well as aid through the volunteer worker, Mrs. Zap. Except for Varda's earnings all household monies passed through his hands to be redistributed to other household members.

In Phase III the field of relevance of affiliation was markedly expanded as Zackaria, Sima, Zackaria-Sima, Isaac, and Varda all functioned as loci of requests and allocations for the department (see Table 2); and as the areas of employment, income, housing, education, intrahousehold relationships, child care, and external household relationships were all brought to the attention of the department. The role of employment in the area-of-living subjects raised by the clients began to diminish. In Phase II 50 percent of such subjects raised by the Sassons concerned employment, while in Phase III employment comprised only 30 percent of the subjects they raised. (This proportion increased in Phase V to 44 percent and then diminished again in Phase VI to 14 percent.) For the Sassons employment was no longer the major focus of affiliation; while for the department, because employment was intimately connected to termination of affiliation, it remained throughout the major focus of affiliation (in Phases II, III, V, and VI employment comprised between 62 percent and 72 percent of all area-of-living subjects raised by the department). As Table 4 indicates, employment was the only area-of-living subject, of all such subjects raised in client-caseworker contacts, which was introduced more often by the department than by the Sassons. While the department attempted to limit the field of affiliation to allocations which would result in

TABLE 4   *Area-of-Living Subjects Raised in Welfare Department-Client Contacts*

Subject[a]	Number of Times Department Raised Subject	Number of Times Clients Raised Subject	Total Times Subject Raised
Employment	38	35	73
Income	9	12	21
Housing	4	12	16
Education	6	12	18
Intrahousehold relationships	0	17	17
Child care	2	14	16
Health	0	3	3
External social contacts	0	2	2
Total	59	107[b]	166[b]

[a]"Employment" includes the general subject of gainful employment, offers of specific jobs, and requests for employment. "Income" refers to monetary payments unconnected with gainful employment. "Housing" includes living space and associated financial obligations and physical appurtenances. "Education" refers to the costs of and opportunities for formal schooling. "Intrahousehold relationships" includes husband-wife and parent-child relationships within the household. "Child care" includes items like clothing, food, and the institutionalization of children. "Health" refers to the physical well-being and associated needs of household members. "External social contacts" refers to contacts between the household and neighbors.
[b]Two general subjects were not coded.

termination, the Sassons were able to realize resources in transactions which furthered the structural involvement of the department in the household.

Zackaria, given his alternative sources of economic reward, also begins to behave more independently in contacts with the department. In comparison to Phase II, Zackaria in Phase III rejects a higher proportion of department requests (see Table 3). On the other hand, other household loci which in Phase III attempt to initiate or intensify links with the department are more cooperative in their transactions (see Table 3). In attempting to restrict the field of affiliation, the department is relatively unresponsive to these other loci, while Zackaria continues to receive a comparatively high proportion of positive responses (see Table 2). While Zackaria is no longer the "good" client of Phase II, and while the department has made the major commitment of monthly welfare payments to the household, Zackaria remains the single best avenue through which to terminate affiliation. The emerging welfare career-line is highly variable during Phase III. The department furnishes the labels and contents of the welfare career, while pressing for termination; Zackaria and his household receive the allocations and remain comparatively independent of the department's will by relying for subsistence on their alternative economic rewards. I should note again that department allocations provide a basis for client expectations and for subsequent client requests, for it is only after Zackaria begins to receive monthly welfare payments that he begins to speak of not wishing to work and begins to refer to "income"— monetary rewards unconnected to gainful employment.

Phase IV: Closure of Economic Alternatives (1958–1959)

In quick succession three of Zackaria's alternative sources of economic reward were closed, severely restricting his capacity both to resist offers of the department and to realize resources to induce allocations. In turn his actual, rather than officially supposed, dependence on the Welfare Department greatly increased. The first blow came from Mrs. Zap. After five years of unsuccessfully attempting to "rehabilitate" him, she told the department of her efforts in February 1958. Her opinion was that it would be impossible to persuade Zackaria to accept employment. While Mrs. Zap did not withdraw her support from the household, her subsequent efforts were coordinated with the caseworker's, thereby reducing Zackaria's chances of developing each of these sources independently of the other.

Zackaria also experienced difficulties with his peddling activities. His storage facilities in the *moshav* were not equipped with an icebox; the quality of his fish apparently was poor; and he had received a number of warnings from the local Ministry of Health inspector, culminating in his arrest in Beersheba for peddling without proper permit. As well, the *moshav* itself had decided to sponsor fish peddling and refused to entertain an application from the Sasson brothers because they had not been prepared to remunerate the *moshav* for the use of its premises. Zackaria was again placed in a bind. If he did nothing he would lose his peddling. If he went to the caseworker his welfare income might be endangered. I take it as an indication of his commitment to his fish peddling that he approached the caseworker in August 1958 and requested a permit to peddle fish in the Negev. He later admitted to peddling without a permit, but stated that he had only been doing so for a few months. He further intimated that he was thinking of moving permanently to the *moshav*.

This was apparently a tempting inducement for the department. If Zackaria would go gainfully employed, with his family, to the *moshav*, he could be erased from the rolls of the Jerusalem department. (Without a job in the *moshav* Zackaria would still be considered a welfare client, and the department would require the permission of the Negev Regional Welfare Department to transfer him to the latter's welfare rolls. Departments were generally loath to countenance such arrangements, which meant further burdens on their limited budgets.) To dramatize his stated need to move to the *moshav* Zackaria applied for permission to take a second wife with him, but the rabbinical court rejected his illegal request.[50]

He then asked the caseworker for a letter to the effect that the department had never helped him in any way. The caseworker rejected his request, but countered with the offer of a night watchman's job at I£ 110 per month, which he refused.

Meanwhile Mrs. Sasson was pressing for a change of flat. She asked the department to consider herself and her seven youngest children as a separate domestic unit—the equivalent of a de facto separation. She then went to Tel-Aviv for a few weeks and left her children behind, stating that she could no longer dwell in the flat. Upon her return she produced statements by a number of neighbors which attested to the sufferings of the Sassons at the hands of another family of neighbors. She also produced similar statements from the police. The caseworker replied that there were no other three-room flats available in Jerusalem.

Two months later Zackaria admitted to peddling fish without a permit for almost two years and reiterated his desire to move to the *moshav* if he could sell groceries there. The caseworker interceded on his behalf by writing to ask whether the *moshav* would permit Zackaria to use its premises as a base for peddling. The department's investment in the household was increasing, with no sign of relief as the Sasson children grew older.[51]

Mrs. Sasson refused to move to the *moshav*, and instead continued to demand a change of flat. Zackaria offered to take all his children there, but the caseworker insisted that Sima also had to move. Soon after, they declared their joint willingness to move on condition that Zackaria be permitted to sell fish there. But in December 1958 the *moshav* regional council wrote to the Welfare Department refusing Zackaria the permit. Then Zackaria's last alternative source of economic reward was canceled: the Histadrut learned of his peddling and stopped his unemployment insurance payments. He continued to receive welfare payments of I£ 40 per month, while Varda contributed an equivalent amount to the household through Sima. Now Mrs. Sasson had as much money to redistribute within the household as did Zackaria.

This was a major turning point in the relationship between the department and the Sassons, as well as in relationships within the household. Zackaria's loss of economic alternatives, plus the department's knowledge of this, left him less able to resist the demands of the caseworker. Within the household, for the first time since their arrival in Israel, Zackaria was not the breadwinner of the Sassons. Part of this function had been accepted by his eldest daughter, and was later to be shouldered by his wife and other daughters. Therefore Zackaria's position had also weakened relative to his wife and children.

These emergent effects of his relationship with the department paralleled major welfare investments, including monthly payments, which raised the value he placed on termination of affiliation, while making the department more determined to accomplish this. However, the longer his welfare career lasted, the less the department considered him a worthy client who deserved valuable offers in exchange for termination; the offers he received would soon begin to diminish in value. This lengthening of the welfare career-line was due in part to factors external to the relationship, which prevented the department from realizing more valuable offers that it had made to Zackaria.

Phase V: The Consequences of Structural Dependence—
Diminished Responsibility and Bureaucratic Interference (1959–1960)

Having failed to settle the Sassons in the Negev, and cognizant of Zackaria's lack of alternatives, the department continued to press him to accept employment. The value of department offers did not decrease immediately, for the duration and extent of its investment and involvement in the Sassons had generated multiple commitments to the household and an increasing desire to terminate affiliation in exchange for its allocations. These multiple commitments to household loci and areas of living still prevented the department from cutting its losses, and continued to produce offers of comparatively high value.

Zackaria was no longer asked if he was interested in a particular job. He was told that he would receive a fish store, although he objected. The caseworker then turned her attention to Isaac, who was attending a day high school. She insisted that he either work or transfer to a day vocational high school to learn a trade. Isaac refused outright, and then complicated his stance by shifting the responsibility onto his father. He said that he was "born for studies" and that he would not enter the army for his national service until their completion. He reviled his father for the state of the household, but added that there was little his father could do; and he refused to help support the household. I note again that such tactics of complication are themselves emergent properties of the developing relationship, for their strength derives from the involvement of the department in the household. What follows illustrates the dilemma of being committed to the household while desiring termination of affiliation. Although the department ceased to support further army deferments for Isaac, it did support a reduction in his school fees, which he was granted.[52] If Isaac, as the only able-bodied son of the household, were drafted, the Sassons would be entitled to receive financial compensation from the army for the loss of contributions he would presumably have made as a civilian. Such compensation would perhaps reduce pressure on the department by enabling it to reduce allocations. But by supporting a reduction in Isaac's school fees, the department enabled him to continue his education and postpone his national service.

After the meeting with Isaac, the caseworker termed both him and Zackaria "psychopaths," but reiterated to her supervisor that the department should stand firm in obtaining the fish store for Zackaria against all competition "because the family is on the verge of collapse."[53] The use of the informal label "psychopath" appears to have served two purposes. First, it permitted the caseworker to simplify the various contradictions in expectations presented to her without disentangling their complexities. If these persons were "psychopaths" (in other words, incomprehensible), their erratic behavior stemmed from a source external to the caseworker's area of competence; therefore neither she nor the department was responsible. Such terminology also suggested that the clients' responsibility had diminished, since "psychopaths" were not responsible for their own erratic behavior. Then neither department nor clients were accountable, and they could continue their relationship, but with an important difference in emphasis.[54] Diminished responsibility permitted the client to use tactics which might otherwise be severely sanctioned. For the department, diminished responsibility allowed for the normalization of a welfare career-line, although not for client turnover. "Psychopaths" had to be cared for, and that was a department function. In addition, some agency had to assume the responsibility which persons so termed surrendered: "psychopaths" were to be guided and interfered with for their own protection. This in turn legitimized the offering of further benefits to the client. While the progression of redefinitions which Zackaria underwent eased the department's understanding of why affiliation continued, it also rooted Zackaria more firmly in a welfare career. For not long after the caseworker's use of the term "psychopath," monthly welfare payments to the Sassons were raised to I£ 60.

As had happened with the first store offered Zackaria, negotiations over the fish store collapsed: a third party, a private welfare agency which had promised a loan, insisted that it had no available funds. The caseworker then suggested that Zackaria purchase a market stall for I£ 1,000; but he rejected this. Previous offers were to have been underwritten by the department and the private agency. Here the department offered only to intercede to help him obtain loans, and in fact it was unable to negotiate these. Zackaria was then offered a local vegetable-peddling permit, which he rejected; but he countered with a request for a store in his neighborhood so that his younger children could help him.[55] This request would appear to indicate that he was still prepared to accept what he perceived as a fair exchange for termination. However, two weeks later, when the store in the South Market finally became available and was offered to him, he rejected it, stating that he now lived too far away from this store and that his children would be unable to help him. Therefore it may be more correct to state that both the department and Zackaria vacillated over the conditions of termination, and Zackaria vacillated between his desire for worthwhile employment and his emergent desire for the security of a welfare career. When he and the department were able to agree, on at least four significant occasions (offer of foodstuffs store, original offer of store in South Market, move to Negev, and fish store), external factors (interagency competition, construction delays, rejection by the *moshav*, and agency withdrawal) prevented the realization of the employment that Zackaria had accepted.

In August 1959 Zackaria was offered a kerosene-and-ice store which had little utility for him. These were seasonal commodities, and he would have to compete with mobile kerosene vendors who sold from building to building. He did not refuse outright, but complicated his reply by demanding the South Market store he had rejected three months earlier. Rebuffed a number of times, he and Sima staged a sit-in at the department office, and after a few hours the police were called to evict them. The Rehabilitation Office then informed the caseworker that Zackaria had been correct in estimating the difficulty of supporting his household with the proceeds from the kerosene-and-ice store. The Welfare Department, whether in response to this information, to the sit-in, or to both, raised welfare payments to I£ 100 a month.

Given Zackaria's known dependency and the still futile efforts to remove him from the welfare rolls, the department increasingly attempted to interfere in the household. During early 1960, at a series of meetings, the caseworker, her supervisor, and a representative of the Rehabilitation Office attempted to plan a common strategy for handling the Sassons. The Rehabilitation Office caseworker stated that she would refuse to cooperate in finding a store for Zackaria since he had consistently refused previous offers, and she added that it was folly to invest sums in such a client. She suggested that he was suitable only for selling newspapers on a street corner. The supervisor suggested that Zackaria be sent to the *moshav* to work with his brother, employment that would support his household in Jerusalem; failing that, she suggested that Mrs. Zap persuade Zackaria to return to the labor exchange for work. The Welfare Department caseworker suggested that Zackaria's doctor be persuaded to tell him that his illnesses were worsening because he remained idle. These plans are the most substantive evidence of a shift in department policy toward coercion and interference. Much the same general stand was taken on Isaac's refusal to work.[56] Previously Zackaria and Sima had asked the caseworker to persuade the headmaster of Isaac's school not to support another army deferment. Now the supervisor wrote: "I am going to intervene at the recruiting office, and tell them to draft him and direct him to study an occupation. The fact that he wants theoretical studies is disturbing his balance." This the supervisor did, but Isaac was not to enter the army for another two years. It was also decided definitively to tell the Sassons that someone in the household had to begin to work. The department caseworker argued for withdrawal of monthly payments as a threat, but the others adopted the softer line which was later presented to the Sassons: if they refused any further employment arrangements made for them by the caseworker, the department would cease to support them once all their children came of working age. Since the youngest child, Dalia, was then two years of age, the threat was quite toothless; its very weakness indicated the overall commitment to the household as a unit which the department had developed over the previous five years.

The next offer of employment made to Zackaria—selling newspapers—demonstrated how little the department was prepared to allocate in exchange for termination of affiliation. This was no longer an attempt to find him employment suitable to the support of his family, but an attempt to achieve a semblance of "rehabilitation." Yet as long as he continued to receive monthly welfare payments it is difficult to see why he should have accepted this lesser offer, which he did in fact refuse. In other words, although he was dependent upon welfare, the department could not directly utilize its power to coerce him as long as it remained committed to the overall welfare of the household and he remained the major client. This problem was partially alleviated in the subsequent phase, when the department turned Sima into the major client of the household.

Phase V, like Phase IV, is an intermediate period in which the department and the Sassons vacillate in their conception of fair exchange, and in which Zackaria shifts perceptibly toward a welfare-career commitment. The department continues to devalue his moral worth, his sense of responsibility, and finally the value of offers made to him, while retaining its overall commitment to the household. Zackaria had been able to resist department offers and demands in the transactions of Phase III (see Table 3) because he had alternative economic rewards, and he is able to resist the department in the transactions of Phase V because the department's commitment to the household has substantially raised the welfare payments which pass through his hands.

Phase VI: Welfare Dependence and
Department Disengagement (1960–1965)

For the first time the caseworker seriously turned her attention to Mrs. Sasson, and using the withdrawal of some aid as a threat, sent her to the Rehabilitation Office, where she accepted a job in a school kitchen at I£ 100 a month.[57] The department then took the significant step of removing welfare aid from Zackaria's control by making monthly checks payable to Sima, and by directing her to give him I£ 10 per month as an allowance. This action effectively shifted the locus of power within the household. Zackaria, the major household earner, had first become dependent upon the department for subsistence, and then became dependent upon his wife for subsistence.[58] For the next six months Zackaria tried to have the decision reversed by coming to the department office with lists of demands and requests, few of which were supported by Sima. When he threatened divorce the caseworker wrote to the rabbinical court to ask that a reconciliation be effected.

Since two household members (Sima and Lea) were employed, the department lowered monthly payments to I£ 90.[59] In July 1961 Zackaria was again offered a job selling newspapers, and he finally capitulated to the worst offer made to him by the department. While the formal affiliation of Zackaria had been terminated, the department could not erase the household from the welfare rolls because of its extensive involvements and commitments. Zackaria quit his job after two months, stating that the work was too strenuous, and the situation remained as before. He was fifty-four years old. The department then tailored its definition of Zackaria to meet this contingency. He was defined as ''old and weak'' and was offered employment in a bookbindery reserved for persons past the age of retirement. He rejected the offer, but countered with a request for a permit to peddle old clothes.[60]

What followed again demonstrated the flexible parameters of moral and situational constructs like ''old and weak,'' which are formulated to meet utilitarian problems. Seeing that Zackaria was prepared to peddle old clothes, the department ignored its own definition and supported his application: ''This time we have the impression he is serious about it. . . . We have known Mr. Sasson for many years and he is an honest man. . . . We hope that this time he will be able to rehabilitate himself and improve his situation at home.''[61] However, the Rehabilitation

Office, which had previously vetoed a kerosene-and-ice store, had now found such a store near Zackaria's flat, and had arranged for him to obtain it. The Welfare Department agreed to contribute I£ 350, and a private agency agreed to contribute I£ 350 plus a loan of I£ 250, so that Zackaria could begin with operating capital of I£ 950, I£ 700 of which did not have to be repaid.

Zackaria quickly lost the store. Even though it had initiated the venture, the Rehabilitation Office reversed its decision and refused to support his candidature, arguing that his health was too poor and that he could not support his family with the proceeds of such a store. The private agency also refused to invest after its social worker reported that Zackaria was not a suitable candidate; and the offer of the store was withdrawn.

From this point Zackaria completely abandoned any attempts to procure what he perceived as a profitable exchange for his welfare career. I take his unpreparedness to enter into further transactions about employment as an indication that his career-line was firmly directed to obtaining whatever welfare benefits he could still receive. However, his commitment to a welfare career occurred at a time when such a career-line could bring him only diminishing returns, since he had already lost most of the personal and situational resources which had induced department allocations. Zackaria stated openly that he was too ill to work, and that he only desired financial support. The caseworker continued to state that he would have to work. The department did not seem to be "officially" aware that Zackaria's commitment to welfare, and his state of dependency, had been in part nurtured by the department's own manipulation of income distribution within the household, by its attempts to coerce him to accept employment which met neither his needs nor those of his household, and by its failure to realize the allocation of a number of its more valuable offers. Now that his dependency on welfare was complete, the department remained primarily interested in "rehabilitating" him and erasing him from the rolls. But as the field of relevance had widened to include the household and its diverse components, Zackaria's role in the affiliation had diminished in significance for the department; and whether he was "rehabilitated" or not had only limited bearing on the overall department-household affiliation. Henceforth the department was unprepared to offer Zackaria any employment which it considered worthwhile.

For the next two years Zackaria remained out of work, and sporadically tried to induce the department to support him. Other actions he directed against his family. He poured kerosene over clothing and mattresses within the flat and set them alight. He broke doors and furniture and shattered windows, and stole money from his wife for his own use. He took to sleeping during the day and attempted to prevent his wife from sleeping at night.[62] While these events were communicated to the department by the family, the caseworker did not react. By this time three of the Sasson women were employed and earning comparatively well; and the household had never known such material prosperity.[63]

In February 1964 the Rehabilitation Office suggested to Zackaria that he work in SAGE, a sheltered workshop for the elderly indigent. He refused but no longer made any complicating demands: "He complained that he is deprived. . . . He complains about his difficult situation." Two months later welfare payments were reduced to I£ 50 per month, and none of the Sassons vigorously attempted to have this decision reversed.[64]

Zackaria continued to appear at the welfare office to complain about how he was treated within the household: his family had forced him to live by himself in one room and no longer spoke to him. In April 1965 he complained that his wife had thrown him out of the flat, and that his children insulted and beat him.[65] He asked for help in dealing with them. However, the department limited its contact to the subject of employment. Zackaria was told that since he was incapable of helping himself the department recommended that he enter SAGE, regardless of the fact that, at fifty-eight, he was under the retirement age of sixty-five.

In Phase VI Zackaria indicates his commitment to a welfare career, while Sima is directed toward employment.[66] The overall pattern of transactions between department and household reflects for the first time the former's active use of power to press for disengagement from, and termination of, household affiliation. As Table 2 indicates, Phase VI contains the highest proportion of department rejections of client requests. Complementary to this, as Table 3 indicates, in Phase VI clients are more responsive to the department than they were during any previous phase. Furthermore, in Phase VI the clients' commitment to the welfare career-line is indicated by their raising of the subject of a welfare income more often than the subject of employment; this trend, first evident in this phase, continues through Phase VII. While the department continues to raise the subject of employment more often than that of a welfare income, it raises the subject of a welfare income proportionately more often than in previous phases, and this trend also continues through Phase VII.

Phase VII: From Welfare Career to Sheltered Career (1965–)

A few weeks after his plea for help, Zackaria began to work in SAGE.[67] Soon after, Isaac completed his national service, and welfare payments were canceled on the assumption that the able-bodied eldest son should support his parents even though he no longer lived with them.[68] There were also strong pressures to have Zackaria removed from SAGE, which described him as a "real burden, socially, hygienically, and mentally." The head of the Rehabilitation Office agreed that there was "no reason to disturb the atmosphere of the place and to damage, by his presence, the possibility of other old people being absorbed there." But the office could suggest only that he return to selling newspapers. In SAGE Zackaria sat at work, dozed at times, and exerted little effort; but for the first time in four years he had his own limited earnings of I£ 40–50 a month to spend as he saw fit, and he desired to continue in SAGE. The Welfare Department also preferred to keep him working there, since this diminished the likelihood that the household would have to be reinstated on the roll of monthly welfare payments. The Rehabilitation Office then argued that since this was his first regular job in many years his "rehabilitation" was slow, but that with time his demeanor, deportment, and productivity would improve.

However, monthly welfare support of I£ 50 was renewed in May 1966 because both Zackaria and Sima were ill, and they had no other source of income.[69] Varda and Lea had married and ceased to help support the household. Two other daughters, Rachel and Sarah, were studying outside Jerusalem. Two younger sons, Benno and David, were in institutions, while two older sons, Victor and Aharon, were doing their national service. The household consisted of Zackaria, Sima, and their two youngest daughters, Dalia and Zafrira, aged eight and nine. Monthly payments were canceled the following year when both elder Sassons returned to work.

In February 1968 Zackaria fell and broke a leg. Sima refused to care for him. The department noted: "all our efforts to convince his wife to cook and clean for him failed. She refused to do anything for him. He did not wash or change his clothes since he fell down . . . the wife locks the kitchen and does not even allow him to make a cup of tea. . . . The police come every day to bring peace between the parents. They both ask for help in getting a divorce and we refuse." And Mrs. Sasson was recorded as saying that "she cannot continue to live with him because he is stinking, because he collects leftover food from garbage cans and brings it home; because, whenever he can, he steals the children's food and eats it, and he was never ready to support the children." The department arranged for a maid for Zackaria at I£ 50 a month.

In August 1968 Mrs. Sasson underwent minor surgery and was found to be suffering from malignant cancer. Rachel and Sarah returned to the household; one worked as a maid, and the other cared for the two youngest daughters. The department agreed to allocate I£ 50 for household upkeep. But by the end of 1968 Sima was receiving monthly payments of I£ 150, and the department was trying to secure an early pension for her so that support could be reduced. By the spring of 1969 both Rachel and Sarah were working, and monthly payments were reduced to I£ 50. Benno, then fifteen, had been expelled from the retarded children's home "because of sexual aberrations." He was living at home, but neither worked nor studied. Victor had been released from the army, was taking an electrician's course, lived at home, but did not contribute to household upkeep. Zackaria continued to work in SAGE.

The probable pattern of subsequent support had been established. Zackaria was sixty-three and in two years would begin to receive support from the national insurance system. Sima might well not live that long, and with two exceptions all the Sasson children were close to being defined as capable of supporting themselves. Then the Welfare Department would once again attempt to terminate the affiliation of the household. However, from 1957 through 1969 the department had never been able to cancel completely its commitments to various loci within the household.

CONCLUSION

At the outset I suggested that a transactional perspective had analytic strength when applied to the problem of how social relationships could develop between officials of service bureaucracies and their clients when neither party was oriented toward such sustained affiliations, and when, in formal organizational terms, the imbalance in power between the parties heavily favored the service bureaucracy.[70] This chapter has attempted through an extended case study to demonstrate how the sequential process of negotiated transactions over conditions of termination of affiliation could result in the emergence of a client career-line which became wholly oriented toward inducing welfare benefits, while both the relevant service bureaucracy and the client remained oriented for a lengthy period toward termination of affiliation.

The case of the Sassons suggests that the first crucial factor in extending the schedule of affiliation is the nature of the initial affiliation itself: the general obligations of department and client are specified, but the exact allocations to be exchanged for termination of affiliation are not specified. This provides the client with the opportunity to begin negotiations over what he perceives as a fair exchange for termination of affiliation. If the client does not receive what he perceives as a fair exchange, he has easy access to the forum of the welfare office, within which he can attempt to realize resources to induce the department to allocate benefits, first for the sake of meeting his central needs and then for the sake of the benefits themselves.

A second set of crucial factors which operates to extend the schedule of affiliation is the means which the client realizes, inadvertently or deliberately, to induce department allocations. In the case of the Sassons, Zackaria expanded the field of relevance of affiliation by introducing the department to diverse loci of potential investment within the household, and to diverse areas of household living which could fall within the diffuse boundaries of department responsibility. In this case affiliation initially included a single client locus who represented a single solidary household, according to the information available to the department. In the course of transactions the field of relevance of the affiliation expanded to include five somewhat different household loci who at times presented quite different conceptions of the household. Once aware of a diversity of household loci, the department was also made aware of situational coalitions within the household which at times were in opposition to one another: Zackaria versus Isaac, Zackaria plus Sima versus Isaac, Zackaria plus Sima versus Victor, Sima supporting Varda, and Zackaria versus Sima. These shifting coalitions, as well as the one of Zackaria plus Sima versus their neighbors, all served to complicate the expanded field of relevance of affiliation. In addition, during the course of transactions, the initial area of employment was expanded to eight areas of living which were directly connected to five household loci, and which indirectly included and affected the full household of thirteen members. Once the department invested in a particular locus or area of living, this in turn made available or activated further resources for the clients to induce department allocations, and increased the capacity of the clients to negotiate what was perceived as a fair exchange for termination of affiliation. However, as department allocations continued and increased, the affiliation itself became more valuable to the clients, and this raised what was perceived as the value of a fair exchange for termination of affiliation. Furthermore, by becoming aware of diverse household loci and their diverse needs, and by allocating benefits to them, the department became involved in the household in complex and mutually reinforcing ways.

As the duration of affiliation lengthened, the field of relevance was also expanded by the Welfare Department, for it sought contacts with other agencies in searching for the means to terminate affiliation, and its contacts with the Sassons required it to have contact with other organizations. Thus other organizations like the labor exchange, Amidar, the police, and private welfare agencies came to be relevant to the affiliation of the Sassons, as did, within the Welfare Department itself, the Rehabilitation Office and the Youth Office. Both the household components and the external components included within the expanded field of affiliation came to have a say in what conditions of termination of affiliation should apply, and therefore they came to constrain the capacities of the initial client and the department to agree upon the value of a fair exchange for termination.

While on the side of the household the expansion of the field of relevance to include diverse loci generates further resources with which to induce allocations, these loci also come to provide resources which the department can realize to limit affiliation: diverse loci provide the department with alternatives which can be supported or manipulated to limit the resources and affiliation of the initial or major client. Thus attempts by clients to realize resources to induce allocations, and by the department to limit or terminate affiliation, both contain within them elements of constraints which in later phases function to restrict the bargaining capacities of the major parties to the affiliation. These parties come to have less control over the duration and shape of the emergent career-line and over whether it becomes directed toward obtaining welfare benefits for their own sake or toward obtaining a fair exchange for termination.

If the client can open alternative opportunities for economic reward, he can maintain a more independent stance in transactions with the department, in that he can postpone compliance with its demands and offers. Since the potency of such alternatives depends upon their being kept secret from the department, from the point of view of the latter the behavior of the client is puzzling and to some extent "illogical." As the involvement of the department continues to develop through continuing allocations, the officials in contact with the client household seek explanations to clarify their lack of control. I suggested that one such form of explanation is the application of informal stigmatizing designations to clients. Such designations justify the extension of the welfare career, but, like other resources mentioned, they operate contrary to the designs of those who realize them, for they also justify the continuing allocation of welfare benefits. While this latter point would, in the short run, appear to benefit the client, the application of stigmatizing designations also justifies increased department interference in, and coercion of, the client household to seek termination of affiliation. In other words, the feedbacks which emerge from the realization of these and other resources have ramifications for the welfare career which are, in a sense, unintended by either party, and which control the parties' capacities to negotiate a fair exchange for termination of affiliation. The application of stigmatizing labels devalues the worthiness of the client, and may therefore also diminish the value of offers made to him by the department, at a time when the alternative opportunities of the client enable him to hold out for more valuable offers.

As the welfare timetable of the Sassons continued to be lengthened, with multiple department involvements in the household, the affiliation no longer focused upon the problem of the major client, but instead upon the multiple commitments of the department to the household as a unit. Therefore terminating the affiliation of a single household locus did not necessarily result in the severance of relationships with the household. From the standpoint of the department, the costs of continuing affiliation increased with the lengthening of affiliation, and termination of affiliation became more desirable in that respect. Moreover, for the department the rewards of continuing affiliation decreased with time, since it received little return for its extensive investments in the household. In addition, with time the costs of terminating affiliation decreased, for the department appeared to be more prepared to cut its losses, at least with respect to the major client, Zackaria. And with time the rewards for terminating affiliation increased, since this would free the accumulated benefits allocated to the Sassons for other clients of the department. From the standpoint of the client, with time the costs of continuing affiliation decreased, since client resources had already been realized and their effects in the form of benefits were being received. With time the client's rewards for continuing affiliation increased, since more valued benefits continued to be forthcoming. For the client the costs of terminating affiliation rose with time, since this would result in the loss of benefits of progressively greater value, benefits which were predictable and could be relied upon. Finally, the client's rewards for terminating affiliation decreased, as the value of the conditions of termination offered by the department decreased. However, I should also note here that as the department increasingly utilized stigmatizing designations to interfere in the household and to coerce the major client, the personal costs of continuing affiliation for the major client appeared to become overly great, and consequently the costs of terminating affiliation decreased, even though the conditions of termination had diminished in value. In general, I would suggest that the longer affiliation continues, the fairer termination will appear to the Welfare Department, and the less fair it will appear to the client, as the value of what is offered in exchange for termination diminishes.

The diminishing value of what is considered a fair exchange for termination is also related to the changing life-situation of the client; for with closure of economic alternatives, increasing age, worsening health, and changing composition of the household, the range of benefits which the department can make available narrows. One of the implications of this study is that great stigmatization of the client coincides in time with the greater structural dependence of the client upon welfare benefits, and with the greater commitment of the client to the welfare career-line; this situation develops at a time when the client has the least resources with which to induce allocations, and at a time when the department has increased resources with which to press for termination of affiliation. This process is rooted in the dual aspects of the resources realized by parties to influence their relationships—in the fact that the resources on the one hand provide rewards, but on the other contain the seeds of future constraint. It is the sequential resolution of these dialectics, and their consequent effects on subsequent contacts and transactions, which provide for the dynamic emergence of structures like the welfare career-line. Examination of this process may have greater value for the study of official-client relationships than has hitherto been recognized.

ACKNOWLEDGMENTS

Field work in Jerusalem was supported by the Bernstein Israel Research Trust, directed by Professor Max Gluckman. Additional support was provided by the Canada Council. I am especially thankful to the Department of Family and Community Services of the Municipality of Jerusalem, which permitted me unrestricted access to selected files. Previous versions of this paper have substantially benefited from the informed comments of Professor Emanuel Marx, Dr. Richard Werbner, Professor Max Gluckman, Dr. W. W. Sharrock, Dr. Cyril Sofer, Dr. Kingsley Garbett, and Dr. John Lee.

NOTES

1. Weber is especially emphatic on the probabilistic nature of the social relationship. He writes: "let it be repeated, and continually kept in mind, that it is only the existence of the probability that, corresponding to a given subjective meaning complex, a certain type of action will take place, which constitutes the 'existence' of the social relationship" (1964: 119).

2. The exchange theorist Emerson has stressed that only longitudinal studies, whether "historical" or experimental, raise data questions about the "feedback" or emergent effects of ongoing social relations (viz., about the nature of bureaucratic affiliation, in the context of this chapter). See Emerson 1969: 387, 405.

3. In discussing contacts between psychiatrists and patients, and lawyers and clients, where moral or personal accountability is an issue, Scheff (1968: 6) writes: "The fixing of responsibility is a process in which the client offers definitions of the situation, to which the interrogator responds. After a series of offers and responses, a definition of the situation acceptable to both . . . is reached."

4. I follow Kapferer (1972: 163) in maintaining that "transaction" refers to "a unit of activity and its content directed by one individual" toward his counterpart in the course of a social contact. However, I would add that this unit of activity is one which contains an offer-response sequence. Touching on a matter outside the scope of this chapter, which is of necessity restricted to a textual rather than interactional analysis, let me say that I would

restrict interpersonal transactions to sequences of activity which are perceived as such by participants, thereby excluding a wide range of paralinguistic and kinesic phenomena. But I see no particular justification for limiting either transaction (see Barth 1966: 4) or exchange (see Kapferer 1972: 164) to reciprocal interactions. In the course of their everyday activities persons "do" transaction and exchange without necessarily being aware of them as such. I think that "doing" is the correct way to denote such activities without, at the level of description, evaluating the significance of accomplished social action. However, the doing of transaction or exchange has effects which can be evaluated in terms of conceptions like reciprocity or status differentiation and power in relationships.

5. In discussing contacts between doctors and patients in Israeli clinics, Katz et al. (1969: 310) note that "the clients are not so resourceless as they appear. They can offer or withhold cooperation, so cooperation is a resource. They can show deference, or give status, or make known their gratitude—and these may matter to the official, and perhaps even to the organization. They can invoke their 'rights'—even if they aren't quite sure what those are—or appeal to the fact that the organization exists to serve them." There are also bureaucratic situations in which personal attributes like age or state of health will be major resources for clients. Nevertheless, these are not necessarily resources which are immediately communicated to and perceived by officials. They must be stressed in the presentations of clients in order to be realized.

6. This is an oversimplification. While certain resources like age and state of health must be overcommunicated by clients in order to be realized, other resources, like the alternative economic opportunities of clients, must be undercommunicated, viz. kept hidden from officials, if they are to retain their potency.

7. A similar conception of "career" is offered by Roth. He notes that "A career is a series of related and definable stages or phases of a given sphere of activity that a person goes through on the way to a more or less definite and recognizable end-point or goal" (1963: xviii). See also Becker (1967: 22–25) for another similar view of career.

8. Kapferer (1972: 7) credits Blau (1964) for the introduction of the idea of emergent property, and notes, in my view correctly, that "The introduction of this concept marks a departure from other exchange theories such as those of Homans and Barth which view structural and institutional forms as ultimately reducible to their individual components." However, it may be noted here that the idea of emergence appears implicitly in Emerson, when he writes that "It might even be meaningful to talk about the parties being controlled by the relation itself" (Emerson 1962: 34).

9. While the parties relevant to an ongoing career-line will be attributing meanings to what is occurring, the career-line may acquire quite different substantive meanings in retrospect, as the relevant parties continue to try to "make sense" out of what occurred in the light of what is occurring. I will discuss such reinterpretations and their effects in the context of stigmatizing labels applied to welfare clients. For another discussion of retrospective reinterpretation, see Wilson 1970.

10. The welfare department referred to here is the Department of Social Welfare of the Municipality of Jerusalem, recently renamed the Department of Family and Community Services. All further references to "Welfare Department" or "department" are to this public welfare agency.

11. Descriptions of such procedures in American public welfare agencies are found in Piven and Cloward (1972: 149–175), Zimmerman (1969: 345–353), and Jerry Jacobs (1968–1969). Israeli public welfare caseworkers are overburdened, with an average caseload per worker of between three hundred and four hundred files. This has led them to protest that they are "scapegoats" whose task is to explain to their clients the shortcomings of various government agencies. See the *Jerusalem Post,* June 28, 1972.

12. Agencies whose functions are dependent upon a comparatively small group of clients are more likely to adopt a long-term orientation to clients, and to cultivate their affiliations, since termination of affiliation may also mean termination of the contracts of agency caseworkers. Caseworkers hired in Jerusalem to work with disadvantaged youths during a period of tumultuous disturbances may now be fired because the situation has quieted. See the *Jerusalem Post*, February 1, 1973.

13. The spoken term most frequently used by caseworkers is "rehabilitatzia," a transliteration of "rehabilitation." The modern Hebrew term, "shikum," is frequently used on formal occasions and in written communications.

14. On a number of occasions in recent years public welfare caseworkers and senior administrators have threatened to withdraw services, strike, or resign if ongoing budgetary deficits were not covered by the municipalities concerned or by the national Ministry of Social Welfare. See *Jerusalem Post*, November 9, 1971; February 22, 1972; and June 30, 1972.

15. Emphasis on a speedy turnover of clientele in American public welfare agencies has been noted by Hasenfeld (1972: 261) and by Jerry Jacobs (1968–1969: 418). Consider also the following statement signed at the request of the Welfare Department by a man aged fifty-seven, who had been allocated a market stall and a loan to purchase stock: "I declare that by receiving the stall . . . and the money to start it going I see my final *rehabilitation* [i.e., his rehabilitation is in sight] and I will not have any more requests of the social welfare service."

16. For example, when the client mentioned in note 15 complained that he was not earning enough from the market stall to support his household, he received the following reply: "you must work and serve the customers nicely as we have warned you before. All the responsibility for not succeeding rests with you. . . ." That he was then fifty-eight, with a hernia, and with one leg crippled by childhood polio, was not admitted as relevant here.

17. Toren (1969: 168) gives the Israeli example of a mother of young children who requested aid in finding employment, and who was told that it was more important that she care for her children.

18. In a most powerful study of client socialization, Robert Scott (1969: 119) writes: "When those who have been screened into blindness agencies enter them, they may not be able to see at all or they may have serious difficulties with their vision. When they have been rehabilitated, they are all blind men. They have learned the attitudes and behaviour patterns that professional blindness workers believe blind people should have."

19. Robert Scott (1970: 282) notes that experts have much leeway in choosing and emphasizing information about their clients in order to mold a conception of stigma which will accord with the work conditions of the former.

20. I accept Blau's (1964: 117) conception of power as "the ability of persons or groups to impose their will on others despite resistance through deterrence either in the form of withholding regularly supplied rewards or in the form of punishment, inasmuch as the former as well as the latter constitute, in effect, a negative sanction." See also Emerson 1962: 32.

21. In Blau's conception of transaction, "trust" plays a crucial mediating role between the preparedness of one party to make the commitment of investing in another and the expectation that the other will reciprocate or comply (see Blau 1964: 94, 98). In the context of this paper, "trust" has very little currency. In fact, if a welfare client is considered to be a less responsible person, suspicion about his preparedness to reciprocate through compliance and termination should be the norm. The welfare situation is one of power relations in which client compliance rests either upon acceptance of what is perceived as a "fair exchange" or upon the exercise of sanctions. However, in the long term there is a factor which must

mediate between allocations to the client and commitment to the client, whether he reciprocates or not. I will refer to this mediating factor as "involvement," and it bears some resemblance to Emerson's (1962: 39) idea of "motivational investment." In the case study to follow, both "involvement" and "commitment" will be treated as emergent properties of ongoing transactions which permit the career-line to develop.

22. The client is often unaware of or uninterested in the fact that the department is itself dependent upon a host of agencies, organizations, and institutions for the benefits it offers, and that the provision of these benefits depends on changing conditions of supply and demand and on how successful the department is in competing with other agencies. See Hasenfeld 1972.

23. Blau (1964: 120) notes that "Needs . . . do not remain constant. By providing individuals with goods and services that increase their satisfaction, their level of expectations tends to be raised, and while they were previously satisfied without these benefits, they are now desirous of continuing to obtain them." I might also note here that the resources the client can realize to induce further allocations of a particular type may derive their potency from the very nature of the allocations themselves, and so client resources may themselves be emergent properties of the emerging career-line.

24. The degree of openness in a "state of talk" will vary with the context of official-client communications. See Kadushin 1962 and Scheff 1968.

25. As Gergen (1968) has pointed out, such contradictions in the presentation of self are not necessarily indicative of personal disorganization, but instead highlight the capacities of the self for situational adaptation. In arguing for a theory of "multiple selves" he notes that "The prevalent view that the normal behaviour of individuals tends toward consistency is misconceived . . . the more 'natural' state of the organism is one which includes numerous disparities and contradicting tendencies" (pp. 306–307).

26. When two or more clients within a household cooperate on a single demand, the potential for complication greatly increases. Consider the case in which a husband and wife make the same demand, never present their demand together, and alternate their positions on the demand from positive to negative so that both never hold the same position at the same time. The department must then divert time and personnel to solve three problems: (a) that of the husband's demands and his changing position; (b) that of the wife's demands and her changing position; and (c) that of the couple together and their mutually contradictory demands about an issue which concerns them both.

27. In his study of a small Israeli town, Marx (1972: 297) noted that men who attempted to coerce officials were those who "were usually not quite destitute. . . . They could take the risk attending such a course of action: they hoped to gain but could also afford to lose." These were men whose bureaucratic dependence was leavened by alternative sources of economic rewards, and who could therefore manage a more defiant, more independent self-presentation to officials. On the other hand, clients in precarious financial states could not afford the risk of alienating officials, who were virtually their sole source of economic benefits.

28. For example, consider the following letter sent to an illiterate woman after she had been ejected from a welfare office by the police. She had been registered for hospitalization at a nominal rate and had demanded free hospitalization. The letter read: "we cannot accept the way you behaved in the social welfare office. . . . We have the feeling you are trying to obtain by force demands that we cannot accomplish; and to the explanation of the social worker you react with cursing and rude shouts. We hope you will understand and will not force us to use the legal possibilities we have that will cause you a lot of unpleasantness."

29. Blum and McHugh point out that the offering of motives for social behavior does not specify psychological causation, but is an act of social interpretation through which an

observer can "assert how a behavior is socially intelligible by ascribing a socially available actor's orientation" (Blum and McHugh 1971: 100).

30. There are a number of unavoidable weaknesses in the data of the case, about which the reader should be aware. I treat the Welfare Department as organizationally constant through time even though it has undergone major organizational changes during the years of the case. Nevertheless, I think the orientation ascribed to the department is correct throughout. Second, during the course of his welfare career, Zackaria passed through the hands of a number of caseworkers. However, the files I examined did not clearly distinguish between caseworkers, and therefore a potentially important variable, that of differences in approach to the client household, had to be omitted from the analysis. Finally, it is clear from an examination of the files that not all caseworker-client contacts were recorded.

31. All names of persons have been changed, and the contents of certain events slightly altered to ensure anonymity.

32. The Jewish Agency was responsible for the housing, employment, and welfare of immigrants during the first three years after their arrival in Israel. Camps were used as temporary measures until sufficient housing could be constructed.

33. Jerusalem had not participated in the absorption of the mass immigration, but it did begin to receive large numbers of immigrants during the period of 1949–1951 (see Schmelz 1964: 244).

34. Marx (1972: 298) writes that "assaults on officials rarely involve serious physical violence. The assailants generally merely swore and threatened violence and occasionally indulged in violent gestures like lifting a chair." He interprets the use of chairs (p. 197) as an attack upon the symbols of officialdom (viz., using the "seat" of authority to coerce the holders of such seats, thereby denying its exclusiveness and legitimacy).

35. A good example of such cooling procedures is found in Marx 1972: 295–296.

36. This is Zackaria's interpretation of the events, as he explained it to me in 1969.

37. Once Zackaria discovered this particular reward he could use the tactic of not paying rent when he felt unable to. This can be interpreted as a strategy which he adopted with regard to his bureaucratic obligations (i.e., nonpayment to a number of agencies) and a statement about how he perceived his obligations (i.e., he did not consider himself to have obligations to bureaucracy when he assessed the responsibility of officialdom for his difficult position).

38. The activation of personal influence in bureaucratic intercession is generally termed *proteksia* in Israel. Danet and Hartman (1972: 407) write that "In colloquial Hebrew, the concept has been narrowed to exclude all reference to graft, bribery, or the exchange of money—thus including now only the exchange of nonmonetary favours and activation of normative obligations."

39. It is doubtful whether Zackaria would have earned much more in carpentry during this period of Israel's history. While his salary would have been higher, he probably would not have worked more days per month. Possibly the major gain would have been a change in status, from unskilled to skilled.

40. Communications of this kind have been termed "persuasive appeals" by Katz and Danet (1966). In a study of letters written to the Israel customs authority Danet (1971: 856–857) found that "when clients are weak and have little to offer, appeals to altruism are high, and appeals to norms ... are low." Danet also found that persons in low-status occupations and persons who had emigrated from Middle Eastern and North African countries tended to be quite diffuse in their orientation to the customs authority.

41. The term "social case" (*micrei sa'ad* or *micrei sociali*) has somewhat ambiguous referents in Israel. Officially it can refer either to anyone who presents himself at a welfare

office and requests assistance, or to anyone who is actually supported in kind or cash by welfare. In practice it seems to refer more to persons who are becoming longer-term clients. The popular referent of "social case" is someone who cannot function satisfactorily through his own efforts and must request welfare aid as a support. All these references imply stigmatized elements of incapacity.

42. One must always take into account the economic realities within which the department must function, and the limitations these place on the extent to which a disability can be recognized and considered as "a need requiring immediate assistance." I have uncovered a number of instances in which a client was issued a medical certificate stating that the room or flat in which the client lived was highly detrimental to his health, and recommending a change of dwelling. Either no action was taken by the department, or action was taken very slowly. Since flats are scarce and clients are quite indigent, the financial burden for a new dwelling would fall on the department with its limited funds. Therefore impaired health in this context is not recognized as requiring immediate attention.

43. The caseworker noted that Zackaria would not help care for the children because this was "woman's work"; that he was authoritarian toward his children but suffered because they did not heed him; and that the children did not contribute to the income of the household. These attributes reflected what social workers have often accepted as "the breakdown of the traditional Middle Eastern patriarchal family" and consequent generational conflicts. These "negative" attributes were not peculiar to the Sasson household and did not reflect against it; for they expressed, supposedly, a more general process of conflict between "traditional" and "modern" cultures.

44. These offer-response transactions occurred through a series of six contacts between Zackaria and the department. Offer-response transactions noted in the files totalled 168. This total forms the basis of tables later in this chapter; but only the most significant transactions are discussed in the text.

45. Isaac was then sixteen and studied in an elementary vocational school for the mentally retarded. However, I do not know whether he was judged retarded. Because he had begun his formal studies in Israel at a late age, a school for the retarded may have been thought the easiest place for him to catch up with his studies.

46. In his study of an Israeli town, Marx (1972: 307) also found that welfare officials "would refrain from helping the spouses to obtain a divorce, as in all likelihood this would leave those authorities responsible for the maintenance of the minor children."

47. Marx (1972: 317), citing a senior Israeli police official, notes that while conflicts among neighbors are a frequent cause of violence, such cases are rarely taken to court, since the police try to bring the opposing parties to a more amicable resolution.

48. However, the department continued to allocate other benefits to the household: money for food when Sima complained that Zackaria was withholding welfare payments; the installation of electricity at a special rate; money for children's clothing; and the placing of two younger sons, Aharon and Benno, in special day schools after they were judged to be retarded.

49. The police did begin to process this complaint, but later closed the case for lack of evidence.

50. While the matter of divorce had first been presented to the department presumably to draw attention to their plight, by this time the Sassons were seriously contemplating divorce proceedings, and had taken the issue to the rabbinical court. The court was initially bound to seek a reconciliation, and then to ensure that all members of the household were supplied with requisite living facilities. This the Welfare Department was not prepared to guarantee. In addition, Zackaria and Sima shifted their position on divorce. Hence Zackaria's request for a second, viz. compliant, wife.

51. Isaac joined what was described as "undesirable elements." Victor, aged twelve, was serving a two-year reformatory sentence for theft. Aharon, aged eleven, had also been arrested for theft and was on probation.

52. Isaac was then twenty years of age and had received deferments to enable him to complete high school. National service in Israel usually begins at age eighteen.

53. This is further evidence that overall department commitment was no longer to a single client—that the unit of commitment had become the household and its manifold loci and areas of living. Zackaria is not touted for the fish store here because he is a "good" client, but because he is perceived as a linchpin of household viability, which is a matter of concern the department has been induced to accept through numerous transactions. Once Zackaria is no longer perceived as a significant factor in the stability of the household, the value of offers made to him decreases.

54. W. Richard Scott (1969: 127–128) notes the use of quasi-psychiatric terminology in contacts between supervisors and caseworkers "to justify actions aimed at forcing the client to conform to the worker's plans and to the agency's program." However, the use of such terminology here has the unintended effect of prolonging affiliation while justifying more coercive measures to terminate it.

55. The Sassons continued to be allocated lesser benefits by the department. See Handelman 1971: 136.

56. After a number of violent altercations among Zackaria, Sima, and Isaac, during which the police were called, Zackaria and Sima asked that Isaac be institutionalized, and the caseworker promised, "We are either going to rehabilitate him or send him to a mental hospital."

57. The second-eldest daughter, Lea, also began working as a maid and turned over a portion of her earnings to her mother. Lea was then fifteen. The eldest daughter, Varda, now twenty, studied full-time in a teachers' seminary. The department had paid most of her school and board fees.

58. Since Zackaria was no longer a worthy client, the caseworker no longer worried about his "loss of status" within the household.

59. Sima Sasson reacted to this decrease with attempts to reinvolve the department fully in the household: (a) she staged a sit-in and the police were called to evict her from the office; (b) she wrote to the president of Israel recounting her family history, stating that Zackaria's demands for a divorce failed because the department would not permit it; (c) she argued that Victor, now fifteen, should be placed in a kibbutz to be taught to work; (d) she demanded a divorce; (e) she demanded a change of flat; (f) she accused Zackaria of stealing a welfare check, and demanded that the caseworker take the check from him. When the caseworker responded tardily, Sima became abusive and the police were called to evict her again. Her demands were not met even though she employed tactics which had worked in the past. The department was attempting to disengage from its involvement in the household.

60. I doubt whether Zackaria would have defined himself as "old." His counteroffer to peddle should be seen as a partial reaffirmation of his physical capacities rather than as an indication of desire to peddle clothes as such. He could not easily have refused bookbindery employment by claiming to be healthy, since he had just claimed ill health in leaving the newspaper job.

61. This letter was written to the Rehabilitation Office. It is further evidence of the capacity of records to yield contractual accounts which are used for official purposes to establish the legitimacy of a course of action. In this case the application requested bureaucratic support on behalf of the "degenerate psychopath," Zackaria.

62. Marx notes that men whose financial situations are very precarious, and who have no economic alternatives but welfare sources, cannot risk appearing rebellious before officials. Instead they become violent toward persons close to them, like their wives. Marx's contention (1972: 299) appears to be supported by the case of the Sassons, for prior to Zackaria's dependence for subsistence on the department there are no recorded instances of the kind cited in the text.

63. Sima Sasson was then earning I£ 160 monthly. Varda had graduated and was employed as a teacher; and Lea worked as an assistant to a kindergarten teacher. Of the sons, Isaac was in the army, while the others were not employed to my knowledge.

64. The department remained involved in the problem of a divorce for the Sassons. In June 1963 the rabbinical court was prepared to grant one on condition that Zackaria would have a one-room flat to move into. Since the department refused to guarantee funds for such a flat, the divorce was not granted. In March 1964 Zackaria was prepared to turn over all property to Sima and return to France; but the department refused to purchase a ticket for him.

65. At one point the caseworker suggested to her supervisor that Zackaria be removed from the flat and settled elsewhere with department aid, because "his children treat him like a dog." The supervisor reacted vigorously to this expression of department commitment to the household by stating that welfare payments should be reduced and that Zackaria should not receive an allowance. This restored the official balance in favor of continued disengagement, and the caseworker did not again commit such sentiments to the record.

66. Concomitantly, the proportion of times the subject of intrahousehold relationships is raised by clients increases sharply in Phase VI. The matter generally takes the form of opposition between Zackaria on the one hand and Sima and the children on the other. The expressions of opposition appear in part to result from increased department interference within the household, which aggravates existing tensions and which offers Sima the resources to increase her opposition to her husband.

67. Blau (1964: 133) has written that "By exercising power and making demands on subordinates, a superior makes remaining under his power less attractive, and alternatives to it relatively more attractive than they were before, thus decreasing his subordinates' dependence on which his power rests." Zackaria appeared to have decided that the easy working conditions and limited salary of SAGE were more attractive than subsistence from the department through the agency of his wife.

68. By May 1966 the department had offered the Sassons legal aid to force Isaac to support them. The Sassons accepted and their case against Isaac dragged on for another two years before ending inconclusively.

69. Mrs. Sasson had placed her two youngest sons, Benno and David, in institutions. Benno was placed in a home for retarded children. Mrs. Sasson then went to the Committee for Saving Children, a religious, antimissionary voluntary association, and threatened to have David converted to Christianity. The committee placed David in an institution outside Jerusalem.

70. This essay is seen as a step toward a comparative study of factors which give rise to differing forms of welfare career-lines. A crude first attempt, which focuses upon the differential resources realized by a number of clients, is found in Handelman 1971: 163–201.

REFERENCES

Barth, Fredrik. 1966. *Models of Social Organization*. Royal Anthropological Institute Occasional Paper No. 23. London.

Beck, Bernard. 1966–1967. Welfare as a moral category. *Social Problems*, 14: 258–277.
Becker, Howard S., ed. 1967. *The Other Side: Perspectives on Deviance*. New York: Free Press.
_____. 1969. Social-class variations in the teacher-pupil relationship. In B. C. Rosen, H. J. Crockett, and C. Z. Nunn, eds., *Achievement in American Society*. Cambridge, Mass.: Schenkman.
Bittner, Egon. 1965. The concept of organization. *Social Research*, 32: 230–255.
Blau, Peter M. 1964. *Exchange and Power in Social Life*. New York: John Wiley.
Blau, Peter M., and W. Richard Scott. 1962. *Formal Organizations*. San Francisco: Chandler.
Blum, Alan F., and Peter McHugh. 1971. The social ascription of motives. *American Sociological Review*, 36: 98–109.
Burns, Tom. 1958. The forms of conduct. *American Journal of Sociology*, 64: 137–151.
Danet, Brenda. 1971. The language of persuasion in bureaucracy: "modern" and "traditional" appeals to the Israel customs authorities. *American Sociological Review*, 36: 847–859.
Danet, Brenda, and Michael Gurevitch. 1972. Presentation of self in appeals to bureaucracy: an empirical study of role specificity. *American Journal of Sociology*, 77: 1165–1190.
Danet, Brenda, and Harriet Hartman. 1972. On "proteksia": orientations toward the use of personal influence in Israeli bureaucracy. *Journal of Comparative Administration*, 3: 405–434.
Edgerton, Robert B. 1967. *The Cloak of Competence: Stigma in the Lives of the Mentally Retarded*. Berkeley and Los Angeles: University of California Press.
Emerson, Richard M. 1962. Power-dependence relations. *American Sociological Review*, 27: 31–41.
_____. 1969. Operant psychology and exchange theory. In Robert L. Burgess and Don Bushnell, Jr., eds., *Behavioral Sociology: The Experimental Analysis of Social Process*. New York: Columbia University Press.
Garfinkel, Harold. 1967. Good organizational reasons for "bad" clinic records. In *Studies in Ethnomethodology*. Englewood Cliffs, N.J.: Prentice-Hall.
Gergen, Kenneth J. 1968. Personal consistency and the presentation of self. In Chad Gordon and Kenneth J. Gergen, eds., *The Self in Social Interaction*. New York: John Wiley.
Goffman, Erving. 1963. *Stigma: Notes on the Management of Spoiled Identity*. Englewood Cliffs, N.J.: Prentice-Hall.
_____. 1967. *Interaction Ritual: Essays on Face-to-Face Behavior*. New York: Doubleday Anchor.
_____. 1970. *Asylums: Essays on the Social Situation of Mental Patients and Other Inmates*. Harmondsworth, Middlesex: Penguin.
Handelman, Don. 1971. Patterns of interaction in a sheltered workshop in Jerusalem. Ph.D. dissertation, Department of Social Anthropology, University of Manchester.
Hasenfeld, Yeheskel. 1972. People processing organizations: an exchange approach. *American Sociological Review*, 37: 256–263.
Jacobs, Glenn. 1970. Life in the colonies: welfare workers and clients. In Glenn Jacobs, ed., *The Participant Observer: Encounters with Social Reality*. New York: George Braziller.
Jacobs, Jerry. 1968–1969. "Symbolic bureaucracy": a case study of a social welfare agency. *Social Forces*, 47: 413–422.
Kadushin, Charles. 1962. Social distance between client and professional. *American Journal of Sociology*, 67: 517–531.
Kanev, I. 1968. *Social and Demographic Development and the Shape of Poverty in Israel*. Tel-Aviv: Economic and Social Research Institute and Kupat Holim.

Kapferer, Bruce. 1972. *Strategy and Transaction in an African Factory*. Manchester: Manchester University Press.

Katz, Elihu, and Brenda Danet. 1966. Petitions and persuasive appeals: a study of official-client relations. *American Sociological Review*, 31: 811–822.

Katz, Elihu, and S. N. Eisenstadt. 1965. Some sociological observations on the response of Israeli organizations to new immigrants. In S. N. Eisenstadt, ed., *Essays on Comparative Institutions*. New York: John Wiley.

Katz, Elihu, Michael Gurevitch, Tsiyona Peled, and Brenda Danet. 1969. Doctor-patient exchanges: a diagnostic approach to organizations and professions. *Human Relations*, 22: 309–324.

Kay, Herma H. 1969. The offer of a free home: a case study in the family law of the poor. In Laura Nader, ed., *Law in Culture and Society*. Chicago: Aldine.

Kushner, Gilbert. 1968. Indians in Israel: guided change in a new-immigrant village. *Human Organization*, 27: 352–361.

Lyman, Stanford M., and Marvin B. Scott. 1970. Accounts. In *A Sociology of the Absurd*. New York: Appleton-Century-Crofts.

Marx, Emanuel. 1972. Some social contexts of personal violence. In Max Gluckman, ed., *The Allocation of Responsibility*. Manchester: Manchester University Press.

Mayer, John E., and Noel Timms. 1970. *The Client Speaks: Working Class Impressions of Casework*. London: Routledge and Kegan Paul.

Palgi, Phyllis. 1963. Immigrants, psychiatrists, and culture. *Israel Annals of Psychiatry and Related Disciplines*, 1: 43–58.

Piven, Frances Fox, and Richard A. Cloward. 1972. *Regulating the Poor: The Functions of Public Welfare*. London: Tavistock.

Roth, Julius. 1963. *Timetables: Structuring the Passage of Time in Hospital Treatment and Other Careers*. Indianapolis: Bobbs-Merrill.

Scheff, Thomas J. 1968. Negotiating reality: notes on power in the assessment of responsibility. *Social Problems*, 16: 3–17.

Schmelz, O. 1964. The Jewish population of Jerusalem. *Jewish Journal of Sociology*, 6: 243–263.

Scott, Robert A. 1969. *The Making of Blind Men*. New York: Russell Sage Foundation.

———. 1970. The construction of conceptions of stigma by professional experts. In Jack D. Douglas, ed., *Deviance and Respectability: The Social Construction of Moral Meanings*. New York: Basic Books.

Scott, W. Richard. 1969. Professional employees in a bureaucratic structure: social work. In Amitai Etzioni, ed., *The Semi-Professions and Their Organization*. New York: Free Press.

Shokeid, Moshe. 1971a. *The Dual Heritage: Immigrants from the Atlas Mountains in an Israeli Village*. Manchester: Manchester University Press.

———. 1971b. Moshav Sela: frustration and crisis in the process of absorption. In Ovadia Shapiro, ed., *Rural Settlements of New Immigrants in Israel*. Rehovot: Settlement Study Center.

Sjoberg, Gideon, Richard A. Brymer, and Buford Farris. 1966. Bureaucracy and the lower class. *Sociology and Social Research*, 50: 325–337.

Toren, Nina. 1969. Semi-professionalism and social work: a theoretical perspective. In Amitai Etzioni, ed., *The Semi-Professions and Their Organization*. New York: Free Press.

Weber, Max. 1964. *The Theory of Social and Economic Organization*. New York: Free Press.

Weingrod, Alex. 1966. *Reluctant Pioneers: Village Development in Israel*. Ithaca, N.Y.: Cornell University Press.

Weiss Bar-Yosef, Rivka. 1968. Desocialization and resocialization: the adjustment process of immigrants. *International Migration Review,* 2: 27–45.

Wilson, Thomas P. 1970. Conceptions of interaction and forms of sociological explanation. *American Sociological Review,* 35: 697–710.

Zimmerman, Don. 1969. Record-keeping and the intake process in a public welfare agency. In Stanton Wheeler, ed., *On Record: Files and Dossiers in American Life.* New York: Russell Sage Foundation.

———. 1971. The practicalities of rule use. In Jack D. Douglas, ed., *Understanding Everyday Life.* London: Routledge and Kegan Paul.

Transactional Continuity in Mount Hagen

ANDREW STRATHERN

At the end of his book on land and society on Matupit Island in New Britain, A. L. Epstein discusses the familiar problems of continuity and change. The Tolai people, including those on Matupit, had experienced and responded to a complex set of introduced changes since the 1870s. They were deeply involved in cash cropping, wage labor, and new forms of politics, education, and religion, and yet Epstein was able to write that, "if so much of the evidence points to change, what gives the Tolai situation so much of its complexity . . . is the no less striking evidence of persistence and continuity" (1969: 294). The same phenomenon has often been pointed to in other studies of introduced change in societies subjected to colonial rule. These societies do not automatically through time become replicas of Western industrialized societies, despite the apparently diligent efforts of government agencies at certain stages of history to lead them in this direction. Government policies and attitudes change also, especially perhaps with a switch from colonial administration to independence. Resistance to the wholesale adoption of an imported social and cultural model does not, of course, preclude selective adoption, and one approach to the study of change has been to investigate how people make such selections and why, and how the selection results in a changing pattern of allocation of resources. If one is considering the allocation of resources as an index of change, then major transactions in which people engage over time are a good guide to follow, simply because they require much organization and effort from participants in them. In studies of New Guinea Highlands societies, the most obvious context to examine is that of competitive ceremonial exchange, in which both leaders and lesser men are involved and which takes place between groups that are significant units in local-level politics. This chapter sketches some dimensions of continuity in one ceremonial exchange system, the *moka* system of the Mount Hagen area in the Western Highlands District of Papua New Guinea.

In the *moka*, wealth objects such as pigs, valuable shells, and nowadays cash pass from hand to hand through partnerships between men in different political groups, and also as "helping" gifts to men in the same political group. A rule of the *moka* is that the "*moka* maker" in a particular exchange should give more than he has received by way of "solicitory" gifts from his partner (see Strathern 1971b). The *moka* maker must be "generous," and by being so he gains an increment of general prestige as well as specifically placing the recipient in his debt. To give merely an exact return for solicitory gifts, without any addition, brings with it no particular prestige, nor does it provide any basis for the continuation of a partnership. Since the added gifts constitute a debt, which eventually should be paid if the recipient is going to even or reverse the score and thus gain prestige for himself, it is clear that *moka* making presumes both a continuity in relationships between exchange partners and a spirit of rivalry between them. It is clear, too, that there is a possibility of partnerships coming to an end or being weakened if the goals set for them by the rules are not in practice achieved. These possibilities and presumptions are played out in actual relationships both between groups and between individual exchangers, and there is a complicated interplay of group and individual interests involved in each *moka* occasion, when a number of men may combine to give to their partners.

Along with the rule that the *moka* maker must try to give more than he has received goes the fact that *moka* making is a matter of delayed exchange. It takes time to gather or actually produce the goods needed for a successful *moka*. Further, from the same rule one can predict a tendency in the *moka* for an expansion of exchange networks to occur over time, as men seek to increase the size of the gifts they make by drawing more men into partnerships with them. An important concerted *moka* gift between allied groups may thus remain unreciprocated in full for a decade; and although the intervening years will be filled with activities preparatory to the return prestation, nowadays many other changes crowd into everyday life, and it becomes harder to concentrate on the *moka* to the exclusion of other activities. The question of how much longer the *moka* will survive as an institution is raised. As with all institutions, if it is to continue there has to be a way of inducing young people to participate in it. In the *moka* this is done basically by building up partnerships around the relationship with the mother's people, in the "affinal-maternal complex" (Reay 1959). This in turn depends on the continuing interest of the younger generation, and as alternative possibilities open up this interest may wane. A great deal depends on the choices made by leaders and on their influence over younger people. In this chapter I approach the question of continuity largely through a study of what leaders are doing and of the extent to which their views and actions are accepted by others.

To approach the contemporary situation, we need first to sketch some processes of change which have probably occurred in Hagen society since the first exploration of the New Guinea Highlands in the early 1930s. Europeans, coming into Hagen as entrepreneurs, missionaries, and government officers, brought with them a large and continuing supply of pearl shells, which were major wealth items used in the *moka*. In pre-contact times such shells, and others valued as wealth tokens, flowed in smaller numbers through established routes into the Highlands from the coastal areas. The immediate effect of their direct introduction into Hagen by incomers was both to give the Europeans an important status in Hageners' eyes and to inflate the size of payments required in bridewealth and the *moka*. Whereas previously access to valuables was controlled entirely through the trading and ceremonial exchange networks and was dominated by "big-men," it now became possible for men to earn shells from outsiders by offering them labor and goods. In the past it seems likely that the big-men held almost a monopoly over transactions with pearl shells. That monopoly was quickly broken when the Europeans came. Wealth was diffused more widely through the population, although there were also opportunities for some groups and individuals to capture significant advantages in access to the new supply by setting up friendships with incomers, offering them land to settle on, regular labor, pigs, and so on. The big-men responded to the challenge of this situation by developing what had previously been their special skill, the organization of exchange occasions, so as to persuade men who had gained shells from other sources to support them in exchanges they themselves were planning. In this way they attempted to retain their special status and influence even though their monopoly was broken.

Administration officers gradually extended the pacification of groups for several miles around Mount Hagen station in the 1930s and 1940s. As warfare abated or ceased, groups intensified competition through *moka* exchange, in much the same way and for the same reasons as has been suggested for other areas of Papua New Guinea (for example, Salisbury 1962; Meggitt 1971, 1974; Young 1971, with references given there). Thus the demand for shells remained high and the size and frequency of prestations continued to grow.

The first internal adjustments to the increased supply of valuables can be seen in rates of exchange at the heart of *moka* transactions themselves. One basic transaction is the exchange of shells for a live pig and 2 shells. Previously the "rate" established was that 4 shells equaled 1 pig plus 2 shells, but later 8 shells were required for the pig and 2 shells. Such a change of rates meant that the value of pigs rose in comparison to that of shells. This inflation of shell payments was accompanied by an inversion of the situation of privileged access to shells through trade: previously southern groups had controlled the entry of pearl shells into Hagen, but now the northern groups near to the station were doing so, and southern leaders invented a cargo cult in an attempt to regain the advantage they had lost (Strathern 1971a). The size of payments in shells continued to rise into the 1950s. As particular kinds of shells became altogether too plentiful, they were actually dropped as appropriate items for use in *moka*: cowries, nassa, and green snail were dropped in this way, and only pearl shells remained in regular use by the early 1960s. The shells dropped from the exchange system remained popular as ornaments, however, except for cowries sewn onto ropes which women used to wear swathed round their bodies at dances. In the mid 1960s the only prestation which I saw involving nassa and cowrie shells was made to a remote outlying group, an example of the process whereby people get rid of surplus unwanted goods or valuables by giving them to more conservative or less favored populations nearby.

"Giving up" valuables in this way created some problems, for these items were owed by partners to each other in the *moka*. However, rough equivalences between items can be established. A pearl shell, for example, can be regarded as equivalent to a cowrie-shell rope, and thus debts in cowrie can be paid off in pearl shells. The process continues today with pearl shells themselves. In 1964–1965 over a thousand pearl shells were given by men of two groups to two allied groups, as part of a larger *moka* gift involving some 350 live pigs as well as certain extra items such as cattle. The final return for this gift was made in early September 1974. This time there was no suggestion that pearl shells would be involved. Instead the *moka* makers collected some twelve thousand dollars in cash and used this to purchase cattle and commercially reared pigs as extra gifts, so that their partners would "feel good" and would "forget about" the shells they gave earlier. Again, the pearl shells they received previously they gave to men to the south, living on the slopes of Mount Hagen, who still use them in *moka*; and in return for these shells they received money.

This removal of certain items from the *moka* can be seen both as a response to inflation and as an index of other factors of social change. The switch from shell valuables to cash is particularly interesting here, since it may be read as a continuing choice to make investments in *moka* rather than to concentrate the use of cash on a nexus of marketing and daily consumption activities. Introduced items of high value, such as cattle or cars, which can be and are used for profit-making and business activities, are also circulated in the *moka*. The September 1974 *moka* which I have mentioned featured also the presentation of a Toyota Landcruiser vehicle worth over four thousand dollars to an important big-man (who is also a House of Assembly member).

Why has cash entered the ceremonial system? First, big-men are likely to have realized that if cash becomes a part of ceremonial payments they can control flows of it to a far greater extent than if it remains in an outside nexus of transactions only. Second, Hageners see cash as rather like another kind of imported valuable, like the valuable shells that were imported in the past. When Europeans first brought shells Hageners were delighted, as we have noted earlier. But much later they discovered that shells were not the items Europeans themselves used in transactions to obtain goods, and the quest then became to obtain money, since this was the true "strong thing" of the incomers. Already by 1964 a youngish man expressed a cynical view: "These shells are just the cover for a kind of food that the white man eats. He takes the food inside and eats it and throws the shell away. We pick it up and use it as a valuable." Money is thought of both as the real source of the white man's power and as a direct replacement for pearl shells in the ceremonial system. This opening up of the system to new items has meant that the system can absorb changes into itself and, on the other hand, that it is subject to inflationary pressures as the supply and value of new wealth items fluctuate. *Moka* making consequently remains quite a risky business.

We have seen that it is a cultural rule of *moka* that one attempts to exceed the size of previous gifts and thus to give more than one owes. If this were successfully done, the size of gifts would continually increase until there came a point when resources of organization and production could not cope. A tendency in this direction would be strengthened by inflation of the kind I have described. However, in addition to the process of dropping out items, the way in which debts are counted also puts a brake on the growth in size of prestations. It is the difference between a previous gift and the present one which is counted as the ongoing debt between partners. If A gives x shells to B and B returns $2x$, A does not have to attempt to give 4x shells to B next time. A owes to B x shells and should give these plus an addition, preferably enough to make 2x again. Thus the size of gifts can theoretically be stabilized, while one is still keeping to the rules of *moka*. Nevertheless, given the involvement of big-men in the system, there is a drive toward an increase in scale and particularly toward an increasing complexity of networks involved in the organization of a large *moka*. In a sequence of prestations which I observed in 1964–1965, it was clear that at least some groups were finding it difficult to coordinate events and that weak groups were actually failing in their efforts to make successful *moka*. By September 1974, when the return prestation for the 1964–1965 sequence was finally completed, financial efforts to achieve a large enough gift were further complicated by an intrusion of hostility and suspicion into intergroup relationships which made it very difficult for leading big-men to stage the actual dancing occasion for the prestation. The problems had thus become overtly political, and conflict, instead of being expressed only in debates about financial readiness to make the prestation, centered on accusations and claims of sorcery—killings within the set of clans which were supposed to dance together in celebration of the gift. The *moka* is supposed to be a sign of, and a means of creating, alliances and friendships between groups and individual partners. Its effects, however, can be nullified or reduced by political animosities which may both prevent a proper unity from being displayed among the givers of a *moka* and cause splits among the recipients as a result of jealousy over the size of gifts to different subgroups.

It is clear, when one looks at the history of the post-contact period in Hagen, that the *moka* system received an initial set of stimuli as a result of the coming of the administration. Further political and economic changes, however, have made it problematic whether the institution will continue to survive. On the other hand, it is difficult to see exactly how it could be dropped *in toto*; and, if it were to be dropped, it might reasonably be suggested that problems of integration between groups would almost inevitably emerge. So the question of whether the *moka* has changed its form and content and whether it will continue into the future is one of both academic and practical concern. In answering the question, we need to take into account the differing forms which ceremonial exchange institutions have taken in different parts of the Highlands (see Strathern 1969 and Brunton 1971).

Throughout the Chimbu area, for example, the kind of festival which is of greatest importance is the periodic pig-kill, for which pigs must be reared and fattened over a number of years (Brookfield 1968, 1973; Brown 1972). Pigs have to be pastured in fallow areas and also fed by hand with sweet potatoes (raw or cooked), the staple Highlands crop. As preparations for a festival intensify, increasing amounts of labor and land have to be allocated to the care of pigs. In a situation of change, alternative possibilities for the deployment of resources emerge. In Chimbu the major introduced cash crop was coffee. Once coffee trees have been planted, certain areas of garden land are removed from the cycle of fallowing and reuse for subsistence crops. Fallow periods in other garden areas may then have to be shortened or new garden areas obtained. Since pigs also are supported from the land, it becomes clear that at some point there is likely to be a conflict of choice about priorities in the use of land resources. The first coffee was introduced in Central Chimbu about 1952, its planting encouraged by administration extension workers. By 1961 almost every adult man had at least one coffee patch. New food gardens were made from fallow and fenced against pigs. When caring for both pigs and coffee trees became difficult, a split developed between "traditionalists," who wanted to raise a full herd of pigs for a festival, and "progressives," who wished to concentrate on money making through coffee. Throughout the 1960s the "progressives" gained on the "traditionalists." Garden areas previously reserved for special crops used in ceremonies were planted with coffee or sweet potatoes. People used cash to buy imported foodstuffs or trucks. The "path of innovation" was halted, however, in 1966 by a growing overall shortage of land and a fall in the market price of coffee. Those who wanted to make more money could not expand much further through cash cropping. They and others began turning back to the idea of obtaining both prestige and security by investing in ceremonial exchange. In either case, whether producers continued to concentrate on coffee or turned to pig rearing again, land problems were more acute than before, and the predictable result in the 1970s has been a resurgence of warfare concerning land boundaries between large tribal groups and their neighbors. Over this time span, then, alternatives of choice were held together: it was not impossible to abandon the new and turn back to the old. Further, at a deeper level of analysis, the dichotomy between "traditionalists" and "progressives" hides certain complications (Brown 1972, 1974). What were the basic aims of the "progressives"? Instead of slaughtering pigs for festivals they instituted large-scale parties in which prestations of cooked rice and fish obtained from trade stores were made to allies and friends. Their basic political values thus remained much the same as those of the "traditionalists," although the medium in which these values were expressed was different.

One can see from this account why it is that in Chimbu land problems became central to the question of whether ceremonial exchanges of pigs should continue. First, there was *ab initio* an overall high population density in the area; and second, the raising of large herds of fattened pigs for festivals, which would in any case periodically strain land resources, came sharply into conflict with the expansion of coffee-tree plantings in the mid 1960s.

In Hagen, because of the form the *moka* system takes, the conflict between cash cropping and ceremonial exchange has been less sharp. Moreover, it has been mediated by the introduction of large amounts of money, gained from cash cropping, into the ceremonial exchange system itself. In *moka*, as we have seen, there is an in-built tendency for reliance on a wide network of friends, allies, and supporters, in order to achieve a large-enough gift for one's recipient partners. At least this is how the big-men operate. Hence the group about to give a *moka* does not steadily have to expand its demands on its own land resources over a period of years. Men can obtain the pigs they need by careful management of their auxiliary exchange networks. Indeed, they sometimes do so to the neglect of their own domestic garden production. Up to about half of the pigs a big-man gives away in a *moka* he may himself have received recently in *moka* from other partners. His problem is thus to call in all of his debts that he wishes to within a fairly short period of time, and then to make his own *moka* quickly after that, so as not to overstrain his own garden resources and the labor of his wife or wives. Political delays in the *moka*, occasioned by the leader being too far ahead of his followers in his preparations or by another big-man causing trouble and so splitting the group apart, can prove very costly. If a group becomes involved in too many political disturbances, it cannot effectively mount the plans required to carry through a big *moka* prestation. Hence there is an incentive built into the *moka* for the leaders who have the biggest status in it to ensure that peace is kept as long as an important prestation remains uncompleted.

The use of increasingly large sums of cash to replace valuables in *moka* over the past few years has, as we have noted, both helped to ensure the continuity of the system and exposed it, as it has been exposed before, to inflation. When pearl shells were first brought in large quantities by Europeans, both leaders and ordinary men seized on them with delight, and the big-men rapidly expanded the already existing ethic of peacemaking between groups by means of payments of compensation for killings, followed by full-scale *moka* exchanges. In turn, money is replacing pearl shells and it too is being used to pay compensations for deaths and to strengthen friendships between allies, just as in Chimbu the so-called progressives used cash to stage large parties for their friends and allies. What is basically at issue here, of course, is political security, and it is strictly rational, if one wishes to have sufficient peace and security to pursue economic schemes for money making, to use a large proportion of one's money in attempting to strengthen relationships with allies. It is clear, however, that besides the need for security the desire for prestige is influential in determining the amounts of cash which get involved in *moka*. In 1964 the first "money *moka*" I saw was organized by young men of one particular clan, but with the active participation and approval of older, established big-men; it comprised a gift of £A 600 (the currency was then in pounds) to men of another clan. It was not a successful experiment, in a sense, for a return has never been made to date, but that has not deterred other groups around from following suit, and by the early 1970s sums of money between $1,000 and $2,000 had become a common component of various kinds of ceremonial payments, compensations for deaths following car accidents, compensations to matrilateral kin after the ordinary death of a man, and established *moka* following sequences of transactions from previous years. In 1974, as mentioned already, three clans of a tribe combined together to collect money, reputedly totalling $12,000, in order to buy special pigs and cattle for a *moka* to their allies.

This use of money in *moka* clearly means that the discontinuity between "cash cropping" and "traditional exchange" is broken down. There is also a strong need to put money into compensation payments as fighting in warfare style re-emerges and isolated killings occur. These killings and the cash which has to be used to pay for them are thus renewal points for transactional continuity. For political leaders of all kinds the killings and the cash payments for them present both new opportunities and new problems. In the mid 1960s many of the younger leaders, involved as local government councillors with electoral wards, spoke of the need to give up *moka* and take up cash cropping instead. But by the mid 1970s these men are ten years older themselves and have seen the political environment change from the temporary stability caused by "Kiap rule" ("Kiap" is a Pidgin term for "government officer") to a much more volatile situation, in which groups need to be much more reliant on themselves and their friends and can less effectively call on external force from the police or the government administration officers to sort out their troubles (cf. Strathern 1974). It is not surprising to find that the attitudes of these men have changed.

One of them, for example, has been a representative of his council area in the national Parliament or House of Assembly since 1972. As a politician representing an electorate, he needs wide support. An existing basis for this is provided in networks of exchange between groups and their leaders. He is also interested in making money out of business activities. To do this he requires land, help from workers, freedom to travel, and safety for his vehicles on the roads. Business success brings him not only money but also much jealousy from rivals, and the dangers inherent in this can be corrected only if he, as leader, has popularity and standing. He thus feels additional pressure to engage in ceremonial exchanges which can bring him this kind of support. Conversely, other big-men seek alliances with him, partly because of his new political position and in the hope that he may be able to bring particular benefits to them. He himself in earlier years spoke of his wish to give up *moka* and do modern things, while at the same time in practice he became more and more heavily involved in it. To the outside world he professed concern for the modern style and so was a "progressive"; inside his own electorate and among his allies, however, he has increasingly become a "traditionalist." The dangers to him as a prominent leader were underlined when in 1970 an attempt was made to kill him while he was attending a ceremony for the opening of a new police post. The attempt failed, but some of his own relatives, thinking him dead, rushed out to make another attempted killing in revenge, and a complex series of disputes, Supreme Court trials, compensation payments, and enduring bitterness between certain groups ensued. Since then he has more and more energetically taken part in *moka*, in particular with his mother's people, who are the chief traditional allies of his clan. It was they who provided him personally with a new Toyota Landcruiser in their September 1974 prestation to his group. He particularly seeks out a prominent and knowledgeable older big-man from his mother's tribe who can give him advice on the past situation of fighting, *moka*, and alliance between groups, encapsulated in large numbers of stories and allusions which a clever orator knows how to marshal in relation to contemporary events—and which a leader must be able to recognize when they are brought up by other leaders. Thus the older big-man, rather than being entirely left behind and eclipsed by the younger politician, is actually an important mentor to him. Both in turn now look with some apprehension at younger men who through access to cash, and because cash has been brought into the *moka,* can directly challenge them; and at still younger men, who do not seem to be taking over partnerships from their senior kinsmen in the way that is necessary for a smooth and exact continuation of *moka* links over a span of generations. These young men are criticized as upstarts, card players, beer drinkers, and men who travel about in cars and think of chasing women rather than serious matters of business and *moka.*

Where do the major incentives for continuity remain, then, and what threatens it? First, it is important to remember that through the various fluctuations in the availability and popularity of valuables and cash, pigs have remained a central concern, and still today are at the heart of all important kinds of payments (cf. Meggitt 1974). Second, we have seen how the *moka* has in a sense been given renewed life from time to time by the infusion into it of new kinds of valuables, most recently cash. What will happen when requirements for payments of cash get out of hand remains to be seen. Third, the political situation among groups has grown more tense, and this in itself has induced leaders to invest more in *moka,* which may help to give them some security. Killings provide reasons for fresh exchanges and money provides a new medium in which young men as well as older ones can play their part and excel. There are problems that emerge from this same set of conditions. With the building of roads, the introduction of money, the purchase of vehicles, and regular travel from rural areas into Hagen town, the chances for conflict between physically separated groups have increased. There has thus been a need to fix compensation payments not only between traditional enemies but even between groups which before had nothing much directly to do with one another. In one instance, a whole council area combined to make a payment to another similar council, each council containing some sixteen to eighteen thousand people. At such an expanded political level it is hard to organize payments with success and to convert them into ongoing exchanges on the model of *moka* partnerships. They tend to be once-and-for-all affairs, and although they have a vital function they cannot exactly duplicate the results of *moka* exchanges themselves. The use of money, too, has its dangers. Money can be used for many things. It cannot be kept within the *moka* nexus. This is both useful, in that money earned in other ways can be channeled into *moka,* and awkward, since it can be channeled out again, and at any time it would be possible for people to pull their money right out of *moka* and use it for other purposes. Finally, as has been noted earlier, the development of disruptive disputes and actual fighting between groups which otherwise should be cooperating for *moka* making poses a threat to the successful completion of any given *moka,* although not, in principle, to the system itself, since it is only by exchanging goods after fighting that an ordinary peaceful existence can be renewed.

All activities, including the modern ones of cash cropping and marketing, are likely to be threatened unless peace can successfully be restored after fighting. Similarly, cash cropping cannot be pursued without adequate secure access to land. This in turn cannot be guaranteed unless one's group is strong and united and has friends, and that cannot be achieved other than through the medium of exchange relations. To date, then, any apparent oppositions between cash cropping and ceremonial exchange, individualism and community goals, and traditional and modern activities are mediated by the local political situation among groups. The cash-cropping entrepreneur needs security and help, and so exchanges in the *moka* to attain these requirements; the more traditionally oriented big-men need to be involved in cash cropping too, since they need cash for effective participation in ceremonies. How long this particular compromise in activities will continue to hold is hard to say, but for the meantime the generalization made by one big-man, Ongka, of Kawelka tribe, is a good summary: "Law [that is, modern activities] and custom [traditional activities] both continue, they are in competition with each other, but one will not overcome the other—they will carry on together."

ACKNOWLEDGMENTS

Field work has been carried out in the Mount Hagen area from 1964 to 1974 under the auspices of the University of Cambridge, the Australian National University, and the University of Papua New Guinea. I wish to thank all these institutions for their support.

REFERENCES

Brookfield, H. C. 1968. The money that grows on trees. *Australian Geographical Studies,* 6 (2): 97–119.
———. 1973. Full circle in Chimbu: a study of trends and cycles. In H. C. Brookfield, ed., *The Pacific in Transition: Geographical Perspectives on Adaptation and Change.* London: Edward Arnold, 1973.
Brown, Paula. 1972. *The Chimbu: A Study of Change in the New Guinea Highlands.* Cambridge, Mass.: Schenkman Publishing Co. Distributed by General Learning Press, Morristown, N.J.
———. 1974. Mediators in social change: new roles for bigmen. *Oceania,* 9 (3): 224–230.
Brunton, R. 1971. Cargo cults and systems of exchange in Melanesia. *Mankind,* 8 (2): 11–28.
Epstein, A. L. 1969. *Matupit: Land, Politics and Change Among the Tolai of New Britain.* Canberra: Australian National University Press.
Meggitt, M. J. 1971. The pattern of leadership among the Mae-Enga of New Guinea. In R. M. Berndt and P. Lawrence, eds., *Politics in New Guinea.* Nedlands: University of Western Australia Press, 1971.
———. 1974. "Pigs are our hearts!" The Te exchange cycle among the Mae-Enga of New Guinea. *Oceania,* 44 (3): 165–203.
Reay, M. 1959. *The Kuma: Freedom and Conformity in the New Guinea Highlands.* Melbourne: Melbourne University Press, for the Australian National University.
Salisbury, R. F. 1962. *From Stone to Steel: Economic Consequences of a Technological Change in New Guinea.* Melbourne: Melbourne University Press, for the Australian National University.
Strathern, A. J. 1969. Finance and production: two strategies in New Guinea Highlands exchange systems. *Oceania,* 40 (1): 42–67.

_____. 1971a. Cargo and inflation in Mount Hagen. *Oceania*, 41 (4): 255–265.

_____. 1971b. *The Rope of Moka: Big-Men and Ceremonial Exchange in Mount Hagen, New Guinea*. Cambridge: Cambridge University Press.

_____. 1974. When dispute procedures fail. In A. L. Epstein, ed., *Contention and Dispute: Aspects of Law and Social Control in Melanesia*. Canberra: Australian National University Press.

Young, M. W. 1971. *Fighting with Food: Leadership, Values and Social Control in a Massim Society*. Cambridge: Cambridge University Press.

Notes on Contributors

COHEN, A. P.   Born in 1946. Currently Lecturer in Sociology at the University of Manchester. Previously at Memorial University of Newfoundland and Queen's University (Kingston, Ontario). Has done field work in Newfoundland (1968–1970) and is presently working in Whalsay, Shetland Isles. Author of *The Management of Myths* and various articles.

COMAROFF, J. L.   Born in Cape Town. Lecturer at the University of Manchester. Previously at College of Swansea; doctorate from the London School of Economics. Has worked in Botswana and among the Barolong boo Ratshidi in the South Africa-Botswana borderland. Editor of *Diary of Sol T. Plaatze*; author of articles on Tswana politics and law.

GILSENAN, MICHAEL   Born in 1940. Now at University College, London. B.A. in Oriental Studies (Arabic) and doctorate in Social Anthropology, both from Oxford. Has taught in South Arabia local schools (1958–1959), researched popular Sufism in Cairo (1964–1966), and studied politics and ideology in North Lebanon (1971–1972).

HANDELMAN, DON   Born in 1939 in Montreal. Presently Senior Lecturer at The Hebrew University of Jerusalem. Previously at Tel-Aviv University (1971–1972); Postdoctoral Fellow, Institute of Social and Economic Research, Memorial University of Newfoundland (1973–1974). Doctorate from the University of Manchester. Author of papers on shamanism, face-to-face interaction, expressive behavior, bureaucracy, and urbanism.

HEATH, A. F.   Born in 1942. Fellow of Jesus College, Oxford, and holder of a University Lectureship. Read Classics and Economics at Trinity College, Cambridge; Ph.D. in Sociology, Cambridge. Author of *Rational Choice and Social Exchange*.

KAPFERER, BRUCE   Born in Sydney, Australia. Currently Professor of Anthropology at the University of Adelaide; previously affiliated with the Institute for African Research, University of Zambia, and with the University of Manchester. Has done field work among the Bisa in the Northern Province of Zambia; in the town of Kabwe, Central Province of Zambia (1964–1966); and in Galle, Sri Lanka (1970, 1971–1972). Author of *Corporation Leadership and Village Structure,*

289

Strategy and Transaction in an African Factory, and various articles on healing rituals and urban political and social organization.

MARRIOTT, McKIM   Born in 1924. Professor of Anthropology and of the Social Sciences at the University of Chicago. Doctorate from the University of Chicago, 1955. Has studied Hindi-speaking villagers of western Uttar Pradesh, India (1950–1952, 1968–1969), and a small city in Maharashtra, India (1955–1957).

PAINE, ROBERT   Born in 1926 in Portsmouth, England. Presently Visiting Professor at the University of Stockholm; Henrietta Harvey Professor in Anthropology, Memorial University of Newfoundland. Former Director of Anthropological Research, Memorial University. Has done field work among Coast Lapps and nomadic Reindeer Lapps; current research is on political rhetoric. Author of *Second Thoughts About Barth's "Models"* and numerous other monographs and articles.

PARKIN, DAVID   Born in 1940 in England. Currently at the University of London (SOAS); previously at the Universities of London, Nairobi, and Sussex, and Commonwealth Scholar and Research Associate, EAISR, Kampala, Uganda. Has carried out field research in Uganda and Kenya. Author of *Neighbours and Nationals in an African City Ward* and *Palms, Wine and Witnesses*; editor of *Town and Country in Central and Eastern Africa.*

SALISBURY, RICHARD F.   Born in 1926 in London. Director of the Centre for Developing Area Studies and the Programme in the Anthropology of Development, McGill University. Received doctorate from the Australian National University; past president of the Canadian Sociology and Anthropology Association and the Northeastern Anthropological Association. Has done field work in the New Guinea Highlands, among the coastal Tolai of New Britain, among Wapisiana Indians and bauxite workers in Guyana, and since 1971 among Cree Indians of northern Quebec. Author of a number of books, including *From Stone to Steel* (1962) and *A House Divided* (1976).

SANSOM, BASIL   Born in 1938 in South Africa. Research Fellow with the Australian Institute for Aboriginal Studies; previously (1963–1974) at the University of Manchester. Has done research in oases of the Fezzan and among Druze in Lebanon; worked among the Pedi of South Africa in 1960–1961.

STRATHERN, ANDREW   Professor of Social Anthropology at the University of Papua New Guinea. B.A. and Ph.D. from Cambridge (Classics and Anthropology). Has done extensive field research in the Highlands of Papua New Guinea. Author of *The Rope of Moka* and various articles.

Index